City Cycling

Urban and Industrial Environments

Series editor: Robert Gottlieb, Henry R. Luce Professor of Urban and Environmental Policy, Occidental College

For a complete list of books published in this series, please see the back of the book.

City Cycling

Edited by John Pucher and Ralph Buehler

The MIT Press
Cambridge, Massachusetts
London, England

MIT Press books may be purchased at special quantity discounts for business or sales promotional use. For information, please email special_sales@mitpress.mit.edu or write to Special Sales Department, The MIT Press, 55 Hayward Street, Cambridge, MA 02142.

This book was set in Sabon by Toppan Best-set Premedia Limited. Printed and bound in the United States of America.

Library of Congress Cataloging-in-Publication Data

City cycling / edited by John Pucher and Ralph Buehler.
    p.   cm.—(Urban and industrial environments)
Includes bibliographical references and index.
ISBN 978-0-262-51781-2 (pbk. : alk. paper)
1. Cyling—Handbooks, manuals, etc. 2. City traffic—Handbooks, manuals, etc. I. Pucher, John R. II. Buehler, Ralph.
GV1043.7.C57   2012
796.6–dc23
2012006720

10 9 8 7 6 5 4 3 2 1

John Pucher dedicates this book to his aunt Chris Kerzman, who was the inspiration for his four decades of car-free living.

Ralph Buehler dedicates this book to his wife, Nora, his parents, Liesel and Georg, and his sister, Steffi.

Contents

Contributors

John Pucher, PhD, is a professor in the Bloustein School of Planning and Public Policy at Rutgers University (New Jersey, United States). He conducts research on a wide range of topics in transport economics and finance. For over three decades, he has examined differences in travel behavior, transport systems, and transport policies in Europe, Canada, the United States, and Australia. In recent years, Pucher's research has focused on walking and bicycling and what North American and Australian cities can learn from European cities to improve the safety, convenience, and feasibility of these nonmotorized modes. His research emphasizes walking and cycling for daily travel to increase physical activity and enhance overall public health.

Ralph Buehler, PhD, is an assistant professor in Urban Affairs & Planning at Virginia Tech's Alexandria Center (Virginia, United States). Most of his research has an international comparative perspective, contrasting transport and land-use policies, transport systems, and travel behavior in western Europe and North America. His research examines the influence of transport policy, land use, and sociodemographics on travel behavior; active travel and public health; and public transport demand, supply, and financial efficiency. In 2008, Buehler's dissertation comparing travel behavior in Germany and the United States was selected as best dissertation in planning by the Association of Collegiate Schools of Planning (ACSP).

Adrian Bauman, PhD, School of Public Health, University of Sydney, Australia

Emmanuel de Lanversin, MS Eng, MPP, MS Arch, Department of Infrastructure Planning, French Ministry of Transport, Paris

Jennifer Dill, PhD, Toulan School of Urban Studies & Planning, Portland State University, Oregon

Peter G. Furth, PhD, Department of Civil and Environmental Engineering, Northeastern University, Boston

Jan Garrard, PhD, School of Health and Social Development, Deakin University, Melbourne, Australia

Stacey Guzman, BA, Transportation Sustainability Research Center, University of California at Berkeley

Susan Handy, PhD, Department of Environmental Science and Policy, University of California at Davis

Eva Heinen, PhD, Research Institute for Urban, Housing, and Mobility Studies, Delft University of Technology, the Netherlands

Peter L. Jacobsen, PE, public health consultant, Sacramento, California

Kevin J. Krizek, PhD, College of Architecture and Planning, University of Colorado at Boulder

Kristin Lovejoy, MS, Institute of Transportation Studies, University of California at Davis

Noreen C. McDonald, PhD, Department of City and Regional Planning, University of North Carolina at Chapel Hill

Chris Rissel, PhD, School of Public Health, University of Sydney, Australia

Harry Rutter, PhD, Department of Public Health, University of Oxford, England

Susan A. Shaheen, PhD, Transportation Sustainability Research Center, University of California at Davis and Berkeley

Takahiro Suzuki, MCRP, Japanese International Development Agency, Tokyo

Paul Tranter, PhD, School of Physical, Environmental, and Mathematical Sciences, University of New South Wales, Canberra, Australia

John Whitelegg, PhD, Department of Geography, Lancaster University, England

Hua Zhang, PhD, Transportation Sustainability Research Center, University of California at Berkeley

Preface and Acknowledgments

Recent years have witnessed a booming interest in cycling around the world, both on the part of cyclists themselves and among transportation planners, academic researchers, and a variety of government agencies and nongovernmental organizations seeking to improve the sustainability of cities and transportation systems. After decades of stagnation, cycling levels have doubled or tripled in many American, Canadian, and Australian cities since 1990. Similarly, cycling has been thriving in more traditionally bike-oriented countries in northern Europe, where cycling serves up to a third of all trips.

Academic research on cycling has also boomed in recent years, with a vast increase in research and publications on all aspects of cycling. This book pulls together much of that research in a convenient, up-to-date format that permits readers to assess the state of knowledge and practice along many important dimensions. A key purpose of the book is to enable readers to learn from experience in cities of all sizes, from different parts of the world, and from perspectives of different academic and professional disciplines, with the aim of increasing cycling and making it safer for all segments of society.

This book is intended for everyone with an interest in cycling. All the chapters have been written to be understandable and useful for a wide range of readers, including cyclists as well as cycling researchers. By keeping technical jargon and complicated analysis to a minimum, the authors seek to appeal to the broadest possible audience. Yet even professionals with an extensive background in cycling research will find up-to-date information and analysis they can use to promote cycling and improve cycling safety. The book would be appropriate as a text in university courses on sustainable transportation in general or about bicycling and walking in particular.

The broad audience intended for the book reflects one of the main themes running throughout the book. Cycling should be made feasible, convenient, and safe for everyone: for women as well as men, for all age groups, and for a wide range of physical abilities. The authors of this book take the view that cycling should not be limited to cyclists who are highly trained, fit, and daring enough to do battle with motor vehicles on busy roads. As demonstrated in many chapters, getting children, seniors, and women on bikes requires provision of safer and more comfortable cycling conditions than currently exist in most North American, Australian, and British cities. On the basis of extensive research, the chapter authors provide many specific strategies for increasing the social inclusiveness of cycling in a variety of different environments.

The social diversity advocated by the authors is mirrored in their own diversity. The chapter authors include roughly as many women as men, ranging in age from 25 to 68. They come from eight countries on four continents, thus providing an international perspective throughout the book, representing countries with low but growing cycling levels (Australia and the United States) as well as northern European countries with traditionally high levels of cycling (Germany and the Netherlands). The authors also provide a multidisciplinary perspective drawing on a wide range of academic backgrounds: geography, urban planning, environmental science, transportation planning, civil engineering, and public health.

The authors are indebted to our editors at MIT Press for having initiated the idea for this book and then guiding us along to its completion. In particular, we thank Professor Robert Gottlieb, editor of The MIT Press's Urban and Industrial Environments series, and Clay Morgan, our acquisitions editor for the MIT Press. We also thank Miranda Martin and Kathleen Caruso of the MIT Press as well as manuscript editor Nancy Kotary and the indexer for our book, Tobiah Waldron.

The book benefited from peer review by three anonymous referees, whom we thank for their feedback on the draft book manuscript. Before the book as a whole was peer reviewed, each chapter was sent to experts in the specific topic areas examined by the particular chapters. The chapter referees provided detailed corrections, updates, and additional information that greatly improved the individual chapters before the book was assembled and sent out for overall peer review. We are especially grateful to these eighty-one chapter referees, who appear here in one consolidated list, in alphabetical order and not organized by chapter: Gulsah Akar, Troels Andersen, Lisa Aultman-Hall, David Bassett, Tim Blumenthal, Stefan Böhme, Tom Bogdanowicz, Jennifer Bonham, Eric Britton, Frank Borgman, Noah Budnick, Sebastian Bührmann, Nick Cavill, Andy Clarke, Stuart Clement, Kelly Clifton, Gian-Carlo Crivello, Andy Dannenberg, Adrian Davis, Paul Demaio, Ian Dewar, Jane Dixon, Timothy Ericson, Darren Flusche, Jan Garrard, Norman Garrick, Billie Giles-Corti, Tara Goddard, Paul Goger, Alexandra Goodship, Thomas Götschi, Stephen Greaves, Martina Güttler, Bernhard Gutzmer, Susan Hanson, Gregory Heath, Kristiann Heesch, Eva Heinen, Ria Hilshorst, Christine Hoehner, Peter Jacobsen, John Kaehny, Rich Killingsworth, Sue Knaup, Charles Komanoff, Kevin Krizek, Fabian Kuester, Charles Lloyd, Anne Lusk, Roger Mackett, Noreen McDonald, Tracy McMillan, Peter Midgley, Jeff Miller, John Neff, Barry Pless, Kate Powlison, Mike Pratt, Jonathan Peters, Marni Ratzel, Daniel Rodriguez, Gabe Rousseau, Harry Rutter, Jim Sallis, Warren Salomon, Mark Schlossberg, Cara Seiderman, Patrick Seidler, Shannan Sohlqvist, Rosemarie Speidel, Mio Suzuki, Joey Tabone, Kay Teschke, Anna Timperio, Cor van der Klaauw, Bert van Wee, Lynn Weigand, Owen Weygood, John Whitelegg, Alastair Woodward, Tetsuo Yai, and Yizhao Yang. In addition to the preceding acknowledgments, some of the chapter authors include (at the end of their chapters) a listing of persons and organizations that provided information and advice for their specific chapters.

This book is the result of a team effort requiring intensive cooperation and coordination between the authors of each chapter as well as across the various chapters. The editors would like to thank each of the chapter authors for the time, effort, and thought they invested in their chapters. We also thank the countless individuals and organizations who contributed information, data, photos, and advice throughout the three years it took to produce this book.

1

Introduction: Cycling for Sustainable Transportation

John Pucher and Ralph Buehler

Sustainability and the Renaissance of Cycling

Many countries in western Europe, North America, and Australasia have officially recognized the importance of cycling as a practical mode of urban transportation and endorse the dual objectives of raising cycling levels while increasing safety (Austroads 2011; ECMT 2004; European Commission 2007; NZ Transport 2011; Transport Canada 2003; USDOT 2010). There are many reasons to encourage more cycling. It causes virtually no noise or air pollution and consumes far fewer nonrenewable resources than any motorized transportation mode. The energy cycling requires is provided directly by the traveler, contributing to daily physical activity, aerobic fitness, and cardiovascular health while helping protect against obesity, diabetes, and various other diseases (Buehler et al. 2011; Pucher et al. 2010). Cycling has the potential to reduce roadway congestion because bikes take up a small fraction of the space needed for the use and parking of cars. Moreover, cycling is economical, costing far less than the private car and public transportation in both direct user outlays and public infrastructure investments. Because cycling is affordable by virtually everyone and physically possible for most people, it is socially equitable and has the potential to enhance mobility options for all groups. In short, it is hard to beat cycling when it comes to environmental, economic, and social sustainability.

In recent years, governments at every level have been implementing policies to help realize the potential of cycling to improve the overall sustainability of our transportation systems and the livability of our cities. As discussed in chapter 2, national governments have generally established overall policy goals and guidelines, whereas state and local governments have been primarily responsible for actually implementing and funding efforts to increase cycling. In many cities throughout Europe, North America, and Australasia, cycling facilities and programs have been vastly expanded and improved. The results have been encouraging, as documented in many of the chapters in this book. Even in car-oriented countries such as the United States and Australia, cycling has grown considerably over the past two decades, with some cities experiencing a veritable bike boom. Northern European countries with a historical cycling culture, such as the Netherlands and Denmark, have greatly improved their existing cycling infrastructure and raised their already high levels of cycling. Some European countries without a history of daily, utilitarian cycling, such as France and Spain, have greatly increased cycling in their major cities.

Purpose of the Book

This book examines the cycling renaissance underway in most countries of the western, industrialized world. The purpose of the book is not simply to portray trends in cycling but also to identify which measures are most effective for increasing cycling levels, improving cycling safety, and making cycling possible for all segments of society. Our focus is on promoting daily cycling in cities for utilitarian purposes such as visiting friends and making trips to work, school, shopping, church, and doctors' offices. As documented in many of the chapters, success depends on a coordinated package of mutually supportive infrastructure, programs, and policies. Although cycling infrastructure is essential, it must be supported by a range of complementary measures.

Structure of the Book

Chapter 2 provides a broad overview of cycling trends, safety, and policies in fifteen countries in Europe, North America, and Australasia. The most detailed analysis is for the Netherlands, Denmark, Germany, the United Kingdom, and the United States, the countries for which the available statistics are most comparable. The information presented in chapter 2 is mainly at the country level, in contrast to chapters 12, 13, and 14, which focus on city-specific case studies.

Chapters 3 and 4 examine two of the most important motivations for cycling: improved health and time and cost savings. Chapter 3 provides a comprehensive review of the scientific evidence of the physical, mental, and social health benefits of cycling for daily travel. Even though they rely on a wide variety of locations, timing, study designs, and statistical techniques, virtually all available studies find that cycling is healthy for the individual. In addition, cycling for daily travel can help reduce car use and thus generate societal health benefits by lessening the noise, air pollution, greenhouse gases, and overall traffic danger caused by motor vehicles. Reduced health costs from increased cycling far exceed the costs of cycling infrastructure.

Perhaps the most important factors in choice of travel mode are the time and cost of travel. Although most readers probably assume that the car is always faster than the bicycle, chapter 4 shows that this is not always the case. Effective speed takes into account the time spent earning the money to pay for the ownership and operation of a car. Cars usually have higher operating speeds than bicycles (except on very congested roads), but the car requires much more time to earn the money to pay for its much higher costs. Adding that work time to direct travel time yields effective car speeds that are often lower than cycling speeds, as indicated by calculations of effective speed for cities throughout the world. Thus, saving time may be an important rationale for cycling instead of driving.

Chapters 5, 6, and 7 examine three crucial elements of a cycling system: bicycles, bikeways, and safety. Chapter 5 documents the increase over the past two decades in the variety of bikes and cycling equipment available on the market. Bikes range from cheap, basic designs to expensive, high-performance racing bikes. Perhaps most important is the proliferation of bike designs intended for daily, utilitarian cycling and adapted to the needs of city travel. The increasing choice in bike designs in particular caters to a broader range of cyclist needs, which vary widely depending on age, gender, skill level, cycling location, and trip purpose.

Chapter 6 analyzes a wide range of infrastructure provisions for cyclists: roads with no special provisions for cyclists at all; traffic-calmed residential streets; roads with painted bike lanes; roads with physically separated, protected bike lanes or cycle tracks; and off-road bike paths. This chapter compares the bikeway design standards of various countries. It also assesses the extent to which the greater separation of cycling facilities from motor vehicle traffic in some European countries accounts for the much higher cycling levels and safer cycling there compared to the United States, where most cycling is on roads with no provisions or with unprotected bike lanes.

A crucial factor influencing the decision whether to cycle is safety, both real and perceived. Chapter 7 provides a comprehensive review of the literature on this issue and finds that perceived risks usually exceed the actual risks of cycling. Even more important, exhaustive scientific evidence reviewed in this chapter demonstrates that the health benefits of cycling far exceed traffic safety risks. Nevertheless, much could be done to improve cycling safety. Motor vehicles impose the most serious traffic dangers to cyclists. Thus, the key to improved cycling safety is reducing motor vehicle speeds on shared roadways and providing physical separation of cyclists from motor vehicle traffic on arterials. Although much of the focus of cycling safety has been on bike helmets, this chapter shows that laws requiring helmet use are not an effective strategy.

Chapters 8 and 9 deal with two complementary programs to encourage more cycling. The integration of cycling with public transportation helps cyclists cover trip distances that are too long to make by bike. Public transportation services can also provide convenient alternatives when cyclists encounter bad weather, difficult topography, gaps in the bikeway network, and mechanical failures. Chapter 8 documents the four main approaches to integrating cycling with public transportation: provision of bike parking at train stations and bus stops, bike racks on buses, permission and storage space to take bikes on board trains, and the coordination of bikeway route networks so that paths and lanes lead to public transportation stops.

Chapter 9 examines the worldwide boom in bikesharing programs, which were offered in over 160 cities on five continents in 2011. This chapter describes the successive evolution of the four generations of bikesharing systems over the past four decades: free bikes; coin-deposit bikes; IT-based systems with smart cards; and demand-responsive, multimodal systems. Although most studies report that bikesharing increases cycling, there are concerns about vandalism, bike redistribution, safety, and financing. This chapter examines the advantages and disadvantages

of alternative systems and proposes an improved design that would mitigate some of the problems identified in existing systems.

Chapters 10 and 11 address the special needs and preferences of
women and children. Because recent surveys indicate a falling or stagnant
level of cycling by women and children in some countries, it is essential
to target cycling infrastructure and programs to these groups. Chapter
10 examines spatial variation in women's cycling rates among countries,
cities, and city neighborhoods. Where women cycle as much as men, the
overall bike share of trips is high and cycling safety is excellent. This
chapter considers the many factors that affect women's cycling, finding
that women are often deterred from cycling by concerns about personal
safety and traffic risks. Several strategies are proposed to adapt cycling
policies to the special concerns of women and thus to increase their rate
of cycling.

It is especially important to promote cycling among children because
habits learned while young tend to persist throughout life. As documented in chapter 11, cycling can provide children with a range of
physical, mental, and social benefits, greatly enhancing their mobility and
independence. Unfortunately, cycling rates for children have fallen in
most countries in recent decades. The downward trend can be explained
by increased car ownership among parents, longer distances between
home and school, increasing traffic danger, and parental fears about the
personal safety of their children. This chapter examines ways to reverse
the downward trend in child cycling based on successful policies in some
countries and cities. Improving cycling safety, especially for the trip to
school, is a key approach, but other complementary programs are also
required.

Chapters 12, 13, and 14 examine cycling trends and policies in cities
of different sizes. Smaller cities generally have shorter trip distances as
well as less air pollution, less noise, less traffic, and less stressful traffic
conditions than larger cities. Moreover, their smaller size makes it easier
to coordinate transportation policies and to introduce innovative infrastructure and programs. Promoting cycling in larger cities is more challenging for all the opposite reasons. Heavier traffic, more noise and air
pollution, and longer trip distances discourage cycling as city size
increases. Moreover, larger cities often comprise many local governmental jurisdictions and multiple layers of bureaucracy, making it politically

difficult to develop and coordinate transportation policies on a regional basis. The other important difference is that public transportation services are far more extensive in larger cities than smaller cities. Although cycling and public transportation can work together, as shown in chapter 8, they may also compete with each other over short and intermediate trip distances.

These three chapters highlight the large differences among cities that are not revealed in the national, aggregate data examined in chapter 2. Chapter 12 focuses on four detailed case studies of Davis, California; Boulder, Colorado; Odense, Denmark; and Delft, the Netherlands. The chapter also provides an overview of cycling levels and policies in seventeen other small cities in the United States, Canada, and Europe. Chapter 13 examines cycling in thirteen large cities with metropolitan area populations of at least a million. They include two cities in Australia (Melbourne and Sydney); five cities in the United States (Chicago, Minneapolis, Portland, San Francisco, and Washington); three cities in Canada (Montreal, Toronto, and Vancouver); and three cities in Europe (Amsterdam, Copenhagen, and Berlin). Chapter 14 examines cycling in four megacities with at least ten million inhabitants in their metropolitan areas: London, New York, Paris, and Tokyo. In addition to highlighting the special challenges and potential for cycling in cities of different sizes, these three chapters enable a closer look at how cities have developed their cycling programs over time, coordinating various measures into a package of mutually complementary policies.

Chapter 15 concludes the book with an overview and synthesis of what works best to raise cycling levels and improve cycling safety under a variety of different situations. The wide range of countries and cities examined in this book offer an extensive base of experience for planners and government officials to draw on when developing effective policies to promote cycling.

References

Austroads. 2011. *National Cycling Strategy: Gearing Up for Active and Sustainable Communities.* Sydney: Austroads.

Buehler, Ralph, John Pucher, Dafna Merom, and Adrian Bauman. 2011. Active Travel in Germany and the USA: Contributions of Daily Walking and Cycling to Physical Activity. *American Journal of Preventive Medicine* 40 (9) (September): 241–250.

ECMT (European Conference of Ministers of Transport). 2004. *National Policies to Promote Cycling*. Paris: ECMT.

European Commission. 2007. *Green Paper—Towards a New Culture for Urban Mobility*. Brussels: European Commission.

NZ Transport (New Zealand Transport Agency). 2011. *Planning for Walking and Cycling*. Auckland, New Zealand: NZ Transport.

Pucher, John, Ralph Buehler, David Bassett, and Andrew Dannenberg. 2010. Walking and Cycling to Health: Recent Evidence from City, State, and International Comparisons. *American Journal of Public Health* 100 (10): 1986–1992.

Transport Canada. 2003. *Sustainable Development Strategy 2004–2006*. Ottawa: Transport Canada.

USDOT (U.S. Department of Transportation). 2010. *The National Walking and Bicycling Study: 15-Year Status Report*. Washington, DC: USDOT, Federal Highway Administration.

2

International Overview: Cycling Trends in Western Europe, North America, and Australia

Ralph Buehler and John Pucher

Variation in Cycling Levels among Countries and Cities

There are large differences in cycling levels among countries in western Europe, North America, and Australasia. At the low end, the bike share of trips is only about 1 percent in Australia, Canada, and the United States and about 2 percent in the United Kingdom and Ireland (see figure 2.1). At the upper end, the bike share is 26 percent in the Netherlands, 18 percent in Denmark, and about 10 percent in Germany, Finland, Sweden, and Belgium.

For most of the countries shown in figure 2.1, the bike share refers to daily trips for all trip purposes, as derived from national travel surveys. Australia, Canada, and Ireland do not have national travel surveys, however, and their censuses report only on trips to work. Census data on work trips probably underestimate overall levels of cycling, as is seen most clearly by comparing the two 2009 surveys for the United States. The US Census Bureau's American Community Survey (ACS), which only includes work trips, reports two-thirds as high a bike share (0.6% versus 1.0%) as the National Household Travel Survey (NHTS), which includes all trip purposes.

There are also methodological differences in the travel surveys for the various countries that limit their comparability. Nevertheless, it is clear that cycling rates in most northern European countries are much higher than in North America and Australia. Roughly the same pattern of differences among countries holds for daily distance cycled per capita, ranging from 0.1 km in the United States and 0.2 km in the United Kingdom to 1 km in Germany, 1.6 km in Denmark, and 2.5 km in the Netherlands (European Commission 2005–2007; USDOT 2010b).

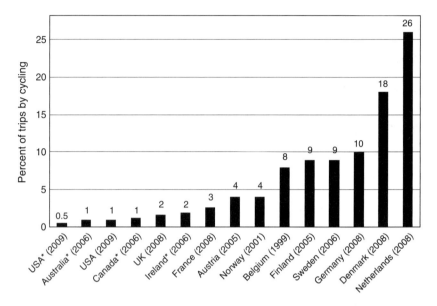

Figure 2.1
Cycling share of daily trips in Europe, North America, and Australia, 1999–2008.
Note: The latest available travel surveys were used for each country, with the survey year noted in parentheses after each country name. The modal shares shown in the figure reflect travel for all trip purposes except for those countries marked with an asterisk (*), which report only journeys to work derived from their censuses. Differences in data collection methods, timing, and variable definitions across countries and over time limit the comparability of the modal shares shown in the figure. *Sources:* Australian Bureau of Statistics 2007; Bassett et al. 2008; German Ministry of Transport 2010; Danish Ministry of Transport 2010; Department for Transport 2010b; European Commission 2005–2007; Pucher and Buehler 2008; Statistics Canada 2010; USDOC 2010; USDOT 2010b.

The national differences presented in figure 2.1 hide variation in cycling levels among cities within each country. Figure 2.2 shows bike mode shares for selected cities in the Netherlands, Denmark, and Germany. Figure 2.3 shows bike mode shares for selected cities in the United Kingdom, the United States, Canada, and Australia. Although there is considerable variation within each country, the largest differences are between the bike-friendly countries in figure 2.2 and the car-dominated countries in figure 2.3.

With few exceptions, the most bike-oriented cities in the United Kingdom, the United States, Canada, and Australia have lower levels of

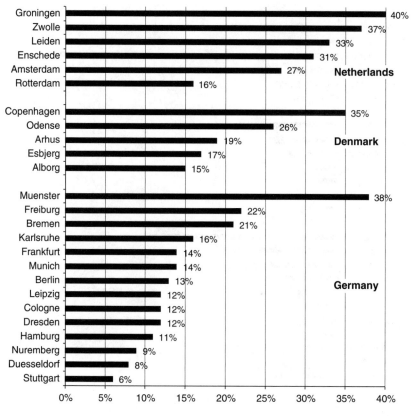

Figure 2.2
Bike share of trips in selected cities in the Netherlands, Denmark, and Germany, 2000–2009. *Sources:* ECMT 2004; City of Berlin 2010; Dutch Bicycle Council 2006, 2010; Socialdata 2009; HWWI 2010.

cycling than the least bike-friendly cities in the Netherlands, Germany, and Denmark. For example, only the small cities of Cambridge (England, United Kingdom), Victoria (British Columbia, Canada), Davis (California, United States) and Boulder (Colorado, United States) have bike mode shares comparable to those in most Danish, Dutch, and German cities. Portland, Oregon, the most bike-oriented large city in the United States, has a bike mode share of 6 percent, the same as Stuttgart, Germany, which is the least bike-oriented German city in our sample. Chapters 12, 13, and 14 provide more detailed analysis of the differences in cycling levels among cities in Australia, North America, and western Europe.

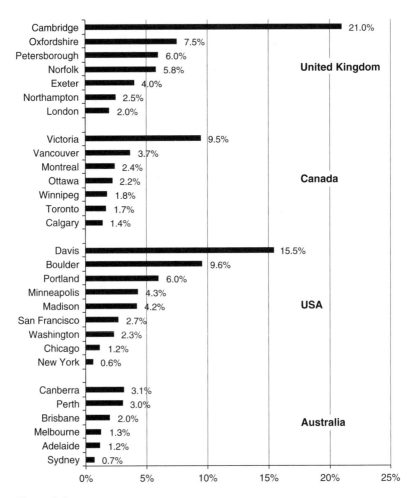

Figure 2.3
Bike share of trips in selected cities in the United Kingdom, Canada, the United States, and Australia, 2000–2009. *Sources:* Australian Bureau of Statistics 2007; Department for Transport 2010b; Statistics Canada 2010, USDOC 2010.

Trip Purpose and Distance

The higher share of trips by bicycle in Dutch, Danish, and German cities may be partly explained by shorter trip distances than in American, Canadian, and Australian cities due to more mixed-use development, less suburban sprawl, and higher population densities in Europe (Heinen, van Wee, and Maat 2010; Krizek, Forsyth, and Baum 2009). In the Netherlands, Denmark, and Germany, 40 percent of all trips are shorter than 2.5 km, compared to only about 30 percent in the United States and the United Kingdom (German Ministry of Transport 2010; Danish Ministry of Transport 2010; Department for Transport 2010b; Statistics Netherlands 2010; USDOT 2010c). However, even within the same trip distance categories, there are large differences among countries in bike mode share. Americans and Britons cycle for only 2 percent of trips shorter than 2.5 km, compared to bike mode shares of 31 percent in Denmark, 29 percent in the Netherlands, and 16 percent in Germany for the same trip distance. For trip distances from 2.5 to 4.5 km, the bike mode share in the United States and the United Kingdom is less than 2 percent, far lower than the 35 percent bike share of trips in the Netherlands, 24 percent in Denmark, and 12 percent in Germany. For trip distances from 4.5 to 6.5 km, the bike mode share is less than 1 percent in the United States and the United Kingdom, but 24 percent in the Netherlands, 15 percent in Denmark, and 7 percent in Germany. In short, the Dutch, Danes, and Germans cycle for much higher percentages of trips than Americans and Britons over all distance categories.

Trip purpose also varies by country. Cycling is mainly for practical, utilitarian purposes in northern Europe, even in the United Kingdom. For example, travel to work or school in the United States accounts for only 15 percent of all bike trips, compared to 28 percent in Germany, 30 percent in the United Kingdom, 32 percent in the Netherlands, and 35 percent in Denmark. Shopping accounts for 10 percent of bike trips in the United States but 20 percent in Germany, 22 percent in the Netherlands, and 25 percent in Denmark. More than 60 percent of bike trips in the United States are for recreational purposes, compared to 38 percent in Germany, 35 percent in the United Kingdom, 27 percent in the Netherlands, and 10 percent in Denmark (German Ministry of Transport 2010; Danish Ministry of Transport 2010; Department for Transport 2010b; Statistics Netherlands 2010; USDOT 2010c).

Who Cycles?

Cycling is common among all demographic groups in Germany, the Netherlands, and Denmark. For example, as shown in chapter 10, women are as likely to cycle as men in Germany (49% of cyclists are women), Denmark (55%), and the Netherlands (56%). By comparison, women account for less than 30 percent of cyclists in the United Kingdom (29%), Canada (29%), the United States (24%), and Australia (21%). Similarly, cycling is common in all age categories in Germany, the Netherlands, and Denmark. As shown in figure 2.4 and discussed further in chapter 11, children and adolescents have the highest cycling levels in all five countries. However, cycling levels are also high among adults in Germany, Denmark, and the Netherlands. Indeed, cycling rates increase for the

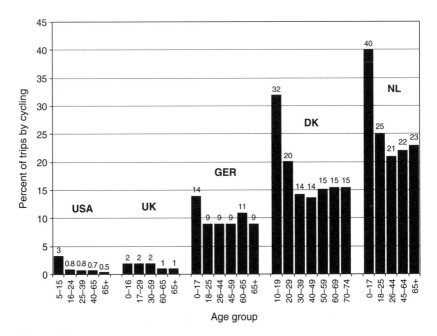

Figure 2.4
Cycling share of trips within each age group in the United States, the United Kingdom, Germany, Denmark, and the Netherlands, 2008 (as percent of trips by all modes for all trip purposes). *Sources:* Bassett et al. 2008; German Ministry of Transport 2010; Danish Ministry of Transport 2010; Department for Transport 2010b; European Commission 2005–2007; Pucher and Buehler 2008; USDOT 2010b.

oldest age groups in Denmark and the Netherlands. Of all trips made by persons 65 and older, the bike accounts for 23 percent of trips in the Netherlands, 15 percent in Denmark, and 9 percent in Germany, but less than 1 percent in the United States and the United Kingdom. Clearly, cycling is physically possible well beyond the age of 65, provided that conditions are safe and convenient.

Impacts of Car Ownership

High levels of car ownership are not necessarily incompatible with high levels of cycling. The Netherlands, Denmark, and Germany are affluent countries where almost all households have cars. Thus, their high cycling levels are not due to an inability to afford a car. Figure 2.5 shows that between 1960 and 2008, car ownership levels increased significantly in all countries. The United States has the highest level in motorization, followed by Germany, Canada, and Australia. The United Kingdom, the Netherlands, and Denmark have the lowest levels of car ownership. Increased car ownership and use discourage cycling by offering direct

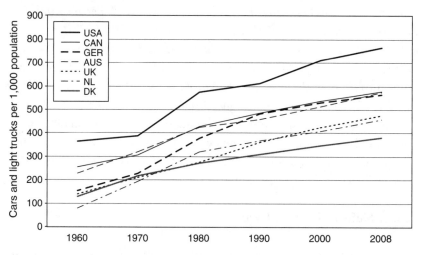

Figure 2.5
Trend in car and light truck ownership per 1,000 population in the United States, Canada, Australia, Germany, the Netherlands, and Denmark, 1970–2008. *Sources:* Bassett et al. 2008; German Ministry of Transport 2010; Danish Ministry of Transport 2010; Department for Transport 2010b; OECD 2003–2007; Pucher and Buehler 2008; Statistics Netherlands 2010; USDOT 2010b.

competition as a mode of travel and worsening traffic dangers for cyclists on roads. Nevertheless, cycling can thrive even in environments with nearly universal car ownership, as shown by the examples of Germany, the Netherlands, and Denmark, provided that car use is restricted from endangering or inconveniencing cyclists. The case of Germany, in particular, shows that high levels of car ownership do not preclude high levels of cycling. Although Germany has 20 percent more cars per capita than the United Kingdom, the bike share of trips in Germany is ten times higher than in the United Kingdom.

Higher taxes on car ownership and use in Europe help explain lower levels of automobile ownership and use compared to the United States, Canada, and Australia. In Europe, taxes account for roughly 65 percent of the gasoline retail price, compared to much lower tax shares in Australia (37%), Canada (32%), and the United States (20%) (IEA 2010). As a result, in 2009 gasoline retail prices per liter were two to three times higher in the Netherlands ($1.87), the United Kingdom ($1.84), Germany ($1.80), and Denmark ($1.78) than in Australia ($1.08), Canada ($0.91), and the United States ($0.65) (IEA 2010). Europeans also pay higher taxes on new car purchases. In Denmark, the tax rate on new car purchases is between 105 percent and 180 percent, depending on the value of the vehicles (DIW 2005). Compared to Denmark, taxes on car purchases are lower in Germany (19%), the United Kingdom (20%), and the Netherlands (20–50%), but still significantly higher than in North America and Australia (AAA 2007; Buehler 2010; Pucher and Buehler 2006). Moreover, better and more convenient public transportation systems in continental Europe—integrated with comprehensive bikeway and walkway networks—reduce the need to drive an automobile (Heinen, van Wee, and Maat 2010; Krizek, Forsyth, and Baum 2009; TRB 2001).

Policy Shifts to Promote Cycling

In the 1950s and 1960s, increasing motorization levels, sprawling urban development, and government policies in most western European countries favored car use and contributed to a sharp decline in cycling. For example, the number of daily bike trips in Berlin fell by 75 percent from 1950 to 1975 (City of Berlin 2003). Other German, Dutch, and Danish cities report declines in the bike share of trips from roughly 50–85 percent in 1950 to only 14–35 percent of trips in 1975 (Dutch Bicycle Council 2006). During that period, many European cities focused on expanding roadway and car parking supply while largely ignoring the needs of cyclists (Hass-Klau 1993b).

Increasing car use in cities led to environmental pollution, roadway congestion, and a sharp rise in traffic injuries and fatalities. Those harmful impacts of car use provoked a dramatic reversal of the transportation policies of most German, Dutch, and Danish cities. Instead of adapting themselves to the car, most cities chose to restrict car use and increase its cost while promoting public transportation, walking, and cycling (Buehler, Pucher, and Kunert 2009; ECMT 2004; Hass-Klau 1993a; Pucher 1995a, 1995b). Greatly expanded and improved cycling infrastructure contributed to a rebound in cycling. Between 1975 and 1995, cycling levels rose by about 25 percent in the same sample of German, Dutch, and Danish cities that had witnessed a drastic decline in cycling prior to 1975 (Dutch Bicycle Council 2006). In Berlin, the number of daily bike trips increased by 300 percent between 1975 and 2008 (City of Berlin 2010). National data also show a considerable increase in cycling since the policy shift of the 1970s. Since 1978, average daily kilometers cycled per inhabitant increased from 0.6 km to 1.0 km in Germany, from 1.3 km to 1.6 km in Denmark, and from 1.7 km to 2.5 km in the Netherlands. Over the same period, daily cycling levels declined in the United Kingdom from 0.3 km to 0.2 km and were roughly constant in the United States (0.1 km) (European Commission 2005–2007; USDOT 2010b).

Cycling Safety

Many studies document that traffic danger is a deterrent to cycling, especially for women, the elderly, and children (ABW 2010, 2012; ITF 2010; McClintock 2002; OECD 2007; WHO 2002). Thus, safer cycling conditions are perhaps the main reason for more cycling among all groups in Germany, Denmark, and the Netherlands. Figure 2.6 compares annual cyclist fatality and injury rates, controlling for kilometers of cycling per year. The Netherlands, Denmark, and Germany have the safest cycling. Cyclist fatality rates in the Netherlands are only a third

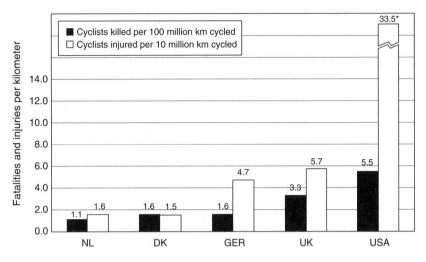

Figure 2.6
Cyclist fatality rates and nonfatal injury rates in the Netherlands, Denmark, Germany, the United Kingdom, and the United States, 2004–2008. *Note:* To control for annual fluctuations, a five-year average (2004–2008) was used for cyclist injuries and fatalities. Trips and kilometers for cycling exposure levels were derived from 2008 travel survey data. *The cyclist injury rate for the United States is off the chart and is thus shown with a discontinuous bar. *Sources:* Bassett et al. 2008; German Ministry of Transport 1991–2010, 2010; Danish Ministry of Transport 2010; Department for Transport 2010a, 2010b; Pucher and Buehler 2008; Statistics Netherlands 2010; USDOT 2006–2010, 2010b.

as high as in the United Kingdom and only a fifth as high as in the United States. Cyclist fatality rates are not quite as low in Denmark and Germany, but still only half as high as in the United Kingdom and less than a third as high as in the United States. Serious cyclist injuries are far more common than cyclist fatalities. However, data on injuries are less reliable than information on fatalities, mainly due to underreporting of injuries in police and hospital reports (OECD 2007). Available data suggest that cyclist injury rates in the United States are twenty times higher than in Denmark and the Netherlands and seven times higher than in Germany.

From 1970 to 2008, the annual number of cyclist fatalities decreased by roughly 70 percent in Denmark, the United Kingdom, Australia, the Netherlands, and Germany (figure 2.7). In contrast, cyclist fatalities in the United States increased sharply in the 1970s and then declined only slowly until the early 2000s. Since then, cycling fatalities in the United

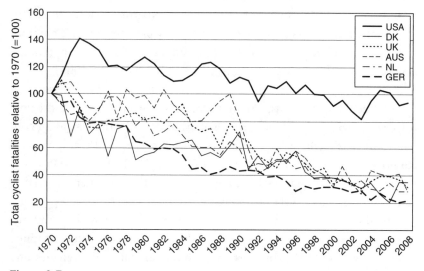

Figure 2.7
Trend in cycling fatalities in the United States, Denmark, the United Kingdom, Australia, the Netherlands, and Germany, 1970–2008 (percent relative to 1970 level). *Sources:* Australian Government 2004, 2011b; ITF 2010; Pucher and Dijkstra 2003.

States have remained near 1970 levels. In Australia, cycling fatalities fluctuated between 1970 and 1989 and then dropped off sharply between 1989 and 1993. That drop coincides with the implementation of Australia's mandatory helmet law for adult bicyclists. It is not clear whether cyclist safety in Australia actually improved or if the mandatory helmet law discouraged cycling, thus reducing cyclist exposure (Robinson 2006). The decline in fatalities in Denmark, Germany, and the Netherlands occurred without mandatory helmet laws and in spite of more cycling. Increasing cycling levels and falling injury and fatality rates support the theory of "safety in numbers" described in chapter 7.

National Cycling Strategies

As discussed in chapters 12, 13, and 14, most policies that increase cycling and make it safer are implemented at the local level. National governments, however, influence cycling through national cycling policies, dedicated funding, traffic regulations, roadway and bikeway design standards, and dissemination of cycling expertise. Motivations for national governments to promote cycling vary but often include environmental and public health benefits, reduced traffic congestion and noise, improved traffic safety, and tourism (ABW 2012; ECMT 2004).

National cycling strategies and master plans vary greatly in content, level of detail, legal status, and financial commitment. Canada is the only case study country without a national cycling policy: the Canadian constitution specifically relegates the responsibility for local transportation to provincial governments (Transport Canada 2011). In the other countries we examined, national cycling policies establish the general goal of increasing cycling levels and making cycling safer. In some countries, national governments postulate specific goals for cycling. For example, the UK National Cycling Strategy of 1996 set the goal of quadrupling cycling levels by 2012. In most cases, however, national strategies and plans do not set specific targets. The German national cycling plan is typical in calling for significant increases in cycling without quantifying goals (German Ministry of Transport 2006a; Danish Ministry of Transport 2011; Department for Transport 2008; Netherlands Ministry of Transport 2006; Transport Canada 2011; USDOT 2010d).

National cycling policies provide a vision for cycling that can guide lower levels of governments in their own efforts to increase cycling and make it safer. In Denmark and the Netherlands, for example, national cycling policies are intended to help local jurisdictions develop their own bicycle plans (Danish Ministry of Transport 2011; Netherlands Ministry of Transport 2006). In most countries, the national cycling policy recommends improved data collection and benchmarking efforts to increase knowledge about cycling. Some national governments coordinate the dissemination of information about best practices or cutting-edge planning tools (e.g., the Danish "ideas catalog").

National Funding for Cycling

Most national cycling policies provide little, if any, dedicated funding to finance implementation of the measures proposed in the national policy. The German national master plan is an exception; it provides annual funds for national cycling promotion (German Ministry of Transport 2002). In the 1990s, the Dutch national master plan provided funds for bike infrastructure to municipalities, but current funding is limited to bike parking at rail stations and requires a 50 percent local government match (Netherlands Ministry of Transport 2006, 2009). Some national governments have also provided dedicated funding for experimental cycling projects, such as the Nonmotorized Transportation Pilot program in the United States, the National Cycle City program in Denmark, and the Canadian Urban Transportation Showcase program (Danish Ministry of Transport 2011; Transport Canada 2010; USDOT 2010a, 2010d).

Local jurisdictions usually have some flexibility in their use of national funds. Cycling projects, for example, are eligible for federal Transportation Enhancement (TE) funds in the United States and the federal Urban Transport (GVFG) funds in Germany (German Ministry of Transport 2005; USDOT 2010d). In many countries, national governments fund cycling infrastructure along national highways, often as part of roadway improvement programs. Moreover, most governments contribute toward funding programs to improve cycling training and safety, such as the Safe Routes to School program in the United States, the Bikeability Program in the United Kingdom, and the dedicated fund for cycling safety in Denmark (Danish Ministry of Transport 2011; Department for Transport 2008; USDOT 2010d). In some countries, part of the national funding is competitive, such as the Cykelpuljen program in Denmark, the Sustainable Transport Fund in the United Kingdom, and the Urban Transportation Showcase Fund in Canada (Danish Ministry of Transport 2011; Department for Transport 2011; Transport Canada 2010).

Traffic Regulation and Training for Drivers and Cyclists

Australian states, Canadian provinces, and American states are responsible for driver's training and traffic regulations for motorists as well as cyclists (ABW 2010; Australian Government 2004; Transport Canada 2011). Following federal recommendations, all Australian states and most territories passed laws requiring cyclists of all ages to wear helmets (see chapter 7). In Canada, four out of thirteen provinces and territories require all cyclists to wear helmets, and two provinces require cyclists under the age of eighteen to wear helmets (Robinson 2006). In spite of federal government endorsement of helmet use in the United States, no state requires bike helmets for adults and only half of states require helmets for children (ABW 2010; Dennis et al. 2010). Denmark, Germany, the Netherlands, and the United Kingdom do not require bike helmets for children or adults but strongly encourage bike helmets for children (ECMT 2004).

All European countries have national traffic signage and regulations. In the Netherlands and Germany, national regulations prioritize the traffic safety of cyclists and pedestrians, with special protection for children and seniors, who are especially vulnerable (German Ministry of Transport 2006b; Pucher and Buehler 2008). Nationally standardized driver's training courses and strict motorist licensing tests in Europe emphasize the importance of protecting vulnerable road users. Driver's training is expensive in western Europe, where obtaining a driver's license typically costs between €1,000 and €2,000 (European Driving Schools Association 2010; KBA 2007). Driver's training in the United States, Canada, and Australia is much less expensive than in Europe and does not stress the legal obligation of motorists to avoid endangerment of pedestrians and cyclists (Australian Government 2011a; Transport Canada 2011; USDOT 2007).

Most children in Germany, Denmark, and the Netherlands participate in cycling training or testing in school (German Ministry of Transport 2002; Danish Ministry of Transport 2011; Netherlands Ministry of Transport 2006). In both Denmark and the Netherlands, safe cycling courses for school children are required by the national government. Safety courses are financed by the national government in Denmark but by municipalities in the Netherlands. About 80 percent of Dutch schools participate voluntarily in a national cycle testing program for children—focusing on practical on-road cycling skills beyond classroom safety lessons (Netherlands Ministry of Transport 2006). In Germany, all states have adopted bike training as an integral part of the school curriculum in the third or fourth grade (German Ministry of Transport 2002). Courses vary from state to state but usually include classroom instruction about cycling safety and traffic regulations, police-administered training sessions on special off-street bike training facilities, and in-traffic cycling training with police officers on local streets. Only a few American, Canadian, and Australian schools provide cyclist training for children, and participation by students is voluntary (Pucher, Buehler, and Seinen 2011; Pucher, Garrard, and Greaves 2011). Nongovernmental organizations such as CAN-Bike in Canada and the League of American Bicyclists in the United States provide cyclist training for all ages and skill levels, but such courses are not offered in most cities (CAN-Bike 2011; LAB 2010). Moreover, they charge a fee and reach only a small percentage of the population.

Speed Limits and Design Standards for Roadways and Bikeways
In all countries, municipalities determine policies such as speed limits and traffic calming of residential streets. Starting in the 1970s, German and Dutch municipalities progressively traffic-calmed almost all neighborhood streets (Hass-Klau 1993a, 1993b; Pucher and Buehler 2008). Speed limits are typically 30 kilometers per hour (km/h) or less, and sometimes as low as 15 km/h or even 7 km/h (walking speed) (Buehler 2010; Hamilton-Baillie 2001). In North America and Australia, speed limits in residential neighborhoods are much higher, and traffic calming is usually limited to a few streets, not area-wide as in European cities. Some North American cities such as Vancouver (British Columbia) and Seattle (Washington) have implemented traffic calming measures for decades, but none as extensively as in Europe (Ewing 1999, 2008; Hamilton-Baillie 2001; Hass-Klau 1993b; Webster and Mackie 1996).

National and state governments are responsible for speed limits and road design on national and state highways. Even in urban areas, such roads are subject to specific national or state standards. Municipalities must seek the approval of higher levels of government to make any physical changes to these national or state roads. National governments or national nongovernmental organizations often publish design guidelines for roadway and cycling facilities. In the United States, for example, the federal government publishes the Manual on Uniform Traffic Control Devices (MUTCD), which must be followed by all states (USDOT 2009). The American Association of State Highway and Transportation Officials (AASHTO) and the National Association of City Transportation Officials (NACTO) publish detailed design guidelines for bicycle facilities in the United States (AASHTO 1999; NACTO 2010). Similar nongovernmental organizations in the Netherlands and Germany regularly update and disseminate guidelines for best practice in bikeway and roadway design in those two countries (CROW 2010; Roadway and Transport Research Center 2007). Canadian provinces and Australian states have their own road and bikeway standards, which are often based on national guidelines (Austroads 2010; TAC 1998).

Trends in Government Support for Cycling

National government funding for cycling varies greatly across countries and over time. For example, in the United States, federal funding for bicycling and walking increased from only $5 million per year in the late 1980s to over $1 billion per year in 2009 (Rails-to-Trails Conservancy 2010). It is not possible to separate funding for bicycling and walking for the United States, but the significant increase in funding for both modes combined reflects the large increase in federal spending on cycling. The British national government strongly supported cycling in the 1990s and early 2000s. However, the Conservative government that came into power in 2010 discontinued most national cycling programs in April 2011 (Department for Transport 2008, 2011). The national governments of Australia and Canada have never played a major role in cycling promotion, with no regular funding at all and only occasional support for experimental programs such as TravelSmart (individualized marketing) in Australia and the Urban Transportation Showcase (for sustainable transportation projects) in Canada (Australian Government 2006; Transport Canada 2010).

The German federal government has been increasing its involvement in cycling in recent decades, both through increased funding and by supporting cycling planning and promotion. Federal funding for cycling more than doubled from about €50 million per year in 1990 to €120 million annually in 2006 (German Parliament 2007). Moreover, the German Ministry of Transport published its first national cycling report in 1998, followed by its national cycling plan in 2002 and the forthcoming national cycling plan 2020 (German Ministry of Transport 2002; German Federal Government 1998). Dutch and Danish national governments provide limited financial support, but cycling is an integral part of national transportation planning in both countries (Danish Ministry of Transport 2011; Netherlands Ministry of Transport 2006, 2009).

National governments have increased their support for cycling over the past few decades with the expectation that a modal shift from driving to cycling would help combat societal problems such as obesity and air pollution. Chapter 3 discusses in detail the range of important individual and societal health benefits of cycling that justify national government support for policies to promote cycling.

As this brief overview of national policies suggests, national governments provide state and local governments with funding as well as technical assistance and coordination of cycling planning and promotion efforts. In all countries, however, state and local governments have the ultimate responsibility for adopting and implementing specific cycling infrastructure and programs. Municipal government policies, in particular, determine the ultimate fate of cycling, as discussed in the detailed city case studies in chapters 12, 13, and 14.

References

AAA (American Automobile Association). 2007. *Your Driving Costs 2007.* Washington, DC: AAA.

AASHTO (American Association of State Highway and Transportation Officials). 1999. *Guide for the Development of Bicycle Facilities.* Washington, DC: AASHTO.

ABW (Alliance for Biking and Walking). 2010. *Bicycling and Walking in the United States: 2010 Benchmarking Report.* Washington, DC: Alliance for Biking and Walking.

ABW (Alliance for Biking and Walking). 2012. Bicycling and Walking in the United States: 2012 Benchmarking Report. Washington, DC: Alliance for Biking and Walking. http://www.peoplepoweredmovement.org/benchmarking.

Australian Bureau of Statistics. 2007. *2001 Census of Population and Housing, Journey to Work Files.* Canberra, Australia: Australian Bureau of Statistics.

Australian Government. 2004. *Monograph 17: Cycle Safety.* Sydney: Australian Transport Safety Bureau.

Australian Government. 2006. *TravelSmart.* Sydney: TravelSmart.

Australian Government. 2011a. *Apply for a Driver's License.* Sydney: Australian Government.

Australian Government. 2011b. *Australian Road Fatality Statistics.* Sydney: Department of Infrastructure and Transport.

Austroads. 2010. *Traffic Control Devices.* Sydney: Association of Australian and New Zealand Road Transport and Traffic Authorities.

Bassett, David, John Pucher, Ralph Buehler, Dixie Thompson, and Scott Crouter. 2008. Walking, Cycling, and Obesity Rates in Europe, North America, and Australia. *Journal of Physical Activity & Health* 5 (6): 795–814.

Buehler, Ralph. 2010. Transport Policies, Automobile Use, and Sustainable Transport: A Comparison of Germany and the United States. *Journal of Planning Education and Research* 31 (3): 76–93.

Buehler, Ralph, John Pucher, and Uwe Kunert. 2009. Making Transportation Sustainable: Insights from Germany. Washington, DC: The Brookings Institution, Metropolitan Policy Program. http://www.brookings.edu/reports/2009/~/media/Files/rc/reports/2009/0416_germany_transportation_buehler/0416_germany_transportation_report.pdf.

CAN-Bike. 2011. CAN-Bike Program. Ottawa: CAN-Bike.

City of Berlin. 2003. *Cycling in Berlin 2003*. Berlin: City of Berlin, Department of Urban Development.

City of Berlin. 2010. *Cycling in Berlin 2010*. Berlin: City of Berlin, Department of Urban Development.

CROW (Information and Technology Centre for Transport and Infrastructure). 2010. *ASVV Recommendations for Traffic Provisions in Built-up Areas*. Amsterdam: CROW.

Danish Ministry of Transport. 2010. *Danish National Travel Surveys*. Copenhagen: Danish Ministry of Transport.

Danish Ministry of Transport. 2011. *Bicycling in Denmark*. Copenhagen: Danish Ministry of Transport.

Dennis, Jessica, Beth Potter, Tim Ramsay, and Ryan Zarychanski. 2010. The Effects of Provincial Bicycle Helmet Legislation on Helmet Use and Bicycle Ridership in Canada. *Injury Prevention* 16 (4): 219–224.

Department for Transport. 2008. *National Cycling Strategy*. London: Department for Transport, Cycling England.

Department for Transport. 2010a. *National Travel Statistics*. London: Department for Transport.

Department for Transport. 2010b. *National Travel Survey*. London: Department for Transport.

Department for Transport. 2011. *Local Sustainable Transport Fund*. London: Department for Transport.

DIW (German Institute for Economic Research). 2005. *Automobile Taxes in Europe 2005*. Berlin: DIW.

Dutch Bicycle Council. 2006. *Continuous and Integral: The Cycling Policies of Groningen and Other European Cities*. Amsterdam: Dutch Bicycle Council.

Dutch Bicycle Council. 2010. *Bicycle Policies of the European Principals: Continuous and Integral*. Amsterdam: Dutch Bicycle Council.

ECMT (European Conference of Ministers of Transport). 2004. *National Policies to Promote Cycling*. Paris: ECMT.

European Commission. 2005–2007. *Energy and Transport in Figures*. Brussels: European Commission, Directorate General for Energy and Transport, Eurostat.

European Driving Schools Association. 2010. *Driver's License Costs in Europe*. Munich: European Driving Schools Association.

Ewing, Reid. 1999. *Traffic Calming: State of the Practice*. Washington, DC: Institute of Transportation Engineers.

Ewing, Reid. 2008. Traffic Calming in the United States: Are We Following Europe's Lead? *Urban Design International* 13:90–104.

German Federal Government. 1998. *First Report about the State of Cycling in Germany*. Berlin: German Federal Government.

German Ministry of Transport. 1991–2010. *German Transport in Figures*. Berlin: German Ministry of Transport.

German Ministry of Transport. 2002. *Ride Your Bike!* Berlin: German Ministry of Transport.

German Ministry of Transport. 2005. *Federal Subsidies for Local Transportation Projects*. Berlin: German Ministry of Transport.

German Ministry of Transport. 2006a. *National Bicycling Plan*. Berlin: German Ministry of Transport.

German Ministry of Transport. 2006b. *German Traffic Law*. Berlin: German Ministry of Transport.

German Ministry of Transport. 2010. *Mobility in Germany 2008/2009*. Berlin: German Ministry of Transport.

German Parliament. 2007. *Road Report 2007*. Berlin: German Parliament.

Hamilton-Baillie, Ben. 2001. *Home Zones—Reconciling People, Places and Transport. Study Tour of Denmark, Germany, Holland, and Sweden, July to August 2000*. Cambridge, MA: Harvard University.

Hass-Klau, Carmen. 1993a. Impact of Pedestrianization and Traffic Calming on Retailing: A Review of the Evidence from Germany and the UK. *Transport Policy* 1 (1): 21–31.

Hass-Klau, Carmen. 1993b. *The Pedestrian and City Traffic*. New York: Belhaven Press.

Heinen, Eva, Bert van Wee, and Kees Maat. 2010. Bicycle Use for Commuting: A Literature Review. *Transport Reviews* 30 (1): 105–132.

HWWI (Hamburg World Economic Institute). 2010. *Haspa Hamburg Study*. Hamburg, Germany: HWWI.

IEA (International Energy Agency). 2010. *Energy Prices and Taxes*. New York: IEA.

ITF (International Transport Forum). 2010. *Traffic Safety Statistics*. Paris: ITF and Organization for Economic Cooperation and Development (OECD).

KBA (German Federal Motor Vehicle Agency). 2007. *The Basics About Driver's Licensing in Europe*. Flensburg, Germany: KBA.

Krizek, Kevin J., Ann Forsyth, and Laura Baum. 2009. *Walking and Cycling International Literature Review*. Melbourne: Victoria Department of Transport.

LAB (League of American Bicyclists). 2010. *Cycling in the USA*. Washington, DC: LAB.

McClintock, Hugh, ed. 2002. *Planning for Cycling: Principles, Practice, and Solutions for Urban Planners*. Cambridge: Woodhead Publishing Ltd.

NACTO (National Association of City Transportation Officials). 2010. *Cities for Cycling*. Washington, DC: NACTO.

Netherlands Ministry of Transport. 2006. *Cycling in the Netherlands*. Rotterdam, The Netherlands: Ministry of Transport, Public Works, and Water Management.

Netherlands Ministry of Transport. 2009. *Cycling in the Chain: The Combination with Public Transport. Cycling in the Netherlands*. The Hague, The Netherlands: Netherlands Ministry of Transport.

OECD (Organization for Economic Cooperation and Development). 2003–2007. *OECD Statistics*. Paris: OECD.

OECD (Organization for Economic Cooperation and Development). 2007. *Underreporting of Road Traffic Casualties*. OECD/ITRAD Special Report. Paris: International Traffic Safety Data and Analysis Group.

Pucher, John. 1995a. Urban Passenger Transport in the United States and Europe: A Comparative Analysis of Public Policies. Part 1. Travel Behavior, Urban Development and Automobile Use. *Transport Reviews* 15 (2): 99–117.

Pucher, John. 1995b. Urban Passenger Transport in the United States and Europe: A Comparative Analysis of Public Policies. Part 2. Public Transport, Overall Comparisons and Recommendations. *Transport Reviews* 15 (3): 211–227.

Pucher, John, and Ralph Buehler. 2006. Why Canadians Cycle More Than Americans: A Comparative Analysis of Bicycling Trends and Policies. *Transport Policy* 13 (3): 265–279.

Pucher, John, and Ralph Buehler. 2008. Making Cycling Irresistible: Lessons from the Netherlands, Denmark, and Germany. *Transport Reviews* 28 (4): 495–528.

Pucher, John, Ralph Buehler, and Mark Seinen. 2011. Bicycling Renaissance in North America? An Update and Re-assessment of Cycling Trends and Policies. *Transportation Research Part A, Policy and Practice* 45 (6): 451–475.

Pucher, John, and Lewis Dijkstra. 2003. Promoting Safe Walking and Cycling to Improve Public Health: Lessons from the Netherlands and Germany. *American Journal of Public Health* 93 (9): 1509–1516.

Pucher, John, Jan Garrard, and Stephen Greaves. 2011. Cycling Down Under: A Comparative Analysis of Bicycling Trends and Policies in Sydney and Melbourne. *Journal of Transport Geography* 19 (2): 332–345.

Rails-to-Trails Conservancy. 2010. *Federal-Aid Highway Program Funding for Pedestrian and Bicycle Facilities and Programs 1973–1991*. Washington, DC: Rails-to-Trails Conservancy.

Roadway and Transport Research Center. 2007. *Guidelines for City Streets*. Cologne, Germany: Roadway and Transport Research Center (FGSV).

Robinson, Dorothy. 2006. No Clear Evidence from Countries that Have Enforced the Wearing of Helmets. *BMJ (Clinical Research Ed.)* 332:722–725.

Socialdata. 2009. *Mobility Indicators of German Cities.* Munich: Socialdata.

Statistics Canada. 2010. *Canadian Census 2006.* Ottawa: Statistics Canada.

Statistics Netherlands. 2010. *Transportation Statistics.* Amsterdam: Statistics Netherlands.

TAC (Transportation Association of Canada). 1998. *Manual of Uniform Traffic Control Devices for Canada.* Ottawa: TAC.

Transport Canada. 2010. *Leading by Example: Urban Transportation Showcase.* Ottawa: Transport Canada.

Transport Canada. 2011. *Transportation in Canada.* Ottawa: Transport Canada.

TRB (Transportation Research Board). 2001. *Making Transit Work: Insight from Western Europe, Canada and the United States.* Washington, DC: TRB, National Research Council, National Academy Press.

USDOC (U.S. Department of Commerce). 2010. *American Community Survey 2009.* Washington, DC: USDOC, US Census Bureau.

USDOT (U.S. Department of Transportation). 2006–2010. *Transportation Statistics.* Washington, DC: USDOT, Federal Highway Administration.

USDOT (U.S. Department of Transportation). 2007. *Motor Vehicle Driver Licenses.* Washington, DC: USDOT, Federal Highway Administration.

USDOT (U.S. Department of Transportation). 2009. *Manual on Uniform Traffic Control Devices (MUTCD).* Washington, DC: USDOT, Federal Highway Administration.

USDOT (U.S. Department of Transportation). 2010a. *Federal-Aid Highway Program Funding for Pedestrian and Bicycle Facilities and Programs 1992–2010.* Washington, DC: USDOT, Federal Highway Administration.

USDOT (U.S. Department of Transportation). 2010b. *National Household Travel Survey 2009. Version 2.0/2010.* Washington, DC: USDOT, Federal Highway Administration.

USDOT (US Department of Transportation). 2010c. *National Household Travel Surve:, Our Nation's Travel.* Washington, DC: USDOT, Federal Highway Administration.

USDOT (US Department of Transportation). 2010d. *The National Walking and Bicycling Study: 15-Year Status Report.* Washington, DC: USDOT, Federal Highway Administration.

Webster, Daniel, and Adrian Mackie. 1996. Review of Traffic Calming Schemes in 20mph Zones. TRL Report 215. Crowthorne, UK: Transport Research Laboratory.

WHO (World Health Organization). 2002. *The World Health Report.* Geneva, Switzerland: WHO.

3

Health Benefits of Cycling

Jan Garrard, Chris Rissel, and Adrian Bauman

Cycling has multiple health benefits, particularly as a form of moderate to vigorous physical activity. Rapid increases in mechanization in the last half of the twentieth century in the industrialized world have engineered physical activity out of daily life for many people. Changes in modes of personal travel have been dramatic, with private motor vehicle trips replacing walking and cycling in many developed and developing countries.

Transportation cycling provides an excellent opportunity for individuals to incorporate physical activity into daily life. Furthermore, cycling for transportation is accessible and appealing to population groups that often have low levels of participation in sport and other forms of leisure-time physical activity. In pro-cycling countries and cities, transportation cycling is undertaken by considerable numbers of children, adolescents, women, older adults, people with low incomes, and nonathletic people in general. Consequently, transportation cycling can make a substantial contribution to improved health through increased physical activity levels across diverse population groups (Buehler et al. 2011). Health benefits also flow from reduced car use, including improved air quality, reduced noise pollution, and reduced greenhouse gas emissions. Improved social capital and community livability enhances quality of life, and "living streets" increase social interaction and reduce crime.

This chapter examines the health benefits of cycling as a form of moderate to vigorous physical activity and the multiple health benefits that flow from human-scale rather than car-dominated urban environments. We use a broad definition of health as incorporating "physical, mental, and social well-being" (World Health Organization 1948). We do not address the injury risks associated with cycling, as this topic is covered in chapter 7.

Physical Health Benefits of Cycling

This section focuses on the epidemiological evidence for the physical health benefits of increased cycling in populations.

Potential for Physical Activity to Improve Health

Regular moderate-intensity physical activity is an important contributor to population health. Epidemiological evidence suggests that accumulating at least thirty minutes each day of moderate-intensity physical activity can contribute to a range of health benefits, with recent recommendations noting that additional benefits can be achieved with up to an hour per day of total physical activity (U.S. Department of Health and Human Services 2008). Health benefits include chronic disease prevention and favorable impacts on antecedent risk factors such as elevated blood pressure and obesity. In addition, physical activity has mental health and social benefits, discussed later in the chapter.

Achieving the recommendations of thirty or sixty minutes per day will generally require adding to leisure-time physical activity other elements of active living, including active transportation, and increasing energy expended in domestic or occupational settings. Utilitarian cycling provides a practical means for inactive people to be active for thirty minutes per day. Most populations have high rates of bike ownership, people generally know how to cycle, and cycling for short trips can contribute to reaching the minimal daily recommendation of thirty minutes of activity. In car-reliant countries, a high proportion of short trips (less than 5 km) are car trips that could be replaced with cycling (Australian Bureau of Statistics 2009a). The energy expenditure of almost all commuting cycling places it at least in the "moderate intensity" category of activity of around 5–8 METs (metabolic equivalent of task, or 5–8 times the energy expenditure at rest) (Ainsworth et al. 2000). This level is around twice as intense as walking and provides an activity that is continuous, expends sufficient energy, and can be performed by most adults and children.

Types of Cycling to Improve Population Health

There are three settings for cycling that could contribute to population levels of physical activity. First is indoor cycling, in gyms or in domestic settings using stationary bicycles. These involve some cost and, above all, personal commitment to use them, and they may be used by individuals who are already active. Second is cycling as a form of recreational physical activity. Most recreational cycling achieves health enhancing levels but is more likely to be a "weekend" or intermittent choice of activity.

Third—and most likely to be of population health benefit—is cycling to get to and from places, including riding to work, to shops, to visit friends locally, or for other regular short trips. Utilitarian cycling is likely to be a more regular or habitual form of physical activity than gym-based or recreational cycling. In the Netherlands, cycling is the activity that contributes most to the total time spent by adults on moderate-to-vigorous physical activity (van Kempen et al. 2010).

Health Benefits: Findings from Epidemiological Studies

Numerous research studies have examined the health benefits of cycling in clinical settings, with special populations, and usually on stationary bicycles. These small-scale or clinical studies show that laboratory-based cycling improves fitness, cardiovascular risk factor levels, and postprandial blood sugar uptake (Oja et al. 2011). The primary focus of this chapter, however, is not on clinical settings but on population-based evidence of the relationship between cycling and improved health.

Cross-sectional studies have shown inverse associations between active commuting and body mass index, lipid levels, and blood pressure (Hu et al. 2002; Wen and Rissel 2008); one study was conducted in a Chinese city where most active commuting was by bicycle (Hu et al. 2002). European studies have shown similar results (von Huth Smith, Borch-Johnsen, and Jørgensen 2007). Japanese workers who commuted using active modes showed a better general health profile (General Health Questionnaire scores) than those using inactive travel modes (Ohta et al. 2007). A German cross-sectional study reported an association between general health and less chronic disease among regular cyclists aged fifty to seventy years (Huy et al. 2008). Further, ecological associations across countries, cities, and US states have noted that obesity rates are inversely related to walking and cycling rates (Pucher et al.

2010; Bassett et al. 2008). These data do not demonstrate a causal relationship but indicate the potential for improved health in active cycling populations.

Population-based studies, usually based on longitudinal cohort designs, have contributed to evidence for the health benefits of cycling. The Copenhagen cohort study identified that cycling to work reduced the risk of all-cause mortality by 28 percent, independent of other types of physical activity (Andersen et al. 2000). Many studies have identified "active commuting" as protective against all-cause or cardiovascular deaths (Hu et al. 2007; Hamer and Chida 2008) but most of these studies asked about "walking or cycling" to work, so the relative protective effects cannot be separated out and distinguished between walking and cycling. For cardiovascular events, active commuting was protective in Finnish adults, though more so for women than men (Hu et al. 2007). In the Zutphen study of elderly Dutch men, physical activity reduced risk and improved metabolic health; in this sample, the most frequent physical activity was cycling, again providing more direct evidence of cycling-specific prevention benefits (Caspersen et al. 1991). Women in the United States who increased their cycling, even by a small amount, significantly reduced their likelihood of weight gain (Lusk et al. 2010). Finally, a meta-analysis of active commuting (walking *and* cycling) and coronary heart disease reported data from eight studies with an 11 percent average risk reduction for developing heart disease and slightly stronger protective relationships in women than men (Hamer and Chida 2008).

Active commuting is inversely related to diabetes incidence (Pucher et al. 2010; Hu et al. 2003). With respect to cancer risk, bicycling alone was not protective for ovarian cancer (Biesma et al. 2006), and there have been inconsistent findings for breast cancer, with no association shown in a study of Chinese women (Matthews et al. 2001), but a German study reporting lower risk among women with high levels of cycling (Steindorf et al. 2003). For colon cancer, a case-control study in older adults reported a 40 percent decreased risk among active commuting men and women (Hou et al. 2004). In this Chinese sample, commuting was mostly cycling, hence conferring most of this observed benefit. Similar results were seen in the Shanghai women's health cohort, in which cycling more than forty minutes a day significantly reduced all-cause and cancer mortality risk (Matthews et al. 2007).

Among children, walking or cycling to school is associated with higher levels of overall physical activity, but most associations are from cross-sectional studies (Lee, Orenstein, and Richardson 2008). A Danish study showed similar cycling-specific findings using objectively assessed physical activity (Oja et al. 2011). Active commuting to school was also associated with increased aerobic fitness in a study of 6,085 English schoolchildren (Voss and Sandercock 2010). Although active commuting to school is associated with increased physical activity, most studies report no association with body mass index or obesity rates (Lee, Orenstein, and Richardson 2008). As is the case for adults, however, ecological associations across countries indicate that obesity rates are inversely related to rates of active travel to school (usually involving high levels of cycling) (Garrard 2009).

The Potential Impact of Increases in Cycling on Physical Activity Prevalence

As shown in chapter 2, rates of cycling at the population level are much higher in many European countries than in the United States, Canada, Australia and the United Kingdom. The potential public health benefits of cycling promotion are therefore high in countries where the population at risk (i.e., noncyclists) is very large. The challenge is to get those with bicycles to use them on a regular basis in order to make a public health impact on the prevalence of "sufficient activity."

In this section, we analyze data adapted from an Australian population data set in which 57 percent of adults met the recommendation for 150 minutes per week of at least moderate-intensity physical activity and 43 percent were "insufficiently active." The data were modeled to assess what difference it would make to the population prevalence of "sufficiently active" adults if a conservatively estimated 20 percent of people cycled more often. The modeling estimated the prevalence of "sufficient activity" if this subgroup of people cycled once, twice, or three times a week for twenty minutes. Then, the analysis was confined to only those who were "insufficiently active" and 20 percent of them adopted these amounts of cycling activity (see figure 3.1). Given a baseline of 57 percent

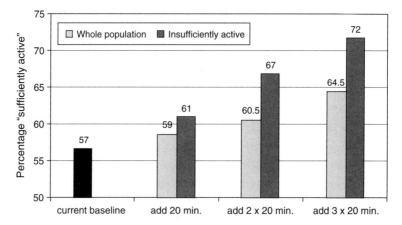

Figure 3.1
Effect of adding episodes of cycling/week on population level (percentage) of "sufficiently active" for (1) 20 percent of the adult population and (2) 20 percent of adult population who are "insufficiently active." *Source:* Data modeled from National Physical Activity Survey, Australia 2000.

"sufficiently active," if 20 percent of Australian adults cycled twenty minutes once, twice, and three times per week, the prevalence of adequately active would increase to 59.0 percent, 60.5 percent, and 64.5 percent, respectively. If only inactive adults were targeted, the prevalence increases would be even larger, to 61.0 percent, 67.0 percent, and 72 percent. Because few population interventions have achieved anywhere near a 5 percent absolute increase in sufficient physical activity, the public health potential for cycling is large, even at modest amounts and frequency of bicycle usage, especially if currently inactive people start cycling. These estimates would be similar for other developed countries with low rates of cycling in which around half the adult population is "insufficiently active." These hypothetical data are compelling, and cycling is accessible, affordable, and achievable by people of all ages. The challenge, therefore, is to establish effective ways to increase cycling in the population.

Psychosocial Health Benefits

The psychosocial benefits of cycling include (1) mental health benefits, (2) social health benefits, and (3) utilitarian cycling as a possible means of reducing health inequalities. These benefits are discussed in the following three sections.

Mental Health and Well-Being

The psychological health benefits of cycling range from preventing and treating anxiety and depression to improving cognitive functioning and increasing subjective well-being. In some cases, the link has been demonstrated for moderate intensity physical activity in general; other studies have looked specifically at cycling. This section focuses on cycling-specific research but also draws on other forms of moderate-intensity physical activity if cycling-specific research is unavailable.

Treatment and Prevention of Mental Health Conditions

A recent systematic review of the relationship between physical activity and depression concluded that exercise improves depressive symptoms in people with depression (Mead et al. 2009). Based on this evidence, UK guidelines for depression management recommend the inclusion of regular exercise in the treatment of mild to moderate depression (NICE 2009). There is also some evidence that regular physical activity may prevent the development of depressive symptoms in older adults (Lindwall, Larsman, and Hagger 2011).

Cognitive Functioning

A number of studies report improved cognitive functioning and educational attainment among young people who are physically active, though none have focused specifically on cycling (Åberg et al. 2009; Sibley and Etnier 2003). Several recent studies have reported significantly higher cardiovascular fitness among young people who cycle to school (Cooper et al. 2008; Andersen et al. 2009), including, in one study, after controlling for nontravel physical activity (Voss and Sandercock 2010). These data provide some indirect evidence that cycling to school may have educational benefits for young people, in addition to the direct health benefits.

These findings are consistent with research into cognitive functioning among older adults. Several US studies have reported that long-term regular physical activity, including walking, was associated with significantly better cognitive function, less cognitive decline, improved motor function, improved memory, and a decreased risk of Alzheimer's disease (Scarmeas et al. 2009; Angevaren et al. 2008).

The prevention of dementia through physical activity has the potential to help mitigate an important and growing global health problem. As shown in chapter 2, countries such as the Netherlands, Denmark, and Germany have established a culture of everyday utility cycling, with bike trips constituting a high proportion of trips by older adults (e.g., 25% of trips by people aged 65 and older in the Netherlands; Pucher and Buehler 2008). However, the impact of cycling rates on dementia in these countries has not been assessed.

Emotional Well-Being

Cross-sectional surveys consistently report that psychological factors such as relaxation, stress reduction, fun, enjoyment, and social interaction are among the key self-reported motivations for commencing and continuing cycling. In an online survey of 2,403 members and contacts of the Australian cycling advocacy organization Bicycle Victoria, key reasons for commencing and continuing cycling included "fun and enjoyment," "getting outside in the fresh air," "relaxation and stress reduction," and "time out for myself" (Garrard, Crawford, and Hakman 2006). Survey participants bicycled for recreation (91%), transportation (58%), and competition (13%).

Cycling usually occurs outdoors, and "green exercise" carried out "in the presence of nature" may improve self-esteem and mood, with a synergistic effect for exercise and exposure to nature (Barton and Pretty 2010). In a detailed qualitative study of the personal and cultural meanings of cycling among twenty-two mainly elderly male cyclists in north-central Italy, participants talked about cycling making them feel healthier, happier, and more youthful, and of the fun and enjoyment of being out and about in the natural environment (Whitaker 2005). In the words of the men, "The bicycle makes the eyes smile" (19), and "I do it because it is my passion, because it is a habit; it is a habit that attached itself affectionately to me" (25).

Enhanced well-being is frequently associated with recreational cycling but is rarely considered in research into travel mode choice, which is predominantly concerned with utility factors such as cost, convenience, and travel time. A study in the United Kingdom reported that compared with other commuter modes, cyclists were more likely to report that their journey to work was pleasant, interesting, and exciting (Gatersleben and Uzzell 2007). However, the context may influence perceptions of stress associated with the cycling commute, with a Belgian study reporting that commuter cycling was associated with increased stress among men in blue-collar jobs (though not among other population subgroups in the study sample; Asztalos et al. 2009).

Young people consistently report a preference for active travel to school, including cycling. Evaluation of the Ride2School program in Victoria, Australia, found that cycling was the most popular mode of travel to school among students in fourth through sixth grades participating in the program; 81 percent "liked" cycling or "really liked [it] a lot" (Garrard, Crawford, and Godbold 2009). "Enjoyment," "Exercise and fitness," and "Quick travel time" were the most frequently cited reasons for preferring cycling to school, indicating that—as for adults— cycling is often perceived to be enjoyable as well as having utilitarian value. As shown in chapter 11, despite young people's preferences for cycling (and walking) to school, in countries such as the United States, the United Kingdom, Canada, Australia, and New Zealand, most children are driven to school, and rates of cycling and walking to school have fallen dramatically over recent decades (van der Ploeg et al. 2008). This disconnection between preferences and behavior indicates high latent demand for cycling but also major barriers to acting on preferred travel modes.

The flip side of the enjoyment of cycling is the psychological distress associated with the actual and perceived risks of cycling in traffic. These are frequently reported barriers to cycling (Horton 2007). The social discrimination and victimization of cyclists as minority road users can also lead to harassment of cyclists (Basford et al. 2002; Garrard, Crawford, and Hakman 2006; Gatersleben and Haddad 2010; Heesch, Sahlqvist, and Garrard 2011; Pucher, Garrard, and Greaves 2011). These factors can contribute to what Horton (2007, 133) refers to as the "fear of cycling."

Social norms and values about being a "good mother" can also label parents (usually mothers) who allow their children to cycle to school as "irresponsible" (Skenazy 2009; Horton 2007). The road safety response to fatalities and serious injuries among motor vehicle occupants is to improve road safety (a societal response) rather than to recommend that people drive less (i.e., take individual responsibility to avoid exposure to risk). As noted in chapter 7, a key aspect of motor vehicle domination is to remove cyclists and pedestrians from the road environment by holding them responsible for the harm caused to them by cars (Jacobsen, Racioppi, and Rutter 2009; Horton 2007).

The research cited previously suggests that for people who choose to cycle, even in adverse conditions, the benefits (including enjoyment) outweigh the concerns. However, negative psychological and social factors can act as major barriers to the promotion of cycling among noncyclists. These particular barriers are likely to decline if cycling becomes more prevalent and safer, and sheds its "minority road user" status.

Social Health Benefits

Human-scale urban environments that support cycling and walking and discourage car use can improve social interactions and increase community attachment, livability, and amenity (Litman and Doherty 2009). The provision of road space to enable high-volume, high-speed car travel comes at a cost to other road users and local residents in terms of community disruption, noise pollution, social isolation, urban sprawl, restrictions on children's independent mobility and opportunities for outdoor play and social interactions (Carver, Timperio, and Crawford 2008; Handy, Cao, and Mokhtarian 2005; Dora and Phillips 2000; Ewing et al. 2003). Appleyard and Lintell's original research, which found that heavy traffic is associated with reduced street-based activities and social interactions between neighbors (Appleyard and Lintell 1980), has been replicated in other settings (Bosselmann and Macdonald 1999; Hart 2008). In response to these findings, and to their widespread omission in transportation planning, Litman has developed a comprehensive framework for transportation planning that includes valuing community cohesion and social connectedness (2009).

There is also evidence that the more compact, permeable urban designs that support cycling and walking lead to crime reduction through increased street activity and "natural surveillance" (Hillier and Sahbaz 2006; Cozens, Saville, and Hillier 2005).

The social interactions that occur as part of recreational and transportation cycling have also been documented (de Geus et al. 2008). In the study of elderly Italian cyclists mentioned earlier, Whitaker (2005) reported that the social connectedness associated with cycling was highly valued among the study sample of older male cyclists.

Cycling also contributes to social inclusion because it provides an affordable and convenient form of personal mobility that is accessible to people who do not own or have access to a motor vehicle. Transportation costs (principally motor vehicle related) account for a high proportion (16%) of household expenditure on goods and services in Australia—second only to expenditure on food and nonalcoholic beverages (17%), and similar to housing costs (16%) (Australian Bureau of Statistics 2006). In the United States, transportation is taking up increasing amounts of household budgets. Although study methodologies have changed over time, the available estimates indicate steady increases in transportation costs from 3.1 percent in 1917–1919 to 15.9 percent in 1984 and 19 percent in 2002 (Australian Bicycle Council 2010).

Psychological and social health also affect physical health. Social isolation, lack of social support, and depression are important risk factors for cardiovascular disease. The increased risk contributed by these psychosocial factors is of similar order to the more conventional coronary heart disease risk factors such as smoking, dyslipidemia, and hypertension (Bunker et al. 2003).

Cycling as a Means of Reducing Health Inequalities

Social gradients in health status exist in most countries, with the poor experiencing substantially higher mortality and morbidity than the rich (Marmot 2001). Many factors contribute to health inequalities, including inequalities in health-enhancing behaviors such as physical activity. However, physical activity through active travel is usually more equitably distributed in populations than leisure-time physical activity. Socioeconomically advantaged population groups are about twice as likely as disadvantaged groups to participate in leisure-time physical activity or sports (Australian Bureau of Statistics 2009b), but this is not the case for transportation cycling and walking (Matthews et al. 2007; Andersen et al. 2000; Berrigan et al. 2006).

In addition to socioeconomically disadvantaged population groups, other priority groups for the promotion of physical activity include women, adolescent girls, and older adults. As shown in chapters 2, 10, and 11, in countries such as Germany, Denmark, the Netherlands, and Japan, a high proportion of young people cycle to school (Garrard 2009), women cycle as frequently as men, and in some cases, the majority of trips taken by seniors (aged 65 and older) are active trips such as cycling and walking (Pucher and Buehler 2008, 2010). These diverse population groups frequently achieve adequate levels of physical activity incidentally, at low cost, and without having to find the time and money to participate in organized sports or fitness programs. The socially inclusive, population-wide participation associated with active travel may help to explain the inverse relationship observed between walking and cycling rates and obesity levels internationally (Pucher et al. 2010; Bassett et al. 2008).

Health in general is better and more equitably distributed when all people have access to the conditions and environments that support health and health enhancing behaviors. Accordingly, improved social integration could be achieved by adopting transportation and road use policies that prioritize public good over private interest by providing more equitable public access to space and mobility, thereby "turning an urban nightmare into a fairer society" (Peñalosa 2010). As Peñalosa states, "A bicycle path is a social statement that a person with a $40 bicycle is as important as anyone with a $40,000 car."

Health Benefits of Reduced Motor Vehicle Use

Although motor vehicle use has a number of positive features, such as the abilities to transport large or bulky heavy items and to cover long distances relatively quickly, these benefits are accompanied by health and social costs. At a personal level, the very sedentary nature of driving or sitting in a motor vehicle is a health hazard. A study of Chinese men found that those who reported riding in a car (as driver or passenger) for more than ten hours a week had an 82 percent greater risk of dying from cardiovascular disease than those who reported less than four hours a week, and similar findings have been reported in the United States (Warren et al. 2010).

Driving to work has been associated with a 13 percent increased risk of being overweight or obese (Wen et al. 2006) after controlling for leisure-time physical activity. Similar associations between time spent driving and obesity have been found in other parts of the world, including the United States (Frank, Andresen, and Schmid 2004), China (Bell, Ge, and Popkin 2002), and Latin America. An Australian study found that men who cycle to work are less likely to be overweight or obese than men who drive to work (Wen and Rissel 2008).

An increase in cycling, when it is associated with a decrease in motor vehicle use, also generates a number of indirect health benefits in the form of reductions in air and noise pollution, road traffic injuries, congestion, and greenhouse gas emissions.

Improved Air Quality
Motor vehicles are a major source of air pollution in most major cities (Bureau of Transport and Regional Economics 2005). In Australia, with a population of about 20 million people, between 900 and 4,500 cases of cardiovascular and respiratory disease occurred due to motor vehicle related air pollution in 2000, costing between AUD$0.4 billion and AUD$1.2 billion (about US$0.4 billion–US$1.3 billion). In addition, air pollution caused by motor vehicles accounted for between 900 and 2,000 premature deaths, with an estimated cost of between AUD$1.1 billion and AUD$2.6 billion (about US$1.2 billion–US$2.7 billion) (Bureau of Transport and Regional Economics 2005). These premature deaths, which are comparable to the number of people killed in road crashes (1,464 in Australia in 2008), have been labeled "the silent road toll." The impact of air and noise pollution is greatest in dense urban centers. Cycling therefore offers significant potential to reduce this cost, as these areas are also the most amenable to cycling because trip distance is likely to be shorter than in outer areas.

Comparative Exposure to Air Pollutants: Cyclists Compared to Motor Vehicle Occupants
One reason motorists sometimes give for not riding a bicycle is that they do not want to be exposed to air pollutants in the road carriageway. Motor vehicles emit a variety of air pollutants that are known to be associated with adverse health effects including fine particles, nitrogen

dioxide and volatile organic compounds (VOCs) (WHO 2005). It is well established that the motor vehicle is a principal source of air pollution in medium and large cities. Less well established is the extent to which cyclists are at higher or lower risk of harmful exposure to air pollutants than other road users. When comparing cyclists' exposures to those of motor vehicle occupants, it is important to consider not only roadway exposure but also the flow rate of pollutants from outdoors to the car interior and vice versa (Knibbs, de Dear, and Atkinson 2009). For car occupants, interior concentrations of pollutants are affected by interior and exterior sources of pollution and the air exchange rate in the vehicle cabin, which in turn is affected by factors such as vehicle speed, ventilation settings, and window positions (Knibbs, de Dear, and Atkinson 2009).

For cyclists, exposure depends on cycling route, location on the roadway, weather, traffic intensity, vehicle and fuel type, speed, and driving style. In addition, the higher respiration rates for cyclists compared with motor vehicle occupants (estimates range from 2.3 to 4.3 times higher) can result in cyclists experiencing greater inhaled quantities of some pollutants than car passengers (Panis et al. 2010). This area of study is complex, with a recent study concluding that further research is required to enable the development of an appropriate model for assessing the relative health impacts attributable to air pollution for cyclists compared with car drivers (van Kempen et al. 2010). What is certain, however, is that reduced motor vehicle use will reduce the health risks of air pollution for all people in urban areas and that choosing low traffic cycling routes can reduce cyclists' exposure to air pollution.

Reduced Noise Pollution

In most urban areas, traffic is the most important source of noise nuisance, which can contribute to insomnia, stress, and hearing damage (Dora and Phillips 2000; Buis and Wittink 2000). There is also emerging evidence of an association between high levels of noise and heart disease (Coghlan 2007). Motor vehicle noise also contributes to reduced community livability (as mentioned previously). In a population survey of crime victimization in Australia, dangerous/noisy driving was the most frequently reported perceived neighborhood problem with crime or nuisance (ahead of vandalism/graffiti, housebreakings, drunkenness, louts/ gangs, car theft, and illegal drugs) (Australian Bureau of Statistics 2010).

Greenhouse Gas Emissions and Climate Change
Transportation is a significant and growing source of the greenhouse gas emissions that contribute to climate change. For example, road transportation is responsible for 22 percent of the United Kingdom's total greenhouse gas emissions (UK Department for Transport 2009). In Australia, transportation emissions rose 30 percent between 1990 and 2005; this level is expected to rise by 67 percent above 1990 levels by 2020 (Department of Climate Change and Energy Efficiency 2008). Cycling, as a zero-emission form of transportation, offers a currently untapped potential to lower emissions in the passenger transportation sector. Unlike a number of high-tech options, bicycles are an equitable, off-the-shelf option that can be deployed immediately. Even with the current limited bicycle infrastructure in Australian cities, cycling to work in 2006 accounted for an estimated 189,392,000 km traveled per year in Australian capital cities, which amounts to a greenhouse gas saving of about 45,000 tons per year relative to single-occupant car travel (Bauman et al. 2008).

The environmental consequences of climate change, which include sea-level rise, degraded air quality, and extreme weather events affect human health both directly and indirectly. Direct health effects include heat-related mortality and morbidity, increased injuries and violence, drowning, vector-, food- and water-borne diseases, food and water shortages and malnutrition, exacerbation of respiratory diseases, and mental health and stress-related disorders (USA Interagency Working Group on Climate Change and Health 2010).

Economic Appraisal of the Health Benefits of Cycling

Transportation services and infrastructure often undergo comprehensive economic appraisals as a basis for investment decision making. However, because many of the benefits of cycling are difficult to measure and are distributed across several sectors, cycling projects tend to be undervalued and consequently underfunded.

Valuing the health benefits of cycling is particularly challenging. As outlined previously, there are multiple health benefits (and some health risks) of cycling that vary across population groups (e.g., men/women, children/adults), time, and place. These benefits can be difficult to quantify and even more difficult to monetize. Nevertheless, some comprehensive benefit-cost analyses (BCAs) of cycling projects that include health benefits have been conducted (ABW 2012). Other studies provide a more general valuation of the health benefits of cycling—for example, estimates of the health cost savings associated with a 10 percent increase in cycling rates.

The World Health Organization's Health Economic Assessment Tool for Cycling (HEAT for cycling) is an example of the latter approach (Rutter et al. 2008). This method has become the standard UK government method for incorporating physical activity benefits into transportation appraisals. It produces an estimate of the mean annual benefit (per cyclist, per trip, and total annual benefit) due to reduced mortality as a result of cycling. The tool consists of a User Guide and Microsoft Excel spreadsheet or direct online system for calculating the health benefit based on parameters entered by the user. The tool uses the "value of statistical life" approach, which estimates reductions in mortality (http://www.heatwalkingcycling.org), and demonstrates health and cost savings for even small increases in population levels of cycling.

A recent report to Cycling England, *Planning for Cycling*, valued the health benefits of a regular commuting cyclist (three times a week for a year) at £679.67 (approximately US$1,070) (SQW Consulting 2008). In the UK Cycling Demonstration Towns project, on average, cycling rates increased by 27 percent in the Cycling Demonstration Towns, and the health benefits (from reduced mortality) were estimated to be around £2.50 for every £1 spent (Cycling England 2010).

Sixteen studies that presented the findings of an economic valuation of an aspect of transportation infrastructure or policy, and included data on walking and/or cycling and health effects in the valuation, were reviewed by Cavill et al. (2008). The benefit-cost ratios (BCRs) were of an impressive magnitude: the median BCR was 5:1, which is far higher than BCRs that are routinely used in transportation infrastructure planning. In the United Kingdom, for example, a BCR of greater than 2 is counted as "high value for money" (Cavill et al. 2008). Health benefits make a sizeable contribution to these BCRs, with a BCA of cycling networks in three cities in Norway reporting that reduced health costs accounted for between two-thirds and one-half of the total benefits (Nordic Council of Ministers 2005).

Few economic appraisals of the health benefits of replacing car trips with cycling trips have included the health benefits of reduced air pollution, noise pollution, and greenhouse gas emissions, although the health benefits of air pollution reduction were included in a study of the impact on walking of the provision of sidewalks (Guo and Gandavarapu 2010).

Summaries of studies that estimate the health value of cycling indicate large variations in health values, reflecting different study types, population groups, appraisal methods, and assumptions (Victoria Transport Policy Institute 2010; Nordic Council of Ministers 2005).

In summary, economic appraisals of the benefits and costs of cycling provision are limited, and few have included the multiple health benefits of cycling (ABW 2012). Nonetheless, the public health benefits of cycling are substantial and make the greatest contribution to overall cycling benefits. These findings indicate that BCAs of transportation infrastructure should routinely include health benefits. There are also indications that BCRs are greatest for cities with low levels of cycling where increases in cycling are easier to achieve than in cities that already have high rates of cycling (Interface for Cycling Expertise 2000).

Conclusions

Cycling has enormous potential to improve public health, particularly in cities and countries that currently have low levels of transportation cycling. Active transportation is consistently associated with meeting recommended levels of physical activity for health (Berrigan et al. 2006) and may flatten out the commonly seen socioeconomic gradient in leisure-time physical activity participation. The potential for active travel to be one of the key solutions to the problem of physical inactivity is well recognized (Shephard 2008) and deserves substantial advocacy and policy focus.

Reduced motor vehicle use also contributes to additional benefits in the form of improved air quality, lower noise levels, reduced greenhouse gas emissions, and improved community livability. When the multiple health and social benefits of a mode shift from private motor vehicle use to cycling are monetized, the economic argument for investing in increased cycling is powerful, with BCRs substantially higher than for investments in alternative forms of transportation infrastructure.

The goal of increased cycling rates in urban areas is achievable, with a number of both developed and developing countries successfully stalling or reversing unhealthy and unsustainable increases in single-occupant car travel for relatively short distances in urban areas. For clean, green, and healthy cities of the future, the road ahead is looking increasingly like a bicycle lane.

References

Åberg, Maria A. I., Nancy L. Pedersen, Kjell Torén, Magnus Svartengren, Björn Bäckstrand, Tommy Johnsson, and Christianna M. Cooper-Kuhn, N. David Åberg, Michael Nilsson, and H. Georg Kuhn. 2009. Cardiovascular Fitness Is Associated with Cognition in Young Adulthood. *Proceedings of the National Academy of Sciences* 106 (49): 20906–209011.

Ainsworth, Barbara E., William L. Haskell, Melicia C. Whitt, Melinda L. Irwin, Ann M. Swartz, Scott J. Strath, William L. O'Brien, et al. 2000. Compendium of Physical Activities: An Update of Activity Codes and MET Intensities. *Medicine and Science in Sports and Exercise* 32 (9 Suppl.): S498–S504.

ABW (Alliance for Biking and Walking). 2012. *Bicycling and Walking in the United States: 2012 Benchmarking Report.* Washington, DC: Alliance for Biking and Walking. http://www.peoplepoweredmovement.org/benchmarking.

Andersen, Lars B., Peter Schnohr, Marianne Schroll, and Hans O. Hein. 2000. All-Cause Mortality Associated with Physical Activity During Leisure Time, Work, Sports, and Cycling to Work. *Archives of Internal Medicine* 160 (11): 1621–1628.

Andersen, L. B., D. A. Lawlor, A. R. Cooper, K. Froberg, and S. A. Anderssen. 2009. Physical Fitness in Relation to Transport to School in Adolescents: The Danish Youth and Sports Study. *Scandinavian Journal of Medicine & Science in Sports* 19 (3): 406–411.

Angevaren, Maaike, Gert Aufdemkampe, H. J. J. Verhaar, A. Aleman, and Luc Vanhees. 2008. Physical Activity and Enhanced Fitness to Improve Cognitive Function in Older People without Known Cognitive Impairment. *Cochrane Database of Systematic Reviews*, no. 3. Art. no.: CD005381. DOI: 10.1002/14651858. CD005381.pub3.

Appleyard, Donald, and Mark Lintell. 1980. The Environmental Quality of City Streets: The Residents' Viewpoint. *Journal of the American Institute of Planners* 38:84–101.

Asztalos, Melinda, Katrien Wijndaele, Ilse de Bourdeaudhuij, Renaat Philip-paerts, Lynn Matton, and Nathalie Duvigneaud. 2009. Specific Associations between Types of Physical Activity and Components of Mental Health. *Journal of Science and Medicine in Sport* 12 (4): 468–474.

Australian Bicycle Council. 2010. *Benefits of Cycling*. Canberra, Australia: Austroads. http://www.austroads.com.au/abc/index.php?type=sep&id=33.

Australian Bureau of Statistics. 2006. *Household Expenditure Survey, Australia: Summary of Results, 2003–04. Cat. No. 6530.0*. Canberra, Australia: Commonwealth of Australia.

Australian Bureau of Statistics. 2009a. *Environmental Issues: Waste Management and Transport Use. Cat. No. 4602.0.55.002*. Canberra, Australia: Commonwealth of Australia.

Australian Bureau of Statistics. 2009b. *Perspectives on Sport. Cat. No. 4156.0.55.001*. Canberra, Australia: Commonwealth of Australia.

Australian Bureau of Statistics. 2010. *Crime Victimisation, Australia, 2008–09, Cat. No. 4530.0*. Canberra, Australia: Commonwealth of Australia.

Barton, Jo, and Jules Pretty. 2010. What Is the Best Dose of Nature and Green Exercise for Improving Mental Health? A Multi-Study Analysis. *Environmental Science & Technology* 44 (10): 3947–3955.

Basford, L., S. Reid, T. Lester, J. Thomson, and A. Tolmie. 2002. *Drivers' Perceptions of Cyclists*. Transport Research Laboratory Report 549. Crowthorne, Scotland: Transport Research Laboratory.

Bassett, David R., Jr., John Pucher, Ralph Buehler, Dixie L. Thompson, and Scott E. Crouter. 2008. Walking, Cycling, and Obesity Rates in Europe, North America, and Australia. *Journal of Physical Activity & Health* 5:795–814.

Bauman, Adrian, Chris Rissel, Jan Garrard, Ian Ker, Rosemarie Speidel, and Elliot Fishman. 2008. *Cycling: Getting Australia Moving: Barriers, Facilitators and Interventions to Get More Australians Physically Active Through Cycling*. Melbourne: Cycling Promotion Fund. http://www.cyclingpromotion.com.au/content/view/333/145/.

Bell, Colin A., Keyou Ge, and Barrie M. Popkin. 2002. The Road to Obesity or the Path to Prevention: Motorized Transportation and Obesity in China. *Obesity Research* 10:277–283.

Berrigan, David, Richard P. Troiano, Timothy McNeel, Charles DiSogra, and Rachel Ballard-Barbash. 2006. Active Transportation Increases Adherence to Activity Recommendations. *American Journal of Preventive Medicine* 31 (3): 210–216.

Biesma, Regien, Leo J. Schouten, Miranda J. M. Dirx, R. Alexanda Goldbohm, and Piet A. van den Brandt. 2006. Physical Activity and Risk of Ovarian Cancer: Results from the Netherlands Cohort Study (The Netherlands). *Cancer Causes & Control* 17 (1): 109–115.

Bosselmann, Peter, and Elizabeth Macdonald. 1999. Livable Streets Revisited. *Journal of the American Planning Association* 65 (2): 165–180.

Buehler, Ralph, John Pucher, Dafna Merom, and Adrian Bauman. 2011. Active Travel in Germany and the USA: Contributions of Daily Walking and Cycling to Physical Activity. *American Journal of Preventive Medicine* 40 (9) (September): 241–250.

Buis, Jeroen, and Roelof Wittink. 2000. *The Economic Significance of Cycling—A Study to Illustrate the Costs and Benefits of Cycling Policy.* The Hague, The Netherlands: VNG Uitgeverij.

Bunker, Stephen J., et al. 2003. Stress and Coronary Heart Disease: Psychosocial Risk Factors. *Medical Journal of Australia* 178 (6): 272–276.

Bureau of Transport and Regional Economics. 2005. *Health Impacts of Transport Emissions in Australia: Economic Costs.* Canberra, Australia: Department of Transport and Regional Services.

Carver, Alison, Anna Timperio, and David Crawford. 2008. Playing It Safe: The Influence of Neighbourhood Safety on Children's Physical Activity: A Review. *Health & Place* 14 (2): 217–227.

Caspersen, Carl J., Bennie P. Bloemberg, Wim H. Saris, Robert K. Merritt, and Daan Kromhout. 1991. The Prevalence of Selected Physical Activities and Their Relation with Coronary Heart Disease Risk Factors in Elderly Men: The Zutphen Study, 1985. *American Journal of Epidemiology* 133 (11): 1078–1092.

Cavill, Nick, Sonja Kahlmeier, Harry Rutter, Francesca Racioppi, and Pekka Oja. 2008. Economic Analyses of Transport Infrastructure and Policies Including Health Effects Related to Cycling and Walking: A Systematic Review. *Transport Policy* 15 (5): 291–304.

Coghlan, Andy. 2007. Dying for Some Quiet: The Truth about Noise Pollution. *New Scientist Magazine* 195 (2618): 6–9.

Cooper, Ashley R., Niels Wedderkopp, Russell Jago, Peter L. Kristensen, Niels C. Moller, Karsten Froberg, Angie S. Page, and Lars B. Andersen. 2008. Longitudinal Associations of Cycling to School with Adolescent Fitness. *Preventive Medicine* 47 (3): 324–328.

Cozens, Paul M., Greg Saville, and David Hillier. 2005. Crime Prevention through Environmental Design (CPTED): A Review and Modern Bibliography. *Property Management* 23 (5): 328–356.

Cycling England. 2010. *Cycling Demonstration Towns: Development of Benefit-Cost Ratios.* London: Department for Transport. http://www.dft.gov.uk/pgr/regional/ltp/demotowns/.

Department of Climate Change and Energy Efficiency. 2008. *Transport Sector Greenhouse Gas Emissions Projections 2007.* Canberra, Australia: Commonwealth of Australia. http://www.climatechange.gov.au/publications/projections/australias-emissions-projections/emissions-projection-2010.aspx#transport.

de Geus, Bas, Ilse de Bourdeaudhuij, Caroline Jannes, and Romain Meeusen. 2008. Psychosocial and Environmental Factors Associated with Cycling for Transport among a Working Population. *Health Education Research* 23 (4): 697–708.

Dora, Carlos, and Margaret Phillips. 2000. *Transport, Environment and Health.* Copenhagen: World Health Organization Regional Office for Europe. http://www.euro.who.int/__data/assets/pdf_file/0003/87573/E72015.pdf.

Ewing, Reid, Tom Schmid, Richard Killingsworth, Amy Zlot, and Stephen Raudenbush. 2003. Relationship between Urban Sprawl and Physical Activity, Obesity and Morbidity. *American Journal of Health Promotion* 18 (1): 47–57.

Frank, Lawrence D., Martin A. Andresen, and Thomas L. Schmid. 2004. Obesity Relationships with Community Design, Physical Activity, and Time Spent in Cars. *American Journal of Preventive Medicine* 27 (2): 87–96.

Garrard, Jan. 2009. *Active Transport: Children and Young People. An Overview of Recent Evidence.* Melbourne: Victorian Health Promotion Foundation. http://www.vichealth.vic.gov.au/en/Publications/Physical-Activity/Active-transport/Active-Transport-Children.aspx.

Garrard, Jan, Sharinne Crawford, and Tara Godbold. 2009. *Evaluation of the Ride2School Program: Final Report.* Melbourne: Deakin University.

Garrard, Jan, Sharinne Crawford, and Natalie Hakman. 2006. *Revolutions for Women: Increasing Women's Participation in Cycling for Recreation and Transport.* Melbourne: Deakin University. http://www.bv.com.au/file/Revs%20exec%20summary%20Final%2012Oct06.pdf.

Gatersleben, Birgitta, and Hebba Haddad. 2010. Who Is the Typical Bicyclist? *Transportation Research Part F: Traffic Psychology and Behaviour* 13:41–48.

Gatersleben, Birgitta, and David Uzzell. 2007. Affective Appraisals of the Daily Commute. *Environment and Behavior* 39 (3): 416–431.

Guo, Jessica Y., and Sasanka Gandavarapu. 2010. An Economic Evaluation of Health-Promotive Built Environment Changes. *Preventive Medicine* 50 (Suppl. 1): S44–S49.

Hamer, Mark, and Yoichi Chida. 2008. Active Commuting and Cardiovascular Risk: A Meta-Analytic Review. *Preventive Medicine* 46 (1): 9–13.

Handy, Susan, Xinyu Cao, and Patricia Mokhtarian. 2005. Correlation or Causality Between the Built Environment and Travel Behavior? Evidence from Northern California. *Transportation Research Part D, Transport and Environment* 10 (6): 427–444.

Hart, Joshua. 2008. Driven to Excess: Impacts of Motor Vehicle Traffic on Residential Quality of Life in Bristol, UK. Master's thesis, Transport Planning, University of the West of England, Bristol.

Heesch, Kristiann, Shannon Sahlqvist, and Jan Garrard. 2011. Cyclists' Experiences of Harassment from Motorists: Findings from a Survey of Cyclists in Queensland, Australia. *Preventive Medicine* 53 (6): 417–420.

Hillier, Bill, and Ozlem Sahbaz. 2006. *High-Resolution Analysis of Crime Patterns in Urban Street Networks: An Initial Statistical Sketch from an Ongoing Study of a London Borough.* London: University College London.

Horton, David. 2007. Fear of Cycling. In *Cycling and Society*, ed. David Horton, Paul Rosen, and Peter Cox, 133–152. Aldershot, Hampshire, England: Ashgate Publishing.

Hou, Lifang, Bu-Tian Ji, Aaron Blair, Qi Dai, Yu-Tang Gao, and Wong-Ho Chow. 2004. Commuting Physical Activity and Risk of Colon Cancer in Shanghai, China. *American Journal of Epidemiology* 160 (9): 860–867.

Hu, Gang, Heikki Pekkarinen, Osmo Hanninen, Zhijie Yu, Zeyu Gou, and Huiguan Tian. 2002. Commuting, Leisure-Time Physical Activity, and Cardio-vascular Risk Factors in China. *Medicine and Science in Sports and Exercise* 34 (2): 234–238.

Hu, Gang, Q. Qiao, K. Silventoinen, J. Eriksson, P. Jousilahti, J. Lindstrom, T. T. Valle, A. Nissinen, and J. Tuomilehto. 2003. Occupational, Commuting, and Leisure-Time Physical Activity in Relation to Risk for Type 2 Diabetes in Middle-Aged Finnish Men and Women. *Diabetologia* 46 (3): 322–329.

Hu, Gang, Jaakko Tuomilehto, Katja Borodulin, and Pekka Jousilahti. 2007. The Joint Associations of Occupational, Commuting, and Leisure-Time Physical Activity, and the Framingham Risk Score on the 10-Year Risk of Coronary Heart Disease. *European Heart Journal* 28 (4): 492–498.

Huy, C., S. Becker, U. Gomolinsky, T. Klein, and A. Thiel. 2008. Health, Medical Risk Factors, and Bicycle Use in Everyday Life in the Over-50 Population. *Journal of Aging and Physical Activity* 16 (4): 454–464.

Interface for Cycling Expertise. 2000. *Study on Cost and Benefits of Cycling Policies (2000)*. Utrecht, The Netherlands: Interface for Cycling Expertise. http://www.i-ce.nl/index.php?option=com_content&task=view&id=39&Itemid=80.

Jacobsen, Peter L., Francesca Racioppi, and Harry Rutter. 2009. Who Owns the Roads? How Motorized Traffic Discourages Walking and Cycling. *Injury Prevention* 15 (6): 369–373.

Knibbs, L. D., R. J. de Dear, and S. E. Atkinson. 2009. Field Study of Air Change and Flow Rate in Six Automobiles. *Indoor Air* 19 (4): 303–313.

Lee, Murray C., Maria R. Orenstein, and Maxwell J. Richardson. 2008. Systematic Review of Active Commuting to School and Children's Physical Activity and Weight. *Journal of Physical Activity & Health* 5 (6): 930–949.

Lindwall, Magnus, Pernilla Larsman, and Martin S. Hagger. 2011. The Reciprocal Relationship between Physical Activity and Depression in Older European Adults: A Prospective Cross-Lagged Panel Design Using Share Data. *Health Psychology* 30 (4): 453–462.

Litman, Todd A. 2009. *Community Cohesion as a Transport Planning Objective*. Victoria, Canada: Victoria Transport Policy Institute. http://www.vtpi.org/cohesion.pdf.

Litman, Todd A., and Eric Doherty. 2009. Transportation Cost and Benefit Analysis: Techniques, Estimates and Implications. 2nd ed. Victoria, Canada: Victorian Transport Policy Institute. http://www.vtpi.org/tca/.

Lusk, Anne C., Rania A. Mekary, Diane Feskanich, and Walter C. Willett. 2010. Bicycle Riding, Walking, and Weight Gain in Premenopausal Women. *Archives of Internal Medicine* 179 (12): 1050–1056.

Marmot, Michael. 2001. Inequalities in Health. *New England Journal of Medicine* 345 (2): 134–136.

Matthews, Charles E., Adriana L. Jurj, Xiao-Ou Shu, Hong-Lan Li, Gong Yang, Qi Li, Yu-Tang Gao, and Wei Zheng. 2007. Influence of Exercise, Walking, Cycling, and Overall Nonexercise Physical Activity on Mortality in Chinese Women. *American Journal of Epidemiology* 165 (12): 1343–1350.

Matthews, Charles E., Xiao-Ou Shu, F. Jin, Q. Dai, J. R. Hebert, Z.-X. Ruan, Y-.T. Gao, and W. Zheng. 2001. Lifetime Physical Activity and Breast Cancer Risk in the Shanghai Breast Cancer Study. *British Journal of Cancer* 84 (7): 994–1001.

Mead, G. E., W. Morley, P. Campbell, C. A. Greig, M. McMurdo, and D. A. Lawlor. 2009. Exercise for Depression. *Cochrane Database of Systematic Reviews*, no. 3. Art. no.: CD004366. DOI: 10.1002/14651858.CD004366.pub4.

NICE (National Institute for Health and Clinical Excellence). 2009. *The Treatment and Management of Depression in Adults*. London: NICE. http://www.nice.org.uk/CG90.

Nordic Council of Ministers. 2005. *CBA of Cycling*. Copenhagen, Denmark: Nordic Council of Ministers. http://www.thepep.org/ClearingHouse/docfiles/CBA%20on%20cycling%20nordic%20council%20report%202005.pdf.

Oja, Pekka, Sylvia Titze, Adrian Bauman, Bas de Geus, P. Krenn, B. Reger-Nash, and T. Kohlberger. 2011. Health Benefits of Cycling: A Systematic Review. *Scandinavian Journal of Medicine & Science in Sports* 21:496–509.

Ohta, Masanor, Tetsuya Mizoue, Norio Mishima, and Masaharu Ikeda. 2007. Effect of the Physical Activities in Leisure Time and Commuting to Work on Mental Health. *Journal of Occupational Health* 49 (1): 46–52.

Panis, Luc Int, Bas deGeus, Gregory Vandenbulcke, Hanny Willems, Bart Degraeuwe, Nico Bleux, Vinit Mishra, Isabelle Thomas, and Romain Meeusen. 2010. Exposure to Particulate Matter in Traffic: A Comparison of Cyclists and Car Passengers. *Atmospheric Environment* 44:2263–2270.

Peñalosa, Enrique. 2010. How to Turn an Urban Nightmare into a Fairer Society, chapter 3, *The Forum*, BBC World Service, April 4, 2010. http://www.bbc.co.uk/programmes/p006xbmx.

Pucher, John, and Ralph Buehler. 2008. Making Cycling Irresistible: Lessons from the Netherlands, Denmark and Germany. *Transport Reviews* 28 (4): 495–528.

Pucher, John, and Ralph Buehler. 2010. Walking and Cycling for Healthy Cities. *Built Environment* 36 (5): 391–414.

Pucher, John, Ralph Buehler, David R. Bassett, and Andrew L. Dannenberg. 2010. Walking and Cycling to Health: A Comparative Analysis of City, State, and International Data. *American Journal of Public Health* 100 (10): 1986–1992.

Pucher, John, Jan Garrard, and Stephen Greaves. 2011. Cycling Down Under: A Comparative Analysis of Bicycling Trends and Policies in Sydney and Melbourne. *Journal of Transport Geography* 19 (2): 332–345.

Rutter, Harry, Nick Cavill, Sonia Kahlmeier, Francesca Racioppi, and Pekka Oja. 2008. *Health Economic Assessment Tool for Cycling (HEAT for Cycling) User Guide*. Copenhagen, Denmark: WHO Regional Office for Europe. http://www.heatwalkingcycling.org.

Scarmeas, Nikolaos, Jose Luchsinger, Nicole Schupf, Adam M. Brickman, Stephanie Cosentino, Ming X. Tang, and Yaakov Stern. 2009. Physical Activity, Diet, and Risk of Alzheimer Disease. *Journal of the American Medical Association* 302 (6): 627–637.

Shephard, Roy. 2008. Is Active Commuting the Answer to Population Health? *Sports Medicine* 38 (9): 751–758.

Sibley, Benjamin, and Jennifer Etnier. 2003. The Relationship between Physical Activity and Cognition in Children: A Meta-Analysis. *Pediatric Exercise Science* 15:243–256.

Skenazy, Lenore. 2009. *Free-Range Kids: How to Raise Safe, Self-Reliant Children*. San Francisco: Jossey-Bass.

SQW Consulting. 2008. *Planning for Cycling. Report to Cycling England*. Cambridge, UK: SQW Consulting.

Steindorf, Karen, Martina Schmidt, Silke Kropp, and Jenny Chang-Claude. 2003. Case-Control Study of Physical Activity and Breast Cancer Risk among Premenopausal Women in Germany. *American Journal of Epidemiology* 157 (2): 121–130.

UK Department for Transport. 2009. *Low Carbon Transport: A Carbon Reduction Strategy for Transport*. Norwich, UK: The Stationery Office. http://www.official-documents.gov.uk/document/cm76/7682/7682.pdf.

U.S. Department of Health and Human Services. 2008. *Physical Activity Guidelines: Advisory Committee Report 2008*. U.S. Department of Health and Human Services. http://www.health.gov/PAGuidelines/Report/.

USA Interagency Working Group on Climate Change and Health. 2010. *A Human Health Perspective on Climate Change*. http://ehp03.niehs.nih.gov/static/climatechange.action.

van der Ploeg, Hidde P., Dafna Merom, Grace Corpuz, and Adrian E. Bauman. 2008. Trends in Australian Children Traveling to School 1971–2003: Burning Petrol or Carbohydrates? *Preventive Medicine* 46 (1): 60–62.

van Kempen, Elise, W. Swart, G. C. W. Wendel-Vos, P. E. Steinberger, A. B. Knol, H. L. Stipdonk, and M. C. B. Reurings. 2010. *Exchanging Car Trips by Cycling in The Netherlands: A First Estimation of the Health Benefits*. Bilthoven, The Netherlands: RIVM, National Institute for Public Health and the Environment.

Victoria Transport Policy Institute. 2010. Transportation Cost and Benefit Analysis II: Safety and Health Costs. Victoria, Canada: Victoria Transport Policy Institute. http://www.vtpi.org/tca/tca0503.pdf.

von Huth Smith, Lisa, Knut Borch-Johnsen, and Torben Jørgensen. 2007. Commuting Physical Activity Is Favourably Associated with Biological Risk Factors for Cardiovascular Disease. *European Journal of Epidemiology* 22:771–779.

Voss, Christine, and Gavin Sandercock. 2010. Aerobic Fitness and Mode of Travel to School in English School Children. *Medicine and Science in Sports and Exercise* 42 (2): 281–287.

Warren, Tatiana, Vaughn Barry, Steven Hooker, Xuemei Sui, Timothy Church, and Steven Blair. 2010. Sedentary Behaviors Increase Risk of Cardiovascular Disease Mortality in Men. *Medicine and Science in Sports and Exercise* 42 (5): 879–885.

Wen, Li Ming, Neil Orr, Chris Millett, and Chris Rissel. 2006. Driving to Work and Overweight and Obesity: Findings from the 2003 New South Wales Health Survey, Australia. *International Journal of Obesity* 30 (5): 782–786.

Wen, Li Ming, and Chris Rissel. 2008. Inverse Associations Between Cycling to Work, Public Transport, and Overweight and Obesity: Findings from a Population Based Study in Australia. *Preventive Medicine* 46 (1): 29–32.

Whitaker, Elizabeth D. 2005. The Bicycle Makes the Eyes Smile: Exercise, Aging, and Psychophysical Well-Being in Older Italian Cyclists. *Medical Anthropology* 24 (1): 1–43.

WHO (World Health Organization). 1948. *WHO Definition of Health*. Geneva: World Health Organization.

WHO (World Health Organization). 2005. *Health Effects of Transport-Related Air Pollution*. Copenhagen: World Health Organisation Regional Office for Europe.

4

Effective Speed: Cycling Because It's "Faster"

Paul Tranter

In the seventh annual New York Commuter Challenge held by Transportation Alternatives in 2008, a cyclist raced against a bus/subway rider and a driver. The bicycle came in a clear winner, taking just over 16 minutes; the car took 22 minutes and the MTA rider took 29 minutes. Transportation Alternatives also measured the carbon footprint of all the commuters: the bike had zero, the transit rider one pound, and the 5-mile (8-km) drive produced six pounds of carbon dioxide. As the cyclist in the race explained, "Bicycling is the fastest and most affordable way to get to work" (Press 2008). That the bicycle was the fastest should come as no surprise to anyone who has visited New York. Yet even cyclists may be surprised to find just how much time bicycles can save in any city when all time costs are considered.

Many cyclists already know they are faster than cars, particularly in peak traffic. The speed advantages of cycling, rather than health, fitness, or environmental reasons, are an important motivator for cyclists. In Copenhagen, the main reason cyclists give for cycling rather than using other modes is that it saves them time because it's faster (Gehl 2009). It is not only in cities such as Copenhagen and New York that cycling can save time. If we take a holistic view of speed, we can see that in most cities throughout the world, cycling is a "faster" mode of transportation than the car. To demonstrate how this can be the case, it is necessary to first examine the concept of "effective speed."

Effective Speed: The Concept

Effective speed is calculated using the standard formula: speed equals distance divided by time. However, in this calculation, *all* the time costs are considered. For car drivers, a significant (and usually ignored) time cost is the time spent at work to earn the money to pay for all the expenses associated with the mode of transportation.

Transport economists have long been aware of the generalized cost of travel, which is the sum of the monetary and the nonmonetary costs of travel. Money costs for motorists include annual registration, fuel, parking, tolls, fines, insurance costs, and other taxes associated with vehicle purchase and ownership. Nonmonetary costs include the time spent taking a journey. In an economic analysis, time is converted to a value in terms of money on the basis of the earning power of the travelers. The concept of effective speed takes a different approach wherein all costs are converted to time, which can then be used to calculate "speed."

To calculate effective speeds for any group and mode of transportation, the key variables are average trip speed (and hence time spent traveling); the costs of the mode of transportation, which include both direct and indirect (or external) costs; the average (median) income (which determines how much time is devoted to earning the money to pay the costs); and any other time devoted to the mode of transportation besides travel (e.g., time spent filling a car with fuel). Tranter and Ker (2007) used the term "social effective speed" to refer to calculations that involve external (indirect) costs (e.g., pollution, congestion) as well as direct costs.

External costs are rarely considered in choices made by individual motorists about their behavior; hence an understanding of external costs is not as influential in affecting travel behavior as an understanding of direct costs. However, as awareness of issues such as the impact of transportation on climate change increases, motorists may be more likely to consider the collective impacts of their individual transportation decisions. The question about whether external costs should be added to effective speed calculations is a question of morality rather than an objective question about methodology. The critical issue is whether individuals should be responsible for the wider impacts of their behavior. Morality suggests that they should. Current behavior in an individualistic society suggests that the majority of citizens ignore these responsibilities. In terms of external costs, this chapter is written for both pragmatists (who accept that external costs are rarely considered by motorists) and for idealists (who argue that external costs should be considered, at least by governments, even if not by individuals). Hence effective speed calculations are provided both with and without external cost estimates.

Perceptions of Travel and Time Costs

In terms of travel times and costs, as Werner Brög explains, "the car is assessed as being better than it really is, its alternatives worse" (Brog 2000, 7). Motorists typically underestimate the costs and overestimate the speeds of their travel. Public transportation users typically do the reverse. Drivers in the United Kingdom estimated the cost of their cars at a level of 40 percent of the cost calculated by the motoring organization RAC (Tranter and Ker 2007). Car drivers in a German study estimated their costs at 42 percent of actual costs and estimated travel times by car at only 82 percent of the actual times (Brog 2000). Not only do car drivers underestimate the time they spend in their cars, but they also rarely consider the total time devoted to these machines. The irrationality of this thinking is illustrated in the following story.

Imagine that you live in a village in the 1800s and that your job each day is to collect water from a nearby stream. This task takes you an hour each day. To "save time," you construct a machine consisting of a system of pulleys, cables, levers, and springs to collect the water for you. With this machine, simply by pulling a lever, you can send your bucket to the stream and have it returned full of water. You appear to have saved yourself an hour each day. However, to get the machine to work, you must spend an hour each day winding up the spring that powers the machine. Should you consider this time in any decision about the effectiveness of the machine?

In modern cities, the equivalent of the time spent winding up the spring in this example is the time motorists spend at work to earn the money to pay for the various costs of their cars. The car will save time only if the time saved in traveling is greater than the work time required to earn the money to pay for the machine. Many motorists—and city governments—seem to ignore this time spent earning money to pay for the transportation costs, that is, the time spent "winding up the spring." Using the concept of effective speed allows this time to be considered.

Development of Ideas behind Effective Speed in the Literature

The ideas behind the concept of effective speed appear in the literature as early as the 1850s. In his famous book *Walden*, first published in 1854, Henry David Thoreau argues that "the swiftest traveller is he that goes afoot" (cited in Atkinson 1937, 47). Thoreau compares his own speed as a pedestrian with the speed of a fellow traveler who plans to go by train to a nearby town: "I start now on foot, and get there before the night. You will in the meanwhile have earned your fare, and arrive there some time tomorrow, or possibly this evening, if you are lucky enough to get a job in season. Instead of going to Fitchburg, you will be working here the greater part of the day. And so, if the railroad reached around the world, I think that I should keep ahead of you" (cited in Atkinson 1937, 47). In 1974, Ivan Illich wrote his thought-provoking book *Energy and Equity*, in which he brought Thoreau's arguments into the twentieth century. Illich explained:

The typical American male devotes more than 1,600 hours a year to his car. He sits in it while it goes and while it stands idling. He parks it and searches for it. He earns the money to put down on it and to meet the monthly installments. He works to pay for petrol, tolls, insurance, taxes and tickets. He spends four of his sixteen waking hours on the road or gathering his resources for it. And this time does not take into account the time consumed by other activities dictated by transport: time spent in hospitals, traffic courts and garages, time spent watching automobile commercials or attending consumer education meetings to improve the quality of the next buy. The model American puts in 1,600 hours to get 7,500 miles: less than five miles per hour. (Illich 1974, 18–19)

In popular literature, there is also evidence of an awareness of the concept of effective speed. In Michael Ende's fantasy story *Momo*, a central theme is the notion of time thieves—the "men in gray"—who encourage citizens to be more efficient with their use of time. One character in the book, a barber, finds that no matter how much time he "saves," there is still never enough time for contact with friends (Ende 1985). The story can be seen as an allegory in which the men in gray represent cars, which steal our time and our money.

In 1990, German sociologist D. Seifried used the phrase "social speed" to describe the average speed of a vehicle after hidden time costs are considered (Whitelegg 1993a, 1993b). Seifried considered the time spent at work to earn the money to pay for the car and its running costs, as well as the external costs of the car. Such external costs include environmental and social costs (e.g., accident costs). Seifried's calculations indicated that when all costs are considered, the "social speed" of a bicycle could be faster than a car.

Kifer (2002) conducted an assessment of the multitude of costs associated with running a car in the United States, including the direct costs used in the calculation of "vehicle operating costs" by motoring organizations as well as various hidden or indirect costs of cars. When only the direct costs to the motorist are considered, the "net effective speed" of US motorists was estimated to be a mere 9.7 mph (assuming a trip speed of 25 mph as the probable US average for cars) (Kifer 2002). (These "direct costs" did not include parking costs, tolls, fines, or vehicle accessories.)

Fisher (2006) explains why the concept of an "efficient car" is a myth, partly because of the huge costs involved in building and maintaining the car and the infrastructure required to keep large numbers of cars moving (e.g., road construction, police, and hospitals). Fisher also points out that the car is based on an incredibly inefficient use of energy. Cars convert only about 20 percent of the energy in fuel into motion. In addition, most drivers weigh only 1/20th of the mass of their cars. Thus, the energy efficiency of a car is about 1 percent for a driver-only situation. Add to this the costs of dismantling and recycling cars and the "herculean efforts nations make or will make to maintain access to oil, and to make good damage caused by greenhouse-effect-based sea-level rises, cyclone and flood damage . . . the efficiency of the car comes down to a few tenths of one per cent" (Fisher 2006, 121–122).

In his book on bioethics, Macer (2006, 75) argued that "most drivers do not realize how low the actual average speed of their local car trips is." Macer asked his university students, "How hard do you have to work to own a car?" Using data on average car speed from Tokyo (19.2 km/h) and Tsukuba (34.5 km/h), he showed that if we account for the work time needed to earn the cost of owning and operating a car, "the average speed of local driving [in Tsukuba] is reduced from about 34.3 to 20.4 km/h, equivalent to vigorous bicycling speed" (Macer 2006). Similar to arguments made in chapter 3, Macer noted that car drivers miss out on the health benefits of the exercise enabled by walking or cycling, yet he did not include any of the external costs of cars in his calculations of speed.

Tranter and coauthors have applied the concept of effective speed to cities in Australia, showing that even in low-density car-dominated cities in a wealthy nation, car travel is not necessarily the "fastest" mode of transport (Tranter 2004; Tranter and May 2006; Tranter and May 2005a, 2005b; Tranter and Ker 2007). Tranter and Ker (2007) introduced external costs into their calculations of effective speed, showing that in Australian cities, cycling is a superior mode of transportation when all costs are considered. More recent research (Tranter 2010) shows that the concept of effective speed can be linked with time pressure and health outcomes. Cities that rely more on private motorized transportation spend more money and hence more time on transportation than cities where active modes of transportation have a greater modal share (Kenworthy and Laube 1999), which has complex negative health outcomes.

This chapter extends the research on effective speed by examining the effective speeds of cars in selected cities throughout the world and then calculating how fast a cyclist needs to cycle in each city to be effectively "faster" than car drivers. Fourteen cities were chosen to represent a range of densities, traffic congestion, and economic development: car-dominated cities in the United States, Canada, Australia, and New Zealand; European cities with medium densities; a high-density, developed Asian city (Tokyo); and three cities in the developing world, one in Africa and two in Asia.

Readers should be aware of a caveat on the arguments in this chapter, which is written on the premise that increasing speed and "saving time" is a worthwhile goal. It is worth considering the possibility that any policy that stresses speed—even effective speed—as the primary transportation goal can conflict with the goal of promoting safe, enjoyable, everyday cycling for more people.

Estimating Effective Speeds

To calculate the effective speeds of cars, data is needed for the total time spent traveling by car drivers, average incomes, and the costs of owning and operating a car. In addition, time spent on other activities associated with operating a car must be considered (e.g., time spent putting fuel in cars). This information is then used to estimate the total time devoted to cars, including the proportion of work time devoted to earning the money to pay for all the costs of transportation. The effective speed is calculated by dividing the distance traveled by the total time. In this chapter, all calculations of effective speed of car drivers are based on "driver only/driver owned" cars, or "dodos," as they are aptly described by Fisher (2006).

To calculate the time spent on each car trip, drivers would need to time their trips from the time they open the car door until the time they leave their car. Data on average trip speeds by cars in cities tend to underestimate the time spent in cars because these times do not include time spent getting into and out of cars or into and out of parking garages or gas stations. In this chapter, unless data were available for a city (e.g., for Tokyo [Macer 2006] or Delhi [Pucher et al. 2007]), Google Maps was used to estimate the average trip speeds by cars in cities. Google Maps is a standardized application available for most cities throughout the world. In some cities, it also has the advantage of providing speeds "in traffic," which represents the peak or rush-hour times during which driving is concentrated. The data here refer to those areas of cities within 15 km from the central business district (CBD) in the city center, which for many cities covers most of the city. This distance represents the upper limit of a commuting distance that cyclists would be willing to travel to the city center. Starting from the center of each city (as defined by Google Maps), averages of trip speeds were taken for three trips in different directions, of around 15 km, and three trips of between 2 and 5 km, from the CBD. Where other estimates of trip speeds were available (e.g., London and Auckland), the Google Maps estimates were shown to be similar or to produce higher average speeds. In London, for example, official estimates of vehicle speeds vary between central, inner, and outer London (16.9 km/h, 22.5 km/h, and 32.4 km/h, respectively) (Evans 2007). These estimates translate into an average of 23.9 km/h over the whole of London. The Google Maps calculation used to calculate effective speeds for London in this chapter was 27.7 km/h. In cases for which Google Maps provided estimates for trip times "in traffic," these times were used in the calculations. For Auckland, an estimate of travel speed of 32 km/h by traffic engineer David Begg was almost identical to the 32.3 derived from Google Maps (One News 2004).

Data on incomes was sourced from publicly available statistics, such as National Statistics (United Kingdom), Australian Bureau of Statistics,

Statistics Canada, the US Census Bureau, Statistics New Zealand, the Directorate of Economics and Statistics (India), or from published articles (e.g., Macer 2006). Average weekly work hours were assumed to be 38 hours. Data on the operating costs of cars came mainly from motoring organizations such as the Royal Automobile Club of Victoria (RACV, Australia), AA (United Kingdom), the Canadian Automobile Association, the Auto Channel (United States), United Danish Motor Owners (Forenede Danske Motorejere), and the Automobile Association of Kenya. In the United States, data were available for the operating costs in different states. In some cases, data were provided by local contacts (e.g., for Cambodia). For Germany, car operating costs were based on recent research that showed that these were 2.26 times higher in Germany than the United States (Buehler 2009). To avoid overestimating the cost for Germany, a figure of two times higher than the United States, rather than 2.26 times, was used in the calculations for car operating costs. Whenever possible, the data for car operating costs was based on a car with one of the lowest operating costs. For example, the RACV identified the Hyundai Getz as the cheapest car to own and operate in Victoria, Australia, at a weekly cost of US$118.44 (or US$6,158.88 per year), and this was used as the basis for estimates for Australian cities. In the US cities, operating costs were based on the Hyundai Accent two-door hatchback. For Copenhagen, car operating costs were based on the Hyundai I20. For India, costs were based on one-third of the value of the purchase price of the cheapest Tata Nano car—marketed as the "cheapest car in the world." The data used in these calculations did not include several costs for car drivers, including costs of home garaging, cost of accessories (e.g., seat covers, floor mats, car wash detergent and polish) infringement fines (e.g., parking fines and speeding fines), or the time spent purchasing the car. Data on parking was sourced from advertised parking sites in each city, and the charges represent fees at the cheaper end of the market for parking on weekdays only. Tolls, when estimated, were based only on payment during weekdays, for the lowest level of tolls payable by motorists traveling to the city center. The costs for bicycles were based on surveys with cyclists in Australia and on data on bicycle costs in other countries. The annual cost of operating bicycles was deliberately overestimated to be approximately the cost of the purchase of a new, high-quality bicycle—around US$1,000 in Australia and the United States. Other time costs associated with cycling were estimated to be: walking from bicycle to work, 5 minutes per day or 30 hours per year; repairs and servicing, 50 hours per year.

The data discussed thus far enable the calculation of "private effective speed" in which calculations are based on the direct costs to individuals (Tranter and Ker 2007). However, external costs of motorized transportation significantly add to the cost of this transportation for the entire community. Even if individual drivers have no concern for their collective impacts on their fellow citizens, governments should be concerned, if only in terms of the total economic costs. The external costs of cars have been estimated to be a significant proportion of the total costs of transport and include the costs of pollution, noise, congestion, greenhouse gas emissions, accident costs above insurance, and "free" or subsidized parking. A recent comprehensive analysis of the direct and external cost of cars in Sydney showed that total direct costs for private motorists were 70 cents per km, and total external costs were 55 cents per km (Glazebrook 2009). Thus one estimate of the value of external costs would be 78.6 percent of the direct costs. In this chapter, a conservative value of 40 percent is used to estimate the external costs of cars for the calculations of the "social effective speed." If the concept of "ecosystem services" is considered, a full costing of fossil fuel use and the far-reaching implications of road building for loss of ecosystem services might increase the external costs enormously. Thus the estimates of external costs of cars used here are likely underestimates, and any effective speeds for cars calculated on the basis of external costs are likely to be overestimates.

Interpreting the Data

The calculations of effective speed for the selected cities show that private effective speeds for car drivers (ignoring the external costs) varied from 18.3 km/h in Canberra, Australia, to a mere 3 km/h in Nairobi. The higher effective speeds in Canberra are a consequence of the combination of high average incomes in Australia, minimal car parking costs in the city compared to other cities, no tolls on roads and minimal traffic congestion in a city designed to facilitate car use on the "unconstrained" part of its congestion trajectory. The low effective speeds in Nairobi (and Delhi and Phnom Penh) are due largely to the low average incomes in these cities and therefore the increased time taken by people to earn enough money to pay for their car costs. In cities such as London and New York (with 8.4 km/h and 9.8 km/h effective speeds, respectively), the relatively low speeds are due mainly to low trip speed and high vehicle operating costs (including parking and tolls). When the external costs are taken into account, the social effective speeds for car drivers range from a high of 15.9 km/h (Canberra) to a low of 2.2 km/h (Nairobi). See tables 4.1, 4.2, and 4.3. In these tables, all income and cost data are converted to US dollars, using the exchange rates of December 18, 2010.

In this chapter, rather than calculating the effective speeds of cyclists in different cities, which would have required detailed data on average cycling speeds, the figures were used to calculate how slow cyclists could cycle and still be effectively faster than a car. If external costs are ignored, then the fastest that a cyclist would need to travel (using the estimates of effective speeds here) would be 21.5 km/h (Canberra), and the slowest would be 3.1 km/h (Nairobi). If external costs are considered, cyclists in Canberra would need to average only 18.3 km/h to be faster than a car driver. In New York, Los Angeles, Tokyo, and Hamburg, cyclists would not need to travel faster than 13 km/h to be faster than a car. In Toronto, a cyclist at an average speed of 14.6 km/h would be faster than a car (when most of the costs are taken into account). Table 4.4 shows the trip speed needed by cyclists to be effectively "faster" than cars, in terms of both "private effective speed" (direct costs only), and "social effective speed" (direct plus external costs considered). In table 4.4, Canberra data are given for the car with the lowest operating costs (Hyundai Getz) and for Australia's top-selling car (Holden Commodore).

The estimates in tables 4.1–4.3 are based on small cars with low operating costs. In Australia, the figures are based on a "light car" with the lowest operating costs as calculated by the RACV for new cars over a five-year period. If, instead of a light car, Australia's number-one-selling car was used as the basis for the calculations, the social effective speed in Canberra would fall to 11.5 km/h. (As of 2010, the Holden Commodore has been "Australia's favourite car" for the last fourteen years.) Therefore, to be effectively faster than the number-one-selling car in Australia, a cyclist in Canberra would need to cycle at only 12.7 km/h. In all other Australian cities, the cyclists could travel slower than this, and still be faster than the top-selling car.

Table 4.1
Data for calculating private effective speed (direct costs only) and social effective speed (direct and external costs) for selected cities in Australasia and North America

	Canberra US$	Sydney US$	Melbourne US$	New York US$	Los Angeles US$	Toronto US$	Auckland US$
Vehicle costs							
Vehicle operating costs	6,159	6,159	6,159	6,405	6,393	6,169	4,304
Parking costs	1,000	4,114	4,114	4,000	4,000	592	708
Tolls		1,029	1,029	1,300			
Total direct costs	7,159	11,234	11,234	11,705	10,393	6,761	5,012
Total direct and external costs	10,022	15,728	15,728	16,388	14,550	9,465	7,016
Average annual income	40,980	40,980	40,980	37,572	37,572	27,569	20,618
Direct costs							
Hours devoted to transportation expenses	315	500	500	568	505	447	443
Direct plus external costs							
Hours devoted to transportation expenses	441	700	700	796	706	626	621
Average trip speeds (km/h)	33.3	23.9	26.3	16.6	26.2	31.3	32.3
Other time devoted to the car							
Walking from car to work (5 min. per day)	30	30	30	30	30	30	30
Wash car (1 hr. per month)	12	12	12	12	12	12	12
Repairs and servicing time	4	4	4	4	4	4	4
Buy fuel, check tires, windshield (10 min. per week)	8	8	8	8	8	8	8
Hours in car per year, based on estimated trip speed	450	628	570	904	573	479	464
Total hours for transportation (direct costs only)	820	1,182	1,125	1,526	1,131	981	962
Total hours for transportation (direct and external costs)	946	1,382	1,325	1,753	1,333	1,160	1,139
Private effective speed (km/h)	18.3	12.7	13.3	9.8	13.3	15.3	15.6
Social effective speed (km/h)	15.9	10.9	11.3	8.6	11.3	12.9	13.2

Table 4.2
Data for calculating private effective speed (direct costs only) and social effective speed (direct and external costs) for selected cities in Europe and for Tokyo

	London US$	Copenhagen US$	Hamburg US$	Tokyo US$
Vehicle costs				
Vehicle operating costs	6,578	6,600	14,448	10,350
Parking costs	6,469	3,156	2,000	920
Tolls	3,234			
Total direct costs	16,281	9,756	16,448	11,270
Total direct and external costs	22,793	13,658	23,027	15,778
Average annual income	25,036	33,595	36,444	63,966
Direct costs				
Hours devoted to transportation expenses	1,186	530	823	321
Direct plus external costs				
Hours devoted to transportation expenses	1,661	742	1,153	450
Average trip speeds (km/h)	27.7	34.2	30.9	19.2
Other time devoted to the car				
Walking from car to work (5 min. per day)	30	30	30	30
Wash car (1 hr. per month)	12	12	12	12
Repairs and servicing time	4	4	4	4
Buy fuel, check tires, windshield (10 min. per week)	8	8	8	8
Hours in car per year, based on estimated trip speed	542	439	485	781
Total hours for transportation (direct costs only)	1,782	1,023	1,363	1,157
Total hours for transportation (direct and external costs)	2,256	1,234	1,692	1,285
Private effective speed (km/h)	8.4	14.7	11.0	13.0
Social effective speed (km/h)	6.6	12.2	8.9	11.7

Table 4.3
Data for calculating private effective speed (direct costs only) and social effective speed (direct and external costs) for selected cities in the developing world

	Nairobi US$	Phnom Penh US$	Delhi US$
Vehicle costs			
Vehicle operating costs	2,958	2,500	1,434
Parking costs	0	0	0
Tolls	0	0	0
Total direct costs	2,958	2,500	1,434
Total direct and external costs	4,141	3,500	2,008
Average annual income	1,200	3,600	1,450
Direct costs			
Hours devoted to transportation expenses	4,496	1,267	1,804
Direct plus external costs			
Hours devoted to transportation expenses	6,295	1,773	2,525
Average trip speeds (km/h)	29.6	35	30.9
Other time devoted to the car			
Walking from car to work (5 min. per day)	30	30	30
Wash car (1 hr. per month)	12	12	12
Repairs and servicing time	4	4	4
Buy fuel, check tires, windshield (10 min. per week)	8	8	8
Hours in car per year, based on estimated trip speed	507	429	485
Total hours for transportation (direct costs only)	5,057	1,750	2,344
Total hours for transportation (direct and external costs)	6,856	2,256	3,065
Private effective speed (km/h)	3.0	8.6	6.4
Social effective speed (km/h)	2.2	6.6	4.9

Table 4.4
Cycling trip speeds (km/h) needed for the effective speed of cyclists to be faster than car drivers

	Direct costs only	Direct plus external costs
Canberra (Getz)	21.5	18.3
Toronto	17.8	14.6
Auckland	17.8	14.7
Copenhagen	16.5	13.4
Canberra (Commodore)	15.7	12.7
Melbourne	14.9	12.5
Los Angeles	14.9	12.4
Tokyo	14.4	12.8
Sydney	14.2	12.0
Hamburg	12.1	9.6
New York	10.6	9.2
Phnom Penh	9.9	7.4
London	8.9	7.2
Delhi	8.0	5.8
Nairobi	3.1	2.2

In every city in the world, it is likely that the effective speed of cars will decline further in coming years. This development will be a result of two factors: first, an increase in congestion—already manifest in Chinese cities with regular gridlock in inner areas (Pucher et al. 2007); and second, a decline in the ability of motorists (and cities) to afford the cost of cars: a consequence of the aftermath of the peaking of global oil supplies (Newman, Beatley, and Boyer 2009). These two factors mean that any city that prioritizes active transportation in their transportation system will be at a considerable advantage over cities that continue with the futile objective of increasing (or even maintaining) the speeds of motorized traffic.

How Increasing Trip Speed Changes Effective Speed
Increasing the trip speeds of cars has little impact on effective speeds because the main time component for many car drivers is not the time spent in cars, but the time spent earning the money to pay for all the costs of cars. If nothing is done to reduce this time component, then effective speeds are not likely to fall. In fact, car drivers who try to save time by driving faster will likely reduce their effective speed because of

the extra costs involved in more hectic driving (more fuel used, more wear and tear on the vehicle, and greater stress on the drivers). City governments' attempts to save time by building faster roads are also futile, as doing so makes virtually no difference to effective speed, even assuming that there was no cost involved. The cost of road building is immense, and if this cost were converted to a time measure (based on average time spent at work to earn the money to pay for it), then building new roads will result in more time spent on transportation rather than less. In the tables of effective speed data, taking London as an example, if average trip speeds could be increased by 10 km/h, this would result in an increase of effective speed for car drivers of a mere 0.7 km/h, assuming that this increase in trip speeds could be achieved at zero cost. However, to increase the trip speed of motorized traffic would require a huge investment in road widening and new highways, including the cost of the demolition of large areas of buildings. In addition to road building costs, there would also be the extra costs of increased pollution from induced traffic, reduced levels of physical activity through active transportation, increased levels of obesity and heart disease, and the loss of social networks as road widening leads to the closure of local shops, schools, and services.

In contrast, any increase in trip speed achieved for cyclists would have a significant positive impact on cycling effective speed. Increases in trip speeds for cyclists could be achieved with minimal cost, for example, by transferring road space to cyclists. For London, if the average trip speed for cyclists increased by 10 km/h, the effective speed would increase by 8.7 km/h because the main time component involved for cyclists is the time spent cycling. As described in chapter 13, in Copenhagen the "green wave" (a series of lights timed so that if cyclists keep pace with the changing lights, they get all the green traffic light signals) is used to increase the average trip speed of cyclists, and the return on this investment for effective speed is far greater than any return on increasing the trip speeds of motorists.

Conclusion: Benefits for Individuals and for Cities

Not only can individuals save time by cycling instead of using the car, but city governments also save money when investment is directed toward cycling. Cities with high rates of active modes of transportation are also cities where city governments spend a lower proportion of their total income on transportation. The level of likely savings is indicated in the differences in the percent of gross regional product (GRP) devoted to transportation in European cities in comparison with Australian cities. European cities spent 8.1 percent of their city's income on transportation, compared with 13.2 percent for Australian cities (Kenworthy and Laube 1999). The amount spent on roads is an important part of this difference between cities. For example, while Copenhagen spent only US$97 per person on roads, Sydney spent US$188.37 (Kenworthy and Laube 1999).

There are many other ways that cycling saves time. Cyclists can often take shortcuts through the city that are not accessible to cars. When cycling is a major proportion of a city's transportation system, local shops and services are more likely to be maintained so that they remain within easy reach. (If cars dominate transportation, local shops, schools, and services close, and people have to travel farther to access them.) Cyclists have less need to spend time at the gym, and every hour spent cycling adds more than an hour to active healthy life. If city residents avoid owning a car by cycling and using public transportation, they could retire ten to fifteen years earlier if they invest the money saved (assuming that they invested the money saved by not owning a car in an investment earning 8 percent per annum over a thirty-year period).

If urban citizens understand the concept of effective speed, many can make transportation mode decisions that will save them time and money and improve their health and well-being. However, some individuals have no choice but to use their cars, and hence major structural changes are needed to enhance urban transportation choices. If city governments wish to invest wisely in transportation, by understanding the concept of effective speed they will also understand the futility of trying to save time through attempts to increase the average trip speeds of private motor vehicles. This argument applies to any city in the world. Those cities that invest most effectively in cycling infrastructure will find that their cities become the "fastest" cities in the world.

Acknowledgments

The following people provided valuable assistance in collecting data or constructive suggestions on the writing of the chapter: Ralph Buehler,

Helmut Holzapfel, Steffen Loft, Alexandra Macmillan, Japeth Ogendi, John Pucher, Phirun Ra, John Whitelegg, and Alistair Woodward. Thanks are also given to the anonymous referees for this chapter.

References

Brög, Werner. 2000. Switching to Public Transport. *UITP: 2nd Asia Pacific Congress*. Melbourne.

Buehler, Ralph. 2009. Determinants of Automobile Use: Comparison of Germany and the United States. *Transportation Research Record: Journal of the Transportation Research Board* 2139:161–171.

Ende, Michael. 1985. *Momo*. Trans. J. Maxwell Brownjohn. Garden City, NY: Doubleday.

Evans, Reg. 2007. Central London Congestion Charging Scheme: Ex-Post Evaluation of the Quantified Impacts of the Original Scheme. Transport for London. http://origin.tfl.gov.uk/assets/downloads/Ex-post-evaluation-of-quantified -impacts-of-original-scheme-07-June.pdf.

Fisher, Frank. 2006. *Response Ability: Environment, Health and Everyday Transcendence*. Melbourne: Vista Publications.

Gehl, Jan. 2009. *2009 Walter Burley Griffin Memorial Lecture*. Canberra, Australia: Walking and Cycling.

Glazebrook, Garry. 2009. Taking the Con out of Convenience: The True Cost of Transport Modes in Sydney. *Urban Policy and Research* 27 (1): 5–24.

Illich, Ivan. 1974. *Energy and Equity*. London: Harper and Row.

Kenworthy, Jeff, and Felix Laube. 1999. *An International Sourcebook of Automobile Dependence in Cities, 1960–1990*. Boulder: University Press of Colorado.

Kifer, Ken. 2002. Auto Costs Versus Bike Costs. Ken Kifer's Bike Pages. http://www.kenkifer.com/bikepages/advocacy/autocost.htm.

Macer, Darryl R. J., ed. 2006. A Cross-Cultural Introduction to Bioethics. Christchurch, NZ: Eubios Ethics Institute.

Newman, Peter, Timothy Beatley, and Heather Boyer. 2009. *Resilient Cities: Responding to Peak Oil and Climate Change*. Washington, DC: Island Press.

One News. 2004. Fresh Idea to Clear Auckland Roads. *TVNZ*, November 27, 2004. http://tvnz.co.nz/view/news_national_story_skin/461230.

Press, Elizabeth. 2008. *Bike vs. Car vs. Transit*. New York: Streetfilms. http://www.streetfilms.org/bike-vs-car-vs-transit/.

Pucher, John, Zhong-Ren Peng, Neha Mittal, Yi Zhu, and Nisha Korattyswaroopam. 2007. Urban Transport Trends and Policies in China and India: Impacts of Rapid Economic Growth. *Transport Reviews* 27 (4): 379–410.

Tranter, Paul J. 2004. *Effective Speeds: Car Costs Are Slowing Us Down.* Canberra, Australia: Department of the Environment and Heritage, Australian Greenhouse Office.

Tranter, Paul J. 2010. Speed Kills: The Complex Links Between Transport, Lack of Time and Urban Health. *Journal of Urban Health* 87 (2): 155–166.

Tranter, Paul J., and Ian Ker. 2007. A Wish Called $quander: (In)Effective Speed and Effective Wellbeing in Australian Cities. *Proceedings of the State of Australian Cities 2007 National Conference.* Adelaide, Australia. http://s3 .amazonaws.com/zanran_storage/www.fbe.unsw.edu.au/ContentPages/ 744449240.pdf.

Tranter, Paul J., and Murray May. 2005a. Questioning the Need for Speed: Can "Effective Speed" Guide Change in Travel Behaviour and Transport Policy? *Proceedings of the 28th Australasian Transport Research Forum.* Sydney.

Tranter, Paul J., and Murray May. 2005b. Using the Concept of Effective Speed as a Stimulus for Travel Behaviour Change and Policy Development. Canberra, Australia: Department of the Environment and Heritage, Australian Greenhouse Office. http://www.environment.gov.au/archive/settlements/transport/ publications/pubs/effectivespeeds.pdf.

Tranter, Paul J., and Murray May. 2006. The Hidden Benefits of Walking: Is Speed Stealing Our Time and Money? Walk 21: 7th International Conference on Walking and Liveable Communities. Melbourne. http://www.walk21.com/paper _search/results_detail.asp?Paper=88.

Whitelegg, John. 1993a. Time Pollution. *Ecologist* 23 (4): 131–134.

Whitelegg, John. 1993b. *Transport for a Sustainable Future: The Case for Europe.* London: Belhaven Press.

5

Developments in Bicycle Equipment and Its Role in Promoting Cycling as a Travel Mode

Kristin Lovejoy and Susan Handy

Efforts to increase utilitarian bicycling—bicycling as an everyday mode of transportation to a destination—have tended to focus on infrastructure, such as bike lanes, cycle tracks, or bike parking. As highlighted in chapters 12, 13, and 14, some communities have combined investments in infrastructure with programs to encourage bicycling and policies that discourage driving. Other approaches aim to increase access to bicycles, including the high-profile bikesharing programs discussed in chapter 9.

Bike planners and researchers have given little attention to the role of bicycle equipment. Some argue that it has a limited role relative to other factors in promoting cycling. An informal survey of bicycling experts in Europe suggests that innovations in equipment would do little to increase the already high levels of bicycling there, especially to the extent that risk of theft already limits the adoption of improved designs. Survey data from the United States suggests that concerns relating to safety and distance are far greater barriers to cycling and must be addressed before concerns over equipment will come into play. But even if this is true, better equipment could improve the experience of bicyclists in many ways, especially in places such as the United States where the typical bicycle does a poor job of meeting the needs of everyday trips. Equipment, defined here to include bicycles and their components, accessories that attach to bicycles, and those that are worn by cyclists, can contribute to greater safety, convenience, comfort, and enjoyment, potentially enhancing the effectiveness of other efforts to promote utilitarian cycling.

How can bicycle equipment help to increase utilitarian bicycling? To answer this question, we first examine what people need when riding bikes for transportation, especially contrasted with riding for sport or recreation. We then describe different types of bicycles and trends and innovations in bicycle components and accessories, including variations across the world. Finally, we conclude with a list of specific equipment—including types of bicycles themselves, accessories that attach to bikes, and those worn by bicyclists—that helps accommodate the particular needs of transportation cyclists.

The Needs of the Utilitarian Bicyclist

The type of equipment best suited to utilitarian bicycling, for which the main purpose of riding is to get somewhere—running errands, chauffeuring children, going out for the evening, or similar trips—is different from bikes tailored to sport or recreational riding. Although these differences may be obvious in countries with a strong culture of everyday utilitarian cycling such as the Netherlands, Denmark, and Germany, they may be overlooked in places like the United States and Australia where many people have experience riding bikes for sport or recreation but the share of all transportation trips made by bicycle is less than 1 percent. It may be a chicken-and-egg problem, as the bicycle industry has tended to ignore the needs of utility cycling in these places, instead catering and marketing to the use of bicycles as toys or sports equipment. It is with these places in mind, where the popular perception of bicycle equipment resides mostly in the sports and recreation-oriented realm, that we highlight the following differences in needs when riding for utilitarian purposes:

• *Desire to wear "normal" clothing*   To seamlessly integrate bicycling with everyday life, someone bicycling for transportation would prefer to wear whatever they would normally wear to their intended destination, just the way drivers, pedestrians, and bus riders do. By contrast, on a recreational outing or when riding for sport, bicyclists might be more willing to wear athletic clothing, special shoes, or a helmet.

• *Need to carry cargo or passengers*   Everyday life requires transporting groceries, books, gym clothes, parcels, and often passengers. By contrast, on a recreational outing or when riding for sport, a bicyclist will likely bring only what is necessary for the activity of riding, carrying at most conveniences such as a water bottle, snacks, or a tire repair kit.

• *Frequent stops and starts*　Utilitarian trips, generally in town, require stops or pauses at stop signs and traffic signals along the way. A rider will likely also want to park at some point, perhaps repeatedly while doing a series of errands. By contrast, when cycling for sport, stopping is counter to the purpose of the activity, so a rider may choose a route based on terrain or scenery with minimal impedances and few stops.

• *Priority of being able to see and be seen*　Because trips in and around town require cyclists to negotiate traffic, they need to be able to look out for traffic and be seen by others, including vehicles, pedestrians, and other bicycles. This requirement persists whenever and wherever an individual might want to go, potentially after dark or in inclement weather. By contrast, for a recreational outing, a rider might choose routes that minimize encounters with other traffic and might forego riding in inclement conditions.

• *Exposure to theft*　Because utilitarian trips often involve stopping and parking at various places, the bicycle and any of its removable components—such as wheels, saddle, or lights, as well as cargo—are frequently vulnerable to theft. This vulnerability creates a need for theft protection and/or a preference for inexpensive bicycles. By contrast, recreational and sport-oriented cyclists can plan outings to avoid leaving a valuable bike in a vulnerable situation.

• *Priority of reliability*　Because utilitarian trips are relatively short and frequent, to be convenient, a bicycle must be immediately and repeatedly ready to use, and it must deliver the rider to his destination without fail. It helps to have a bike that is more resilient to weather and wear. By contrast, for sports or recreation, bicyclists may be motivated to inspect their machines before each outing or frequently adjust tire pressure or finicky gears in order to achieve optimal performance.

In short, the needs of utilitarian bicyclists are the same as those of any other traveler. For individuals to choose cycling, the experience must be competitive with other modes of travel—such as driving, transit, or walking—with respect to travel time and cost, as well as safety, logistical convenience, bodily comfort, enjoyment, and whatever other considerations come into play for particular individuals. Along with proper infrastructure and other policies supporting cycling, the right equipment can help make cycling more competitive with other modes of travel. For instance, fenders and chain guards make it easier to cycle in everyday clothing. Stopping and starting is easier if the saddle height and frame geometry enable the rider to easily reach the ground with his foot. We explore many other ways that bicycle equipment can help accommodate everyday travel needs in the following sections.

Types of Bicycles

The variety of types of bicycles available today reflects the diverse ways that they are put to use for sport, recreation, and utility as well as technological advancements in components, materials, and manufacturing techniques. But the basic design has changed little in the last 120 years. Precursors came in many forms, including hobbyhorses, velocipedes, ordinaries, high-riders, pennyfarthings, and boneshakers, among others. But bicycles entered the mainstream only after technical innovations afforded a safer, more comfortable, and more convenient ride, a historical development that demonstrates the importance of equipment to the overall appeal of cycling. What was known as the "safety bicycle" incorporated a cog and drive chain that allowed the wheels to revolve multiple times per revolution of the pedals (avoiding the need for either a giant wheel or overly rapid pedaling). It also incorporated pneumatic tires, rather than metal or wooden wheels, for a much smoother ride. Combined with low-cost manufacturing techniques—and perhaps the lucky whim of fashion—this practical design caught on with the masses, and bicycling enjoyed sudden popularity in the mid-1890s for both transportation and recreation. With only a few improvements—notably, the addition of the freewheel and brakes just after the turn of the twentieth century—the basic design has changed little in the intervening years.

Today, transportation-oriented bicycles are variously referred to as transport bikes, utility bikes, city or town bikes, roadsters, "normal" bikes (in places like the Netherlands), or Dutch bikes (outside the Netherlands), among other names (see table 5.1). Their distinguishing attribute is that they are designed primarily for practical transportation as opposed to sport or recreation: everyday riding, in normal clothes, in a variety of weather conditions, and with minimal maintenance. Of course, most bicycles may be used for a variety of purposes, and any one bicycle may have a mix of characteristics from one or more of these types. Repurposing is especially common in places like the United States, where utilitarian bicycling has been less prevalent and transportation-oriented bicycles have historically been harder to find. Some riders may choose to have just one bicycle and use it for different purposes on different days, requiring a bike to straddle categories; others may choose to own a "stable" of bicycles, each with different features suited to different sorts of riding or trip purposes (Ballantine 2001).

The differences in types of bicycles ridden for transportation in the United States and in Europe are substantial. A 2006 study of the types of bicycles used by students and employees commuting to the university in Davis, California, where utilitarian cycling is among the highest in the United States (see chapter 12) and where most trips are less than fifteen minutes over flat terrain, 43 percent of respondents reported using mountain bikes, 24 percent road bikes, 18 percent hybrids, 10 percent cruisers, and 5 percent other styles to commute (n = 3147; Congleton 2009). In contrast, a 2008 survey of residents in four Dutch cities showed that 97 percent owned at least one geared "normal" bike (utility-oriented bike), among any other types of bikes they may have owned. In addition, 28 percent owned at least one bike without gears, 23 percent a hybrid, 13 percent a mountain bike, 12 percent a road bike, and 1 percent another style (n = 4172; Heinen 2011).

Though transportation-oriented bicycles have seen the fewest technological changes compared to other categories of bicycles, newer models are much lighter than a century ago, and some incorporate updated components. For instance, hub gears, hand-controlled disk brakes, and LED-powered lights (discussed later in this chapter) have become increasingly common on utility bikes throughout the world over the last decade. Even in the United States, renewed interest in utilitarian bicycling in recent years has given rise to new suppliers of bicycles with a retro aesthetic but modern components. Major US suppliers also see "bikes targeting transportation users" as "the next big thing" and are offering more models with features typically seen on Dutch-style bikes, such as enclosed chain drives, hub gears, and upright step-through frames (Wiebe 2010, 30).

As a particular type of utility bike, cargo bikes—which have built-in capacity for extra baggage and cargo—have benefited from innovations that make carrying heavy loads easier, including lighter materials and

Table 5.1
Typical types of bicycles

Terms used	Intended purpose	Typical attributes
Utility bike Transport bike Normal bike Dutch bike Roadster Town or city bike	Utility	Traditional transportation bike, with a mid-weight, possibly step-through frame, swept-back handle bars positioned somewhat higher than the saddle, 26- or 28-inch wheels, medium-width smooth-tread tires (around 1.5 inches or 37 mm), a three- or eight-speed hub gear, a partial or fully enclosed chain guard, fenders, racks, lights, and a kickstand.
Hybrid Commuter bike Urban bike Street bike Town or city bike	Utility Recreation	Usually a mix of components from road and mountain bikes, such as derailleur gears, partially raised handlebars, slick tires, and direct-pull ("V") or disc brakes. May have a partial chain guard, rack, fenders, and lights.
Road bike Racing bike	Sport Recreation	Designed for maximum speed, with a light frame, 650 or 700 mm wheels (about 28 inches), narrow high-pressure slick tires (23 to 25 mm), dropped handlebars, and sixteen or more speeds, derailleur gears, light rim brakes, small clipless pedals (or toe-clips).
Mountain bike (MTB) All-terrain bike (ATB)	Sport Recreation	Designed for off-road use, with a smaller, sturdy, but light frame, 26-inch wheels, wide and knobby tires (1.5 inches), flat handlebars, and higher gearing—up to thirty speeds—derailleur gears, powerful direct-pull ("V") brakes or disc brakes, perhaps front or full suspension.
Fixed-gear ("fixie")	Recreation Utility	Single-speed bikes that have no freewheel, such that the pedals must move anytime the wheels are moving, often with a lightweight diamond frame, narrow handlebars, and optionally no hand brakes. Especially fashionable in North America in the 1990s and 2000s.

Table 5.1
(continued)

Terms used	Intended purpose	Typical attributes
Cargo bike Freight bicycle Carrier cycle Bakfiets	Utility	Two- or three-wheeled, with a special rack, tray, open or enclosed box, platform, or basket for carrying large or heavy cargo, positioned either low behind the front wheel or between parallel wheels in the front or rear. Often with stronger wheel and frame construction and lower gear ratios to accommodate heavy loads. May incorporate electric assistance.
Electric-assist Electric bicycle E-bike	Utility	Especially popular for utility, commuter, and cargo bicycles; an electric motor supplements pedal power, usually powered by a rechargeable battery.
Small wheel Moulton	Utility	Twenty-inch (or smaller) wheels and a frame that has no top tube (F-frame), designed to be easy to mount and maneuver. Often incorporating front and/or rear suspension, and outfitted with fenders and a rack. Especially fashionable in the United Kingdom and Europe in the 1960s and 1970s.
Folding Folder Breakaway	Utility	Bicycles designed to fold or break into pieces easily into a compact form that can be carried onto public transit or indoors after use. Usually with small wheels and no top tube.
Cruiser Beach cruiser "Paperboy"	Recreation Utility	Heavy and durable, with very wide handle bars, a low mattress saddle, single speed, partial or fully enclosed chain guard, coaster brakes, and extra-wide (2-inch) balloon tires. Especially fashionable when first developed in the 1950s and 1960s, and widely used now on some college campuses and in coastal communities in the United States.

Table 5.1
(continued)

Terms used	Intended purpose	Typical attributes
Recumbent · Recliner	Recreation Utility	Places the rider in a laid-back position low to the ground for both ergonomic and aerodynamic advantage. Designs vary, with the pedals either higher, lower, or in line with the hips, with varying wheel sizes and wheelbase lengths, and steering mechanisms.
Pedicab Rickshaw	Utility Recreation	Usually three-wheeled, designed for one rider to power the drive train, with seating capacity for idle passengers positioned either in front of or behind the rider. Like a cargo bike, but with seating in the cargo area.
Enclosed bicycle Velomobile Human-powered vehicle (HPV)	Utility Recreation	Any range of pedal-powered vehicles with a full or partial enclosure, a fairing or a lightweight shell, for the purposes of aerodynamics or to protect the rider from the elements.
Touring	Recreation	Any model of bike with adjustments made to handle long distances with a heavy load, such as stronger wheels, slick tires, and multiple mounting points for racks and bags.
Tandem Quadracycle Other multirider bikes	Recreation	Varied designs accommodating multiple riders contributing power to the drive train, including traditional tandems (two wheels, one rider in front of the other) and quadracycles (four wheels, riders sit side by side).

brakes and gears that perform well under a heavy load. Their numbers have been growing in recent years in places where bicycling has long been prevalent, such as the Netherlands (where this type of bike is called a *bakfiets*) and especially in Denmark, where an estimated 25 percent of Copenhagen families with two or more children own one (Colville-Andersen 2011). Handy for multiple purposes, these bicycles are increasingly used to chauffeur children in lieu of child seats mounted on conventional bicycles. Even in the United States, cargo bikes are en vogue if not widespread in some urban centers, where they are used for ferrying passengers, delivery of goods, and street-food vending. Functionally similar are trailers that pull behind the bicycle with a separate wheelbase, often used for children or cargo. (See figures 5.1 and 5.2.)

One of the newest areas of innovation for utility bikes is electric assistance in various forms. The earliest models date back almost to the earliest bicycles, first appearing in the 1890s, but renewed interest starting a century later has led to a resurgence of innovation and production in recent years (Morchin and Oman 2006). Models range from those resembling conventional bikes with pedals with an electric motor that can be engaged optionally, such as on hills or in wind, to models that resemble electric scooters. The market for electric bikes, or e-bikes, is booming in China, where there are an estimated 120 million on the road, especially of the latter variety, but interest is growing in Europe and the United States (Goodman 2010; Chu 2010; Morchin and Oman 2006). An estimated 26 million electric bicycles were sold worldwide in 2010, including 23 million in China, 1.5 million in other parts of Asia, 847,000 in western Europe, and 275,000 in the United States (Pike Research 2011). Especially when combined with cargo capacity, these types of bicycles become even more competitive with automobiles as a transportation mode, perhaps enabling trips that might not have been otherwise feasible by bicycle. Older riders or those with long commutes are seen as an especially likely target market for electric bikes. Although some bicycling advocates question the legitimacy of bicycles with power assistance, e-bikes are legally classified as bicycles in most parts of the world, up to a maximum wattage or speed capacity (varying by country and jurisdiction).

A solution to another of the bicycle's disadvantages relative to vehicular travel is to enclose the bicycle in a protective shell, shielding the rider from the elements, a concept revisited throughout the last century. Recumbent or semi-recumbent bikes are especially well suited to the application, due to their low profile. Velomobiles, or fully enclosed recumbents optimized for aerodynamics, are sometimes raced in human-powered vehicle competitions, though similar technology is also practical for everyday riding, with even just a partial fairing or windshield providing substantial protection from precipitation (Ballantine 2001). Four-wheeled, pedal-powered two-seaters designed with full and partial enclosure were codeveloped with motor vehicles in the early 1900s.

Figure 5.1
Examples of bicycles equipped for carrying things. *Credit:* Kristin Lovejoy.

Figure 5.2
Examples of bicycles equipped for traveling with children. *Credit:* Kristin Lovejoy.

Despite being at most a futuristic or fringe phenomenon to date, enclosure—like electric assistance—is an area of innovation with the potential to revolutionize the role of bicycles in meeting travelers' needs (Herlihy 2004).

Design Developments in Bicycle Components

This section provides an overview of notable design developments in bicycle equipment and an assessment of how well they serve utilitarian bicycling. Although low-tech options still prove to be best in many cases, new designs expand the options available, making it easier for riders to find bicycles that meet their needs. A number of technological developments have sprung from bicycles designed for special purposes. For instance, competitive road racing produced bicycles streamlined for speed, including lightweight materials, derailleur gears, and drop handlebars for a more aerodynamic posture. Mountain biking produced bicycles with thick "knobby" tires, suspension technology, and disc brakes. Although not all such developments have been useful for utilitarian bicycling, some have been adopted more widely. For this reason, the industry for recreational and competitive bicycles has played an important role in spurring and incubating new technologies for transportation-oriented bikes. *Richard's 21st-Century Bicycle Book* by Richard Ballantine (2001) is a good resource for more information on component design and other topics. Figure 5.3 diagrams the parts of a typical bicycle, some of which are referenced in the sections that follow.

Frame

It is likely that every possible way that a frame might join the wheels, saddle, and handlebars of a bicycle has been explored over the course of the bicycle's history, though the classic diamond shape is the most familiar. The shape of the frame affects the riding position, ease of reaching the ground during stops and starts, and ease of mounting and dismounting. The steeper the angle of the seat tube—that is, when the pedals are more underneath the saddle rather than forward of the saddle—the more the rider's weight is shifted forward into the arms, enabling a hunched, aerodynamic position typical on road racing bikes (see figure 5.4). By contrast, if the pedals are farther forward, the rider's weight is shifted

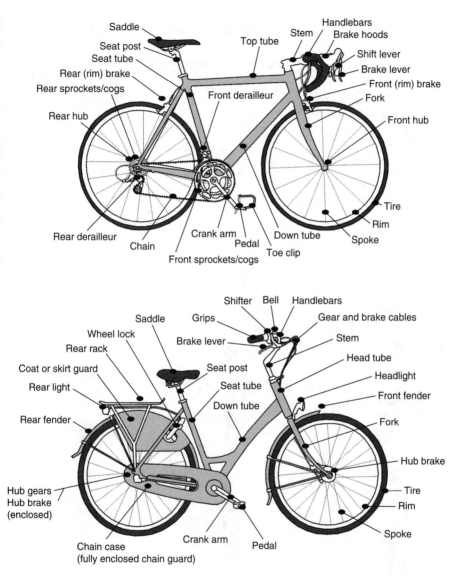

Figure 5.3
Parts of a typical road bike (top) and transport bike (bottom). *Credit:* Kristin Lovejoy.

Dutch-style transport bike	Hybrid or mountain bike	Road/racing bike
• Handlebars are higher than the saddle and swept back • Greater horizontal distance between the saddle and pedals • Step-through frame with no top tube • All of the rider's weight is in her seat • Rider's foot may reach the ground while sitting on the saddle	• Handlebars are level or above the saddle and forward of the stem • The rider is bent at about 45 degrees from vertical • Some of the rider's weight is in her arms • The rider must come out of the saddle for her foot to reach the ground	• Handlebars are level with or lower than the saddle • The rider is bent in an aerodynamic posture • Even more of the rider's weight is in her arms • The seat tube is more steeply angled, with the saddle perched more directly above the pedals • The rider must angle her neck to view the road and come out of the saddle for her foot to reach the ground

Figure 5.4
Rider's posture while sitting and stopping on different types of bicycles. *Credit:* Kristin Lovejoy.

back onto the saddle, accommodating (if combined with the proper handlebar position) a more upright position preferred by some riders. If shifted far enough, the rider can fully extend her legs when pedaling but put her feet flat on the ground when stopped without lifting out of the saddle at all. In addition, a low or absent top tube enables the rider to "step through" over the frame rather than swing her leg over the back of the bicycle when mounting and dismounting. It also provides extra clearance between the legs during frequent stops and starts. Although they are sometimes referred to as "ladies' frames" for accommodating women's skirts, step-through and mixte frames have long been common on utility bicycles for both genders. An altogether different option is recumbent frames, which are both comfortable and fast, though their low profile makes it harder for riders to see and be seen in traffic. Balance can also be tricky, but models with the pedals positioned lower than the hips with a larger (standard-size) rear wheel are more stable, as are tricycles.

Frame materials can also affect how a bike functions. Steel is generally heavier with more flex but may be more durable as well as cheaper and easier to handcraft or repair. Aluminum alloys, used widely on bikes manufactured in the last few decades, are stronger and thus can be made thinner and lighter with more rigidity. Because of their expense, materials such as carbon fiber and even bamboo and flax have been considered but not widely adopted. Because carbon fiber composites are not only very rigid and light, they could potentially be molded into any shape, such as a single-piece shell designed to enclose all messy and vulnerable components, like the chain drive, cables, brakes, lights, and wires. In theory, this could be very practical for the rider and potentially reduce costs associated with bicycle assembly (Herlihy 2004; Ballantine 2001; Morchin and Oman 2006).

Handlebars

The shape and position of the handlebars and stem and the extension of the frame can greatly affect the fit of a bike and thus the physical comfort of the rider. How far the rider has to reach influences how upright the rider sits. The most popular handlebar shape for utility bikes is mostly flat with the ends curving toward the rear of the bike. However, riders may opt for the drop handlebars traditionally found on road bikes that enable at least two riding positions, or flat handlebars traditionally found on mountain bikes, or any other shape that is comfortable, ranging from narrow to wide, curvy to flat, sweeping up, down, back, or not at all.

Wheels and Tires

Wheels and tires are important, on the one hand for cushioning and responsiveness, and on the other because they are vulnerable to failure. "Nowhere else on the bike can you so easily and so greatly alter performance for so little cost," suggests Richard Ballantine (2001, 66). Different materials and configurations of hubs, spokes, rims, tubes, and tires all offer different performance advantages, but the overall quality of construction may be the most important factor for utilitarian riding. Cheap wheels can fail within months, suffering punctures, broken spokes, or out-of-trueness. In addition, weight matters more on the wheels than anywhere else on the bike because the gyroscopic inertia of the spinning wheels magnifies whatever energy is required for acceleration or braking.

Inflation pressure and type of tire are the easiest ways to alter a wheel's performance. In general, wider tires are more comfortable and provide more traction (because more surface area is in contact with the pavement), but also have lower tire pressure and are less efficient. Narrower tires are stiffer with higher pressure and are more vulnerable to punctures, but they are also faster and more responsive. Knobby mountain bike tires are of little use on pavement and produce more rolling resistance. Because wheels can transform the function of a bicycle, having multiple sets of wheels enables a bicyclist to use the same bicycle for multiple purposes. For example, putting smooth-tread tires on a mountain bike can improve its performance as a utilitarian bicycle.

Suspension

Suspension technologies enhance both comfort and efficiency by cushioning the rider and damping up and down movement. Lower-pressure tires, padded handlebar grips, and cushy saddles provide simple forms of damping. Inventors have experimented with more sophisticated suspension throughout the last century, but the technology leapt forward with the popularization of mountain biking in the 1990s. An oil-damped spring, an elastomer block or rubber ball, or compressed air—commonly incorporated into the fork, stem, seat post, rear frame, or some combination thereof—can absorb shock from the terrain or insulate the rider against shocks from the bike. For utilitarian purposes, suspension seat posts are fairly popular; additional suspension is not usually deemed worth the additional cost, weight, and complexity, though some riders may prefer greater cushioning, and suspension technologies are still evolving rapidly.

Transmission

Almost all bicycles have been chain-driven since the late 1800s, the main difference between them being the type and number of different gear ratios. Single-gear bikes have the advantage of being simple, reliable, and potentially lighter and have long been the standard where utilitarian riding is common, such as in the Netherlands, Denmark, Japan, and China, and on flatter terrain. But many riders prefer multiple gears for easier acceleration from a stop, for going faster once moving, and for hilly terrain. Even in places like Amsterdam and Copenhagen, bicycles with multiple gears are increasingly common, as the technology for gears continues to improve. In particular, three-gear bicycles have been common in Europe since the 1980s, and bicycles with more gears seem to be growing in popularity as the technology improves.

The oldest design for variable-gear transmission is a hub gear, with three or more gear ratios enclosed in the rear hub shell. The enclosure of moving parts reduces maintenance needs and improves longevity, and the addition of a chain guard protects clothing. The rider can also shift whether stopped or pedaling. However, historically hub gears had the disadvantage of energy loss—as much as 20 percent in some gears on some models (Ballantine 2001). For this reason, racing cyclists began employing derailleur gears in the 1930s, and they have since become common on recreation-oriented road bikes, mountain/all-terrain bikes, and hybrids, as well as on some utilitarian bikes in Europe. Despite being efficient, derailleur gears have several shortcomings that make them less practical for utilitarian riding. The chain, moving back and forth across laterally mounted sprockets of different sizes, is difficult to enclose. Exposed to the elements, the chain and often finicky shifting mechanism need regular maintenance to function properly; they also tend to catch clothing. In addition, riders can shift gears only while pedaling, and the transition can sometimes lag. This issue is especially inconvenient for biking in traffic, where the rider often needs to downshift while stopped. With these drawbacks, and with continued improvements to hub gear technology, state-of-the-art gears for utility bikes are the modern descendants of the classic hub gears, which offer smooth, reliable shifting between eight gears or more and are well suited to stop-and-go conditions.

For both hub and derailleur gears, the technology of shift control continues to evolve. For example, on some bikes spring-tension indexed shifters, integrated alongside hand brakes, require only the smallest finger twitch to change gears. Wireless electronic shifters are a recent innovation, so far marketed only on high-end road bikes, though they may prove appealing to utility bicyclists in the future.

Alternatives to chain-driven bicycles have been explored throughout the history of the bicycle, but few have caught on. For instance, belt-driven systems have recently reappeared in improved form on high-end mountain bikes as well as mid-priced bikes marketed to urban commuters. In theory, this technology has the advantage of needing no lubrication and is therefore clean, as well as strong, quiet, lightweight, and durable, though perhaps not a significant improvement over the enclosed chain-drive systems to which the Danish and Dutch are accustomed. Electric assistance is one area of innovation in bicycle transmission that may have revolutionary potential, at least in some markets, as discussed previously.

Pedals (and Shoes)

For utilitarian bicycling, full platform pedals are the most versatile, in that they support a broad area of the foot, can be used with any footwear, and are identical right side up or upside down. Other designs have been introduced for aerodynamics and optimal stroke power, but at the cost of convenience and comfort. For instance, securing the foot to the pedal using toe-clips or "clipless" pedals ensures that the foot is optimally placed and enables the rider to pull on the up stroke as well as push on the down stroke for marginal efficiency gains and control, such as in a "track stand" maneuver. However, they require specialized footwear that usually has very stiff soles. Conventional toe-clips can be used with most any footwear, but the pedals must still be used with the correct side facing up and require an extra maneuver to slip one's toe in and out of the clip at each start and stop, an encumbrance avoided on utility bikes in much of the world.

Brakes

Like hub gears, hub (or drum) brakes are popular for utilitarian bicycling because they are fully enclosed, making them reliable, long lasting, and just as effective in wet conditions and dry conditions. Consisting of pads or rollers that press outward on the inside of the hub shell, these brakes may be engaged either by using a hand lever or by pedaling backward (called coaster brakes). Hands-free braking can be practical if one's hands are occupied, such as by holding an umbrella or other item while traveling (though many jurisdictions require or recommend both hands on the handlebars). However, hub brakes are heavy and sometimes weaker than rim or disc brakes, and they can burn out on long downhill rides if engaged continuously. Rim (caliper) brakes are simple and light; a variety of subtypes, ranging from traditional cantilever to direct-pull ("V") brakes, offer different mechanical advantages. However, because they are exposed, rim brakes require maintenance, adjustment, and pad replacement. Furthermore, performance is often reduced in wet conditions, sometimes abysmally. Disc brakes developed for mountain biking are highly effective in wet and dry conditions though also expensive and heavy like hub brakes. Hub brakes are the most common systems on Dutch and Danish utility bikes, though disc brakes are becoming more popular. Most American bikes, as well as recreation- and sports-oriented bikes elsewhere, have rim brakes of some sort, with disc brakes now common on upscale mountain bikes and some commuter bikes.

Apart from coaster brakes, most brakes are engaged by tensing cables using hand levers of various designs. However, some use hydraulic fluid, much like automobile and motorcycle brakes, pushing fluid from the brake lever at the handlebars to the brake caliper at the wheel. Their power may make them attractive for some utility applications, such as on a bakfiets or other cargo bicycle on hilly terrain.

Other Equipment

Although they are not technically a part of the bike itself, accessories such as lights, fenders, locks, and baskets serve critical functions and are arguably a utilitarian bike's defining features—it would be incomplete without them, and almost any bike becomes a utilitarian bike with their addition. Other useful accessories include kickstands, fairings, chain guards, trouser clips, child seats, trailers, all forms of racks, bags and totes, helmets, clothing, and—for some—hydration systems, computers, pumps, and maintenance kits. The basic design or technology of many of these has not changed in decades. For instance, aside from new models made of plastic, fender design is basically the same as a century ago, as essential today as ever in protecting the rider from mud and water kicked up from the road by revolving wheels. However, innovations have occurred in some bike accessories, including—but not limited to—lights, locks, helmets, and the textiles used for clothing and totes, all discussed here.

Racks, Baskets, and Trailers

If not built into the bike itself (as a cargo bike or bakfiets), additional capacity for carrying personal items, parcels, or passengers can be incorporated by way of racks, baskets, bags, child seats, and trailers attached to a standard bicycle (see figure 5.1 and 5.2). Although simpler versions are timeless (such as a simple basket affixed to the handlebars), innovations have enabled even lightweight racks to handle heavier loads, positioning to minimize interference with the bicycle's handling when fully loaded, and one- or two-wheeled trailers for either greater stability or agility.

Lighting Systems

Lights serve two different functions: to help the rider see, which requires a bright, concentrated beam, and to help the rider be seen by others, which requires diffuse light that is persistently visible from many angles and is ideally eye-catching and recognizable. For urban riding, in which there is often enough ambient light for the rider to see but there are also many other road users who may have difficulty seeing him, the latter feature is especially important. The former can be important for cycling in darker areas.

Lighting systems differ in many ways: type of bulb, power source, use of wires, and whether they are permanently affixed to the bicycle. Classic filament-based bulbs provide a relatively bright directed beam, but new HID (high-intensity discharge) lights are the brightest, and LED (light-emitting diode) lights can be almost as bright while consuming much less energy. Dynamo generators, the oldest power-source technology, use a friction mechanism either at the hub or the rim (the "bottle" type) to generate electricity that runs through a wire to wherever the light is mounted. A downside of this design is drag, somewhat greater at the rim than the hub, though some new frictionless models use magnets to generate electricity without any contact. In addition, though old designs illuminate only when the wheels are turning, modern generators using low-energy LEDs and a capacitor remain illuminated for several minutes after the bicyclist stops. Generator lights are usually permanently attached to the bike, which is an added convenience but also means that the whole system is exposed to the elements. Delicate wiring can be especially vulnerable to wear. Some designs avoid wiring by positioning the lights low at the wheel near the generator. Popular for their limitless power supply, generator lights of various types are common on utility bikes in the Netherlands, Denmark, and Germany; the fact that they are required by law in some places has helped spur some of the technical innovations in recent years, making them the state of the art for bicycling lighting systems, though maintenance issues present an ongoing design challenge.

Battery-powered lights have the advantage of flexibility, despite requiring periodic replacement or recharging of the batteries. They come in all shapes and sizes, are usually wireless, can be attached anywhere on the bicycle or the rider, and are usually easily detachable. If they are detachable, they must be attached and removed with each use (to avoid theft), but this also means that they are kept safe from the elements and tampering. In places where generator systems are common or required by law, battery-powered LEDs often serve as supplemental lights or as a quick fix on bicycles whose main lighting system is not functioning. In markets such as the United States, the United Kingdom, and Australia, where few bikes are equipped with generator systems, they are used almost exclusively.

Reflectors—mounted on the pedals, spokes, seat tube, handlebars, or incorporated as reflective paint or textiles—illuminate only when light is shined upon them, such as when caught in the beam of headlights.

Advances in retroreflective materials have made them increasingly effective, at little effort and cost to the rider, as a way to increase visibility.

Locks

Bicycle theft and tampering is a fact of life in most places with a substantial number of bicyclists and is especially a concern for utilitarian riders, who often must leave bicycles in vulnerable locations. Lock technology has evolved to evade the common techniques of larceny, including systems that are part of the bicycle and ones that attach separately. The former are more convenient for the rider but are often not sufficient. Among the latter, riders trade off features such as weight versus efficacy, and size (for instance, a more compact "U" shape is harder to cut as well as lighter) versus the ability to fit around more things in one loop (for instance, the frame, pole, and wheel). Some communities have experimented with GPS systems for tracking stolen bicycles, but none have proved cost-effective for broad adoption. Because of insufficient security, risk of theft often limits the type of bicycle equipment people choose to use, especially for certain types of destinations, such as train stations. Whether a failure of policy or of lock technology, this issue could undermine the usefulness of well-designed bicycles and components if people are too worried about theft to utilize them.

Clothing, Helmets, and Totes

The need for special clothing or personal accessories is counter to the idea that bicycling should function just like any other mode of transportation, fitting seamlessly with everyday life before and after the ride. However, because of their exposure to the elements as well as traffic, bicyclists can benefit from textiles designed to keep them cool, warm, or dry, as needed, or with retroreflective properties for enhanced nighttime visibility. Options have expanded in recent decades, and waterproof wicking synthetics and retroreflective properties masked in tasteful neutral tones are now available. Such materials are also now used in bags, totes, detachable panniers, and messenger bags designed for cyclists. Helmets have become cheaper, lighter, thinner, and more comfortable over the years, and an expanding array of style-oriented helmets and helmet covers help make them appear more like an accessory than just a hardhat (see, for instance, Binkley 2010).

Meeting Utilitarian Needs

The preceding section provided an overview of recent developments in bicycle equipment; table 5.2 catalogs all types of equipment— new or old, high-tech or low-tech—that can help accommodate the specific needs of people using bikes for transportation, as identified earlier. Because the needs of individual riders vary, the list is not exhaustive of the myriad ways that bicycle equipment can make a difference to utilitarian riders, nor will all of this equipment be important to all riders. However, the availability of such equipment makes utilitarian bicycling more feasible and more desirable for more people on more occasions.

Conclusions

Bicycle equipment, old and new, has an important role to play in enhancing the feasibility and desirability of utilitarian bicycling. Traditionally styled utilitarian bicycles dominate in countries where bicycling is a common mode of transportation, and they serve their purpose well. Where utilitarian bicycling is less common, such as the United States, the United Kingdom, and Australia, bicycles designed for recreation have been the norm, but traditional bicycles are making a comeback, sometimes with innovations originally intended for competitive and sport bicycles. This trend bodes well for bicycling in these places: the greater the degree to which bicycle equipment meets the needs of travelers, the more likely they are to choose bicycling.

Of course, bicycle infrastructure and the overall bicycling environment influence this choice as well, as shown in chapters 6, 12, 13, and 14. Infrastructure can make bike equipment less important or reduce the number of functions it must serve. For example, good bicycle paths make cycling safer, possibly reducing bicyclists' reliance on helmets and other safety equipment. The provision of secure bike parking reduces the need for heavy-duty locks and secured components. On the other hand, equipment can also make up for some deficiencies in infrastructure. For example, suspension systems can smooth out the ride when pavement is bumpy. Ultimately, bicycling is most likely where the environment and equipment together ensure that the traveler's needs are met.

Table 5.2
Bike equipment for utilitarian bicyclists' needs

Goal	Bike components	Other gear
Safety		
Protection from vehicle traffic	• Well-functioning brakes	• Helmet • Visibility-enhancing accessories (see below)
Visibility of the bicyclist	• Upright geometry • Bright or reflective frame paint	• Lights and reflectors (diffuse and multidirectional) • Flags • Bell or horn • Bright or reflective clothing
Rider's ability to see traffic	• Upright riding position	• Headlights (concentrated beacon) • Rear mirror
Reliable functionality	• Quality manufacturing • Designs favoring reliability over performance • Moving parts enclosed or encased from the elements (e.g., hub gear) • Duplicate brakes (front and rear, or hand-brake on fixed-gear bikes)	• Patch kit, emergency tools, air, or pump
Logistical convenience		
Ability to carry things	• Pedal brakes for hands-free braking • Cargo bike with built-in storage • Electric-assist bikes for extra heavy loads or long distances	• Easy-to-carry bags, backpacks, and totes • Front or rear baskets, panniers, rack bags • Trailer
Ability to carry passengers	• Multi-person bicycle, such as tandem, tricycle, or quadracycle • Pedicab (one rider, with room for one or more passengers) • Owning a "stable" of bikes, including extra guest bicycles	• Trailer or trail-a-bike • Front or rear child seat • Front or rear rack, seat, or platform that accommodates passengers

Table 5.2
(continued)

Goal	Bike components	Other gear
Logistical convenience		
Ability to surmount distance and hills	• Multiple gears • Electric-assist bicycles • Lightweight frame and components • Weight-forward frame and drop handlebars for aerodynamic posture	
Link to other modes	• Lightweight (for carrying upstairs/onto vehicles) • Folding bike • Quick-release wheels for fitting onto racks or in trunks • Theft-proofing for long-term storage at transit stations: nondetachable parts (no quick-release)	• Theft-proofing for long-term storage at transit stations, including good locks
Ease of maneuvering	• Upright geometry and proper fit for ease of putting foot to the ground for frequent stops and starts • Step-over frame shape • Appropriate number of gears (fewer is simpler and more lightweight; more allows for easier starts, stops, and hill climbing) • Preferred brake system (hand brakes, multiple lever positions/interrupter brakes, pedal brakes for hands-free) • Preferred shifter system (grip shift, thumb shifters, bar-end shifters) • Lightweight materials (frame and components) • Chain guard or enclosed drive chain and transmission for no-fuss with pant leg	• Minimize detachable add-ons (permanently mount all components for less on-and-off hassle) • Any removable add-ons are small and lightweight (mini U-lock, beacon LED lights, etc.) • Clothing and gear is cross-purpose (something you do or would wear/use off the bike)

Table 5.2
(continued)

Goal	Bike components	Other gear
Logistical convenience		
Theft resistance	• Nondetachable parts (no quick-release) • Built-in locks (e.g., wheel locks)	• Good locks • Seat chain • Accessories are either permanently attached or easily removed when parking • GPS tracking technology
Low maintenance needs	• Enclose or encase moving parts (e.g., hub gear, belt drive system) • In general, designs favoring reliability over performance	• Long-lasting batteries or generator lights
Bodily comfort		
Posture/reach	• Geometry of frame, stem, and handlebars that is comfortable • Brakes and shifters easily reached from an upright position	
Seat comfort	• Seat shape is comfortable for rider (wide, cut-out, or other) • Seat design incorporates springs, padded foam, gel, or other cushioning • Seat post that absorbs vibrations (see below)	• Padded seat cover • Plastic seat cover (to keep dry) • Padded biking shorts
Minimal vibrations and shaking	• Suspension (spring, elastomer, or other suspension technology in fork, seat post, frame, or stem) • Shock-absorbing frame, post, or fork material (steel absorbs more than rigid aluminum; carbon fiber absorbs more than metal)	• Padded handlebar tape • Padded seat or seat cover • Padded gloves • Padded biking shorts

Table 5.2
(continued)

Goal	Bike components	Other gear
Bodily comfort		
Protection from rain	• Pedal brakes (for hands-free braking while carrying an umbrella) • Enclosed fairing (such as on an HPV)	• Fenders • Plastic seat cover (to keep seat dry) • Clothing: rain jacket, poncho, rain pants or rain skirt, especially cross-purpose or stylish gear that rider is willing to wear off the bike, or easily accommodates "normal" clothes underneath • Accessories such as spats, shoe covers, boots, gloves, helmet cover, and visor • Umbrella
Protection from grime	• Hub gears • Enclosed drive chain of any kind	• Fenders • Chain guard • Clothing (as above) • Ankle strap or clamp for pant leg
Temperature control		• Warm, ventilated, or wicking clothing; especially cross-purpose or stylish gear that rider is willing to wear off the bike, or easily accommodates "normal" clothes underneath
Manageable exertion	• Sufficient gear ratio options for the rider's ability and/or the terrain • Lightweight frame and components • Electric assistance	

Table 5.2
(continued)

Goal	Bike components	Other gear
Enjoyment		
Fun riding	• Whatever components the bicyclist feels are fun	• Whatever gear the bicyclist feels is fun
Style	• Bike itself is stylish or attractive • Flat pedals accommodate varied footwear	• Personalized paint, stickers, or spoke cards • Baskets, chain guards, and other gear that allow riding with "normal" clothes and personal items • Cross-purpose or "normal" clothes and personal items (purse, brief case, etc.) • Stylish helmets, jackets, and bags

The effectiveness of bicycle equipment in supporting utilitarian bicycling also depends on the interplay between consumers and manufacturers. Aspiring bicyclists may have little idea of what type of bicycle would be best for them or even where to find such a bicycle. Women interviewed for a study in Australia, for example, were unaware of improvements to bicycles since their childhood that might enhance their enjoyment of bicycling (Garrard, Crawford, and Hakman 2006). In the United States, nearly three-fourths of bicycles are purchased at mass merchant outlets such as Walmart (National Bicycle Dealers Association 2010), where the selection is usually limited to less expensive, low-quality bicycles rather than the higher priced, better-quality bicycles in bicycle shops. Given limited consumer interest, it is no wonder that manufacturers have catered to the demand for recreational bicycles while largely ignoring, at least until recently, the utilitarian bicycling niche. As utilitarian bicycling gains popularity in these and other countries and as consumers develop more appreciation for the value of utility-oriented and high-quality equipment, increases in both demand and supply should make good utilitarian bicycles more accessible to more people.

Historically, except in the places where bicycling is truly commonplace, interest in cycling has fluctuated substantially with the winds of fashion. Fashion clearly played a role in the golden age of cycling at the turn of the twentieth century, and more recently, surges of interest in cycling have coincided with certain bicycle equipment coming into vogue, such as ten-speeds in the 1980s, mountain bikes in the 1990s, and fixed-gear bikes in the 2000s. Lately, bicycles have become trendy again, featured in fashion magazines and mainstream advertising campaigns, in the form of classic Dutch-style utility bicycles dressed up with sartorial chic. This trend may help utilitarian cycling catch on in more places, perhaps especially among young urban professionals. Policy makers now face the challenge of capitalizing on the momentum of the trend to make cycling a lasting norm rather than a passing fashion.

Acknowledgments

The authors thank the many experts who provided perspectives on the use, development, and role of bicycle equipment in their local communities and more broadly, including Gustaf Alströmer, Andy Besold, Graham Bradshaw, Ralph Buehler, Nick Cavill, Mikael Colville-Andersen, Jan Garrard, Billie Giles-Corti, Eva Heinen, Susan Knaup, Thomas Krag, Emmanuel de Lanversin, Karel Martens, Paul Martin, Noel McFarlane, Jason Moore, Galen Nishioka, Kate Powlison, Piet Rietveld, Randy Rzewnicki, Warren Salomon, Rosemary Speidel, Chris Stevens, Hans Voerknecht, Yunshi Wang, Jonathan Woolley, Jillian Woolmer, and Yan Xing.

References

Ballantine, Richard. 2001. *Richard's 21st-Century Bicycle Book*. New York: The Overlook Press.

Binkley, Christina. 2010. The Season of Biker Chic: Touring Cities Stylishly on Two Wheels, With Stops for Accessories. *Wall Street Journal*, July 23, W3.

Chu, Kathy. 2010. Electric Bikes Enhance Pedal Power; Millions on Road in China; in the U.S., Not So Much. *USA Today*, February 11, 3B.

Colville-Andersen, Mikael. 2011. Personal communication, March 16.

Congleton, Christopher. 2009. Results of the Fall 2007 UC Davis Campus Travel Assessment. Institute of Transportation Studies, University of California, Davis, Research Report UCD-ITS-RR-09–01.

Garrard, Jan, Sharyn Crawford, and Natalie Hakman. 2006. *Revolutions for Women: Increasing Women's Participation in Cycling for Recreation and*

Transport. Final report. School of Social Health and Development, Deakin University, Burwood, Victoria, Australia. October.

Goodman, J. David. 2010. An Electric Boost for Bicyclists. *New York Times*, January 31, B1.

Heinen, Eva. 2011. Unpublished data provided via personal communication, March 20.

Herlihy, David V. 2004. *Bicycle: The History*. New Haven, CT: Yale University Press.

Morchin, William C., and Henry Oman. 2006. *Electric Bicycles: A Guide to Design and Use*. Hoboken, NJ: John Wiley & Sons, Inc.

National Bicycle Dealers Association. 2010. Industry Overview 2010: A Look at the Bicycle Industry's Vital Statistics. http://nbda.com/articles/industry-overview-2010-pg34.htm.

Pike Research. 2011. Personal communication with Dave Hurst, Pike Research Senior Analyst, March 16.

Wiebe, Matt. 2010. Market Slides: 2009 Imports Hit New Lows. *Bicycle Retailer & Industry News*, July 1.

6

Bicycling Infrastructure for Mass Cycling: A Transatlantic Comparison

Peter G. Furth

For the bicycle to be useful for transportation, bicyclists need adequate route infrastructure—roads and paths on which to get places. In the 1890s, when bicycling first became popular, bicyclists' chief need was better paved roads. In the present era, however, it is not poor pavement but fast and heavy motor traffic that restricts cyclists' ability to get places safely (Jacobsen, Racioppi, and Rutter 2009), as discussed in chapter 7.

European and American policies have strongly diverged on how to address this challenge. In many European countries, including the Netherlands, Germany, Denmark, and Sweden, cyclists' need for separation from fast, heavy traffic is considered a fundamental principle of road safety. This policy has led to systematic traffic calming on local streets and, along busier streets, the provision of a vast network of "cycle tracks"—bicycle paths that are physically separated from motor traffic and distinct from the sidewalk. Cycle tracks (see figures 6.1–6.3) may be at street level, separated from moving traffic by a raised median, a parking lane, or candlestick bollards; at sidewalk level, separated from the sidewalk by vertical elements (e.g., light poles), hardscape, a change in pavement or a painted line; or at an intermediate level, a curb step above the street, but also a small curb step below the sidewalk.

The success of this combination of traffic calming and cycle tracks has been well documented; for example, chapter 2 shows that the percentage of trips taken by bicycle, though less than 1 percent in the United States, exceeds 10 percent in several European countries, reaching 26 percent in the Netherlands; at the same time, their bicycling fatality rates (fatalities per million km of bicycling) are much lower than in the United States (Pucher and Dijkstra 2000; Pucher and Buehler 2010). In contrast,

Figure 6.1
One-way cycle track in The Hague. *Credit:* Peter Furth.

Figure 6.2
Raised crossing carries a two-way cycle track across a minor street at an intersection in Delft. *Credit:* Kim Niedermaier.

Figure 6.3
Cycle track in Montreal is separated from travel lane by bollards and a parking lane. *Credit:* Peter Furth.

the United States has mainly pursued a policy of integrating bikes with traffic, so that getting places by bike usually requires riding in streets with heavy traffic. Therefore, utilitarian bicycle use in the United States is, for the most part, limited to that fraction of the population that is "traffic-tolerant."

This first section of this chapter contrasts American and European policy regarding the provision of bicycle infrastructure. The second section analyzes different kinds of bikeways. The chapter ends with a discussion about funding for bicycle infrastructure and a conclusion.

Policy Regarding Separation from Traffic

The imperative of separating cyclists from fast and heavy motor traffic seems obvious in light of their vulnerability and their large speed and mass differential from motor traffic. Unlike motor vehicles, bicycles do not benefit from cage construction, crumple zones, or airbags (CROW 2007, 31). Separating people from danger is a fundamental principle of industrial safety. As discussed in chapter 11, this is particularly important for children, whose size, limited cognitive ability, and impulsiveness make it especially dangerous for them to integrate with traffic. As shown in chapter 3, in addition to objective risk of injury, the noise and danger of traffic imposes stress on cyclists that makes it difficult to relax and enjoy the outdoors. Many people choose bicycling because it's enjoyable; when bicycling involves constant traffic stress, that enjoyment can be lost.

The combined concerns of safety and comfort make separation from traffic stress a critical factor in attracting people to cycling. In many North American surveys, the chief reason given for not cycling more is the danger posed by motor traffic (Winters et al. 2011). Cyclists willing to ride in heavy traffic represent a small fraction of the population; the mainstream population has been characterized as traffic-intolerant (Furth 2008). At a global level, the correlation is strong; in every country with high levels of bicycle use, bicycle infrastructure that separates bicyclists from fast and heavy motor traffic is widespread (Pucher and Dijkstra 2000; Pucher and Buehler 2008), and in countries lacking routine separation, bicycle use is low. Within the United States, cities with more dedicated bicycling infrastructure tend to have more bicycle use (Dill and Carr 2003; Buehler and Pucher 2012).

Bicycling can make important contributions to societal goals related to public health, energy independence, climate change, air quality, traffic congestion, mobility, economy, and quality of life. However, meaningful progress toward any of these goals can be achieved only with *mass cycling*. Route facilities that appeal to only the traffic-tolerant population are not enough. A goal of any bicycle infrastructure program must be to provide sufficient separation from traffic stress that it attracts the mainstream population.

Bicycling infrastructure can be classified into four levels of separation:

1. *Shared streets and shared lanes*   No dedicated bicycling space.

2. *Bike lanes*   Separation by roadway striping.

3. *Separated paths*   Cycle tracks and shared-use paths along a road, physically separated from moving motor traffic by a barrier such as a curb or parked cars.

4. *Standalone paths* Bike paths or shared-use paths in an independent right-of-way, such as in a park or along an abandoned rail corridor.

Higher levels of separation typically involve both greater construction cost and greater amounts of space. Therefore, governments have a natural tendency to prefer lower levels of separation unless constrained by criteria aimed at meeting user needs.

Dutch and Other European Separation Guidelines

The need for clear policy concerning separation from traffic stress is well understood in European countries that have achieved a high modal share for bicycling. The most recent Dutch criteria regarding separation, developed as part of the national road safety program "Sustainable Safety" (Wegman and Aarts 2006) and the Dutch *Design Manual for Bicycle Traffic* (CROW 2007), are summarized in table 6.1. In urban areas, physical separation in the form of a cycle track is expected on any street with more than two lanes, as well as on any urban street whose speed limit exceeds 50 km/h (31 mph) and any rural road whose speed limit exceeds 60 km/h (37 mph).

For bikes to operate in mixed traffic, urban streets should meet three criteria:

Speed limit should be 30 km/h (19 mph) or less. Moreover, streets may be given this low a speed limit only if they are outfitted with traffic calming measures such as frequent sharp turns, speed humps, or very narrow roadways that make the speed limit self-enforcing.

Traffic volume should be 5,000 motor vehicles per day or less. Moreover, bike lanes are preferred when daily traffic volume exceeds 4,000 vehicles per day. Above this rate, two effects make shared streets stressful (Furth 2008). First, during peak hours, cyclists will experience the "overtaking squeeze"—when a cyclist and two motor vehicles traveling in opposite directions from one another want to pass the same point at the same time—more than once per minute. Second, motorist delay from being blocked by bikes rises to a level that tempts motorists to pass aggressively.

The road should have no car lanes marked, including no centerline. Lane striping should never channel cars toward the part of the road that bicycles normally use; therefore, marked centerlines are inconsistent with

Table 6.1
Dutch bicycle facility selection matrix

Lane configuration	Average daily traffic (vehicles/day)	Street type and speed limit			
		Urban local street 30 km/h (19 mph)	Urban through street 50 km/h (31 mph)	Rural local road 60 km/h (37 mph)	Fast traffic road 70+ km/h (44+ mph)
Two-way traffic with no centerline	<2500	Mixed traffic[a]	Bike lane[b] or cycletrack[c]	Advisory bike lane[d]	Cycle track or low-speed service road
	2000–3000			Bike lane[b] or cycle track[e]	
	3000–5000	Bike lane or cycle track			
	>4000	Bike lane or cycle track	Bike lane or cycle track[c]		
Two lanes (1 + 1)	any	Bike lane or cycle track	Bike lane or cycle track[c]		
Four lanes (2 + 2) or more	any	(Does not exist)	Cycle track or low-speed service road		

Source: CROW 2007.

a. For designated bike routes, a bike lane or advisory bike lane is optional.

b. May be an advisory bike lane on road sections with no centerline.

c. Cycle track is preferred if there is parking; cycle track is recommended for designated bike routes.

d. Although CROW (2007) gives "mixed traffic" for this cell, the default layout for roads in this category is to mark advisory bike lanes.

e. Cycle track is preferred for designated bike routes.

cars and bikes sharing space. Mixed traffic on multilane roads is never acceptable.

The Dutch *Design Manual* recommends bicycle lanes for a rather limited set of circumstances: roads with two lanes and no parking lanes. Where such streets have a parallel parking lane, cycle tracks are preferred; guidance recommends eliminating the bike lanes, making the road correspondingly narrower, and using the redeemed space to create sidewalk-level cycle tracks (Wegman and Aarts 2006, 162; CROW 2007, 118). Bike lanes are used less and less in the Netherlands because they are almost never part of any new road designs and on many older roads, they are being converted to cycle tracks.

On streets too narrow for exclusive bike lanes, many European countries use "advisory bike lanes" (see figure 6.4). Using dashed lines, they divide the street into a central driving zone that is too narrow for two cars and a pair of edge zones that are in effect bike lanes that cars may

Figure 6.4
Advisory bicycle lanes on a two-way street in Delft; note advisory lanes paved red and marked with dashed lines. *Credit:* William G. Gray Jr.

use when encountering opposing traffic. This treatment applies only to streets with one line of traffic per direction and no marked centerline.

King (2003) compared separation criteria used by select international and US jurisdictions. The criteria used in Denmark, Germany, and the United Kingdom are similar to the Dutch criteria in that with increasing traffic volume and speed, they recommend increased separation, moving from mixed traffic to bike lanes and then to cycle tracks. American guidelines are anomalous in that separated paths are never recommended.

Lack of Separation Criteria in the United States

The American Association of State Highway and Transportation Officials' *Guide for the Development of Bicycle Facilities* (AASHTO 1999) has no criteria regarding when cyclists should be separated from fast or heavy traffic. There is no limit to the traffic speed or number of lanes for which a road may have bike lanes or even be designated as a "shared roadway." In the United States, "Share the Road" and "Bike Route" signage are often applied to multilane arterials with heavy traffic, and bike lanes are often marked on multilane arterials with speed limits of 35, 45, and even 55 mph. For example, on San Diego's Camino del Norte, a 55 mph (90 km/h) divided highway, bike lane users are expected to weave across one lane of 55 mph traffic and then ride 900 feet (275 m) in a bike lane sandwiched between four lanes of traffic on the left and two lanes on the right.

The AASHTO *Guide* implicitly justifies its lack of criteria for separation by asserting a dichotomy between users who care more about speed and users who care more about separation from traffic. The Dutch do not see these differences as presenting a conflict; they require that bicycle facilities offer both a high level of separation from traffic stress and a direct route with as few stops as possible. The AASHTO *Guide*, in contrast, is almost doctrinal about the impossibility of meeting both needs with the same facility, stating that "no one type of bicycle facility or highway design suits every bicyclist and no designated bicycle facility can overcome a lack of bicycle operator skill" (AASHTO 1999, 6). It describes a corridor presenting two alternatives: a four-lane, 55 mph (90 km/h) highway with a 5-foot (1.5-m) shoulder and a parallel bicycle route consisting of neighborhood streets linked by short sections of shared-use path. While recognizing that the latter route would be preferred by children and "less confident adults," it states that "most experienced and many casual adult riders will continue to use the shoulder [of the highway] for the sake of speed and convenience" (AASHTO 1999, 7). This example reflects a gross misunderstanding of user needs, as well as a false assumption that travel on neighborhood streets and paths must be slow.

This lack of separation criteria combined with the tendency of government to prefer the lowest-cost solution has meant that the starting point of American policy regarding bicycle infrastructure is not a mandate to meet cyclist needs. Rather, the government's position is that its responsibility is satisfied by allowing bikes to share the road; anything beyond that is optional. If a bike lane or shared road subjects riders to more traffic stress than most people are willing to tolerate, it isn't the fault of the facility, but rather the "lack of bicycle operator skill." If a road's bike lanes vanish on an intersection approach because the road space is "needed" for a left-turn lane or for parking and cyclists are thrust into mixed traffic, that may be regrettable, but—according to American guidelines—it is acceptable.

Where user needs drive infrastructure policy, engineers are motivated to find innovative solutions, as one can find in bicycle-friendly cities across Europe. As examined in chapter 12, Davis, California, stood out for decades as a rare American city displaying this "bicycling for all" attitude. Inspired by a community leader's half-year stay in the Netherlands in the 1960s, Davis made itself a "city of bicycles" (Buehler and Handy 2008), building a bicycling network that includes 50 miles (80 km) of separated and standalone paths, including more than a dozen grade-separated crossings, as well as becoming the first American city to have bike lanes and traffic signals for bicycles. By 1980, when the national bicycle share of commute-to-work trips was less than half a percent, it was 28 percent in Davis. Unlike most American communities its size, Davis has no regular school bus service because bicycling is the usual mode for children to get to school. By 2000, as the population more than doubled and Davis's family-friendly reputation attracted many people working in distant cities such as Sacramento and Berkeley, the bike share for work trips fell to 14 percent; however, for residents working in Davis and the surrounding county, the bike share for work trips was still 25 percent (Buehler and Handy 2008; Pucher, Dill, and Handy 2010; chapter 12, this volume).

In the last decade, several US cities—spearheaded by Portland, Oregon, and New York City—have embraced the European philosophy of providing bicycle facilities targeted to mainstream, traffic-intolerant cyclists (Mapes 2009; Pucher, Buehler, and Seinen 2011). Since 1994, Portland has installed hundreds of miles of bike lanes, bike paths, and bike routes along quiet local streets using traffic-calming measures such as speed humps and diverters (see chapter 13, this volume). The result has been a six-fold increase in bicycle use and an explosion in bicycle culture, giving Portland a reputation as America's leading bicycling city (Birk 2010; Pucher, Dill, and Handy 2010; Pucher, Buehler, and Seinen 2011). New York City hired consultants from Copenhagen to help them design cycle tracks and installed 15 miles of cycle tracks between 2007 and 2010 (see chapter 14, this volume). However, adopting European design practices has not been easy (Birk 2010) because of the influence of a little-known but influential philosophy that asserts that separating cyclists from motor traffic is both dangerous and an attack on cyclists' right to ride in the road, an ideology known as "vehicular cycling."

Vehicular Cycling Theory and Opposition to Bikeways

It is impossible to understand American cycling infrastructure policy without understanding the influence of John Forester's vehicular cycling (VC) theory, which posits that "cyclists fare best when they act as, and are treated as, operators of vehicles" (Forester 1992, 2001). VC proponents argue that separating bicycles from motor traffic is inherently unsafe except along a road with no intersections (e.g., along a seawall). They assert a dichotomy between "objective safety" (crash risk) and "perceived safety," claiming that although people may feel more secure riding in their own space, such as in a bike lane or a separated path, they are in fact at greater risk of collision with motor vehicles than if they mixed with traffic as would, for example, a motorcycle. According to VC theory, when approaching any intersection, it's safer to ride where motor vehicles ride, because that's where motorists are going to look. Their reasoning contains an element of truth—intersection safety undoubtedly depends on visibility and driver expectations. However, the idea that separation *must* be dangerous ignores the massive evidence of the European experience, and the engineering solutions developed to improve intersection safety for cyclists. It also ignores the patent dangers of riding a slow, small vehicle that lacks a protective cage in mixed traffic.

Vehicular cycling theory is preoccupied with a collision type called the "right hook," which occurs when a through-going cyclist conflicts with a right-turning motorist approaching from behind. According to VC theory, bicyclists should prevent right hooks by "controlling the travel lane," that is, occupying a lane position that blocks cars from passing. On an urban street, one should keep to the right between intersections (letting faster traffic pass) but then shift into a lane controlling position on each intersection approach. If intersections are frequent, cyclists should simply stay in the center of the travel lane. VC proponents downplay the risk of collision with same-direction traffic such as being hit from behind or sideswiped and train cyclists to ignore harassment from motorists angry with them for blocking a lane. Cycle tracks and bike lanes, which guide cyclists to stay to the right even through intersections, are therefore anathema to vehicular cycling. Forester (n.d.) teaches that they are not only inherently dangerous but are also part of the "cyclist inferiority superstition" and emphasizes cyclists' rights to operate like any other vehicle.

Forester's antibikeway philosophy has had a pervasive influence within the American bicycle advocacy community. State and local bicyclist organizations have frequently advocated against bike lanes and separated paths; Forester himself served as president of the California Association of Bicycling Organizations and of the League of American Wheelmen, now the League of American Bicyclists. In many cases, bicycle planners hired by state and local government have been VC adherents who used their influence to prevent rather than promote bikeways. Two examples are Boston and Dallas, both named the worst cycling city in America by *Bicycling* magazine (Boston in 1999 and 2006, Dallas in 2008), neither of which had any bike lanes until new bicycle coordinators were appointed in 2007 and 2009, respectively. When a citizens' group exposed Dallas's bicycle planner for remarking, "As long as I'm the Bike Coordinator for the city, Dallas will never have on-street bike lanes" (Bike Friendly Oak Cliff 2008), he defended his position by writing, "I do not worry about 'Is it popular?' or 'Is it politically correct?' or 'Is it the current style?' No. Instead I ask myself, 'Does this action endanger people more than the other alternatives?'" (Summers 2008).

Opposition to Separated Paths

Adult bicycling had a renaissance in the United States in the late 1960s with the popularization of the ten-speed bike and the earth movement. Responding to demand for bicycling facilities, California produced a bikeway planning guide whose first edition took a positive view toward European practices, recommending sidewalk-level bikeways, separated bike lanes, and regular bike lanes (UCLA Institute of Transportation and Traffic Engineering 1972, 44–47, 59–62, 70). Forester, then active in bicycle racing clubs, saw such bikeways as a threat to cyclist's right to ride in the road and a hindrance to fast bicyclists and responded by advancing his VC theory.

At the time, Forester's theory had no empirical support. The California guide cites a Danish study that found that the injury rate on an arterial with cycle tracks was 60 percent lower than on a similar arterial lacking cycle tracks (Council for Traffic Safety Research 1969). Until now, only one credible American study (Wachtel and Lewiston 1994) at first glance appears to support his theory. It compares the rate of motor vehicle–bicycle collisions for cyclists who rode in the street versus on sidewalks that had been designated as bikeways on three Palo Alto, California, streets, and found the crash risk 80 percent greater on the sidewalk bikeway. However, this study considers only crashes at intersections (including driveway junctions) and therefore gives a distorted view of overall safety. Lusk et al. (2011) showed that when between-junction crashes are accounted for along with crashes at intersections, the sidewalk bikeway's crash risk was not statistically different from the risk of riding in the street. Furthermore, because much of the risk associated with sidewalk riding was due to the relatively few cyclists who rode along the left side of the street, they found that for cyclists who used the right-side sidewalk—a discipline enforced by the one-way cycle tracks common in Europe—riding on a sidewalk bikeway carried only half the risk of riding in the street.

Detractors of separated paths frequently cite Moritz (1997), who found that sidewalk riding carries five times the accident risk of bicycling in the street. Apart from the fact that separated paths are different from sidewalks, this finding is not scientifically valid even for sidewalks, both because of a faulty study design and an inadequate sample. This study used a survey in which respondents reported their mileage and crash frequency on different types of facilities (standalone paths, bike lanes, streets without bike lanes, and "other"). Because the study had been designed for other purposes, the questionnaire never mentioned "sidewalk"; results reported for sidewalks are based on responses for facility type "other." Moreover, facility type "other" accounted for only twelve reported crashes.

Montreal presents a unique North American test bed for the safety of separated paths. Inspired by a city official's visit to Amsterdam, it constructed 15 miles of separated two-way paths in the 1980s. Lusk et al. (2011) examined nine years of injury data on six representative cycle tracks and parallel alternative routes and found that injury risk on cycle tracks was 28 percent less than cycling in the street. They also found that the cycle tracks carried 2.5 times more cyclists than the alternative routes.

Residents of European countries with extensive cycle track networks find it astonishing that a theory could persist that separated paths are dangerous. How to overcome the evidence of the massive European experiment, in which, for decades, millions of cyclists have ridden daily on cycle tracks, with crash rates far lower than in the United States and a far greater appeal to vulnerable populations such as children and seniors (Pucher and Dijkstra 2000; Pucher and Buehler 2008, 2010)? Forester, who has never visited the Netherlands as an adult, attempts an explanation: "The Dutch produced a very dangerous bikeway system, compared to cycling on the road, but they have overcompensated for those dangers by installing protective measures that make it extremely inconvenient, again compared to cycling on the road" (Truewheelers 2000). What Forester does not explain is why, if the measures used to make Dutch bikeways safe are so inconvenient, *why* do so many people use them?

American Policy against Separated Paths
Perhaps the most far-reaching impact of Forester's philosophy was getting an effective ban on separated paths written into the AASHTO *Guide for the Development of Bicycling Facilities.* As mentioned earlier, California's first guide had recommended, among other treatments, separated bike

paths at both the street and sidewalk level. Along with bike lanes, such separated paths were considered "Class II bikeways," defined as designated cycling space within the road right-of-way. ("Class I bikeways" are standalone paths, and "Class III bikeways" are shared streets.) However, in spite of a complete lack of empirical evidence against separated paths, California's guide was changed to denounce those separated path treatments; "Class II bikeways" came to mean bike lanes and nothing more. The AASTHO *Guide* then followed the revised California guide, stating that bike lanes should never be placed behind parking lanes and that sidewalk-level bikeways should be used only where there are virtually no intersections, such as along a seawall or while crossing a long bridge (AASHTO 1999, 20, 33–35, 58). Forester credits his movement for keeping European-style separation out of the United States:

When bicycle traffic increased in the 1960s, motorists worried that "their roads" would be plugged up by bicycles. The motor-minded California legislature attempted (1970–2) to bring in the Dutch-style sidepath system to get cyclists off the roads. The motoring establishment thought that they would have great public support, because they believed, as if it were one of the laws of nature that everybody knew was true, that the prime safety requirement for cyclists was staying out of the way of same-direction motor traffic. However, at this time there were cycling spokesmen able to make scientific challenges to their designs, to demonstrate how dangerous these designs are and how much safer vehicular cycling is. This was the start of the American bikeway debate. Cyclists managed to convince the government that it would be held liable for accidents caused by the most obviously dangerous designs, which were then withdrawn. However, the designs which were not so obviously dangerous [bike lanes] were retained as the basis of the governmental bicycle transportation policy. (Forester, n.d.)

Having essentially dismissed separated paths, the AASHTO *Guide* offers designers a meager toolbox for bike facilities: bike lanes or nothing, unless there happens to be an available off-road corridor for a standalone path. And because the design community has by and large felt obligated to follow the *Guide*'s recommendations, the ban on separated paths has been self-perpetuating because committees that control national guidelines tend to accept evidence from US safety studies only, and without American examples whose safety performance could be studied, Forester's assertions that separated paths are dangerous have stood unrefuted.

Undoubtedly, a reason for AASHTO's embrace of VC principles is that they don't call for any money or roadway space being devoted to bicycling. VC demands are music to their ears: "You don't have to build us any bikeways; in fact, doing so would actually harm cyclists. All bicyclists want is wide roads, smooth pavement, and modified drain covers so that our bicycle wheels won't get caught."

Recently, however, a few American municipalities have begun to embrace separated paths for cyclists. Cambridge, Massachusetts, whose bicycle planner studied in Copenhagen, installed a pair of one-way sidewalk-level cycle tracks in 2003. New York City captured the imagination of the country in 2007 when they installed the first of several European-inspired "protected lanes," street-level cycle tracks between the curb and a parking lane (see chapter 14, this volume). Officials report that it has seen a 57 percent increase in number of cyclists and a 50 percent decline in total crashes. Other US cities that have built cycle tracks since 2007 include Indianapolis, Portland, Washington, and Minneapolis.

At this writing, the AASHTO *Guide* is under revision. A review draft suggests that the next edition will mute its criticisms of separated paths; however, it still won't recommend them or offer design guidance for them. Frustrated by AASHTO and aware of engineers' need for guidance as more cities embrace European practices, the National Association of City Transportation Officials (NACTO), led by member cities Portland and New York, developed its own *Urban Bikeway Design Manual* (NACTO 2011), with guidance on several different forms of cycle tracks as well as several other European-style treatments. Its publication may be a major turning point for American bicycling.

Bicycle Route Facility Types

This section describes the principal types of bicycle route facility, with a focus on how they can be applied to create low-stress bike routes that will serve the mainstream population.

Standalone Paths

Standalone paths are usually built in green settings in parks, along rivers and canals, and along abandoned rail rights-of-way. In the United States, they are typically shared with pedestrians and other nonmotorized users, though dual path systems (one path for pedestrians, one for bikes) are standard in Europe and are sometimes used in the United States as well. By providing a largely intersection-free route, standalone paths appeal to the dual user needs of separation from traffic stress and minimizing delay. Standalone paths enjoy strong political support because few Americans can picture themselves as bicycle commuters, but most can see themselves as recreational path users, whether on a bicycle or on foot. Nevertheless, in urban areas, standalone paths are often heavily used for commuting and other utilitarian transportation.

Standalone paths are by nature limited to where a right-of-way exists. Nevertheless, the potential network of standalone paths in North American cities is large. Most American cities developed along river and rail corridors, making paths in such corridors ideal for commuting; examples can be found in many cities. Large parks can also be ideal path settings; Minneapolis and the National Capital region are examples of urban areas with historically strong parks programs that feature many miles of greenway paths.

Building new paths can be expensive, with estimates ranging from $300,000 to $1.5 million per mile ($200,000 to $1,000,000 per km) or more if bridges are involved. However, some cities have found ways to stretch their path dollars. As noted in chapter 12, Boulder, Colorado, has a network of more than a hundred miles of bike paths, largely along its creeks, including seventy-four underpasses (Pucher, Dill, and Handy 2010). This development took advantage of regulations for flood control that paid for expanding the bridges over the creeks; including paths with these undercrossings involved little incremental cost. Some cities have found that they can develop standalone paths at almost no direct cost by requiring that developers complete any part of the city's path network plan that lies within their development. For example, Davis, California, on seeing the popularity of a "greenbelt" path voluntarily built by one housing developer, began to require that successive developers add to the greenbelt network as the city expanded (Buehler and Handy 2008). Scottsdale, Arizona, and Eagle, Idaho, suburbs of Phoenix and Boise, have each adopted an extensive plan of shared use paths, mostly following existing irrigation canals; developers are required to build path sections lying in their development area.

Narrower Travel Lanes

Where no off-road corridor exists, cyclists must be accommodated in road rights-of-way. Gaining acceptance for 10-foot-wide travel lanes has been a key to several US cities' ability to find space for bikeways. Many city and state highway departments consider anything below 12 feet (3.65 m), the standard lane width for freeways, to be substandard, even though the AASHTO highway design guide (AASHTO 2004, 311–312) allows considerable flexibility regarding lane widths and several US cities routinely use 10-foot-wide lanes on arterials with heavy bus traffic. Potts, Harwood, and Richard (2007), in an extensive study sponsored by the Federal Highway Administration (FHWA), found that on urban and suburban arterials, 9- and 10-foot (2.7- and 3.0-m) travel lanes had the same safety performance as 11- and 12-foot travel lanes, except on undivided multilane arterials.

Cycle Tracks

Cycle tracks form the greater part of the cycling network in cities in the Netherlands and Denmark. The few examples in North America include two-way "sidepaths" in Boulder, one-way "raised bike lanes" in Eugene and Bend, Oregon, "protected bike lanes" in New York between the curb and a parking lane (some one-way, some two-way), and several two-way "bike paths" in Montreal that are at street level and separated from travel lanes by parking lanes, raised medians, and bollards.

Riding on a cycle track involves paying attention to traffic for a few moments when crossing an intersection, then relaxing until the next one. Most people find the quality of this experience far superior to riding in an environment in which one has to pay constant attention to traffic. Having only discrete points that demand attention to traffic conflicts makes cycle tracks better suited to children's cognitive abilities. Cycle tracks also offer cyclists an environment with less traffic noise and cleaner air compared to riding in the road (Kendrick et al. 2011).

A challenge of cycle track design is ensuring safety at intersecting streets and driveways. Motorists' expectation of conflicting bicycle traffic can be enhanced by marking bicycle crossings through intersections, just as crosswalks mark the pedestrian path (NACTO 2011). At minor street intersections, a preferred treatment in Sweden, Denmark, and the Netherlands is to keep the cycle track and sidewalk elevated at sidewalk level through the crossing (see figure 6.2). Elevated crossings clearly signal cyclists' priority over cross traffic and act as a speed hump, reducing both the likelihood and severity of crashes with motor vehicles (Garder,

Leden, and Pulkkinen 1998). Where intersecting cycle tracks meet at signalized intersections, making the cycle tracks continuous around each corner gives cyclists a protected place to queue far in advance of motorists (Markenlei 2011).

Intersection risk along main arterials can be reduced by limiting the number of minor intersections. Access management—limiting driveways and minor intersections on streets whose main function is to carry through traffic—is a well-recognized safety practice in both Europe and the United States, though the American legal framework makes it more difficult to apply. In the Netherlands, most arterials built after World War II have infrequent intersections and no driveways, with the result that cycle tracks along these arterials have long, conflict-free sections between intersections. For older urban arterials with frequent intersections, it used to be questioned whether a bike lane might be preferable to a cycle track (CROW 1994, 81); since 1997, however, the cycle track option has been declared superior (CROW 2007, 119). This change in policy occurred partly because of the success of elevated crossings and partly because research found that a disproportionate share of cycle track crashes involved mopeds, which since a legislative change in 1997 ride in the roadway, not the cycle track, in urban areas. Since 2000, the trend in Dutch cities has been to replace arterial bike lanes with cycle tracks where space permits; Markenlei (2010) provides an excellent visual example.

At signalized intersections, bike signals (green, yellow, and red bicycles)—common in Europe, and also used in Montreal, Portland, and New York—can control the cycle track when the time that it's safe for bikes to cross differs from the time that the parallel traffic phase is green. Dutch arterials frequently have right-turn lanes controlled by a green arrow so that cyclists and right-turning motorists can have separate green phases. Cycle tracks along one-way avenues in New York's cycle tracks, located on the left in order to avoid conflicts with bus stops, use a mirror image scheme to resolve the conflict with left-turning traffic.

Cycle tracks should be wide enough to permit passing or side-by-side cycling. However, space constraints can make this goal difficult to achieve on some streets. Narrow, one-way cycle tracks are better suited to placement at sidewalk level (a common configuration in Germany) so that cyclists can pass one another using the sidewalk when it is clear of pedestrians. Intersections also provide passing opportunities.

Two-way cycle tracks achieve some economy of space because they offer passing opportunities without a passing lane; also, their wider layout makes snow removal easier. For these reasons, Montreal's cycle tracks are almost all two-way. However, two-way cycle tracks bring more complications to intersections and are therefore not permitted in Copenhagen, even though they are ubiquitous a few kilometers away in Malmo, Sweden's number one cycling city. The Dutch *Design Manual* (CROW 2007, 120) favors one-way cycle tracks but recognizes that two-way cycle tracks may be preferred in order to facilitate a safer alignment in general (e.g., if one side of a street has few intersections because it borders a river or railroad), eliminate the need for cyclists to cross a wide street twice, or where there isn't enough space for a pair of one-way cycle tracks. Also, where wrong-way riding on a one-way cycle track is prevalent, it is common Dutch practice to formally convert it to two-way, because with the conversion comes signs and markings that heighten motorists' expectations of two-way cycling. Dutch cities continue to build two-way cycle tracks; recently, some have made it a policy to convert all of their cycle tracks to two-way.

Bike Lanes

This section presents both a defense and a criticism of bike lanes. On one hand, bike lanes are an inexpensive and space-efficient means of accommodating bikes. Lane lines are an effective means of channeling traffic, and because bike lanes are usually so narrow that motorists have no incentive to drive in them, they can provide bicyclists a reserved zone for riding despite the lack of a barrier from motor traffic. On the other hand, the close proximity to moving traffic makes bike lanes more stressful to ride in than a cycle track, especially where traffic is fast or turbulent. Bike lanes offer no protection against illegal parking, often expose cyclists to "dooring" (when a parked car's door suddenly opens, colliding with a passing bike), and present complications at intersections with heavy right-turning traffic.

The Magic of Lines

Vehicular cycling proponents have opposed bike lanes because they guide cyclists to stay to the right, when they would prefer that cyclists be educated to shift frequently between a position on the right (allowing faster traffic to pass) to a lane-controlling position (to block cars and thus prevent a right hook collision). They have argued that the bike lane function could be met by providing a wide outside lane (14–15 feet or 4.3–4.6 m wide)—wide enough for a bike and car to ride side by side, but also narrow enough for a bicyclist to control the lane by riding in the middle. Through their influence, wide outside lanes became a recognized bicycle facility in the United States in the 1990s. Bike lane supporters have countered that wide lanes don't give cyclists the same sense of security as a bike lane and make roads more dangerous by encouraging higher speeds.

This debate led to several "wide lane conversion" studies observing motorist and cyclist behavior when wide outside lanes were divided into a travel lane and a bike lane. Hunter and Feaganes (2005), Duthie et al. (2010), and Parkin and Meyers (2010), studying road sections without parking, found that with a bike lane, cyclists rode further from the curb—evidence of less fear of cars approaching from behind. They also found that motorists passing a bike encroached less on the adjacent travel lane, revealing less stress on their part. For motorists, a line marking the boundary between bicycling and driving zones makes it easier from a distance to gauge a cyclist's lateral position and predict their path.

With cyclists and motorists thus adjusting their position, the average separation between a cyclist and passing motorist becomes smaller. Parkin and Meyers (2010) misinterpreted that resulting smaller average separation as an indication of worse safety, a counterintuitive result that was widely picked up by the press ("bike lanes worsen safety!"). However, safety is not a matter of average separation distance, but of the likelihood of zero or scant separation. Although none of these studies reports on the distribution of separation distance, they show a strong decline in the variability of motorist position, its main component, which can decrease the probability of near-zero separation even if mean separation decreases. Moreover, the clear shift in position by cyclists, whose accumulated experience is bound to include low-probability events such as vehicles passing with scant clearance, suggests that marking bike lanes improves objective as well as perceived safety.

The second argument that vehicular cyclists have advanced against bike lanes is that where they lie along parking lanes, they increase cyclists' risk of dooring by "guiding them" to keep to the right rather than control the lane. To eliminate the dooring hazard, a bike lane should reach 14.5 feet (4.4 m) from the curb (NACTO 2011); however, many bike lanes reach only 12 or 13 feet from the curb, and a cyclist riding in the middle of such a lane is at risk of dooring. Van Houten and Seiderman (2005) tested the effect of marking bike lanes on motorist, cyclist, and parked car position on a 44-foot-wide street with parallel parking. In the first stage, the only marked line was a double yellow centerline; in the final stage, bike lane lines divided each half of the road into a 7-foot-wide parking lane, a 5-foot-wide bike lane (thus the "reach" was 12 feet), and a 10-foot-wide travel lane. Marking the bike lane shifted bicyclists an average of 2.4 inches (6 cm) further from parked cars and decreased the fraction of cyclists riding in the most vulnerable position, less than 9.0 feet (2.7 m) from the curb, by 12 percent. The likely mechanism for this shift is that the added lines serve to confine and push motor traffic toward the centerline, giving cyclists more confidence about riding further to the left. Thus, when user behavior is accounted for, bike lanes are more effective in reducing the dooring hazard than having an undivided shared lane.

Landis, Vattikuti, and Brannick (1997) and Harkey, Reinfurt, and Knuiman (1998) developed models of cyclists' comfort based on ratings given by cyclists. Both found that marking bike lanes had a strong positive effect on cyclists' perceived safety beyond the effect that could be attributed to available roadway space. With either model, subdividing a wide outside lane into a travel lane and a bike lane improves level of service by 90 percent of a grade change on a scale of A (best) to F. Based on these studies, several state highway departments, including Florida and Massachusetts, no longer recommend wide outside lanes as a form of bicycle accommodation.

Bike Lane Criteria for Low-Stress Cycling

In some traffic environments and with adequate width, lines alone can be sufficient to create a low-stress bicycling environment. Zwolle, the Netherlands (Ligtermoet 2010), and Davis, California, are cities in the population range of 50,000 to 120,000 that have achieved high levels of bicycle use relying mainly on a combination of wide bike lanes (2 m) and standalone paths with grade separated crossings. Marked buffers make bike lanes effectively wider (figure 6.5), providing a degree of separation that begins to approach that of a cycle track. Portland has recently

Figure 6.5
Bike lane in Delft is wide, paved red, and has marked buffers on both sides.
Credit: Peter Furth.

installed a pair of 6-foot bike lanes with 2-foot buffers marked on either side in an attempt to provide a low-stress, yet low-cost, bicycling facility.

However, in many traffic environments, bike lanes can subject users to far more traffic stress than the mainstream population will accept. This is why Dutch criteria shown earlier in table 6.1 recommend bike lanes for only a limited combination of traffic speeds, volumes, and number of travel lanes. In addition, low-stress bike lanes should satisfy criteria related to right-turn conflicts and clearance from parked cars.

Because of the variability in parking lane width (widths of 7–12 feet are common in the United States), the key dimension for a bike lane next to a parking lane is not its width but its reach from the curb. Because of the dooring hazard, 14.5 feet is the desirable reach for a bike lane next to a parking lane. Before any smaller reach is considered, other road dimensions (e.g., travel lanes, median offset) should be reduced to their minimum, because a smaller reach represents a safety compromise.

Unfortunately, the AASHTO Guide (1999, 22) calls a configuration with a 13-foot reach (8 feet of parking, 5 feet of bike lane) "desirable" for a bike lane next to a high-turnover parking lane. Designers unfamiliar with cyclists' needs have often followed these dimensions even where space for a greater reach was available.

The most recent Dutch guidelines are blunt: "Cycle lanes are not recommended in combination with parking bays" (CROW 2007, 118). If there must be a parking lane next to a bike lane, Dutch guidelines recommend marking a buffer between the parking lane and the bike lane. They also suggest that a superior solution is to narrow the road by eliminating the bike lane and using that space to make a cycle track at sidewalk level.

Where there is heavy right-turning traffic, a common solution is to use a "pocket bike lane" positioned between a through lane and a right-turn lane. With this configuration, the conflict between cyclists and right-turning cars is resolved at a weaving point upstream of the intersection. For a pocket bike lane to qualify as low-stress, the right-turn lane must begin abruptly to the right of the bike lane, with the bike lane continuing straight and uninterrupted, so that cyclists' priority at the weave point is unambiguous. Additionally, the right-turn lane should be short so that cars driving in it can't go fast. Unfortunately, many pocket bike lanes in the United States do not have these properties. On many arterials, the right travel lane becomes a right-turn lane, forcing cyclists to weave across a lane of full-speed traffic to get from their curbside bike lane to a pocket bike lane.

An alternative to pocket bike lanes, frequently used in the Netherlands and Germany, is a "refuge cycle track," a short section of elevated cycle track on an intersection approach (figure 6.6). Refuge cycle tracks give cyclists a more secure place to queue and, by using separate signal phases, allow them to pass through the intersection without any conflict with right-turning cars.

Contraflow on One-Way Streets

Contraflow bicycling, in which streets are designated as two-way for bicycle travel even though they are one-way for motor traffic, improves safety and mobility for cyclists in many ways. Contrary to often-heard objections, contraflow is consistent with the "rules of the road": traffic

Figure 6.6
Refuge cycle track in Rotterdam gives cyclists a protected place to queue far in advance of the cars' stopline and bundles motor vehicle conflicts with pedestrians and bicycles at a single point. *Photo:* Kevin Levesque.

in either direction keeps to its right, and the street functions like any other two-way street, except that motor vehicles aren't permitted in one direction. Contraflow allows cyclists, who—like pedestrians—operate under their own power, to avoid around-the-block detours. On many one-way streets, cyclists already ride contraflow in considerable numbers, often using the sidewalk; legalizing contraflow helps reduce sidewalk cycling, and the signs and markings that come with formalization improve safety at intersections by raising driver expectations.

In many cities, one-way restrictions keep through traffic from using neighborhood streets, making those neighborhood streets a far safer bicycling environment than riding on the arterials. Brussels's designated bicycle network relies heavily on contraflow for creating bike routes along low-traffic streets. For the same reason, the bicycle network plan for Brookline, Massachusetts, calls for contraflow on fourteen streets, of which two have been implemented as of early 2012.

Germany, France, Belgium, and the Netherlands have all followed the progression of first forbidding bicycle contraflow, then allowing it by exception, and ultimately making contraflow the default treatment for one-way streets in residential areas and in historic downtowns (Covelier 2008). Blanket application of contraflow is seen as a remedy to the injury done to cycling by one-way schemes introduced in the 1970s to facilitate traffic and parking. German research a few years after contraflow was legalized in several communities in 1997 found that most sites had no bicycle collisions and that where they occurred, their frequency and severity was no worse for contraflow cyclists than for with-flow cyclists (Alrutz et al. 2002). Recognizing the successful continental European experience with contraflow, recent British guidance is: "Where one-way systems are introduced, consideration should always be given to maintaining two-way working for cycles through contraflow, if it can be safely accommodated" (Department for Transport 2008, 37).

Contraflow can be implemented with three levels of separation from opposite direction traffic. One extreme is to use a barrier, making the contraflow lane a cycle track, as on University Avenue in Madison, Wisconsin. A second is to mark a contraflow lane using a continuous lane line that acts as a centerline, separating opposite direction travel. The most common treatment in Europe does not mark any lane line or centerline, consistent with the standard treatment used on two-way local streets; it uses only signs and sometimes intermittent markings to alert road users to two-way bicycle traffic. This treatment, recently applied in Washington, D.C., allows contraflow on streets too narrow to have an exclusive bike lane.

European experience has shown no problem with bicycle contraflow next to a parking lane. The risk of injury from dooring to a contraflow cyclist is much smaller than when riding with the flow because (1) the cyclist rides next to the passenger side doors, which are used far less often; (2) the car occupant faces the cyclist; and (3) if a contraflow cyclist hits an opening door, the impact tends to close the door rather than open it further.

In the United States, although the *Manual on Uniform Traffic Control Devices* (FHWA 2009a) recognizes contraflow bicycling, the AASHTO *Guide* discourages it, and only a handful of applications exist. Views persist that contraflow promotes lawlessness and that it will lead to head-on collisions, even though the opposite-direction encounters that contraflow legitimizes are no different than those that occur countless times per day on millions of local two-way streets. For example, Boulder, Colorado, officials insisted that a one-block contraflow lane on 13th Street be separated by a raised median, even though the block has only one lane for motor traffic and is so short (600 feet or 180 m between stop signs) that traffic speed is low.

Road-Sharing and Lane-Sharing Treatments: Advisory Lanes and Sharrows

On streets too narrow to mark exclusive bike lanes, both Europeans and Americans have developed treatments to make road sharing safe and less stressful. In Europe, the common treatment is advisory bike lanes, described earlier (figure 6.4). They give cyclists almost the same low-stress environment as an exclusive bike lane, because the markings make it plain that the edge zones are for cyclists and that motorists may enter them only where there is a gap in cyclist traffic. Minneapolis introduced the first US application of advisory lanes in 2011.

The principal American road-sharing treatment is sharrows ("shared lane arrows"), a bicycle silhouette topped by a double chevron, usually marked every 200 feet (65 m) in the middle or right third of a travel lane in order to encourage cyclists to ride at a safe distance from parked cars. Sharrows are used on both two-lane and multilane roads. A San Francisco study (Alta Planning + Design 2004) showed limited effectiveness; when influenced by an overtaking car, sharrows shifted the average cyclist position to the left by only 4 inches (10 cm), indicating that sharrows do little to increase cyclists' willingness to control the lane. Surveys also showed that few cyclists or motorists understood their meaning. Although some cyclists feel that sharrows give them legitimacy when controlling the lane, there is a danger that sharrows will become a cop-out, a way for a city to claim that it's created bike routes without really doing anything to improve bicycling conditions.

Advisory lanes in Europe have proven acceptable to mainstream cyclists, including children and seniors, but there is no such evidence for sharrows. A subtle but fundamental difference is that advisory lanes are a *shared road* treatment, but sharrows—which almost always leave the centerline and (on multilane roads) lane lines intact—are a *shared lane* treatment. The European approach delineates the bicyclists' space and allows motor vehicles to share it, as guests, when they need to. The American approach delineates motor vehicle lanes and then asks cyclists to ride in the middle of them.

Bike Routes Using Quiet Streets

Local streets, which typically have low traffic speeds and volumes, are vital for people to have access to the bicycle network. In addition, local streets can be used to form main bicycle routes. The concept is more complex than it may first appear, because the very factors that keep through traffic from using local streets—for example, being discontinuous or labyrinthine—also make them unsuitable for through bicycling.

Creating a bike route along quiet streets can be approached from two directions. One is to take an existing long, continuous street and apply measures to divert and slow traffic while allowing bikes to pass through. The West Coast cities of Berkeley, Palo Alto, and Portland have taken advantage of their grid street network to make selected streets "bicycle boulevards" using partial street closures and median barriers to divert through motor traffic, along with traffic circles and speed humps to slow traffic (Walker, Tressider, and Birk 2009; Pucher, Dill, and Handy 2010; Pucher, Buehler, and Seinen 2011). Another diversion treatment is applying reversing one-way restrictions in conjunction with bicycle contraflow (Department for Transport 2008, 38).

The second approach is to connect discontinuous local streets using bicycle-pedestrian links such as short sections of path to connect cul-de-sacs or provide a shortcut through parks or bridges and underpasses to overcome barriers such as highways and streams. Many new European suburbs make extensive use of this strategy, making local streets that are discontinuous for cars but continuous for bikes and pedestrians.

Bike routes that follow quiet streets often need safety treatments where they cross main roads such as median refuges or signalization. Where they meet main streets at T junctions, a short section of cycle track may be needed on the main street until the path can resume on the next local street. If bikes have to ride in the road along the main street, intersection safety is better if the route involves a left turn onto the main street.

Routes that follow local streets can be difficult to follow, necessitating wayfinding signs or markings. The Netherlands has a well-developed system of wayfinding signage that American cities, led by Portland, have begun to emulate.

Traffic Calming in City Centers and Beyond

The historic road network's focus on city centers makes them strategic for bicycling. If the city center is dominated by cars, it can effectively cut one side of the city off from the other. Several European cities employ traffic diversion schemes to prevent through traffic through the historic center, forcing cars to leave the center at the same access point where they entered. Where these diversions are permeable to bikes, it can make the entire central area open to low-stress bicycling (Pucher and Buehler 2008; Pucher, Dill, and Handy 2010) without a need for bike-specific treatments such as bike lanes or cycle tracks.

Houten, a "new town" suburb of Utrecht in the Netherlands, has extended this model to encompass the entire town of 45,000 people. Two ring roads surround the town, meeting to form a figure eight. Within the rings, through traffic by car is not possible; to get from one side of town to another, cars must use the ring road. The ring roads have many access points, preventing any large concentration of traffic on the interior streets. The interior streets have turns every 75 m or less, making the 30 km/h speed limit self-enforcing. Without bike lanes or cycle tracks apart from standalone paths through parks, the town is a paradise of low-stress bicycling, with 40 percent of trips made by bike, earning it the title "Bicycle City" by the national Bicyclists Union in 2008.

Network Density

So far, this section has described treatments that can be used to create low-stress bicycle routes. To be effective, these routes must form a network connecting neighborhoods with destinations such as employment sites, schools, shopping areas, recreation areas, and train stations.

In built-up areas, the network must inevitably take the form of a fine mesh. The Dutch *Design Manual* recommends a mesh of 250 m (about one-sixth of a mile) (CROW 2007, 65); however, the mesh at this level is mostly for local access. More important is the spacing for *through* bicycle routes, which can be measured at linear barriers such as rivers and wide roads. For example, in Delft, the average spacing of bike routes across barriers is 400 m (0.25 miles) at the provincial highway and at the extended Zuidwal, and 750 m (0.45 miles) at the railroad, main canal, and freeway. With this dense a mesh, access to all neighborhoods and meaningful destinations is virtually assured.

Funding Bicycling Infrastructure

The development of bicycling infrastructure in the United States has been hindered by three principal barriers, as illustrated poignantly in Birk's (2010) story of Portland's birth as a bicycle-friendly city. One is lack of popular interest, something that has clearly turned around in many American cities. Second is national engineering guidance biased in favor of vehicular cycling, which may also have reached a turning point with the publication of the NACTO bikeway design guide (NACTO 2011). The remaining hindrance is the political question of funding for bikeway improvements.

Although developing a high-quality bicycle network is inexpensive compared to a highway or rail network, it still requires considerable investment. Interviews with officials from three Danish cities revealed annual per capita expenditures on bicycle route infrastructure of between $11 to $27; Dutch officials quote a national average of €37 ($50), plus an equal amount spent on bicycle parking and noninfrastructure programs—and these are countries that already have an excellent existing network. In the United States, Portland has estimated that a citywide network of low-stress bike routes would require an investment of $773 million to put all residents within 0.25 miles (400 m) of a low-stress bikeway, or $329 million to reach 80 percent of the population (Gotschi 2011); Austin estimates that its bikeway network will cost $250 million. Spread over twenty years, these investments would involve spending between $20 and $66 per capita per year.

What mechanisms might be invoked to secure this level of funding? The first is bicycle accommodation laws and policies, which require providing bicycling infrastructure on road construction projects. In the United States, bicycle and pedestrian needs must be "considered" on federally funded road projects; as of early 2012, Congress is considering legislation that would mandate their accommodation. Because bicycling by nature occurs mostly on nonregional streets, accommodation or "complete street" policies are especially important at the local level. A small but growing number of states and local jurisdictions have adopted "complete street" policies (ABW 2012).

Second, engineering guidelines should stop discouraging separated bike paths and should include criteria for separation from traffic that responds to the needs of traffic-intolerant users. Without those changes, accommodation or "complete street" requirements have little actual impact. For example, because Massachusetts until recently recognized "wide outside lanes" as a form of bicycle accommodation, the state's accommodation law was satisfied on several projects by simply making the outer travel lanes a bit wider.

Third, planning regulations can require that land development projects include bicycling infrastructure. We have already cited examples of cities requiring developers to build regional paths within their developments; traffic mitigation requirements can also ensure that appropriate route sections and crossings be provided as part of private development projects.

A fourth mechanism is piggybacking on infrastructure projects. In addition to the earlier example of Boulder taking advantage of flood control projects to build underpasses for bike trails, Portland is using $20 million from a large stormwater project to turn several local streets into "neighborhood greenways" with low-stress bike routes. Marking bike lanes when streets are repaved is the most popular piggybacking scheme.

In many cities, one can see scattered sections of bike lane here and there as repaving and mitigation opportunities have been exploited. Clearly, reactive mechanisms alone are insufficient; deliberate funding is also needed in order to supply vital links that cannot be realized opportunistically. Some examples in the United States include Washington, D.C., where approved projects in 2010 amounted to $8 per capita per year, and Oregon, which since 1971 has required that 1 percent of state highway funds be devoted to bicycles and pedestrians—a factor that has helped make Portland, Eugene, and Corvallis among the most bicycle-friendly cities in the United States.

In most communities, the federal government has been the main source of funding for bicycling infrastructure through programs such as Transportation Enhancements, Recreational Trails, and Congestion Mitigation and Air Quality. Yet over the period 2000–2008, annual federal expenditure for bicycle and pedestrian projects combined rose from $1 to a paltry $1.50 per capita (FWHA 2009b). That level of funding would enable a city of 500,000 people to develop less than one mile of path per year; a single bridge could consume twenty years' funding. Clearly, another funding model is needed. In 2005, the Non-Motorized Transportation Pilot Program provided one-time funding of $25 million to four different communities in order to demonstrate the ability of better infrastructure to encourage more walking and bicycling. That amounted to $170 per capita for Columbia, Missouri, but only about $8 per capita for Minneapolis. The Rails-to-Trails Conservancy and other advocates are currently trying to garner support for an expanded program providing $25 to $75 million to each of forty communities.

Conclusion

For bicycling to contribute meaningfully to societal goals in the areas of public health, livability, traffic congestion, and energy use, it has to appeal to the mainstream, traffic-intolerant population. Bicycling infrastructure in many parts of Europe has been successful in achieving mass cycling because it respects the fundamental human need to be separated from traffic stress. This chapter has shown how the antiseparation vehicular cycling ideology has stymied America's development of bicycling infrastructure and how that influence is waning as American communities begin to embrace the European attitude and infrastructure designs. A huge challenge still remains for how the needed infrastructure will be funded. A promising model is to build as much as possible with whatever funds can be found and to trust that the resulting growth in bicycle ridership will create the public pressure and political climate that makes additional funding possible. It is this writer's opinion that the turning point will be when children begin again riding bikes to school in large numbers. When bicycle infrastructure and children's safety become intertwined, funding for bicycle infrastructure will be secure.

References

AASHTO (American Association of State Highway and Transportation Officials). 1999. *Guide for the Development of Bicycle Facilities*. Washington, DC: AASHTO.

AASHTO (American Association of State Highway and Transportation Officials). 2004. *Geometric Design of Highways and Streets*. Washington, DC: AASHTO.

ABW (Alliance for Biking and Walking). 2012. *Bicycling and Walking in the United States: 2012 Benchmarking Report*. Washington, DC: Alliance for Biking and Walking. http://www.peoplepoweredmovement.org/benchmarking.

Alrutz, D., W. Angenendt, W. Draeger, and D. Gündel. 2002. Traffic Safety on One-Way Streets with Contraflow Bicycle Traffic. Strassenverkehrstechnik 2002 (6): 1–16.

Alta Planning + Design. 2004. San Francisco's Shared Lane Pavement Markings: Improving Bicycling Safety. San Francisco: San Francisco Department of Parking and Traffic.

Bike Friendly Oak Cliff. 2008. Building the Cause for Change. http://bikefriendlyoc.wordpress.com/2008/11/18/building-the-cause-for-change.

Birk, Mia. 2010. *Joyride: Pedaling toward a Healthier Planet*. Portland, OR: Cadence Press.

Buehler, Ralph, and John Pucher. 2012. Cycling to Work in 90 Large American Cities: New Evidence on the Role of Bike Paths and Lanes. *Transportation* 39 (2): 409–432.

Buehler, Ted, and Susan Handy. 2008. Fifty Years of Bicycle Policy in Davis, California. *Transportation Research Record* 2074:52–57.

Council for Traffic Safety Research. 1969. *Cycle Track Implications for Road Safety*. Copenhagen: Council of Traffic Safety Research.

Covelier, Luc. 2008. The City Is Nothing without Bicycle Contraflow. FUB (French Federation of Bicycle Users). *Vélocité* 97:12–14.

CROW. 1994. *Sign Up for the Bike: Design Manual for a Cycle-Friendly Infrastructure*. Ede, The Netherlands: CROW.

CROW. 2007. *Design Manual for Bicycle Traffic*. Ede, The Netherlands: CROW.

Department for Transport. 2008. *Cycle Infrastructure Design*. London: The Stationary Office.

Dill, Jennifer, and Theresa Carr. 2003. Bicycle Commuting and Facilities in Major U.S. Cities: If You Build Them, Commuters Will Use Them. *Transportation Research Record* 1828:116–123.

Duthie, Jennifer, John F. Brady, Alison F. Mills, and Randy B. Machemehl. 2010. Effects of On-Street Bicycle Facility Configuration on Bicyclist and Motorist Behavior. *Transportation Research Record* 2190:37–44.

FHWA (Federal Highway Administration). 2009a. *Manual on Uniform Traffic Control Devices*. Washington, DC: FHWA.

FHWA (Federal Highway Administration). 2009b. Federal-Aid Highway Program Funding for Pedestrian and Bicycle Facilities and Programs. http://www.fhwa.dot.gov/environment/bikeped/bipedfund.htm.

Forester, John. 1992. *Effective Cycling*. Cambridge, MA: MIT Press.

Forester, John. 2001. The Bikeway Controversy. *Transportation Quarterly* 55 (2): 7–17.

Forester, John. N.d. The Bicycle Transportation Engineering Organization that Ought to Be. http://www.johnforester.com/BTEO/Organization.htm.

Furth, Peter G. 2008. On-Road Bicycle Facilities for Children and Other "Easy Riders": Stress Mechanisms and Design Criteria. Transportation Research Board Annual Meeting CD-ROM, paper 08–1074.

Garder, P., L. Leden, and U. Pulkkinen. 1998. Measuring the Safety Effect of Raised Bicycle Crossings Using a New Research Methodology. *Transportation Research Record* 1636:64–70.

Gotschi, Thomas. 2011. Costs and Benefits of Bicycling Investments in Portland, Oregon. *Journal of Physical Activity & Health* 8:S49–S58.

Harkey, David L., Donald W. Reinfurt, and Matthew Knuiman. 1998. Development of the Bicycle Compatibility Index. *Transportation Research Record* 1636:13–20.

Hunter, William, and John R. Feaganes. 2005. Wide Curb Lane Conversions: The Effect on Bicycle and Motor Vehicle Interaction. *Transportation Research Record* 1939:37–44.

Jacobsen, Peter L., Francesca Racioppi, and Harry Rutter. 2009. Who Owns the Roads? How Motorized Traffic Discourages Walking and Bicycling. *Injury Prevention* 15:369–373.

Kendrick, Christine M., Adam Moore, Ashley R. Haire, Alexander Y. Bigazzi, Miguel Figliozzi, Christopher M. Monsere, and Linda George. 2011. The Impact of Bicycle Lane Characteristics on Bicyclists' Exposure to Traffic-Related Particulate Matter. Transportation Research Board Annual Meeting CD-ROM, paper 11–3070.

King, Michael. 2003. Urban Bicycle Facility Selection Guides. Transportation Research Board Annual Meeting CD-ROM, paper 03–3520.

Landis, Bruce W., Venkat R. Vattikuti, and Michael T. Brannick. 1997. Real-Time Human Perceptions: Toward a Bicycle Level of Service. *Transportation Research Record* 1578:119–126.

Ligtermoet, Dick. 2010. *Continuous and Integral: The Cycling Policies of Groningen and Other European Cycling Cities*. Rotterdam: Fietsberaad.

Lusk, Anne C., Peter G. Furth, Patrick Morency, Luis F. Miranda-Moreno, Walter C. Willett, and Jack T. Dennerlein. 2011. Risk of Injury for Bicycling on Cycle Tracks versus in the Street. *Injury Prevention* 17:131–135.

Mapes, Jeff. 2009. *Pedaling Revolution*. Corvallis, OR: Oregon State University Press.

Markenlei. 2010. Cycling Amsterdamsestraatweg, Utrecht, The Netherlands. http://www.youtube.com/watch?v=FOkbz4tm324.

Markenlei. 2011. Junction Design the Dutch—Cycle-Friendly—Way. http://www.youtube.com/watch?v=FlApbxLz6pA.

Moritz, William E. 1997. Survey of North American Bicycle Commuters: Design and Aggregate Results. *Transportation Research Record* 1578:91–101.

NACTO (National Association of City Transportation Officials). 2011. *Urban Bikeway Design Guide*. http://nacto.org/cities-for-cycling/design-guide/.

Parkin, J., and C. Meyers. 2010. The Effect of Cycle Lanes on the Proximity between Motor Traffic and Cycle Traffic. *Accident: Analysis and Prevention* 42 (1): 159–165.

Potts, Ingrid B., Douglas W. Harwood, and Karen R. Richard. 2007. Relationship of Lane Width to Safety for Urban and Suburban Arterials. *Transportation Research Record* 2023:63–82.

Pucher, John, and Ralph Buehler. 2008. Making Cycling Irresistible: Lessons from the Netherlands, Denmark, and Germany. *Transport Reviews* 28 (4): 495–528.

Pucher, John, and Ralph Buehler. 2010. Walking and Cycling for Healthy Cities. *Built Environment* 36 (5): 391–414.

Pucher, John, Ralph Buehler, and Mark Seinen. 2011. Bicycling Renaissance in North America? An Update and Re-Assessment of Cycling Trends and Policies. *Transportation Research Part A: Policy and Practice* 45 (6): 451–475.

Pucher, John, and Lewis Dijkstra. 2000. Making Walking and Cycling Safer: Lessons from Europe. *Transportation Quarterly* 54 (3): 25–50.

Pucher, John, Jennifer Dill, and Susan Handy. 2010. Infrastructure, Programs, and Policies to Increase Bicycling: An International Review. *Preventive Medicine* 50:S106–S125.

Truewheelers. 2000. Descriptions of Dutch and Danish Cycling and Design Standards without Rose-Colored Glasses. http://www.truewheelers.org/cases/vassarst/dutch.htm.

Summers, P. M. 2008. Why I Do What I Do the Way I Do. *Smart Cycling Dallas*, November 17, 2008. http://cycledallas.blogspot.com.

UCLA Institute of Transportation and Traffic Engineering. 1972. *Bikeway Planning Criteria and Guidelines*. Reprint. Washington, DC: Federal Highway Administration, U.S. Department of Transportation. http://katana.hsrc.unc.edu/cms/downloads/BikewayPlanningGuidelines1972.pdf.

Van Houten, R., and C. Seiderman. 2005. How Pavement Markings Influence Bicycle and Motor Vehicle Positioning: Case Study in Cambridge, Massachusetts. *Transportation Research Record* 1939:1–14.

Wachtel, Alan, and Diane Lewiston. 1994. Risk Factors for Bicycle-Motor Vehicle Collisions at Intersections. *ITE Journal* 64 (9): 30–35.

Walker, Lindsay, Mike Tressider, and Mia Birk. 2009. *Fundamentals of Bicycle Boulevard Planning and Design*. Portland, OR: Center for Transportation Studies, Portland State University.

Wegman, Fred and Letty Aarts. 2006. *Advancing Sustainable Safety*. Leidschendam, The Netherlands: Institute for Road Safety Research.

Winters, M., G. Davidson, D. Kao, and K. Teschke. 2011. Motivators and Deterrents of Bicycling: Comparing Influences on Decisions to Ride. *Transportation* 38:153–168.

7

Cycling Safety

Peter L. Jacobsen and Harry Rutter

Improving cycling safety is obviously important for reducing injuries to people riding bicycles. Moreover, safer cycling would encourage more people to cycle because risk averse and vulnerable groups are deterred from cycling by fear of injury and thus do not enjoy the health benefits of the physical activity of cycling.

As this chapter will show, cycling is not intrinsically dangerous, although it may appear so because of the risks of severe injury or death imposed by drivers. People cycle less than they would if the dangers imposed by motorized traffic were reduced. They judge the risks of injury from riding bicycles—whether accurately or not—and respond accordingly. A review of the literature from the fields of medicine, public health, city planning, public administration, and traffic engineering shows that the real and perceived danger and discomfort imposed by motor traffic discourage cycling (Jacobsen, Racioppi, and Rutter 2009). Although measuring behavioral effects is difficult, there is an inverse correlation between the volume and speed of traffic and the level of cycling. Interventions that reduce traffic speed and volume may therefore increase cycling, with consequent improvements in public health. In addition, the risk to an individual cyclist of being seriously injured decreases as the level of cycling within an area increases (Jacobsen 2003). A climate of fear around cycling may therefore lead to lower levels of cycling, making it more risky for those who continue to cycle, and so on in a vicious circle.

Hence the most important issue in bicycle safety is that the danger posed by motorized traffic discourages cycling. Society loses not only the health benefits that cycling affords through increased physical activity but also the wider social and environmental benefits of nonmotorized transport.

Health Risk Compared to Health Benefit

As noted in chapter 3, virtually all scientific studies show that the health benefits of cycling far offset the traffic dangers. In Copenhagen, cycling to work has been found to decrease the risk of dying by over 25 percent in any one year (Andersen et al. 2000). Copenhagen has some of the world's best cycling infrastructure, and Denmark has one of the world's lowest fatality rates per distance cycled (de Hartog et al. 2010), so it may not provide a generalizable example. In Shanghai, women who cycled to work were found to have a 35 percent reduction in risk for all-cause mortality (Matthews et al. 2007) although Shanghai provides a more dangerous cycling environment than Copenhagen. A similar level of health benefit from cycling was documented among people with type 2 diabetes in Finland (Hu et al. 2004).

A study based on cycling in the Netherlands found that people who switched their main mode of travel from driving to cycling gained nine times more years of life than they lost as a result of increased inhaled air pollution and traffic injuries. The authors repeated their calculations for the United Kingdom, where the risk of a fatal bicycle injury is about 2.5 times greater than in the Netherlands, and still found that the gain would be seven times greater than the risks. Comparing the physical activity benefit to only the injury risk (omitting the pollution factor) showed that the cyclist in the Netherlands would gain 35 times more years of life (de Hartog et al. 2010).

That the health benefits to cyclists so consistently and greatly exceed the risks of being killed in a traffic crash needs to be prominent in any discussion of bicycle safety. To avoid losing the societal health benefits of cycling, injury-prevention programs should take an objective approach to the true level of danger for cyclists. Instead of overplaying the risks, they should work synergistically with activity-promotion programs to reduce the dangers created by motorized traffic.

Danger Is Imposed on Cyclists

Most of the risk of severe injury while cycling is not intrinsic to the activity; motorists impose it on cyclists. Cycling is a benign activity that often takes place in dangerous environments. The majority of injuries to cyclists do not involve a motor vehicle and typically do not cause severe injuries, which are far more likely to arise in the far smaller number of collisions with vehicles.

The potential for injury is related to the kinetic energy involved, which is proportional to the mass of the moving object multiplied by the square of its velocity. A 2-tonne vehicle traveling at 50 km/h has more than 200 times the kinetic energy of an 85-kg male on a 15-kg bicycle traveling at 15 km/h.

Injury data support this observation. At speeds below 20 mph (32 km/h), cyclists and pedestrians are rarely killed in collision with vehicles (Kim et al. 2007, Rosén, Stigson, and Sander 2011). This physiological tolerance for injury is central to Sweden's Vision Zero road safety approach that identifies the importance of protecting pedestrians and cyclists from motor vehicles exceeding 30 km/h (19 mph) (Johansson 2009).

The important role of motor vehicles in severe injuries and fatalities for cyclists is seen in a range of injury data. As the injury severity increases, a greater proportion of injuries is attributable to motor vehicle collisions. Although only 15 percent of the injured cyclists presenting at emergency rooms were hit by motor vehicles, 36 percent of those hospitalized were (Rivara, Thompson, and Thompson 1997). A range of studies has shown that approximately 90 percent of cyclist deaths involve motorists (Nicaj et al. 2009; Rowe, Rowe, and Bota 1995; McCarthy and Gilbert 1996; Spence et al. 1993). It is clear that protecting the health of cyclists requires measures to prevent motorists from colliding with them.

Fatalities and serious injuries that result in chronic health impairment are a much more important target for prevention than minor injuries. However, because the minor injuries occur much more frequently than fatal and severe injuries, their greater numbers may overwhelm injury data. It is thus essential to separate out severity from volume of injuries, as the two are not interchangeable. Some measures, such as that of disability-adjusted life years (DALYs) used by the World Health Organization (WHO), allow equivalence between small numbers of deaths and severe injuries, and larger numbers of minor injuries. But because minor injuries to cyclists typically have no impact on long-term cycling behavior, their aggregate impact is trivial compared to serious injuries that prevent or dissuade people from cycling. The health benefits of cycling are so great that this can have a major impact over a person's life.

The key characteristics of cyclist collisions with motor vehicles differ for fatal and minor injuries. For example, motorist and cyclist intoxication are both associated with fatal injuries, but not with minor injuries. Because minor injuries greatly outnumber fatal injuries and alcohol intoxication is not associated with increased risk of minor injuries, the importance of alcohol may be overlooked if all injury severities are aggregated (Kim et al. 2007).

A study of cyclist injuries in Belgium that defined minor injuries as those for which hospital visits lasted less than twenty-four hours found them to be surprisingly common: 148 minor bicycle-related injuries per million kilometers (Aertsens et al. 2010). This rate is 2,000 to 7,000 times as high as the rate for fatalities, which is 0.072 fatalities per million kilometers in the United States, 0.032 in Germany, and 0.020 in the Netherlands (Pucher and Dijkstra 2003). It is important that none of the cyclists with minor injuries studied in Belgium gave up cycling permanently: 30 percent indicated greater concern about cycling but did not stop, and although 5 percent did stop cycling, this was the case for an average of only thirteen days. From a public policy perspective, if minor injuries do not discourage physical activity, they represent primarily a financial cost and should not be considered a significant health issue.

Risk Factors for Collisions

Of the three main elements determining serious cyclist injuries—the road design and condition, the motorist, and the cyclist—the cyclist is the most studied. It may be that the cyclist is simply the easiest element to study: the victim may, for example, be well documented in medical records. In contrast, studying streets often requires extensive fieldwork, based on specialist understanding of road design and operation. Studying motorist characteristics is even more difficult because such inquiry may require the use of police databases, which—due to privacy concerns—are not readily available to researchers. Also, accurately identifying the relative contributions of motorists and cyclists is skewed by the legal perspective underpinning the collection of police and other data in these circumstances. These data will reflect the requirements of law enforcement and civil liability and may be constrained both by the demands of the legal burden of proof and a particular worldview among people collecting the data. As a result of these factors, discussions of causality in motorist-cyclist crashes may be biased against the cyclist.

There is an ethical issue when comparing dangerous behavior by motorists to risky behavior by cyclists. The driver endangers the cyclist, not vice versa, and it is rare for a cyclist or pedestrian to injure another road user (Elvik 2010). The language of injury causation is often distorted, with a tendency to blame the victim. This is especially seen in injuries among children, where normal childhood behavior may incorrectly be regarded as irresponsible, rather than motorists traveling too fast for the situation (Roberts and Coggan 1994). Blame for causation of the collision is a backward-looking approach, but preventing future collisions requires a forward-looking approach, as seen in the Vision Zero philosophy, which requires adaptation and learning from crashes and injuries to build safety into the transport system (Fahlquist 2006). Some injury prevention specialists object to determining blame at all, claiming that it is uninformative and does not help analysis (Elvik 2011b). Because society tends to acquiesce in blaming children for their injuries, the real causes—dangerous neighborhood and roadway design and dangerous driver behavior—are not usually addressed.

By far the biggest risk factors for cyclist deaths are motor vehicle speed and mass. Heavy-duty trucks are unwieldy in urban situations, with the driver unable to see large areas around the truck, and are especially dangerous to cyclists (Kim et al. 2007; McCarthy and Gilbert 1996).

Although popular opinion suggests that traffic injuries result from "accidents," which are unavoidable, possibly even random events, there is considerable scientific evidence that collisions between a cyclist and a motorist are both predictable and avoidable. Motorists who collide with cyclists share several distinct characteristics:

• They are overwhelmingly male: over 90 percent of the drivers who kill cyclists in London (McCarthy and Gilbert 1996) and New York City (Komanoff and Smith 2000) are men.

• They tend to be uninsured: drivers without insurance are 40 percent more likely to cause severe injuries to cyclists than insured drivers (Moore et al. 2011).

• Those who cause deaths are disproportionately likely to be intoxicated or traveling at excessive speed (Kim et al. 2007).

Improving motorist behavior could greatly reduce severe injuries and fatalities among cyclists. It is also worth noting that the risks cyclists face from motorists are not constant but decrease as the level of cycling in an area increases (Jacobsen 2003).

Cyclist Characteristics

To identify possible approaches to improving road safety, it is helpful to divide injured cyclists into three broad groups: children, sober adults, and adults intoxicated with drugs or alcohol. The aggregation of these different categories of cyclists into a single pool disguises the important patterns of injury causation specific to each, impeding the development of truly effective injury-prevention programs.

Children

The age profile of cyclists has changed over the last forty years; they used to be mostly children, whereas today they are increasingly adults. In the early 1970s, 91 percent of injured cyclists were under the age of 20 (Williams 1976), but in a 1997 study, only 59 percent of injured cyclists were under 20 years old (Rivara, Thompson, and Thompson 1997). This shift likely reflects a decrease in bicycle use by children, rather than safer conditions for child cyclists (Jacobsen, Racioppi, and Rutter 2009).

Collision patterns vary substantially based on the age of the cyclist involved. Children on bikes are typically hit when emerging from driveways onto minor roads or when riding through intersections. Adult cyclists are often hit from behind or by an oncoming motorist turning across their path (Williams 1976).

Intoxicated Cyclists

Alcohol-intoxicated riders are considerably more likely than sober cyclists to be severely injured or killed. In one study in Portland, Oregon, although only 15 percent of killed and hospitalized adult cyclists had elevated blood alcohol levels, half of the adult cyclists with fatal injuries were intoxicated (Frank et al. 1995).

Of 200 injured cyclists reviewed during a study at a regional trauma center in Austin, Texas, 40 either had measurably elevated blood alcohol levels or themselves reported having consumed alcohol. The intoxicated cyclists were much more likely to have been injured at night or in the rain and to have been admitted to the hospital. Only 1 of the 40 (2.5%) alcohol-consuming cyclists had worn a helmet, compared to 44 percent of the others. Both cyclists who incurred severe brain injuries were intoxicated, and the average hospital care cost of the alcohol-consuming cyclists was twice that of their sober counterparts (Crocker et al. 2010).

Nevertheless, of all road users killed in a study of over 1,000 road-traffic fatalities between 2000 and 2006 in England and Wales, cyclists were the least likely to have consumed alcohol or drugs. Of the cyclists tested, 33 percent showed the presence of alcohol and/or drugs, compared to 55 percent of drivers, 52 percent of car passengers, 48 percent of motorcyclists, and 63 percent of pedestrians (Elliott, Woolacott, and Braithwaite 2009). More cyclist fatalities are due to intoxicated motorists than intoxicated cyclists (Kim et al. 2007).

Net Health Benefits of Increasing Cycling

In an earlier section, we showed that on an individual basis, increased cycling benefits health. Does that effect hold for a large mode shift from driving to cycling?

Comparing the health burden of motorized traffic in the United States with the Netherlands shows a correlation between motor vehicle use and health. Across the developed world, road traffic injuries rank fifth as a cause of ill health across the population (Murray and Lopez 1997), but they rank third in the United States (McKenna et al. 2005) and thirteenth in the Netherlands, which has one of the highest levels of cycling in the world (Melse et al. 2000).

A shift from driving to cycling raises the question of the balance between protecting its users—where a car excels—against causing little harm to others and benefiting the rider's own health—where a bicycle excels. A heavier vehicle protects its users from injury, but the heavier and faster the vehicle, the more kinetic energy and hence injury potential it has (Elvik 2010). Determining the total burden of injury resulting from a shift in travel modes involves weighing the shift in danger that vehicles impose on other road users against the protection they afford their occupants.

Collisions between cyclists and pedestrians are rarely fatal. In a German study, ten pedestrians and two cyclists died in bicycle-pedestrian collisions, a tiny fraction (0.1%) of the total of approximately 8,000 traffic fatalities during the study period (Graw and König 2002).

The consequence of a shift from driving to cycling is further complicated because the risk to an individual cyclist of being injured is nonlinearly related to the amount of cycling: as the level of cycling increases, so do total injuries, but at a lower rate. In general, doubling cycling increases cyclist injuries by only a third (Jacobsen 2003). In contrast, halving car use approximately halves the number of single- and multiple-vehicle crashes. Although the exact nature of the relationship is unclear, the total number of crashes would probably decrease if there were a large enough shift from motor vehicles to bicycles (Elvik 2009).

A series of studies has modeled the likely health consequences of a shift from personal motor vehicles to bicycles (Austroads 2010; AVV 2006; Dutch Bicycle Council 2006; Lindsay, Macmillan, and Woodward 2010; Stipdonk and Reurings 2010). In most cases, road traffic fatalities varied up or down by only a small amount, and adding in the physical activity benefits of active travel resulted in health benefits that far outweighed any minor increases in injuries.

Empirical observations bear out the findings of these models. A number of cities—including London, Bogotá, Berlin, Amsterdam, Copenhagen, Odense, and Groningen—have successfully developed bicycle infrastructure and other programs to encourage cycling and simultaneously reduced the levels of deaths and injuries among cyclists. Portland, Oregon, experienced an increase in reported crashes of 14 percent, but over the same period, the number of cyclists entering the downtown area increased by more than 300 percent (Pucher, Dill, and Handy 2010).

A nationally funded initiative in Odense, Denmark, allocated 20 million Danish kroner or approximately 120 kroner per person (US$25) in an attempt to increase cycling, reduce injuries, and improve health. Fifty projects were developed and implemented during the four years of the program, including physical improvements, changes to regulations, and marketing campaigns. It resulted in 20 percent more cycling trips, replacing car trips and public transit use, while reducing injuries to cyclists by 20 percent. The project was estimated to save much more money than it cost (Troelsen, Jensen, and Andersen 2004).

Helmets

Use of bicycle helmets is a central element of many campaigns intended to improve cyclist safety. But helmets do not create safety; only a safe environment, free from the dangers created by motorized traffic and poorly designed roads, can do that. Reducing danger and increasing safety are prerequisites for encouraging both cycling and walking (Gehl 2010, Jacobsen, Racioppi, and Rutter 2009). Because promoting and wearing helmets might promulgate a false perception that cycling is an unusually risky activity (Lorenc et al. 2008)—which would reduce cycling (Jacobsen, Racioppi, and Rutter 2009)—it may actually decrease health across a population. The risk of being injured by a motorist increases as the level of cycling decreases (Jacobsen 2003), and that increased fear might leave those who do cycle at greater risk.

Bicycle helmets were first marketed to the general population in the 1980s. An early analysis asked cyclists about their crashes and found that helmeted cyclists had a 90 percent reduced risk of death (Dorsch, Woodward, and Somers 1987). A retrospective case-control study found that helmeted cyclists had an 85 percent reduction in risk of head injury (Thompson, Rivara, and Thompson 1989). More recent evidence has, however, led to a reappraisal of the benefits of wearing bike helmets. Elvik has reported that three previous meta-analyses were in broad agreement that helmeted cyclists have a reduced risk of head injury, yet his own meta-analysis that combined the risk of injury to head, face, or neck found that helmets provide only a small protective effect. Moreover, this effect is evident only in older studies—newer studies showed no net protective effect (Elvik 2011a). The reasons for these much lower estimates of protective effect seen in the most recent studies are not known, but they may result from changes in helmet construction, as well as the methods used in the meta-analyses (Elvik 2011a).

The dramatic difference in injuries between helmeted and bareheaded cyclists reported in the earliest studies has not been seen in population-level research. In a study of six jurisdictions where cyclists were compelled to wear helmets, resulting in a large increase in the proportion of cyclists wearing them, the ratio of head injuries to other injuries did not noticeably decrease (Robinson 2006). It may be that people who choose to wear helmets are especially cautious and safety-minded (Elvik 2011a; Farris et al. 1997). Indeed, one analysis has found that bareheaded cyclists "tend to be in higher impact crashes than helmet users, since the injuries suffered in body areas other than the head also tend to be much more severe" (Spaite et al. 1991, 1515). The authors concluded that helmet use may be a "marker" for cyclists who tend to be in less severe crashes, rather than contributing to reductions in the level of injury (Spaite et al. 1991). It is also worth noting that intoxicated cyclists rarely wear helmets and tend to be involved in disproportionately severe crashes (Crocker et al. 2010, Kim et al. 2007; Spaite et al. 1995).

Analysts in observational studies must be wary of the pitfalls of selection bias—"muddling characteristics of the chooser with the benefits of the choice" (Westmont 2004). Such selection bias is clearly a risk for research into cycling helmets, especially because bareheaded and helmeted cyclists differ so much in terms of characteristics associated with the likelihood and severity of crashing.

Another possible reason for not achieving the dramatic reduction in injuries initially identified for helmets could be that cyclists take more chances as a consequence of wearing them, a phenomenon known as risk compensation (Elvik 2011a; Phillips, Fyhri, and Sagberg 2011). In addition, motorists might treat cyclists differently in response to the clothing and equipment they wear—for example, by driving closer to helmeted cyclists (Walker 2007).

Yet another possible reason could be because the studies examined different injury severity patterns. The retrospective studies examined emergency room visits, which are dominated by minor injuries, whereas the population-level study examined hospital admissions, which are characterized by serious injuries. When the authors of the most-quoted retrospective study more closely examined cyclists' injuries, they found that hospitalizations and deaths were outnumbered by emergency room visits by 9:1, with helmets having no apparent effect on hospitalization rates (Rivara, Thompson, and Thompson 1997). They also found—as did Kim et al. (2007)—that helmeted riders had fewer deaths. Given the lack of impact of helmet use on hospitalization rates, it may be that the difference in death rates is attributable to differences in the cyclists (such as risk-taking behavior) rather than a protective effect of helmet wearing.

Even the best helmet provides limited protection. In the United States, a helmet is tested with a mass of 5 kilograms (11 pounds) at an impact velocity of 5.4 meters per second (12 mph) (Consumer Product Safety Commission 1998). As discussed earlier, a car colliding with a cyclist at a speed below 20 mph rarely causes a fatal injury. Because the energy transferred in the impact is a function of mass multiplied by the square of the velocity, a head hitting the ground at 12 mph involves only 36 percent of the energy of the same head hitting a motor vehicle with a combined velocity of 20 mph; at higher velocities, the disparity is even greater.

Laws requiring cyclists to wear helmets are controversial. The European Cyclists' Federation actively opposes them, as does RoadPeace, the British charity for road crash victims (ECF 2011; RoadPeace 2010). Not only have such laws failed to bring about reductions in rates of head injuries (Robinson 2006), but they also reduce the level of cycling (Robinson 1996) and the health benefits of physical activity. Because the risk that an individual cyclist will be struck by a motorist increases as the level of cycling decreases, compulsory helmet laws could have the perverse effect of increasing deaths—not just risk of death—among those who continue to cycle (Komanoff 2001).

Conclusion

The issue of safety presents a complex set of challenges for cycling. Both real and perceived dangers discourage cycling, and the safety of cycling is related to the number of cyclists on the roads. Proactively addressing cyclist safety thus creates a virtuous circle in which more safety increases the numbers of cyclists and the presence of more cyclists improves their safety.

Cyclist safety is largely an artifact of traffic safety and to a large extent out of the control of cyclists themselves. Serious injuries mostly result from collisions with vehicles; for sober adult cyclists, motorists are primarily responsible for those collisions.

Notwithstanding these difficulties, many cities and countries have managed to increase the level of cycling while simultaneously reducing the proportion of injuries to cyclists. By implementing a wide variety of policies to improve safety, Germany and the Netherlands have both significantly reduced cyclist deaths. These countries have greatly expanded their cycle networks, implemented traffic calming, restricted or otherwise discouraged vehicle use in urban areas, and developed traffic regulations strongly favoring pedestrians and cyclists (Pucher and Dijkstra 2003; Pucher and Buehler 2008).

An impressive range of cities has also successfully encouraged cycling while simultaneously reducing injuries. The list includes big cities (London), small cities (Boulder, Colorado), and developing cities (Bogotá). Cyclists respond to a variety of interventions to encourage them to ride and feel comfortable (Pucher, Dill, and Handy 2010). Cyclist safety is not improved through single interventions but from the accumulation of many individual and collective actions, illustrated by the activities and ideas expressed throughout this book. Improving the safety of cyclists should focus on the causes, not the victims, of danger. Although the risks should not be ignored or trivialized, it is important to emphasize that cycling is a fundamentally safe and healthy activity that not only benefits the individual cyclist but also promotes safety among other road users and a healthier environment for the entire population.

References

Aertsens, Joris, Bas de Geusb, Grégory Vandenbulcke, Bart Degraeuwe, Steven Broekx, Leo De Nocker, Inge Liekens, et al. 2010. Commuting by Bike in Belgium: The Costs of Minor Accidents. *Accident Analysis and Prevention* 42 (6): 2149–2157.

Andersen, Lars Bo, Peter Schnohr, Marianne Schroll, and Hans Ole Hein. 2000. All-Cause Mortality Associated with Physical Activity During Leisure Time, Work, Sports, and Cycling to Work. *Archives of Internal Medicine* 160 (11): 1621–1628.

Austroads. 2010. *The Road Safety Consequences of Changing Travel Modes.* Sydney: Austroads.

AVV (Transport and Travel Advisory). 2006. *Promoting Bicycle Use: Consequences for Traffic Safety.* Rotterdam, The Netherlands: AVV.

Consumer Product Safety Commission. 1998. Safety Standard for Bicycle Helmets; Final Rule. *Federal Register* 63 (46). http://www.cpsc.gov/businfo/frnotices/fr98/10mr98r.pdf.

Crocker, Patrick, Omid Zad, Truman Milling, and Karla A. Lawson. 2010. Alcohol, Bicycling, and Head and Brain Injury: A Study of Impaired Cyclists' Riding Patterns R1. *American Journal of Emergency Medicine* 28 (1): 68–72.

de Hartog, Jeroen Johan, Hanna Boogaard, Hans Nijland, and Gerard Hoek. 2010. Do the Health Benefits of Cycling Outweigh the Risks? *Environmental Health Perspectives* 118 (8): 1109–1116.

Dorsch, Margaret M., Alistair J. Woodward, and Ronald L. Somers. 1987. Do Bicycle Safety Helmets Reduce Severity of Head Injury in Real Crashes? *Accident; Analysis and Prevention* 19 (3): 183–190.

Dutch Bicycle Council. 2006. *Promoting Bicycle Use: Consequences for Traffic Safety*. Utrecht, The Netherlands: Dutch Bicycle Council.

ECF (European Cyclists' Federation). 2011. *Helmets and Reflective Vests*. Brussels: ECF. http://www.ecf.com/road-safety/helmets-and-reflective-vests/.

Elliott, Simon, Helen Woolacott, and Robin Braithwaite. 2009. The Prevalence of Drugs and Alcohol Found in Road Traffic Fatalities: A Comparative Study of Victims. *Science & Justice* 49 (1): 19–23.

Elvik, Rune. 2009. The Non-Linearity of Risk and the Promotion of Environmentally Sustainable Transport. *Accident Analysis and Prevention* 41 (4): 849–855.

Elvik, Rune. 2010. Why Some Road Safety Problems Are More Difficult to Solve than Others. *Accident Analysis and Prevention* 42 (4): 1089–1096.

Elvik, Rune. 2011a. Publication Bias and Time-Trend Bias in Meta-Analysis of Bicycle Helmet Efficacy: A Re-Analysis of Attewell, Glase, and McFadden, 2001. *Accident Analysis and Prevention* 43 (3): 1245–1251.

Elvik, Rune. 2011b. Book Review: Anders af Wåhlberg: Driver Behaviour and Accident Research Methodology; Unresolved Problems. *Safety Science* 49 (5): 751–752.

Fahlquist, Jessica Nihlén. 2006. Responsibility Ascriptions and Vision Zero. *Accident; Analysis and Prevention* 38 (6): 1113–1118.

Farris, Christine, Daniel W. Spaite, Elizabeth A. Criss, Terence D. Valenzuela, and Harvey W. Meislin. 1997. Observational Evaluation of Compliance with Traffic Regulations among Helmeted and Nonhelmeted Bicyclists. *Annals of Emergency Medicine* 29 (5): 625–629.

Frank, Edmund, Pamela Frankel, Richard J. Mullins, and Natasha Taylor. 1995. Injuries Resulting from Bicycle Collisions. *Academic Emergency Medicine* 2 (3): 200–203.

Gehl, Jan. 2010. *Cities for People*. Washington, DC: Island Press.

Graw, Matthias, and H. G. König. 2002. Fatal Pedestrian-Bicycle Collisions. *Forensic Science International* 126 (3): 241–247.

Hu, Gang, Johan Eriksson, Noël C. Barengo, Timo A. Lakka, Timo T. Valle, Aulikki Nissinen, Pekka Jousilahti, and Jaakko Tuomilehto. 2004. Total and

Cardiovascular Mortality among Finnish Subjects with Type 2 Diabetes. *Circulation* 110 (6): 666–673.

Jacobsen, Peter L. 2003. Safety in Numbers: More Walkers and Bicyclists, Safer Walking and Bicycling. *Injury Prevention* 9 (3): 205–209.

Jacobsen, Peter L., Francesca Racioppi, and Harry Rutter. 2009. Who Owns the Roads? How Motorised Traffic Discourages Walking and Bicycling. *Injury Prevention* 15 (6): 369–373.

Johansson, Roger. 2009. Vision Zero—Implementing a Policy for Traffic Safety. *Safety Science* 47 (6): 826–831.

Kim, Joon-Ki, Sungyop Kim, Gudmundur F. Ulfarsson, and Luis A. Porrello. 2007. Bicyclist Injury Severities in Bicycle-Motor Vehicle Accidents. *Accident Analysis and Prevention* 39 (2): 238–251.

Komanoff, C. 2001. Safety in Numbers? A New Dimension to the Bicycle Helmet Controversy. *Injury Prevention* 7 (4): 343–344.

Komanoff, Charles, and Michael J. Smith. 2000. *The Only Good Cyclist: NYC Bicycle Fatalities—Who's Responsible?* New York: Right of Way.

Lindsay, Graeme, Alexandra Macmillan, and Alistair Woodward. 2010. Moving Urban Trips from Cars to Bicycles: Impact on Health and Emissions. *Australian and New Zealand Journal of Public Health* 35 (1): 54–60.

Lorenc, T., G. Brunton, S. Oliver, K. Oliver, and A. Oakley. 2008. Attitudes to Walking and Cycling Among Children, Young People and Parents: A Systematic Review. *Journal of Epidemiology and Community Health* 62 (10): 852–857.

Matthews, Charles E., Adriana L. Jurj, Shu Xiao-ou, Hong-Lan Li, Gong Yang, Qi Li, Yu-Tang Gao, and Wei Zheng. 2007. Influence of Exercise, Walking, Cycling, and Overall Nonexercise Physical Activity on Mortality in Chinese Women. *American Journal of Epidemiology* 165 (12): 1343–1350.

McCarthy, Mark, and Katie Gilbert. 1996. Cyclist Road Deaths in London 1985–1992: Drivers, Vehicles, Manoeuvres and Injuries. *Accident Analysis and Prevention* 28 (2): 275–279.

McKenna, Matthew T., Catherine M. Michaud, Christopher J. L. Murray, and James S. Marks. 2005. Assessing the Burden of Disease in the United States Using Disability-Adjusted Life Years. *American Journal of Preventive Medicine* 28 (5): 415–423.

Melse, Johan M., Marie-Louise Essink-Bot, Pieter G. N. Kramers, and Nancy Hoeymans. 2000. A National Burden of Disease Calculation: Dutch Disability-Adjusted Life-Years. *American Journal of Public Health* 90 (8): 1241–1247.

Moore, Darren N., William H. Schneider, IV, Peter T. Savolainen, and Mohamadreza Farzaneh. 2011. Mixed Logit Analysis of Bicyclist Injury Severity Resulting from Motor Vehicle Crashes at Intersection and Non-Intersection Locations. *Accident Analysis and Prevention* 43 (3): 621–630.

Murray, Christopher J. L., and Alan D. Lopez. 1997. Alternative Projections of Mortality and Disability by Cause 1990–2020: Global Burden of Disease Study. *Lancet* 349 (9064): 1498–1504.

Nicaj, L., C. Stayton, J. Mandel-Ricci, P. McCarthy, K. Grasso, D. Woloch, and B. Kerker. 2009. Bicyclist Fatalities in New York City: 1996–2005. *Traffic Injury Prevention* 10 (2): 157–161.

Phillips, Ross Owen, Aslak Fyhri, and Fridulv Sagberg. 2011. Risk Compensation and Bicycle Helmets. *Risk Analysis* 31 (8): 1187–1195.

Pucher, John, and Lewis Dijkstra. 2003. Promoting Safe Walking and Cycling to Improve Public Health: Lessons from the Netherlands and Germany. *American Journal of Public Health* 93 (9): 1509–1516.

Pucher, John, and Ralph Buehler. 2008. Making Cycling Irresistible: Lessons from the Netherlands, Denmark, and Germany. *Transport Reviews* 28 (4): 495–528.

Pucher, John, Jennifer Dill, and Susan Handy. 2010. Infrastructure, Programs, and Policies to Increase Bicycling: An International Review. *Preventive Medicine* 50 (S1): S106–S125.

Rivara, Frederick P., Diane C. Thompson, and Robert S. Thompson. 1997. Epidemiology of Bicycle Injuries and Risk Factors for Serious Injury. *Injury Prevention* 3 (2): 110–114.

RoadPeace. 2010. *Safer Cycling: Why Helmets Are Not the Answer.* London: RoadPeace.

Roberts, Ian, and Carolyn Coggan. 1994. Blaming Children for Child Pedestrian Injuries. *Social Science & Medicine* 38 (5): 749–753.

Robinson, Dorothy L. 1996. Head Injuries and Bicycle Helmet Laws. *Accident Analysis and Prevention* 28 (4): 463–475.

Robinson, Dorothy L. 2006. No Clear Evidence from Countries that Have Enforced the Wearing of Helmets. *British Medical Journal* 332 (7543): 722–725.

Rosén, Erik, Helena Stigson, and Ulrich Sander. 2011. Literature Review of Pedestrian Fatality Risk as a Function of Car Impact Speed. *Accident Analysis and Prevention* 43 (1): 25–33.

Rowe, Brian H., Alison M. Rowe, and Gary W. Bota. 1995. Bicyclist and Environmental Factors Associated with Fatal Bicycle-Related Trauma in Ontario. *Canadian Medical Association Journal* 152 (1): 45–53.

Spaite, Daniel W., Elizabeth A. Criss, David J. Weist, Terence D. Valenzuela, Daniel Judkins, and Harvey W. Meislin. 1995. A Prospective Investigation of the Impact of Alcohol Consumption on Helmet Use, Injury Severity, Medical Resource Utilization, and Health Care Costs in Bicycle-Related Trauma. *Journal of Trauma* 38 (2): 287–290.

Spaite, Daniel W., Mark Murphy, Elizabeth A. Criss, Terence D. Valenzuela, and Harvey W. Meislin. 1991. A Prospective Analysis of Injury Severity among Helmeted and Nonhelmeted Bicyclists Involved in Collisions with Motor Vehicles. *Journal of Trauma* 31 (11): 1510–1516.

Spence, Laura J., Evelyn H. Dykes, Desmond J. Bohn, and David E. Wesson. 1993. Fatal Bicycle Accidents in Children: A Plea for Prevention. *Journal of Pediatric Surgery* 28 (2): 214–216.

Stipdonk, Henk, and Martine Reurings. 2010. *The Safety Effect of Exchanging Car Mobility for Bicycle Mobility.* Leidschendam, The Netherlands: SWOV (Institute for Road Safety Research).

Thompson, Robert S., Frederick Rivara, and Diane C. Thompson. 1989. A Case-Control Study of the Effectiveness of Bicycle Safety Helmets. *New England Journal of Medicine* 320 (21): 1361–1367.

Troelsen, Jens, Soren Underlien Jensen, and Troels Andersen. 2004. *Evaluation of Odense—Denmark's Cycling Showcase City.* Odense, Denmark: City of Odense.

Walker, Ian. 2007. Drivers Overtaking Bicyclists: Objective Data on the Effects of Riding Position, Helmet Use, Vehicle Type and Apparent Gender. *Accident Analysis and Prevention* 39 (2): 417–425.

Westmont, Karen. 2004. Review of Nicholas P. Retsinas and Eric S. Belsky, eds., Low-Income Homeownership: Examining the Unexamined Goal. *Urban Affairs Review* 39 (4): 522–525.

Williams, Allan F. 1976. Factors in the Initiation of Bicycle Motor Vehicle Collisions. *American Journal of Diseases of Children* 130 (4): 370–377.

8

Integration of Cycling with Public Transportation

John Pucher and Ralph Buehler

Coordinating cycling with public transportation is mutually beneficial, enhancing the benefits of both modes and encouraging more cycling as well as more public transportation use (Brons, Givoni, and Rietveld 2009; Givoni and Rietveld 2007; Hegger 2007; Martens 2004 and 2007; TRB 2005; USDOT 1998). Bicycling supports public transportation by extending the catchment area of rail stations and bus stops far beyond walking range and at much lower cost than neighborhood feeder buses and park and ride facilities for cars. Access to public transportation helps cyclists make trips longer than possible by bike alone. Public transportation services can also provide convenient alternatives when cyclists encounter bad weather, difficult topography, gaps in the bikeway network, and mechanical failures.

This chapter focuses on efforts to integrate cycling with public transportation in Europe and North America but also includes examples from Japan and Australia. For many decades, both cycling and public transportation have been important means of travel in northern European cities, providing a historically strong rationale for coordinating these two modes of urban transportation. Consequently, efforts to integrate cycling with public transportation began much earlier in Europe than in North America. Significant proportions of rail passengers in Europe reach their stations by bike: 39 percent in the Netherlands, 25 percent in Denmark, and 9 percent in Sweden (Hegger 2007; Martens 2007). Similarly, 20 percent of metro and suburban rail passengers in the Tokyo metropolitan area cycle to their stations (MLITT 2008a).

In the past, bike-and-ride in North America was limited by low overall levels of cycling and public transportation use in most cities, just the reverse of the situation in northern Europe and Japan (Bassett et al. 2008; Pucher and Buehler 2010). In recent years, however, levels of cycling and public transportation use have reached record highs in both the United States and Canada. Between 1995 and 2008, public transportation trips rose by 38 percent in the United States and by 46 percent in Canada (APTA 2009, 2011a). The total number of bike trips to work increased by 57 percent in the United States from 2000 to 2009 and by 43 percent in Canada from 1996 to 2006 (USDOC 2010a, 2010b; Statistics Canada 1996–2010). From 2001 to 2009, the bike share of access trips to public transportation in the United States tripled, from only 1 percent to 3 percent (Pucher et al. 2011). In some cities, cycling has grown so much that the demand for bike-and-ride facilities exceeds the available supply (TRB 2005). To meet the rising demand, almost all large American and Canadian cities have been rapidly implementing the sorts of measures already used in Europe and developing innovative approaches of their own (Pucher and Buehler 2009).

This chapter has three main purposes: (1) to describe the range of measures to integrate cycling with public transportation; (2) to examine trends over time and differences among countries in their efforts to harmonize the two modes; and (3) to report evidence on the effectiveness of such measures for actually raising cycling levels. As shown by specific examples from cities around the world, different approaches are needed in different contexts, and possible conflicts with public transportation must be taken into account.

The chapter is organized according to the four main categories of measures to coordinate cycling with public transportation: (1) bike parking at rail stations and bus stops; (2) provisions for taking bikes on board trains and buses; (3) bike rental facilities near public transportation stops; and (4) the coordination of bike routes with public transportation. Table 8.1 provides an overall summary and guide to the sections that follow.

Bike Parking at Train Stations and Bus Stops

By far the most common measure to integrate cycling with public transportation is the provision of bike parking at rail stations and bus stops, especially in Europe and Japan, where buses do not have bike racks and trains are often too crowded to accommodate bikes on board. Bike parking is almost always provided at train stations in city centers as well as at outlying stations along the rail network (Dutch Bicycle Council 2010; Netherlands Ministry of Transport 2009). In the Netherlands, Denmark, and Germany, many residents use a bike to reach the nearest suburban rail station, park it there, and then take the train to the city center, where they continue their trip with another bike they have parked at the main train station (City of Muenster 2004; North Rhine Westphalia Ministry of Transport 2004; Pucher and Buehler 2008).

Although bike parking is sometimes provided at major bus terminals, route interchanges, and key stops, most bike parking is at rail stations (figure 8.1). For example, in 2010 there were 325,000 bike parking spaces at train stations in the Netherlands and 76,196 bike parking spaces at train stations in Denmark (Danish Ministry of Transport 2010; Netherlands Ministry of Transport 2010; ProRail 2011). There are no

Figure 8.1
There are 325,000 bike parking spaces at train stations in the Netherlands, such as here in Delft. It is estimated that 180,000 additional parking spaces will be needed by 2020. *Photo:* Eva Heinen.

Table 8.1
Integration of bicycles with public transportation

Parking at public transportation stops

	Description	Examples and extent of implementation
Train stations vs. bus stops		
Parking at rail stations	Bike racks, lockers, cages, or bike stations next to or inside rail and metro stations in cities as well as outlying stations along the rail network.	Most important form of integration with public transport in Europe and Japan, with large amounts of bike parking at most suburban rail and many metro stations, often in form of bike stations: • 800,000 bike parking spaces at metro and suburban rail stations in Tokyo • 325,000 bike parking spaces at Dutch train stations; 76,000 at Danish train stations • 32,000 bike parking spaces at commuter rail and subway stations in Berlin; 45,000 in Munich • 38,000 bike-and-ride parking spaces in the United States, 26,500 of which are at rail stations • 1,100 bike parking spaces at transit stops in Vancouver, Canada
Parking at bus stops	Usually simple, but sometimes sheltered bike racks at bus stops. Typically provided at major bus terminals, route interchanges, and key stops.	Less common in North America and mostly restricted to northern Europe, due to lack of bike racks on buses in Europe

Table 8.1
(continued)

Parking at public transportation stops

	Description	Examples and extent of implementation
Types of parking facilities		
Unsheltered/ sheltered	Unsheltered bike parking without roof to protect bikes from weather. Sheltered bike racks with simple roofs, but also bike lockers, bike stations, and bike parking within rail station buildings.	Most parking in unsheltered bike racks on sidewalks, plazas or open parking lots Trend toward sheltered parking, at least covered with a roof of some sort • Chicago offers sheltered or indoor parking at 83 of its 143 subway and elevated rail stations
Guarded	Improved security of bike parking facilities featuring guards and often video surveillance.	Trend in northern Europe (esp. the Netherlands, Germany, Denmark) toward guarded parking to prevent theft, both in special facilities such as bike stations as well as outdoor parking that is guarded by attendants: • 85,000 guarded bike parking spaces at Dutch train stations • 11,000 guarded bike parking spaces near three train stations in Groningen
Bike lockers	Box-like metal or plastic container for secure bike storage, often at rail stations, usually rented on a monthly basis. Typically holding one or two bikes per container. Newer fully electronic lockers can be rented without subscription.	Usually at train or metro stations, especially in North America, where it is the main form of sheltered, secure bike parking: • 2,100 bike lockers including 330 electronic bike lockers at rail stations in the San Francisco Bay Area • 1,300 bike lockers at Washington's 86 Metrorail subway stations • 15,500 bike lockers at train stations in the Netherlands

Table 8.1
(continued)

Parking at public transportation stops

	Description	Examples and extent of implementation
Bike cages	Secure, covered, locked cage with fencing for safety and sometimes camera surveillance. Electronic key card access available without subscription. Can hold hundreds of bikes.	Many rail stations in northern Europe provide such bike cages: • 82 bike cages in Denmark, of which 42 are in Copenhagen metropolitan area • Some in North American and Australian cities: 9 in Boston, Massachusetts (about 900 spaces), 5 in Portland, Oregon (344 spaces), and 35 in Melbourne, Australia (910 spaces)
Bike stations	Full-service facilities offering secured, sheltered bike parking in addition to bicycle rentals, bicycle repairs, showers, accessories, bicycle washes, and bicycle touring advice. Bike stations are usually adjacent to train or metro stations, but sometimes in commercial districts of city centers.	• 98 full service bike stations (85,000 spaces) at rail stations in the Netherlands; new bike station at Amsterdam's Central Station accommodates 10,000 bikes • 106 bike stations (32,000 spaces) in Germany; 3,300 spaces in Germany's largest bike station in Muenster • 28 bike stations in Switzerland (7,783 spaces) with 12 more bike stations planned • 15 bike stations in North America, with largest in Chicago (300 spaces); 6 bike stations in San Francisco Bay Area • Bike stations next to main rail terminals in Washington (150 spaces) and Toronto (180 spaces) • 2 bike stations with 1,200 spaces in Brisbane, Australia, including 1 at downtown transport hub with 420 parking spaces, 35 showers, and laundry service • Technologically advanced bike stations with automatic deposit and retrieval of bikes in Tokyo

Table 8.1
(continued)

Taking bicycles on vehicles

	Description	Examples and extent of implementation
Bike racks on buses	Device on which bikes can be mounted, typically on the front of buses. Some buses provide special space for bikes on board buses (mainly for folding bikes), in luggage compartments, or separate bike trailers.	Bike racks most common in North America, with 72% of American and 80% of Canadian buses equipped with bike racks • 100% of buses with bike racks in Vancouver, Portland, Chicago, San Francisco, Minneapolis, and Washington, DC • No bike racks on buses in Montreal and New York City Bike racks are rare in Europe and Australia
Bikes on rail cars	Often special space on rail cars reserved for bikes, sometimes with bike racks or hooks. Many systems prohibit bikes during peak hours. Some systems charge special fees for bike transport.	Bikes usually permitted during off-peak hours on most suburban rail, metro, and light rail systems in Europe, North America, and Australia Fees for bringing bikes on board rail vehicles are rare in North America but usual in Europe • In the San Francisco Bay Area, Caltrain's lead cars provide special accommodations for 16–32 bikes, depending on time of day and direction of travel; most ferry lines in the Bay Area also permit bikes on board with no extra fee • Berlin allows bicycles on trains at any time, but charges a fee (€1.70/$2.20) • All 27 light rail vehicles in Minneapolis equipped with onboard interior vertical racks that accommodate 4 bikes per vehicle

Table 8.1
(continued)

Renting bicycles

	Description	Examples and extent of implementation
Bike rentals	Traditional bike rental at counter in train stations. Separate contract for each rental. Rental periods range from one day to several weeks.	• Provision of traditional bike rentals at virtually every major Dutch, Danish, German, and Swiss train station and many suburban stations; especially in regions regularly frequented by tourists
Public bike rentals	Short-term bike rentals at train stations to extend catchment area of public transport. Often membership based or with discounts for public transport passengers with monthly and annual tickets.	• Most widely implemented in Europe, using Smart Card technology, with OV-Fiets public transport bicycle rentals at 200 Dutch rail stations and Call-a-Bike rentals at 50 German train stations • In the Netherlands, payment is made via a special account linked to a season ticket for public transport or a special OV-Fiets membership card • In Germany, bikes can be rented by cell phone at public transport stops, paid for by the minute, and left at any busy intersection in the city • 5,000 rental bikes at train stations in Tokyo

Table 8.1
(continued)

Renting bicycles

	Description	Examples and extent of implementation
Bikesharing	Short-term bike rental with pickup and return at special bike kiosks distributed across cities and often close to public transport stops. Typically membership based, but sometimes one-day guest passes also available. Often the first 30 minutes are free, but fees increase sharply with length of rental period to incentivize short-term rentals.	• New generation of bicycle rental systems such as Vélib' in Paris, Vélo'v in Lyon, Bicing in Barcelona, Bixi in Montreal, Nice Ride in Minneapolis, and Capital Bikeshare in Washington, D.C., with many rental stations near metro and train stations

Coordinating bike routes with public transport

	Description	Examples and extent of implementation
Bike routes leading to public transport stations/stops	Bike paths, lanes, and on-street routes that lead to public transport stations and stops, thus facilitating the bike's role as feeder and collector for public transport.	• Large bike route networks in European cities typically include easy access to public transport stops; less common in North America and Australia • The routing of on-street bikeways in Chicago and the Washington, D.C., bike plan took the location of transit stations into account • Bay Area Regional Bicycle Plan as well as the Bike Plans of BART and Caltrain encourage coordination of bike routes and facilities with public transportation • Explicit coordination of bike routes with public transport stops with the goal of establishing a seamless link between the two modes in Portland

Table 8.1
(continued)

Coordinating bike routes with public transport

	Description	Examples and extent of implementation
Bike routes that parallel public transport routes	Bike paths, lanes, and on-street routes that parallel public transport routes. Bike routes parallel to public transport routes can facilitate access to transit stops and can help avoid conflicts between buses and bicycles.	• Hiawatha LRT line parallels an off-street bike path for most of its length in Minneapolis • Waterfront Trail in the Greater Toronto Area parallels the busy GO Rail Lakeshore corridor • Bike routes often parallel San Francisco MUNI bus routes and intersect with transit stops • In Vancouver, the construction of the Millennium, Expo, and Canada SkyTrain lines included traffic-protected, parallel bike routes to foster bicyclist access to public transport • TransLink in Vancouver promotes cycling in central corridors where bus and rail vehicles are the most crowded and where cycling has the potential to divert some of the overload and thus reduce crowding
Shared bus-bike lanes	Bus-only lanes usually in downtown environments that allow bicycle travel and sometimes allow access for taxis. Private cars and trucks are banned from these lanes.	• Shared bus-bike lanes have been used in many European cities • Extent of shared bus-bike lanes: 308 km in London, 210 km in Paris, and 80 km in Berlin • There are also shared bus-bike lanes in Australian cities including Melbourne and Sydney and North American cities including Toronto, Philadelphia, and Washington, D.C.

national statistics available for Germany, but in 2011 there were 31,600 bike-and-ride parking spots at rail stations in Berlin and 45,000 in Munich (City of Berlin 2011; City of Munich 2011). In 2009, there were more than 800,000 bike parking spaces at metro and suburban rail stations in the Tokyo Prefecture itself and over 2.1 million bike-and-ride parking spaces in the Greater Tokyo metropolitan area (MLITT 2009). By comparison, there were only 38,280 bike-and-ride parking spaces in the entire United States in 2010, of which 26,495 were at rail stations (APTA 2011b).

In recent years, cities throughout Europe, North America, and Japan have been increasing the quantity and quality of bike parking at public transportation. Netherlands Railways installed more than 80,000 additional bike parking spaces between 2005 and 2010 and plans to add 180,000 more spaces by 2020 (Netherlands Ministry of Transport 2011). In the United States, there was a 45 percent increase in bike-and-ride parking between 2006 and 2010, thanks partly to special federal government funding for infrastructure investments that promote integration of cycling with public transportation (APTA 2006, 2008a, 2011b; Clarke 2003; Pucher and Buehler 2009; USDOT 2007). Bike-and-ride parking supply almost doubled in Canada over the same period, increasing by 97 percent (APTA 2006, 2008a, 2011b; CUTA 2008). Comparable time-series data on bike parking supply are not available for other countries, but virtually all the cities we surveyed reported substantial growth and plans for further expansion.

As shown in table 8.1, there are many different kinds of bike parking, ranging from simple bike racks on sidewalks near public transportation stops to advanced, full-service bike stations. Bike racks come in a wide variety of designs including the inverted-U, A-rack, post-and-ring, wave design, two-tiered racks, and decorative racks (APBP 2010). The general trend has been toward designs that fully support the bike and permit locking of both the frame and one or both wheels to the rack. Bike parking can be sheltered to varying extents, either through simple coverings similar to bus shelters or more extensive protection through expansive roofing, partial enclosure, or fully indoor parking.

European cities have been at the vanguard of providing sheltered bike parking immediately adjacent to or within train stations (German Institute for Urbanism 2010; Dutch Bicycle Council 2010; Netherlands

Ministry of Transport 2009; Pucher and Buehler 2008). Most metro and suburban rail stations in Dutch, Danish, and German metropolitan areas offer sheltered and/or secure bike parking of some sort. Chicago has been the North American leader, offering sheltered or indoor parking at 83 of its 143 subway and elevated rail stations, with the specific design tailored to each station's particular situation (Pucher and Buehler 2009). The placement of bike racks inside the stations provides weather protection and greater security because they are usually within easy sight of station attendants and other passengers.

The serious problem of bike theft in most countries has increased the demand for secure parking. Many cities in the Netherlands offer guarded parking lots for bikes, with a personal attendant to discourage theft and vandalism. For example, the city of Groningen has more than 11,000 guarded bike parking spaces at its three railway stations, charging a fee of €99 ($140) per year (Dutch Bicycle Council 2010). Many guarded facilities at train stations in the Netherlands have been upgraded to full-service bike stations. Guarded bike parking is available in most commercial centers and at many schools.

The alternatives to personally guarded parking are bike lockers or bike cages. Bike lockers are sturdy metallic or plastic boxes that hold one or two bikes and are usually rented in advance on a monthly basis. Recently, some public transportation systems have been installing electronic bike lockers, which are available on a first-come, first-serve basis and permit daily or hourly rental. Bike lockers are by far the main form of secure bike parking in North American cities. The San Francisco Bay Area leads, with 2,096 bike lockers at its rail stations (including 326 electronic lockers), followed by Washington, D.C., with 1,300 bike lockers (Pucher and Buehler 2009). In 2010, there were 15,546 bike lockers at train stations in the Netherlands (ProRail 2011).

Bike cages provide less security than bike lockers because anyone with a keycard can gain access to the bikes parked there, but they require less space and are cheaper to construct. The security of cages has been improved by the installation of surveillance cameras in some cities. The public transportation system in the Boston metropolitan area offered nine bike cages in 2011 (called Pedal & Parks) holding 50–150 bikes each, or about 900 bikes in total. Portland had 5 bike cages in 2011 (called regional bike-transit facilities) at key stations, providing parking for 344 bikes in total. Both the Boston and Portland bike cages feature keycard access and surveillance cameras, and a few provide limited services, moving them closer to bike stations than simple bike cages. Many rail stations in northern Europe provide bike cages, and there are some in Australian cities as well (see table 8.1). In 2011, for example, there were 82 bike cages in Denmark, of which 42 were in the Copenhagen metropolitan area. Melbourne's metro and suburban rail network had 35 bike cages in 2011, with a total capacity of 910 bikes. Whatever their limitations, bike cages provide much better shelter and security than unprotected bike racks on sidewalks or train platforms.

Bike stations improve on bike cages by providing a personal attendant, better shelter from the weather, and a range of services such as bike repairs, bike rentals, and sometimes showers and clothes lockers. They are the most secure and most advanced form of bike parking at public transportation stations. As of 2011, there were 98 full-service bike stations in the Netherlands (with 84,660 parking spaces), 106 in Germany (31,846 spaces), and 28 in Switzerland (7,783 spaces) (Council of Bike Friendly Cities 2011; German Institute for Urbanism 2010; German National Cycling Club 2011; ProRail 2011; Association of Swiss Bike Stations 2011). Dutch and German cities began constructing bike stations in the mid-1990s; North American cities have only recently adopted this European innovation. Muenster, Germany, has one of the best and most famous bike stations (figure 8.2). Built in 1999 immediately adjacent to the main train station, the innovative Radstation offers secure, indoor parking for 3,300 bikes as well as bike repairs, bike rentals, accessories, showers, storage lockers, bike washes, touring advice, and direct access to all train platforms (City of Muenster 2004). Amsterdam is currently constructing three new bike stations at its central train station that will accommodate more than 10,000 bikes when completed in 2015. Groningen plans to build a new central railway station with more than 20,000 bike parking spaces. The San Francisco Bay Area led North America with six bike stations in 2011 (1,098 total parking spaces), but there were also bike stations in Washington, Toronto, Chicago, Minneapolis, Portland, and Seattle. As of 2011, the only bike stations in Australia were in Brisbane at two of its busway stations, with a total of 1,170 spaces (City of Brisbane 2011). Tokyo provides massive amounts of bike parking at its rail stations, including some technologically

Figure 8.2
This bike station in Muenster, Germany, holds 3,300 bikes and provides secure bike storage as well as bike rentals, repairs, accessories, touring advice, bike washes, storage lockers, and direct access to all train platforms and bus stops. In 2011, there were 106 bike stations in Germany and 98 in the Netherlands, but only 15 in all of North America. *Photo:* Peter Berkeley.

advanced bike stations that store thousands of bikes and enable the automatic deposit and retrieval of bikes in less than a minute (MLITT 2008b, 2009).

There are few scientific studies of the impact on cycling levels of parking at public transportation stops, but they confirm its importance. Martens (2004, 2007) and Givoni and Rietveld (2007), for example, find that the provision of good bike parking at train stations in northern Europe encourages more cycling as well as more public transportation use. Taylor and Mahmassani (1996) report that secure bike lockers at public transportation stations significantly increase cycling levels. Similarly, Wardman, Tight, and Page (2007) found that provision of bike parking significantly increases the likelihood of cycling and that secure bike parking has an even larger impact. Studies by Hegger (2007),

McClintock and Morris (2003), Pucher and Buehler (2009), and the Netherlands Ministry of Transport (2009) all confirm the expected symbiotic relationship between cycling and public transportation. Finally, a comprehensive report by the Transportation Research Board found that the provision of bike parking costs less than a tenth as much per public transportation passenger as park and ride provisions for cars (TRB 2005).

Provisions for Taking Bikes on Board Trains and Buses

Surveys suggest that cyclists in North America generally prefer to take their bikes with them on board trains and buses so they can use their bikes at both ends of the trip as well as reduce the risk of bike theft and vandalism (Pucher and Buehler 2009). Thus, most buses in North America are now equipped with external racks holding two or four bikes (figure 8.3). The percentage of buses with bike racks almost tripled in the United States in the past decade, from 27 percent in 2000 to 72 percent in 2010 (ABW 2012; APTA 2010). New York City is the only

Figure 8.3
Except for New York and Montreal, all major cities in North America provide bike racks on buses free of charge to cyclists, as here in Minneapolis. More than 50,000 buses (72% of all buses) in North America now have bike racks. *Photo:* Metro Transit.

major American city without bike racks on its buses (Pucher et al. 2010). Except for Montreal, most buses in Canadian cities are equipped with bike racks (Pucher, Buehler, and Seinen 2011). Virtually all North American cities now offer the use of bike racks on buses free of charge, having eliminated fees that were initially charged by some public transportation systems. In sharp contrast, almost no buses in European and Australian cities have bike racks. Few public transportation systems anywhere permit bikes to be taken inside buses unless they are compact, folding bikes.

Public transportation systems in Europe and North America generally permit bikes on light rail, metro, and suburban rail trains, except during peak hour periods when crowding makes it infeasible (TRB 2005; Dutch Bicycle Council 2010; Pucher and Buehler 2009). Most rail systems designate particular cars of trains, and parts of cars, for bikes and increasingly offer special accommodations such as bike racks, bike hooks, special bike holding areas near doors, and special bike cars (APTA 2008b; TRB 2005; Pucher and Buehler 2009). The Caltrain suburban rail line to San Francisco, for example, features special cars with accommodations for 16–32 bikes (figure 8.4). Fees for bringing bikes on board rail vehicles are rare in North America but usual in Europe. Thus, in some respects, public transportation systems in North American are more bike-friendly than European systems in allowing bikes on buses and trains free of charge, partially offsetting the much better bike parking facilities at public transportation stops in Europe.

Most studies of bikes on board public transportation focus on the impacts of bike racks on bus usage and find positive results, generating more passenger fare revenue than the costs of installing bike racks (Hagelin 2007; TRB 2005). The limited evidence available suggests high utilization rates for bikes on board where permitted but insufficient capacity to handle bikes during peak hours. There have not yet been any rigorous statistical studies of the impacts on bicycling levels of bikes on board, but they are probably positive because it helps cyclists cover long portions of trips by public transportation while using their bikes to reach public transportation stops and access destinations (USDOT 1998; TRB 2005; Pucher and Buehler 2009).

Figure 8.4
Most trains allow bikes on board except during rush hours, but in the San Francisco Bay Area, suburban trains permit bikes at all times with no charge and provide two special bike cars such as this one, accommodating 80 bikes. Cyclists ride on the second level of the same cars, just above their bikes. *Photo:* San Francisco Bicycle Coalition.

Bike Rental Facilities at or Near Train Stations

Bike rentals at public transportation stations facilitate integration of the two modes by providing bikes for trips to and from the train station. Public transportation passengers are more likely to have their own bikes for the trip from home to the origin station and less likely to have a bike at the destination station, often near the city center. Thus, most bike rental programs have focused on provision of bike rentals at stations in the city center.

There are three kinds of rental systems that have developed over time to serve the needs of public transportation passengers wanting to use bikes for access to stations: (1) traditional hourly or daily bike rentals from rental offices with an attendant; (2) automated and/or discounted bike rentals using wireless GPS technology and/or membership cards with memory chips; and (3) various kinds of public bikesharing systems, such as those described in detail in chapter 9.

The first type of bike rental, traditional hourly or daily rentals, has existed for many decades at northern European train stations, especially in countries with high levels of cycling. Such facilities are used mainly by recreational riders or sightseeing tourists, not by local residents for daily rentals. Although such rental bikes obviously provide access to and from the train station, they usually must be returned to the same station where they are rented. They are not practical for hourly use or for regular commutation on a daily basis.

A second type of bike rental is the public transportation bike, which was developed in the Netherlands (OV-Fiets) and Germany (Call-a-Bike). Both of these systems focus on providing access by bike from the train station to the final destination of the passenger. Unlike the bikesharing systems described in chapter 9, they charge for even brief periods of use, but in a more convenient way than traditional bike rentals. Moreover, they offer discounts for regular public transportation passengers. Some German cities offer an attractive combination ticket that covers both the public transportation trip and the bike rental (Dutch Bicycle Council 2010; German Railways 2011; Netherlands Ministry of Transport 2009).

The German Railways Call-a-Bike program in Berlin is especially innovative. It permits anyone with a mobile phone and credit card to rent one of more than 3,000 German Rail bikes placed throughout the city. The customer simply dials the Call-a-Bike number, provides credit card information (charged per minute of bike use), and then receives the access code to unlock the bike (German Railways 2011). The bike can be left at many different locations instead of being returned to the point of origin. The same Call-a-Bike service is offered by German Railways in other major cities, including Hamburg, Cologne, Frankfurt, Karlsruhe, Stuttgart, and Munich, with a total of more than 10,000 such rental bikes. Call-a-Bike is also available at all Intercity Express (ICE) train stations, but unlike the citywide services, customers must return the bike to the same station where it was rented (German Railways 2011).

OV-Fiets is an even more extensive public transportation bike program in the Netherlands. In 2011, there were more than 200 OV-Fiets rental locations at Dutch railway stations providing quick and easy discount bike rentals. Payment is made via a special account linked to a season ticket for public transportation or a special OV-Fiets membership card (OV-Fiets 2011). Tokyo has a similar system with about 5,000 rental bikes located at its train stations (MLITT 2008b, 2009).

As analyzed in detail in chapter 9, public bikesharing systems have been rapidly proliferating in cities around the world. Virtually all existing public bikesharing programs have located many of their docking stations near public transportation specifically to provide access to and from stations. Surveys in Paris indicate that many public transportation riders rely on the cheap and convenient availability these public access bikes to get to and from public transportation (TNS Sofres 2009). In that respect, bikesharing systems are also a way to integrate cycling with public transportation.

Coordination of Bike Routes with Public Transportation

Full integration of cycling with public transportation also requires that bike paths and lanes lead to key nodes in the public transportation network. The coordination of bike routes with public transportation is especially necessary in North America, where both cycling facilities and public transportation services are sparse. Yet there is little if any explicit coordination of routes in most American and Canadian cities. By comparison, the networks of bike routes and public transportation lines in Dutch, Danish, and German cities are generally so dense that they almost inevitably overlap to some extent. In addition, however, bike lanes and paths in northern Europe are explicitly designed to connect daily travel destinations in cities, including bus stops and train stations (Dutch Bicycle Council 2010; Pucher and Buehler 2007, 2008). Most bike paths in North America are intended for recreational cycling. They are usually located along rivers, canals, and lakes or in parks and greenways, and thus do not generally provide access to offices, schools, stores, and public transportation stations (Pucher and Buehler 2006).

Another aspect of coordination is locating cycling facilities so as to avoid conflicts with passengers getting on or off buses. In many Dutch, German, and Danish cities, bike lanes and paths curve behind bus stops or are located far enough away from the street that cyclists are not in the way of bus passengers (Pucher and Dijkstra 2000). North American cities have either ignored such conflicts or adopted the simple solution of locating bike lanes on streets without bus service, as in San Francisco (Pucher and Buehler 2009). In New York City, bike lanes are placed on the left side of one-way streets to avoid conflicts with buses picking up passengers from the right lane (NYCDOT 2011).

Many European cities take the opposite approach by offering shared bus-bike lanes. For example, there are 308 km of bus-bike lanes in London, 210 km in Paris, and 80 km in Berlin (Pucher and Buehler 2007, 2008; City of Paris 2008; TfL 2011). Because most bus lanes usually have extra capacity, they can be an ideal supplement to the overall network of cycling facilities. European cities with bus-bike lanes require special training for bus drivers to minimize the dangers of cyclists traveling in the same lane.

Public transportation services are generally most crowded in the city center, which is also where trips tend to be the shortest due to the concentration of activities. Cycling facilities have the potential to relieve the overcrowding of buses and trains. In Vancouver, New York, and London, for example, bike planners have focused on improving cycling facilities on the most heavily traveled corridors in the center to divert some of the excess demand from public transportation to cycling. Yet another type of coordination is the alignment of bike paths parallel to public transportation lines, as in Minneapolis and Vancouver, to enable use of public transportation for excessively long or unpleasant portions of the trip or in cases of mechanical breakdowns or physical exhaustion.

There have not been any scientific studies of the impacts of such coordination of bike and public transportation routes, probably because it would be difficult to quantify the impacts and to control for the many other explanatory factors. Clearly, however, route coordination is an important aspect of integrating cycling with public transportation.

Discussion and Conclusions

Over the past few decades, most European and North American cities have made impressive progress integrating cycling with public transportation. European cities have focused on increasing the quantity and quality of bike parking at public transportation stations. North American cities have placed more emphasis on facilitating bikes on board, either by installing bike racks on buses or permitting them on rail vehicles. Even in the United States and Canada, however, bike parking at transit stops has been vastly expanded over the past ten years, with large increases in the number of racks as well as improvements in the convenience, security, and shelter of bike parking.

Although cycling and public transportation have considerable synergies, there are potential conflicts as well. On some routes, cycling and public transportation may compete with each other over short distances. In some Dutch and German cities, for example, there is evidence that provision of very low-cost semester and annual tickets for students shifts some cyclists to public transportation (Dutch Bicycle Council 2010; Schwanen 2002; Pucher and Buehler 2007).

Another potential conflict involves taking bikes on board rail vehicles. Bikes can cause problems during peak hours when all available capacity is needed to accommodate passengers and there is no extra room for bikes. Taking bikes on buses is much less of a problem, because bike racks are external and do not reduce passenger-carrying capacity. But even bike racks can be filled to capacity during the peak, forcing cyclists to wait for later buses.

Paradoxically, a bike-and-ride program can become problematic where it is most successful. Capacity problems are most likely to arise in cities with well-used public transportation and high levels of cycling. Thus the European approach to bike-and-ride has favored the provision of ample, sheltered, secure bike parking at transit stops instead of accommodating bikes on transit vehicles. Similarly, in North American cities with overcrowding of rail vehicles during rush hours, the focus should be on providing improved bike parking at rail stations. There is a need for more and better parking, including sheltered and secure spaces (Litman 2009). Indeed, an increasing number of American and Canadian cities are now installing multiservice bike stations at their major transit terminals, as is already common in Dutch and German cities. Similar to the concept of "complete streets," an appropriate goal of public transportation in North America should be to provide "complete stations" that fully accommodate the needs of cyclists. "Complete stations" would make rail platforms more accessible to cyclists, which would also improve accessibility for persons with disabilities.

As cycling and public transportation continue to grow in the coming years, so will the demand for bike-and-ride provisions. Although the necessary investments obviously require money, they are far less expensive than park-and-ride facilities for cars, which are not only more expensive per passenger attracted but also less environmentally friendly and less socially equitable than bike-and-ride. Improving bike-and-ride facilities unquestionably contributes to the overall sustainability of the urban transportation system and merits increased government funding.

References

ABW (Alliance for Biking and Walking). 2012. *Bicycling and Walking in the United States: 2012 Benchmarking Report*. Washington, DC: Alliance for Biking and Walking. http://www.peoplepoweredmovement.org/benchmarking.

APBP (Association of Pedestrian and Bicycle Professionals). 2010. *Bicycle Parking Guidelines*. 2nd ed. Washington, DC: APBP.

APTA (American Public Transportation Association). 2006. *2006 Transit Infrastructure Database*. Washington, DC: APTA.

APTA (American Public Transportation Association). 2008a. *2008 Transit Infrastructure Database*. Washington, DC: APTA.

APTA (American Public Transportation Association). 2008b. *2008 Public Transportation Vehicle Database*. Washington, DC: APTA.

APTA (American Public Transportation Association). 2009. *2009 Public Transportation Fact Book*. Washington, DC: APTA.

APTA (American Public Transportation Association). 2010. *2010 Public Transportation Vehicle Database*. Washington, DC: APTA.

APTA (American Public Transportation Association). 2011a. *Transit Statistics*. Washington, DC: APTA.

APTA (American Public Transportation Association). 2011b. *2010 Transit Infrastructure Database*. Washington, DC: APTA.

Association of Swiss Bike Stations. 2011. *Bike Stations in Switzerland*. Bern, Switzerland: Association of Swiss Bike Stations.

Bassett, David, John Pucher, Ralph Buehler, Dixie Thompson, and Scott Crouter. 2008. Walking, Cycling, and Obesity Rates in Europe, North America and Australia. *Journal of Physical Activity & Health* 5 (6): 795–814.

Brons, Martijn, Moshe Givoni, and Piet Rietveld. 2009. Access to Railway Stations and its Potential in Increasing Rail Use. *Transportation Research Part A, Policy and Practice* 43 (2): 136–149.

City of Berlin. 2011. *Cycling in Berlin*. Berlin: City of Berlin, Department of Urban Development.

City of Brisbane. 2011. *Bike Parking and Facilities*. Brisbane, Australia: City of Brisbane, Brisbane City Council.

City of Muenster. 2004. *Bicycling in Muenster*. Muenster, Germany: City of Muenster, Department of City Planning.

City of Munich. 2011. *Cycling in Munich*. Munich: City of Munich, Department of Urban Development.

City of Paris. 2008. *Traffic in Paris in 2008*. Paris: City of Paris, Department of Transport.

Clarke, Andy. 2003. Green Modes and U.S. Transport Policy: TEA-21. In *Sustainable Transport: Planning for Walking and Cycling in Urban Environments*, ed. Rodney Tolley, 433–440. Cambridge: Woodhead Publishing.

Council of Bike Friendly Cities. 2011. *Bike Stations in Western Germany*. Duesseldorf, Germany: Council of Bike Friendly Cities.

CUTA (Canadian Urban Transit Association). 2008. *Canadian Urban Transit Fact Book*. Toronto: CUTA.

Danish Ministry of Transport. 2010. *Overview of the Number of Passengers, Car Parking Supply and Bike Parking Spaces at Danish Train Stations*. Copenhagen: Danish Ministry of Transport.

Dutch Bicycle Council. 2010. *Bicycle Policies of the European Principals: Continuous and Integral*. Amsterdam: Dutch Bicycle Council.

German National Cycling Club. 2011. *Bike Stations*. Bremen, Germany: German National Cycling Club.

German Institute for Urbanism. 2010. *Parking at the Train Station*. Berlin: German Institute for Urbanism.

German Railways. 2011. *Call a Bike*. Berlin: German Railways.

Givoni, Moshe, and Piet Rietveld. 2007. The Access Journey to the Railway Station and Its Role in Passengers' Satisfaction with Rail Travel. *Transport Policy* 14 (5): 357–365.

Hagelin, Christopher. 2007. Integrating Bicycles and Transit through Bike-to-Bus Strategy. Transportation Research Board Annual Meeting CD-ROM, paper 07-3130. Washington, DC: National Academy of Sciences.

Hegger, Ruud. 2007. Public Transport and Cycling: Living Apart or Together? *Public Transport International* 2:38–41.

Litman, Todd. 2009. *Bicycle Parking, Storage, and Changing Facilities*. Victoria, Canada: Victoria Transport Policy Institute.

Martens, Karel. 2004. The Bicycle as a Feedering Mode: Experiences from Three European Countries. *Transportation Research Part D: Transport and Environment* 9 (4): 281–294.

Martens, Karel. 2007. Promoting Bike and Ride: The Dutch Experience. *Transportation Research Part A: Policy and Practice* 41 (4): 326–338.

McClintock, Hugh, and Dave Morris. 2003. Integration of Cycling and Light Rail Transit. *World Transport Policy and Practice* 9 (3): 9–14.

MLITT (Ministry of Land, Infrastructure, Transport, and Tourism). 2008a. *Tokyo Person Trip Survey 2008*. Tokyo: Government of Japan.

MLITT (Ministry of Land, Infrastructure, Transport, and Tourism. 2008b. *Progress Report on Improving Cycling Conditions*. Tokyo: Government of Japan.

MLITT (Ministry of Land, Infrastructure, Transport, and Tourism. 2009. *Bikes Parked at Public Transport Stations*. Tokyo, Japan: Government of Japan, Japan Cabinet Office.

Netherlands Ministry of Transport. 2009. *Cycling in the Netherlands*. The Hague: Netherlands Ministry of Transport.

Netherlands Ministry of Transport. 2010. *Action Plan: Growth on Track*. The Hague: Netherlands Ministry of Transport.

Netherlands Ministry of Transport. 2011. *The Future of Bike Parking*. The Hague: Netherlands Ministry of Transport.

North Rhine Westphalia Ministry of Transport. 2004. *Bike Friendly Cities*. Duesseldorf, Germany: North Rhine Westphalia Ministry of Transport.

NYCDOT (New York City Department of Transportation). 2011. *Bicyclists*. New York: NYCDOT.

OV-Fiets (Public Transport Bike). 2011. *Bike Rentals at Dutch Train Stations*. Utrecht, The Netherlands: OV-Fiets.

ProRail. 2011. *Bike Parking at Train Stations in the Netherlands: Current, Required, and Planned Parking Supply*. Utrecht, The Netherlands: ProRail.

Pucher, John, and Ralph Buehler. 2006. Why Canadians Cycle More Than Americans: A Comparative Analysis of Bicycling Trends and Policies. *Transport Policy* 13 (3): 265–279.

Pucher, John, and Ralph Buehler. 2007. At the Frontiers of Cycling: Policy Innovations in the Netherlands, Denmark, and Germany. *World Transport Policy and Practice* 13 (3): 8–57.

Pucher, John, and Ralph Buehler. 2008. Making Cycling Irresistible: Lessons from the Netherlands, Denmark, and Germany. *Transport Reviews* 28 (4): 495–528.

Pucher, John, and Ralph Buehler. 2009. Integrating Bicycling and Public Transport in North America. *Journal of Public Transportation* 12 (3): 79–104.

Pucher, John, and Ralph Buehler. 2010. Walking and Cycling for Healthy Cities. *Built Environment* 36 (5): 391–414.

Pucher, John, Ralph Buehler, Dafna Merom, and Adrian Bauman. 2011. Walking and Cycling in the United States, 2001–2009: Evidence from the National Household Travel Surveys. *American Journal of Public Health* 101 (S1): S310–S317.

Pucher, John, Ralph Buehler, and Mark Seinen. 2011. Bicycling Renaissance in North America? An Update and Re-Assessment of Cycling Trends and Policies. *Transportation Research Part A: Policy and Practice* 45 (6): 451–475.

Pucher, John, and Lewis Dijkstra. 2000. Making Walking and Cycling Safer: Lessons from Europe. *Transportation Quarterly* 54 (3): 25–50.

Pucher, John, Lewis Thorwaldson, Ralph Buehler, and Nick Klein. 2010. Cycling in New York: Innovative Policies at the Urban Frontier. *World Transport Policy and Practice* 16 (1): 7–50.

Schwanen, Tim. 2002. Urban Form and Commuting Behavior: A Cross European Comparison. *Tijdschrift voor Economische en Sociale Geografie* 93 (3): 336–343.

Statistics Canada. 1996–2010. *Where Canadians Work and How They Get There*. Ottawa: Statistics Canada.

Taylor, Dean, and Hani Mahmassani. 1996. Analysis of State Preferences for Intermodal Bicycle-Transit Interfaces. *Transportation Research Record* 1556: 86–95.

TfL (Transport for London). 2011. Cycling Revolution London: End of Year Review. London: TfL.

TNS Sofres. 2009. *Vélib Satisfaction Survey*. Paris: TNS Sofres.

TRB (Transportation Research Board). 2005. *Integration of Bicycles and Transit. TCRP Synthesis Report 62*. Washington, DC: TRB, National Research Council.

USDOC (U.S. Department of Commerce). 2010a. American Fact Finder: 1990 Decennial Census, Journey to Work. Washington, DC: USDOC, US Census Bureau.

USDOC (U.S. Department of Commerce). 2010b. American Fact Finder: 2009 Decennial Census, Journey to Work. Washington, DC: USDOC, US Census Bureau.

USDOT (U.S. Department of Transportation). 1998. *Bicycles and Transit: A Partnership that Works*. Washington, DC: USDOT, Federal Transit Administration.

USDOT (U.S. Department of Transportation). 2007. *Bicycle Parking and Storage*. Washington, DC: USDOT, Federal Highway Administration.

Wardman, Mark, Miles Tight, and Matthew Page. 2007. Factors Influencing the Propensity to Cycle to Work. *Transportation Research Part A, Policy and Practice* 41 (4): 339–359.

9

Bikesharing across the Globe

Susan A. Shaheen, Stacey Guzman, and Hua Zhang

Concerns about global climate change, energy security, and unstable fuel prices have caused many decision makers and policy experts worldwide to closely examine the need for more sustainable transportation strategies. Sustainable strategies include clean fuels, vehicle technologies, transportation demand management, and integrated land use and transportation strategies (Shaheen and Lipman 2007). Bikesharing—the shared use of a bicycle fleet—is one mobility strategy that could help address many of these concerns. In recent years, interest in this evolving concept has spread across the globe. At present, there are an estimated 135 programs in approximately 160 cities around the world with more than 236,000 bicycles on four continents and over 35 more planned in 16 nations in 2011.

Despite rapid global motorization, worldwide bicycle use has generally increased over the past thirty years. Indeed, as shown in chapter 2, bicycling in Dutch, German, and Danish cities increased between 20 to 43 percent between 1975 and 1995 (Pucher and Buehler 2008). In fact, bicycle trips in Berlin alone quadrupled between 1970 and 2001 (Pucher, Dill, and Handy 2010). Although cycling growth and trends vary worldwide, bikesharing offers a transportation alternative to increase bicycle use by integrating cycling into the transportation system and making it more convenient and attractive to users.

The principle of bikesharing is simple. Individuals use bicycles on an "as-needed" basis. Bikesharing is short-term bicycle access, which provides its users with a sustainable and environmentally friendly form of public transportation. This flexible short-term usage scheme targets daily mobility and allows users to access public bicycles at unattended bike stations. Bicycle reservations, pickup, and dropoff are self-service. Commonly concentrated in urban settings, bikesharing programs provide multiple bike station locations that enable users to pick up and return bicycles to different stations. Bikesharing programs typically cover bicycle purchase and maintenance costs as well as storage and parking responsibilities (similar to carsharing or short-term auto use) (Shaheen, Cohen, and Chung 2009).

By addressing the various aspects of bicycle ownership, bikesharing programs encourage cycling by providing hassle- and maintenance-free bicycle access. Individuals who may not otherwise use bicycles (i.e., tourists or individuals who do not own a bicycle or have access to bicycle storage) are able to enjoy cycling benefits without the responsibility of ownership. Access to multiple bikesharing locations makes short distance travel within participating cities more convenient. Furthermore, making a large number of bicycles available for use at various locations may increase the number of individuals who use cycling to meet their daily mobility needs. A stronger bicycle presence can contribute to an overall acceptance of bicycle use for trips that are not solely recreational but also more practical (i.e., commuting to work, running errands). A stronger bicycle presence may also foster a safer cycling environment. As discussed in chapter 7, having more cyclists on the road improves motorist behavior because drivers become more aware of cyclists and are less likely to collide with them (Jacobsen 2003).

Besides individual user perks, bikesharing also offers environmental, social, and transportation-related benefits. For instance, bikesharing provides a low-carbon solution to the "first mile/last mile" problem (i.e., the issue of connecting the short distance between home and public transit and/or transit stations and the workplace). Thus, bikesharing has the potential to play an important role in bridging the gap in existing transportation networks, as well as encouraging individuals to use multiple transportation modes. Bikesharing benefits can include (1) increased mobility options, (2) cost savings from modal shifts, (3) lower implementation and operational costs (e.g., in contrast to shuttle services), (4) reduced traffic congestion, (5) reduced fuel use, (6) increased use of public transit and alternative modes (e.g., rail, buses, taxis, carsharing, ride sharing), (7) increased health benefits, and (8) greater environmental awareness. The ultimate goal of bikesharing is to expand and integrate cycling into transportation systems so that it can more readily become a daily transportation mode.

In recent years, bikesharing has also expanded to college and work campuses throughout North America. Indeed, there are approximately seventy college/university bikesharing programs operating throughout North America, with another eight planned in 2011. Examples of college/university programs worldwide include CibiUAM at the Universidad Autonoma de Madrid (UAM) in Spain and Velocampus Leeds at the University of Leeds in the United Kingdom. The focus of this chapter, however, is on public systems that are open to residents and visitors, as opposed to closed systems that are accessible only to students and employees of a university or major employer. Furthermore, the authors do not address bike rental programs, which traditionally target users interested in leisure-oriented mobility and are most prevalent in areas with a high tourist concentration. In general, bike rental systems consist of a single or limited number of bike stations that are operated by a service attendant and require users to return rented bicycles to the original bike station.

Over the last forty-six years, bikesharing's evolution has been categorized into three key phases (also known as bikesharing generations) (DeMaio 2003). These include the first generation, called "White Bikes" (or "free bikes"); the second generation: coin-deposit systems; and the third generation or information technology (IT)–based systems (Gradinger 2007). In this chapter, the authors propose a fourth generation, *demand-responsive, multimodal systems*, which builds upon the third.

This chapter is organized into five sections. First, the authors present a history of first- and second-generation bikesharing systems in Europe and North America. Next, third-generation (or IT-based systems) activities are discussed in Europe, the Americas, and Asia. Third, bikesharing business models, impacts, and lessons learned from third-generation systems are discussed. Next, a fourth bikesharing generation is proposed with an eye toward future developments and innovation. Finally, the authors conclude with a summary and recommendations for future bikesharing research.

Bikesharing: The First and Second Generations in Europe and North America

In this section, the authors provide an overview of first- and second-generation bikesharing in Europe and North America. Asia and South America's experience with bikesharing does not begin until the third generation, IT-based systems, which is addressed later in this chapter.

Bikesharing in Europe

Early European bikesharing systems were small-scale, operated as non-profits, and focused on social and environmental issues. In July 1965, the Provos—an organization involved with anarchist politics, the youth movement, and environmental issues—released their "White Bike Plan" in Amsterdam (Home 1991). Fifty bicycles were painted white, left permanently unlocked, and placed throughout the inner city for the public to use freely. However, these bikes were often stolen or damaged. Thus, the White Bike Plan failed soon after its launch.

White Bikes (or Free Bikes): First Generation

Despite Amsterdam's experience, the bikesharing concept caught on and became the first generation of bikesharing known as White Bikes (or free bike systems) (DeMaio 2009). In a free bike system, the bicycle is the main program component. Other distinguishing characteristics of first-generation bikesharing include that bicycles were usually painted one bright color, unlocked, and placed haphazardly throughout an area for free use.

Other cities that implemented a free bike system were La Rochelle, France, in 1974 and Cambridge, England, in 1993. The free bike system in Cambridge, called "Green Bike Schemes," launched with almost 300 shared bicycles that were eventually stolen, resulting in program failure (Midgley 2009b). However, the La Rochelle initiative, called "Vélos Jaunes" or "Yellow Bikes," proved to be successful.

La Rochelle's Mayor, Michel Crépeau, created Vélos Jaunes. Similar to Amsterdam's White Bike Plan, Vélos Jaunes was launched as an environmentally progressive measure and became the first successful bikesharing program in France.

Coin-Deposit Systems: Second Generation

Problems with free bike systems (namely bike theft) led the city government and the City Bike Foundation of Copenhagen, Denmark, to launch a bikesharing service that was different from previous systems. This initiative led to the second generation of bikesharing, known as coin-deposit systems. The main components of this generation are (1) distinguishable bicycles (usually by color and special design); (2) designated docking stations in which bikes can be locked, borrowed, and returned; and (3) small deposits to unlock the bikes.

In May 1995, "Bycyklen" (City Bike) was launched as the first large-scale urban bikesharing program in Europe. This initiative included 1,100 specially designed bicycles that were locked and placed throughout downtown Copenhagen at designated city bike racks (New Mobility Agenda 2008). Bicycles were unlocked with a 20 Danish kroner coin deposit (US$3) that was refunded upon bicycle return. Today, Bycyklen of Copenhagen is famous because it continues to operate with more than 2,000 bicycles and 110 city bike racks, and it led to the second generation of bikesharing.

Copenhagen's coin-deposit model led to a series of European bikesharing programs including: "Bycykler" in Sandnes, Norway (1996); "City Bikes" in Helsinki, Finland (2000); and "Bycykel" in Arhus, Denmark (2005). The experience of the coin-deposit systems demonstrated that second-generation systems were more expensive to operate than earlier systems. Nonprofit groups were frequently created to administer the bikesharing programs. In many cases, local governments also provided bikesharing funding.

Incorporating designated bicycle stations and coin-deposit locks into second-generation systems created a much more reliable bikesharing system. Although amounts vary by country, coin deposit fees are generally low (around US$4). Also, these systems do not issue a time limit for bicycle use, which means that bikes are often used for long time periods or not returned at all. The major problem with coin-deposit systems is bicycle theft, which can be attributed to customer anonymity. Although bikesharing began as a way to reduce motor vehicle use, Bonnette (2007, 20) indicates that "both the first and second generation [bikesharing schemes] provided welcome opportunities to cycle but did not provide adequate enough support nor reliable service to alter motorized transportation choices and influence people to make significant changes." The shortcomings of second-generation systems later gave rise to the third generation of bikesharing.

Bikesharing in North America

Although the history of bikesharing in North America is shorter than in Europe, North America has transitioned through three bikesharing generations. In 1994, the United Community Action Network (a small nonprofit that works on environmental and livability issues) launched the first North American bikesharing program in Portland, Oregon, called "Yellow Bike." Sixty bicycles were left unlocked at Pioneer Square in Portland and were available for anyone to use (O'Keefe and Keating 2008). This program closed in 2001, however. Soon after, Yellow Bike evolved into "Create-A-Commuter" at the Community Cycling Center. The City of Portland plans to launch a new bikesharing program in 2013.

Soon after Yellow Bike's introduction, Boulder, Colorado, launched the "Green Bike Program" in 1995. The City Transportation Management department ran this program. At the time, 130 bicycles were provided for free use. This system eventually ended due to bike theft.

Coin-Deposit Systems: Second Generation

In 1996, the twin cities of Minneapolis and St. Paul launched the "Yellow Bike Project." Created by a local health club's law firm, it was the first coin-deposit system (or second-generation system) in North America. This program employed 150 bicycles that were placed at designated locations. To use this program, users made a one-time, refundable US$10 deposit, signed a waiver, and received a Yellow Bike Card that facilitated bike use. This program was eventually canceled.

St. Paul's Yellow Bike Project was soon followed by multiple North American bikesharing systems that employed the coin-deposit model. Programs included "Olympia Bike Library" in Olympia, Washington (1996); "Yellow Bike" in Austin, Texas (1997); "Red Bikes" in Madison, Wisconsin (which launched as a free bikesharing system in 1995 and evolved into a coin-deposit model a few years later); "Freewheels" in Princeton, New Jersey (1998); and "Decatur Yellow Bikes" (DYB) in Decatur, Georgia (2002).

Third Bikesharing Generation: Europe, the Americas, and Asia

Since its inception in 1965, bikesharing activity has expanded to include five continents: Europe, Asia, Australia, North America, and South America. At present, Europe is the leading hub for bikesharing growth, development, and success.

As of March 2011, there were approximately 135 bikesharing programs operating in an estimated 160 cities around the world, with more than 236,000 shared bicycles. Eighteen European nations currently support bikesharing. The Americas operate programs in Canada, Mexico, the United States, Argentina, Brazil, and Chile. Asia, which represents the fastest growing bikesharing market, operates programs in China, South Korea, and Taiwan. Table 9.1 provides an overview of available bikesharing data worldwide. Researchers compiled the data for this table via expert interviews, phone calls, and emails with bikesharing system operators worldwide.

Evolution from Second- to Third-Generation Bikesharing

The first generation of bikesharing introduced an innovative mobility option, but the notable failure of this approach demonstrated the need for a new model that deterred theft and incentivized bicycle return. Second-generation bikesharing programs introduced a more viable alternative by integrating the use of coin-deposit locks. Building upon this innovation, third-generation programs gained worldwide popularity by incorporating advanced technologies for bicycle reservations, pickup, dropoff, and information tracking. Though a significant number of bikesharing programs currently operate as third-generation models, existing and developing bikesharing programs are exploring or exhibiting the potential for continuous improvements in what the authors call "fourth-generation" systems. See table 9.2 for an overview of the bikesharing generations.

The four main components of third-generation bikesharing programs are (1) distinguishable bicycles (color, special design, and/or advertisement); (2) docking stations (e.g., flex or fixed stations); (3) kiosk or user interface technology for checking bikes in or out; and (4) advanced technology (e.g., mobile phone, magnetic strip card, smartcards) (City-Ryde, n.d.). See figure 9.1 for an overview of third-generation bikesharing

Table 9.1
Worldwide bikesharing programs

Country	Programs	Bicycles	Stations
Argentina	1	560	15
Australia	2	2,600	200
Austria	3	1,500	82
Belgium	1	2,500	180
Brazil	2	452	43
Canada	1	6,100	490
Chile	1	150	15
China	19	123,172	4,422
Czech Republic	1	30	16
Denmark	3	2,650	187
France	29	36,830	3,141
Germany	5	13,330	811
Ireland	1	550	44
Italy	19	3,763	362
Japan	1	150	15
London	1	6,000	400
Luxembourg	2	400	64
Mexico	1	1,200	90
Monaco	1	10	2
Norway	1	1,660	154
Poland	1	155	13
Romania	1	300	3
Slovenia	1	300	31
Spain	25	14,048	1,142
South Korea	2	2,031	185
Sweden	2	1,500	110
Switzerland	1	600	45
Taiwan	2	5,000	61
United States	4	3,122	313
United Kingdom	2	6,091	420
Total	**136**	**236,754**	**13,056**

Notes: The authors count one program for each system that spans multiple cities in one country. Bikesharing in Germany has fixed stations and flex stations. In total, there are approximately 62 fixed stations in Germany. Seven cities also use flex stations as bikesharing stations.

Table 9.2
Bikesharing generations

First generation: Free bike systems (White Bikes)
• Components
◦ Bicycles
• Characteristics
◦ Distinct bicycles (usually by color)
◦ Located haphazardly throughout an area
◦ Bicycles unlocked
◦ Free of charge
Second generation: Coin-deposit systems
• Components
◦ Bicycles
◦ Docking stations
• Characteristics
◦ Distinct bicycles (color or special design)
◦ Located at specific docking stations
◦ Bicycles have locks
Third generation: IT-based systems
• Components
◦ Bicycles
◦ Docking stations
◦ Kiosks or user interface technology
• Characteristics
◦ Distinct bicycles (color, special design, or advertisements)
◦ Located at specific docking stations
◦ Bicycles have locks
◦ Smart technology is used for bicycle checkin/checkout (mobile phones, mag-stripe cards, or smartcards)
◦ Theft deterrents (program specific; members are required to provide ID, bankcard, or mobile phone number to identify users). Failure to return bicycle incurs charges to recover bicycle cost and may also include high punitive costs. Nonmembers are generally required to pay a large deposit to ensure bike return, under risk of losing their deposit
◦ Programs paid for as a membership service, typically free for the first specific time interval with gradually increasing costs enforced

---

Figure 9.1
Three main components of third-generation bikesharing systems, as shown here in Paris, France. *Credit:* Tristan Nitot (flickr.com/photos/nitot/).

components. Information technology makes third-generation bikesharing programs distinct by enabling programs to track bicycles and user information, which has helped to deter bike theft. The next sections summarize third-generation bikesharing in the three main regions of the world.

European Overview
European experience provides a robust history of bikesharing planning, implementation, and operations. More recent growth of third-generation bikesharing programs can be attributed to innovations tracing back to this understanding.

In 1998, the first citywide IT-based system appeared when Clear Channel, a large outdoor advertising company, launched its first "Smart-Bike" program in Rennes, France. To access free bicycles for up to three hours, SmartBike required users to complete a smartcard application. After eleven years of service, the Rennes system, more commonly known as "Vélo à la Carte," came to an end in May 2009. This program has been replaced by "LE vélo STAR," which operates with 900 bicycles and 81 stations.

The program that later popularized third-generation bikesharing is "Vélo'v" in Lyon, France. Launched by JCDecaux in 2005, Vélo'v now operates with more than 4,000 bicycles in Lyon and Villeurbanne.

In 1974, the city of La Rochelle launched Vélos Jaunes. By 2006, the program included 120 bicycles and 12 stations. In 2009, La Rochelle replaced Vélos Jaunes with a second, fully automated system (i.e., bicycle pickup and dropoff is via self-service with a smartcard) called "Yélo." Yélo, which currently operates with 350 bicycles and 50 stations, employs smartcards that enable full integration with the public transportation network.

In 2010, London also launched the "Barclays Cycle Hire" system (with BIXI as the service provider). At present, users have access to 6,000 bicycles at 400 bike stations.

Today, the most widely known third-generation bikesharing system is "Vélib'" in Paris, France. To date, Vélib' operates with 20,600 bicycles and 1,451 bicycle stations available every 300 meters. Vélib' operates on a fee-based system in which the first thirty or forty-five minutes of cycling is free to users (depending on user subscription).

Between 2007 and 2008, Vélib' reported that 20 million trips were made through its program. Averaging 78,000 trips per day, usage rates for Vélib' require that the program operate as efficiently as possible to maintain and distribute the bicycles.

As of March 2011, there were eighteen European nations operating bikesharing programs: Austria, Belgium, the Czech Republic, Denmark, France, Germany, Italy, Ireland, London, Luxembourg, Monaco, Norway, Poland, Romania, Spain, Sweden, Switzerland, and the United Kingdom.

Americas Overview

Although North American bikesharing experience is more limited, Washington, D.C.'s "SmartBike" pilot program demonstrated that bikesharing is feasible. Launched in 2008 with 120 bicycles and 10 stations, Smart-Bike marked the beginning of North America's experience with IT-based systems. By January 2009, the program reported 1,050 subscribers. As highlighted in chapter 13, in 2010, SmartBike DC came to an end and "Capital Bikeshare" was launched. Capital Bikeshare operates in Arlington County, Virginia, and Washington, D.C., with 1,100 bicycles and 114 stations. As of May 2012, it was the largest bikesharing program in the United States.

For several years, however, the largest IT-based system in North America was BIXI (BIcycle-TaXI) in Montreal, Canada, which started in May 2009 and had 5,000 bicycles and 400 stations as of May 2012. The planned 2013 launch of bikesharing in New York City with 10,000 bikes will overtake Montreal, but BIXI was a pathbreaking development and set the example that other cities are now following. After the cancellation of their second-generation bikesharing program—the Yellow Bike Project—the city of Minneapolis launched "Nice Ride" Minnesota in June 2010, with BIXI as the service provider. This system currently operates with 700 bicycles and 73 stations.

In May 2011, BIXI launched in Toronto and currently operates with 1,000 bicycles and 80 stations. The program also expanded into the Ottawa-Gatineau area and operates with 100 bicycles and 10 stations. It is important to note that technological advances in the BIXI program mark a shift toward the fourth-generation of bikesharing described shortly.

Between late spring and fall 2012, fifteen new bikesharing programs plan to launch in the United States and one in Canada. In 2013, New York City is planning to implement North America's largest bikesharing program. Financed in part by $41 million from Citibank, Citi Bike is scheduled to offer 10,000 bikes and 600 docking stations (NYCDOT 2012).

In 2010, Mexico City launched "EcoBici," which currently operates with 1,200 bicycles and 90 docking stations. Prior to Ecobici's launch, city officials agreed to build 186 miles of bike lanes by 2012 to encourage cycling.

Bikesharing activity in South America started in 2008. At present, Argentina, Brazil, and Chile are the only nations with fully operating programs. Colombia is in the process of planning its own bikesharing system.

In 2008, Brazil launched two bikesharing programs—"UseBike" in São Paulo and "Samba" in Rio de Janeiro. Following Samba's launch in Brazil, Chile started a bikesharing program, which currently operates with 180 bicycles and 18 stations.

Asian Overview

Asia's bikesharing history is limited to third-generation, IT-based systems. Despite its more limited experience, Asia is the fastest growing market for bikesharing today. The first bikesharing program to launch in Asia was "TownBike" in Singapore in 1999 (known as "Smart Bike" from 1999 to 2004). This program ended in 2007.

The second bikesharing program in Asia was the "Taito Bicycle Sharing Experiment," which operated in Taito, Japan, from November 2002 to January 2003. It was the first bikesharing pilot in Japan and was funded by the national government's Social Experiment grants. The program employs 130 bicycles at twelve locations. Users accessed bicycles by magnetic striped membership cards, which helped prevent theft.

At present, bikesharing programs are operating in South Korea, Taiwan, and mainland China. South Korea's city government launched its first bikesharing program, "Nubija," in Chongwan in 2008. It now operates with more than 3,500 bicycles and 160 stations. Similar to other programs, Nubija does not charge users a fee for the first hour of use.

"C-Bike" in Kaohsiung City launched in 2009 as the first bikesharing program in Taiwan. At present, this program offers 4,500 bicycles and 50 bike stations. Following Kaohsiung's program, the Taipei government partnered with Giant to launch their bikesharing system, "YouBike," in 2009. This program is completely automated and offers 500 bicycles at ten locations.

The largest and most famous bikesharing program in Asia is the "Public Bicycle" system in Hangzhou, China, which was launched by the Hangzhou Public Transport Corporation in 2008 (see figure 9.2). This system was the first IT-based system in mainland China. With a population of 4.24 million people (in the urban area), Hangzhou's high population density makes it a promising bikesharing location. Today, Hangzhou's system operates with 60,600 bicycles and more than 2,400 bike stations.

Figure 9.2
Hangzhou, China, has the world's largest public bikesharing system, with more than 60,000 bikes. *Credit:* Hua Zhang.

According to a survey by the Hangzhou Public Transport Corporation, bicycles are used six times per day on average, and no bicycles were lost during its first year of implementation (Hangzhou Public Transport Corporation, n.d.).

The Hangzhou Public Bicycle System has surpassed Vélib as the largest bikesharing program in the world. It has sparked great interest in bikesharing in mainland China. Indeed, Chinese cities with bikesharing programs include Shanghai, Wuhan, Guangzhou, Nanjing, Dujiangyan, Foshan, Haiko, Shenzhen, Qingzhou, Suzhou, Yantai, Wuxi, Yinchuan, Jiangyin, Zhoushan, Tongliang, Nanchang, and Chizhou.

In May 2010, the city of Melbourne, Australia, launched its first bikesharing program, known as "Melbourne Bike Share" (with BIXI as the equipment provider). It currently operates with 600 bicycles and 50 docking stations, and users must abide by mandatory cycle helmet-wearing laws. Many bikesharing commentators speculate that these mandatory helmet laws have hindered the success of Melbourne's program, as helmet laws tend to deter casual cyclists.

Business Models, Impacts, and Lessons Learned from Third-Generation Bikesharing Systems

The success of third-generation programs has made it the most prominent bikesharing model worldwide. Furthermore, its successes have increased bikesharing markets to include a growing number of bikesharing vendors, providers, service models, and technologies.

Business Models and Vendors

Bikesharing providers range from local governments to transportation agencies, advertising companies, for-profit groups, and nonprofit groups (DeMaio 2009). Bikesharing is funded through advertising, self-funding, user fees, municipalities, and public-private partnerships (CityRyde 2009). Table 9.3 provides an overview of bikesharing business models and providers.

Table 9.3
Bikesharing providers and business models

Provider	Standard operating model	Program example
Advertising company	Provide bikesharing services in exchange for rights to advertise on city street furniture and billboards	• SmartBike (US) • Cyclocity (France)
Public transportation agencies	Provide bikesharing services under the guidance of a public authority to enhance the public transportation system	• Hangzhou Public Bicycle (China) • Call a Bike (Germany)
Local governments/ public authority	Directly design and operate a bikesharing program for the well-being of cities or a local government purchases bikesharing services that are provided by others	• City Bikes (Denmark) • Nubija (South Korea) • YouBike (Taiwan) • Shanghai Public Bicycle (China)
For-profit	Provide profitable bikesharing services with minimal government involvement	• Nextbike (Germany)
Nonprofit	Provide bikesharing services under the support of public agencies or councils	• BIXI (Canada) • Hourbike (UK) • Wuhan Public Bicycle (China)

The most prominent funding sources for third-generation bikesharing are municipalities and advertising partnerships (in which advertising companies provide bikesharing services in exchange for advertising rights on city street furniture and billboards). In Barcelona, Bicing funds bikesharing through advertising, but it also uses revenue from parking fees (i.e., parking meters) to cover the costs. According to Midgley (2009b), local governments operate 27 percent of European bikesharing systems. In addition, JCDecaux and Clear Channel—the two biggest outdoor advertising companies—operate 23 percent and 16 percent of bikesharing programs, respectively. Public agencies also are becoming an increasingly important provider of bikesharing programs. As mentioned earlier, a public transportation agency operates the Hangzhou bikesharing system under local government guidance. Furthermore, nonprofit bikesharing programs, which typically require public support at the startup stage, are likely to remain a prominent model for the foreseeable future.

At present, major bikesharing vendors include JCDecaux, Clear Channel Adshel, BIXI, Véolia Transportation, Cemusa, and B-Cycle (City-Ryde 2009). Examples of other providers include Nextbike, OYBike, B-igloo, and Domoblue. Several major bikesharing systems include BIXI in Canada, Public Bike System Company (PBSC) in the United States, Bicincittà by Comunicare in Italy, and Cyclocity by JCDecaux in France (Midgley 2009a). Furthermore, increasing use of advanced technologies in third-generation bikesharing has led to a growing market for technology vendors. IT-based systems became popular after the largest outdoor advertising company, Clear Channel, launched SmartBike in Rennes, France. Other companies that provide automated IT-based systems include Biceberg (underground bicycle parking); BIXI Public Bike System (bicycles and bike station); Ebikeshare (bicycles and bike station); LeisureTec Bike Station (bicycle stations); Q I Systems CycleStation (kiosks and smartcards); Sekura-Byk (bicycle racks and smart card systems); and Urban Racks (bicycle racks) (International Bicycle Fund, n.d.).

Social and Environmental Impacts

At present, research on the environmental and social benefits of bikesharing, particularly before-and-after behavioral trends, is limited. However, many bikesharing programs have conducted user-based surveys that document program experience.

One impact of bikesharing is its potential to provide emission-free transportation. SmartBike, for instance, estimates that more than 50,000 SmartBike trips cover a total of 200,000 kilometers (km) per day throughout Europe, and USA SmartBike calculates that a car covering this same distance would produce 37,000 kilograms of carbon dioxide (CO_2) emissions per day (SmartBike 2008). With an average of 78,000 trips per day and approximately 20 minutes per trip, Vélib' users cover an estimated 312,000 km per day. A car covering this same distance would have produced approximately 57,720 kg of CO_2 per day. As of August 2009, BIXI users covered an estimated 3,612,799 km, which translates into 909,053 kg of reduced greenhouse gas (GHG) emissions. As of October 2009, the Hangzhou Public Bicycle Program generated 172,000 trips per day. With an average trip lasting approximately thirty minutes, Hangzhou program users covered an estimated 1,032,000 km per day. An automobile covering this same distance would produce 190,920 kg of emissions. If successful, these data suggest that increased bikesharing activity has the potential to yield notable GHG emission reductions. However, emission reductions are difficult to estimate. Factors such as bicycle redistribution systems and previous user behavior (i.e., not all bikesharing users were previously automobile users) may reduce emission reduction estimates.

Nevertheless, the potential of bikesharing programs to reduce vehicle emissions is promising when one considers current data on modal shifts. For instance, after the 2007 launch of Bicing in Barcelona, the city's bicycle modal share rose from 0.75 percent in 2005 to 1.76 percent in 2007 (Romero 2008). Following the 2007 launch of Vélib', the bicycle mode share in Paris increased from about 1 percent in 2001 to 2.5 percent in 2007 (Nadal 2007). Furthermore, a recent survey of SmartBike (Washington, D.C.; now Capital Bikeshare) members found that bikesharing attracted nearly 16 percent of individuals who would otherwise have used personal vehicles for trip making (District of Columbia Department of Transportation 2009). Vélo'v in Lyon, France, reports that bicycle use replaced 7 percent of trips that would otherwise have been made by private vehicles (Bührmann 2007). In Paris, 20 percent of Vélib' users also reported using personal vehicles less frequently (The Vélib' Letter 2008).

Although few studies evaluate behavioral shifts, available data suggest notable changes. For example, during the first year of Vélo'v, Lyon documented a 44 percent increase in bicycle riding (Bührmann 2007). Ninety-six percent were new users who had not previously bicycled in the Lyon city center. In addition, bicycle riding in Paris also increased by 70 percent with the launch of Vélib'.

The growth and evolution of bikesharing programs worldwide has led to increased public awareness of bikesharing and its potential social, environmental, financial, and health-based benefits. Along with increased bikesharing awareness, public perception of bicycling as a transportation mode also has evolved. A 2008 Vélib' survey, for instance, found that 89 percent of program users agreed that Vélib' made it easier to travel through Paris. According to SmartBike, nearly 79 percent of respondents reported that bikesharing use in Washington, D.C., was faster or more convenient than other options. In Montreal, the initial public reaction to BIXI was skeptical. However, the heavy presence of BIXI bicycles has led Montreal residents to embrace the new system. In general, cities that have implemented successful bikesharing programs appear to have improved the image of bicycling as a viable transportation mode. Given the early and limited impact data, more research is needed on the social and environmental benefits of bikesharing.

Lessons Learned

The last forty-six years of bikesharing planning, implementation, and operations have led to a range of lessons learned. In this section, we address six key lessons learned: (1) bicycle theft and vandalism, (2) bicycle redistribution, (3) information systems, (4) insurance and liability considerations, (5) role of supportive infrastructure and partnerships (e.g., bike-transit connection), and (6) prelaunch considerations.

Bicycle Theft and Vandalism

Early bikesharing programs learned that user anonymity created a system prone to bicycle theft. Third-generation bikesharing introduced electronic smartcards to access bicycles from their racks. Smartcards record user identification information as well as bike usage (e.g., time, duration, location, kilometers). This improvement solved previous issues of user anonymity and facilitated bicycle tracking, which reduced bike theft and vandalism. Despite such innovations, a 2009 study of Vélib' reported that since its launch in 2007, 7,800 bicycles had disappeared and another 11,600 bicycles had been vandalized. High rates of theft raise concerns because Vélib' bicycles are expensive. Indeed, it currently costs the program €400 (US$519) to replace each bicycle. Although existing technologies such as global positioning systems (GPS) and radio frequency identification tracking developments can greatly decrease bicycle theft, such technology increases implementation costs. In contrast to Vélib', Hangzhou's bikesharing system and BIXI in Montreal have experienced low theft and vandalism rates. To curb theft and vandalism, Hangzhou's system employs inexpensive bikes (400 RMB, or US$60). A high density of bicycles—free for the first hour—makes cycling more convenient, which can decrease the need to steal a bicycle. To curb the impact of vandalism, BIXI allocates 8–9 percent of its budget to address theft. By the end of 2009, less than 3 percent of BIXI's budget to address vandalism and theft had been used (Crivello 2009). Overall, emerging fourth-generation models should consider more robust bicycles that include more effective locking mechanisms to further deter theft.

Bicycle Redistribution

Vélib's experience highlights the need for bicycle redistribution (i.e., bicycles must be redistributed to key demand locations frequently after use). To manage its 20,600 bicycles, Vélib' uses twenty natural-gas-powered vehicles to transport bikes from one station to another. As bikesharing programs grow and cover larger areas, emerging systems must find ways to address redistribution issues that have been raised in Vélib's experience. For instance, BIXI and Hangzhou also employ trucks to redistribute bicycles. In addition, BIXI is redesigning redistribution trucks to include on-board computers that can provide drivers with real-time information on bicycle stations to facilitate a speedier and more efficient response to bicycle shortages and station overcrowding. As cities launch larger programs, it is important that emerging fourth-generation systems (described in the following section) incorporate technological improvements for bicycle redistribution.

Information Systems

One of the most revolutionary changes introduced by third-generation bikesharing programs is the use of real-time information systems. Today, the majority of third-generation programs provide users with real-time information on station parking and bicycle availability through the Internet (e.g., an individual program website or websites such as Google Maps) by directing text messages to mobile phones or phone-based hotlines. Such technologies should continue to be improved and be included in current and future bikesharing programs to facilitate a more efficient and user-friendly system.

Insurance and Liability Considerations

The growth of bikesharing programs also has raised questions regarding insurance and liability. For instance, helmet use is not mandatory for most bikesharing programs, which may conflict with insurance liability laws. As of 2007, Vélib' reported an estimated six fatalities. In contrast, Nextbike has encountered three accidents (user injuries), and BIXI and Hangzhou each had one accident in 2009. The authors are aware of two programs that currently provide insurance for users: Hangzhou and Bicing. In the case of Hangzhou bikesharing, the service covers any injury that occurs due to bikesharing use (Tao 2009). Bicing provides public liability insurance, which includes all damage or harm resulting from the service (such as equipment and users) to a third party. This policy also covers harm to users. At present, the main obstacle to insurance coverage is high cost.

Role of Supportive Infrastructure and Partnerships

Overall, a comprehensive city bikesharing strategy—from cycling infrastructure to public transit connections—is needed to encourage bikesharing growth. Cities that have successfully implemented bikesharing programs have also expanded their cycling infrastructure. For instance, bike lanes in the city of La Rochelle grew from 130 km in 2003 to 150 km in 2005 (Midgley 2009a). Bike lanes in Paris expanded from 122 km in 1998 to 399 km in 2007 (Pucher, Dill, and Handy 2010). The city of Barcelona had less than 10 km of bike lanes in 1990, which increased to 155 km of bike paths by 2008 (Romero 2008). In Germany, cycling networks increased from 12,911 km in 1976 to 31,236 km in 1996 (Pucher and Buehler 2008).

Bikesharing partnerships are also crucial to encouraging bikesharing growth. Typical partnerships are established between bikesharing programs and public transit. For instance, bike parking is often made available at metro and subway stations, near bus stops, train stations, and other forms of public transportation. "Call a Bike" in Germany not only places bicycles at rail stations, but also offers financial incentives to users with a Bahn rail card. Partnerships also include the use of linked smartcards that allow users to access various transportation modes with a single linked transit card. This approach encourages multimodal connections to complete a trip. However, a fully integrated linked transit card is hard to establish because it requires various public transportation departments to sync their schedules, establish connecting facilities, and create a single pricing scheme.

A comprehensive bikesharing strategy (i.e., safety campaigns, linked transit options, cycling policies) is crucial in promoting bikesharing's current and future growth.

Prelaunch Considerations

Bikesharing programs around the world agree that successful systems are those that address the specific needs of their users and market segments prior to and after deployment. Programs such as BIXI have found that bicycle availability is not easy to predict. BIXI addresses this issue by employing mobile bicycle stations that can be relocated according to usage patterns. BIXI also has identified prelaunch marketing as a critical action for success. "Hourbike" (in the United Kingdom) has noted pricing as key to establishing a profitable business model. Furthermore, the implementation of incremental usage fees encourages bicycle users to plan short trips to avoid high fees.

The city of Paris implemented other prelaunch strategies that have encouraged bikesharing success. For example, prior to Vélib's launch, the city's mayor lowered vehicle speed limits, built more bike paths, and changed street directions by creating more one-way streets. These modifications helped reduce private vehicle traffic by 20 percent.

Spain established a national funding program known as the Spanish Institute for Energy Diversification and Saving (IDEA). As part of this effort, various Spanish cities received funding and support for bikesharing. In Germany, the department of transportation also established a national funding program to promote bikesharing efforts. In 2009, fifteen funding awards were granted for bikesharing programs.

To address other prelaunch concerns—including bicycle flow, number of docking stations needed, and bicycle redistribution practices—mathematical tools and models have now been created (see Shu et al. 2010). Such tools allow cities to evaluate various bikesharing scenarios to assess program viability before launch and during operation.

As third-generation bikesharing markets continue to expand worldwide, current models of implementation, operations, and technology provide key insights for future systems. In the next section, the authors propose a fourth bikesharing generation: "demand-responsive, multimodal systems."

The Future

Advances and shortcomings of previous and existing bikesharing models have contributed to a growing body of knowledge of this shared mode. Such experiences are making way for an emerging fourth-generation bikesharing model or demand-responsive, multimodal systems. These systems build upon the third generation and emphasize (1) flexible, clean docking stations (or no docking stations, e.g., German railways); (2) bicycle redistribution innovations; (3) smartcard integration with other transportation modes, such as public transit and carsharing; and (4) technological advances (e.g., GPS tracking, touchscreen kiosks, solar power, electric bikes). The main components of fourth-generation bikesharing are the bicycle, docking station, kiosk/user interface, bicycle distribution system, and linked public transit smartcard.

BIXI in Canada marks the beginning of bikesharing's fourth generation. One of BIXI's major innovations includes mobile bicycle docking stations, which allow stations to be transferred to different locations according to usage patterns and user demands. Another improvement that BIXI offers is the use of solar-powered stations, which further reduce emissions and the need to secure access to an energy grid to support operations.

Fourth-generation systems also might consider omitting fixed docking stations and opting for flex stations in which users employ mobile phone technology and street furniture for bicycle pickup and dropoff. With such a system, users receive a code on their mobile phone to unlock bicycles. Users leave bicycles at major intersections and inform the program where the bicycle is locked. This approach allows bicycles to be available throughout an entire city and minimizes the amount of infrastructure needed to operate a program.

Call a Bike in Germany operates a hybrid system in which flex and fixed stations are used. Between March and May 2010, the city of Berlin launched a pilot program that consisted of fixed and flex stations within a defined parking area. Buffalo Carshare is set to launch a "Social Bicycles" (SoBI) pilot program in August 2012 whereby users will be able to call or use a smartphone application to locate a bicycle. If successful, reducing the need for bicycle docking stations may allow bikesharing to be more accessible in cities around the world, as it would dramatically decrease the cost of starting and operating a program. However, flex stations can pose problems, such as difficulty locating bicycles because they are not confined to defined stations or hubs.

Another area of improvement for fourth-generation systems is bicycle redistribution innovations (DeMaio 2009). Vélib's use of specially designed vehicles for bicycle relocation represents a first step toward addressing this issue. However, employing larger, designated vehicles for bicycle transportation increases implementation costs and is not an emission-free solution. In the future, bikesharing services will continue to deploy more efficient redistribution methods (e.g., automated technologies that facilitate demand-responsive bike relocation). Bikesharing models may also incentivize user-based redistribution (i.e., the rider performs bicycle redistribution) by employing demand-based pricing in which members receive a price reduction or credit for parking bicycles at empty docking locations.

A third feature of fourth-generation systems is the seamless integration of bikesharing with public transportation and other alternative modes, such as taxis and carsharing (for more information on carsharing, see Shaheen, Cohen, and Chung 2009; Shaheen and Cohen 2007; Millard-Ball et al. 2005) via smartcards, which support numerous transportation modes on a single card. Launched in 2009 in La Rochelle, France, Yélo uses a smartcard that is fully integrated with the public transportation system. In 2010, the city of Guangzhou, China, launched the "Guangzhou Public Bike Initiative." This system is also fully integrated with the city's bus rapid transit (BRT) and metro stations (Shaheen et al. 2011). However, creating a program that coordinates various forms of transportation on a single card is challenging and costly, as it requires multiple agency involvement.

Another area for improvement is bicycle security, which can be addressed by ongoing technological advancements. For instance, GPS integration could deter bike theft and facilitate bike recovery. However, GPS units are costly and can potentially increase financial losses if bikes with built-in GPS are vandalized or stolen. Finally, to target a larger scope of bikesharing users, fourth-generation systems may be more likely to incorporate electric bicycles, which enable longer-distance trips; encourage cycling on steeper hills and slopes; and lessen physical exertion requirements, particularly when users are commuting or making work trips in business attire.

Conclusion

Bikesharing emerged in Europe as a transportation mode forty-six years ago. Since its inception, bikesharing systems have evolved to address geographic and technological demands. Bikesharing has expanded to include five continents: Europe, North America, South America, Asia, and Australia. Bikesharing growth has undergone three evolutionary stages including: first-generation White Bikes (or free bike systems), second-generation coin-deposit systems, and third-generation IT-based systems. Building upon third-generation systems, the authors also propose an emerging fourth-generation system: demand-responsive, multimodal systems.

Notable growth in third-generation bikesharing programs has led to a diversity of business models ranging from advertising to nonprofits. Despite limited research on the social and environmental benefits of bikesharing, recent surveys document (1) reduced auto use, (2) behavioral shifts toward increased bicycle use for daily mobility, and (3) a growing perception of the bicycle as a convenient transportation mode.

Other important benefits include GHG emission reduction and individual and citywide cost savings. Operating and maintaining personal automobiles includes fuel costs, insurance and registration fees, and maintenance-related expenses. In contrast, bikesharing programs cover bicycle purchase, maintenance, and storage or parking expenses. For cities, it is less costly to implement bicycle infrastructure than vehicle infrastructure. However, programs such as Vélib' have demonstrated that bicycle theft and vandalism can offset bikesharing cost savings.

Other benefits include positive health effects due to bicycle use (Pucher and Dijkstra 2003; Pucher and Buehler 2010). However, health benefits are often overlooked due to safety concerns. At present, cities with higher numbers of motorists experience increased cycling accidents. Bikesharing programs can help reduce traffic congestion and vehicle fuel use. However, obstacles such as limited trip length, lack of cargo space, exposure to weather conditions, and user issues (i.e., limited height adjustment on bicycles) reduce the number of potential bikesharing users.

As bikesharing continues to expand, lessons from previous and current bikesharing programs have led to a greater understanding of implementation and operational procedures. Indeed, this understanding has facilitated the success of bikesharing programs in cities with varying needs and characteristics. For instance, bikesharing has proven successful in Hangzhou—a city with a developed cycling culture and high levels of cycling prior to bikesharing introduction. Conversely, Mexico City—a city with historically low levels of cycling—has also launched a successful program.

Bikesharing has addressed a range of goals. For instance, bikesharing was launched to address high emission levels in China and traffic congestion in Mexico City. In Montreal, it was deployed to complement existing transportation options. Despite city size or cycling levels, the introduction of various bikesharing technologies, business models, and varying operational costs means that developed and developing cities have more options to launch a program that addresses issues and needs specific to their city. However, more in-depth understanding and research on bikesharing are needed, including bikesharing's social and environmental benefits; a better understanding of the environments in which it works best (e.g., cities in which biking is not already popular as a daily mode, where private storage is limited, and the potential in developing countries); sustainable business models; operations; advanced technology applications (i.e., the potential of electric bicycles); and the role of public policies in supporting its ongoing growth.

Acknowledgments

The California Department of Transportation, Honda Motor Company, and the Mineta Transportation Institute funed this research. The authors would like to thank Melissa Chung for her assistance in gathering data and Gian-Carlo Crivello (BIXI), Xuejun Tao (Hangzhou Public Bicycle System), Mareike Rauchhaus (Nextbike), and Tim Caswell (Hourbike) for their expert interviews.

Note

Perhaps more than any other aspect of cycling, bikesharing is rapidly changing, with increases in the number and size of bikesharing systems as well as changes in system and vendor names. The information in this chapter reflects the situation at the time of writing in early 2012.

References

Bonnette, Brittany. 2007. The Implementation of a Public-Use Bicycle Program in Philadelphia. Urban Studies senior thesis. University of Pennsylvania. http://www.bikesharephiladelphia.org/PDF%20DOC/PUBBonnetteThesis.pdf.

Bührmann, Sebastian. 2007. *New Seamless Mobility Services: Public Bicycles Policy Notes (NICHES Policy Note 4)*. Cologne: Rupprecht Consult Forschung and Beratung GmbH.

CityRyde. 2009. *Bicycle Sharing Systems Worldwide: Selected Case Studies*.

Crivello, Gian-Carlo. 2009. Telephone interview conducted by Stacey Guzman, October 29.

DeMaio, Paul. 2003. Smart Bikes: Public Transportation for the 21st Century. *Transportation Quarterly* 57 (1): 9–11.

DeMaio, Paul. 2009. Bike-Sharing: Its History, Models of Provision, and Future. *Journal of Public Transportation* 13 (4): 41–56.

District of Columbia Department of Transportation. 2009. SmartBike DC Survey Results. http://www.metrobike.net/index.php?s=file_download&id=29.

Gradinger, Kyle. 2007. The Evolution of Bike Sharing Programs. Bike Share Philadelphia. http://www.bikesharephiladelphia.org/learn/history/.

Hangzhou Public Transport Corporation. N.d. Hangzhou Public Bicycle. http://www.hzzxc.com.cn.

Home, Stewart. 1991. *The Assault on Culture: Utopian Currents from Lettrisme to Class War*. Edinburgh: AK Press.

International Bicycle Fund. N.d. Bicycle Parking & Storage Suppliers. http://www.ibike.org/engineering/parking-equipment.htm#High-Tech.

Jacobsen, Peter L. 2003. Safety in Numbers: More Walkers and Bicyclists, Safer Walking and Bicycling. *Injury Prevention* 9 (3): 205–209.

Midgley, Peter. 2009a. The Role of Smart Bike-Sharing Systems in Urban Mobility. *Journeys LTA Academy*, no. 2: 23–31.

Midgley, Peter. 2009b. Shared Smart Bicycle Schemes in European Cities. Global Transport Knowledge Partnership (gTKP). http://www.uncrd.or.jp/env/4th -regional-est-forum/Presentations/28_PS4_gTKP.pdf.

Millard-Ball, Adam, Gail Murray, Jessica Ter Schure, Christine Fox, and Jon Burkhardt. 2005. Car-Sharing: Where and How It Succeeds. Transit Cooperative Research Program Report 108. Washington, DC: Transportation Research Board of the National Academies.

Nadal, Luc. 2007. Bike Sharing Sweeps Paris Off Its Feet. Sustainable Transport. Institute for Transportation and Development Policy, No. 19: 8–12.

New Mobility Agenda. 2008. World City Bike Implementation Strategies: A New Mobility Advisory Brief. http://www.ecoplan.org/library/prospectus.pdf.

NYCDOT (New York City Department of Transportation). 2012. New York City Bike Share. New York: City of New York. www.nyc.gov/bikeshare/.

O'Keefe, Thomas, and Joe Keating. 2008. The Yellow Bike Story. http://c2.com/ybp/story.html.

Pucher, John, and Ralph Buehler. 2008. Cycling for Everyone: Lessons from Europe. *Transportation Research Record: Journal of the Transportation Research Board* 2074: 58–65.

Pucher, John, and Ralph Buehler. 2010. Walking and Cycling for Healthy Cities. *Built Environment* 36 (5): 391–414.

Pucher, John, and Lewis Dijkstra. 2003. Promoting Safe Walking and Cycling to Improve Public Health: Lessons from the Netherlands and Germany. *American Journal of Public Health* 93 (9): 1509–1516.

Pucher, John, Jennifer Dill, and Susan Handy. 2010. Infrastructure, Programs, and Policies to Increase Bicycling: An International Review. *Preventive Medicine* 50 (S1): 106–125.

Romero, Carlos. 2008. Spicycles in Barcelona. Spicycles Conference, Bucharest, Romania. http://spicycles.velo.info/Portals/0/FinalReports/Barcelona_Final _Report.ppt.

Shaheen, Susan A., and Adam P. Cohen. 2007. Growth in Worldwide Carsharing: An International Comparison. *Transportation Research Record: Journal of the Transportation Research Board* 1992:81–92.

Shaheen, Susan, Adam Cohen, and Melissa Chung. 2009. North American Carsharing: A Ten-Year Retrospective. *Transportation Research Record: Journal of the Transportation Research Board* 2110:35–44.

Shaheen, Susan, and Timothy Lipman. 2007. Reducing Greenhouse Gas Emissions and Fuel Consumption: Sustainable Approaches for Surface Transportation. *Journal of International Association of Traffic and Safety Sciences (IATSS) Research* 31 (1): 6–20.

Shaheen, Susan, Hua Zhang, Elliot Martin, and Stacey Guzman. 2011. Hangzhou Public Bicycle: Understanding Early Adoption and Behavioral Response to Bikesharing in Hangzhou, China. *Transportation Research Record. Journal of the Transportation Research Board* 2247: 33–41.

Shu, Jia, Mabel Chou, Qizhanag Liu, Chung-Piaw Teo, and I-Lin Wang. 2010. Bicycle-Sharing System: Deployment, Utilization, and the Value of Re-distribution. http://www.bschool.nus.edu.sg/Staff/bizteocp/BS2010.pdf.

SmartBike. 2008. *Facts*. http://www.smartbike.com/facts.

The Vélib' Letter. 2008. Today, We Know You Better! Newsletter 10. Tables in chapter 9. http://velib.centraldoc.com.

Tao, Xuejun. 2009. Telephone interview conducted by Hua Zhang, November 9.

10

Women and Cycling

Jan Garrard, Susan Handy, and Jennifer Dill

The use of bicycling as a mode of transportation varies markedly across countries and cities, as described in chapters 2, 12, 13, and 14, but there are also some striking variations across demographic groups. In bicycle-friendly cities and countries, cycling is an inclusive, population-wide activity that includes large numbers of children, seniors, and women. In contrast, in car-oriented cities with low levels of cycling, the majority of cyclists are young to middle-aged men. These demographic differences are especially striking for transportation cycling. In Australia and the United States, women constitute about one-third of recreational cyclists but only about one-quarter of commuter cyclists (Australian Sports Commission 2010; Pucher, Garrard, and Greaves 2011; Pucher et al. 2010).

Several explanations have been proposed to account for these marked gender differences in utilitarian cycling, including: activity preferences ("women just don't like cycling"); more serve-passenger trips (e.g., chauffeuring children); and greater concern about personal safety and traffic risks. These factors all help explain lower cycling among women. The question, however, remains: why do these factors appear to constrain women in low-cycling countries more than women in high-cycling countries? So strong is the association between cycling mode share of transportation and female rates of cycling that some observers have suggested that gender equity in cycling is an indicator of a cycling-friendly environment (Baker 2009). Similar patterns are also observed for children (Garrard 2009) and older adults (Pucher and Dijkstra 2003; Pucher and Buehler 2010), though these are not as well documented as the gender differences in cycling.

This chapter documents the benefits of cycling for women, describes patterns of female participation in cycling geographically and temporally, explores reasons for the highly variable rates of female cycling, and discusses strategies for establishing cycling as a viable transportation option for women.

Benefits of Cycling for Women

Replacing car trips with cycling trips delivers multiple benefits for health, the environment, transportation efficiency, and community livability (Forsyth, Krizek, and Rodríguez 2009; Giles-Corti et al. 2010). For women, cycling to work has been shown to significantly improve physical performance (de Geus, Joncheere, and Meeusen 2009) and to reduce the risk of all-cause mortality (Matthews et al. 2007), cancer mortality (Matthews et al. 2007), coronary heart disease[1] (Hu et al. 2007; Hamer and Chida 2008), colon cancer, possibly breast cancer (Steindorf et al. 2003; Matthews et al. 2007), and weight gain (Lusk et al. 2010).

Although many of the physiological health benefits of cycling are similar for men and women, women stand to gain more from improved conditions that support utility cycling because in many countries they are less likely to be adequately active than men (Sisson and Katzmarzyk 2008). Many women do not enjoy or do not have the time or resources to participate in structured sport and exercise activities (Graco, Garrard, and Jasper 2009; Kavanagh et al. 2007). When physical activity is a "nonathletic," habitual part of everyday life that does not require additional exercise time, women are more likely to achieve physical activity parity with men. In the Netherlands, where men and women cycle for transportation at comparable levels, cycling is the activity that contributes most to the total time spent by adults on moderate-to-vigorous physical activity (van Kempen et al. 2010).

The importance of incidental physical activity in the form of active transportation has been demonstrated most convincingly for young people, particularly adolescents. Studies in the United Kingdom report that adolescent girls who travel actively to school are several times more likely to meet physical activity guidelines than those who do not (Smith et al. 2010; Voss and Sandercock 2010). In the study by Voss and Sandercock (2010), the greatest benefits were for cycling compared with walking and for girls compared with boys: girls were nearly eight times more likely to be classified as "fit" if they cycled to school, after adjusting for other factors.

In addition to the physical health benefits of utility cycling, women may benefit more than men from balanced transportation systems that include provision for accessible, safe cycling. Women's travel patterns differ in key respects from those of men. For example, based on data from the 2002 national travel survey in Germany, in multiperson households with children, 13.5 percent of the trips undertaken by women who worked full time were to serve other passengers (usually children); the comparable figure for men in full-time employment was 8.5 percent of trips (Nobis and Lenz 2005). In the United States, female workers with children in the household made more trips per day than male workers with children did, though they traveled fewer miles. In two-worker households, women were twice as likely as men to pick up or drop off children during their commute (McGuckin and Nakamoto 2005). When conditions preclude children and older adults traveling independently, including by bicycle, it is more often women who serve the travel needs of other family and community members (Gossen and Purvis 2005). Consequently, when cycling-friendly conditions support independent bicycle trips by children and other dependents, women are the principal beneficiaries of a reduction in these particular household responsibilities.

Cycling Benefits for Women: A Historical Perspective

Although the health benefits of cycling for women are now clear, many experts argued the opposite when women first began bicycling more than a century ago. The introduction of the safety bicycle in the 1890s made the bicycle more accessible to everyone, particularly women, when compared to the highwheelers, which were ridden primarily by men. The prospect of more women riding bicycles prompted a public debate on the health benefits or harms of women cycling. Garvey (1995, 74) explains that "nearly every book on bicycling from the period includes a discussion, citing medical authorities, of bicycling's effects on women's health."

The health reasons given against women cycling fell into two broad areas. First, the physical effort was too strenuous for women—a reason that was also given for why women should not participate in other exercise or sport (Garvey 1995). Bicycling was purported to have negative effects on a woman's reproductive system, as well as leading to gout, tuberculosis, epilepsy, and other ailments (Strange and Brown 2002). The second line of argument related to sexual health. Fears that women would experience orgasm while sitting astride the bicycle saddle were detailed in several medical journals at the time. Other publications, however, included medical arguments supporting the health benefits of moderate amounts of bicycling for women, who were often characterized as being weak and invalid, sometimes suggesting that cycling could improve their fitness for motherhood (Garvey 1995).

Historically, cycling has also been seen as contributing to women's emancipation. During the bicycle "craze" of the late 1800s, bicycling was directly linked to women's freedom and independence. However, at the time, this was often perceived as a threat, with many organizations actively trying to discourage or prevent women from cycling (Herlihy 2004). Strange and Brown (2002, 616) explain that "the bicycle posed a challenge to the doctrine of separate spheres by offering women a way to escape the physical confines of the home."

Some women advocates at the time sought to assuage fears by suggesting that cycling could be feminine and reinforce traditional female roles; others saw the bicycle as a tool for reform. Elizabeth Cady Stanton, a leading figure in the early women's rights movement in the United States, saw the bicycle as a reason for dress reform, explaining that it was ridiculous and unnatural for women to be wearing dresses and tight corsets while riding. Her arguments were not just about dress, however. Stanton argued that the bicycle would inspire courage, self-respect, and self-reliance in women (Strange and Brown 2002). Prominent nineteenth-century American women's rights advocate Susan B. Anthony was another proponent of women's cycling, explaining to the *New York World* in 1896: "Let me tell you what I think of bicycling. I think it has done more to emancipate women than anything else in the world. It gives women a feeling of freedom and self-reliance. I stand and rejoice every time I see a woman ride by on a wheel . . . the picture of free, untrammeled womanhood" (Harper 1983, 859).

The notion that the bicycle helps women gain independence and equality is still relevant today in many developing countries, where the bicycle may provide access to health care or other daily needs, though this is still seen as a threat by some men (Welke and Allen 2004).

Patterns of Cycling for Women

Geographic Variations

The association between bicycle mode share of everyday travel and female participation in utility cycling is evident nationally, as well as for cities, regions, and local areas. In countries such as the United States and Canada that have low overall bicycle mode share of trips, the majority of cyclists are male. In contrast, countries with relatively high bicycle mode share have few (in some cases, opposite) gender differences in cycling (see figure 10.1). Similar patterns occur across cities (see figure 10.2) and within local jurisdictions (see figure 10.3). In Melbourne, Australia, 2006 census data for the journey to work indicate that inner-city areas tend to have relatively high rates of both cycling and female participation in cycling (figure 10.3). These areas tend to have better cycling infrastructure and close proximity to the central business district,

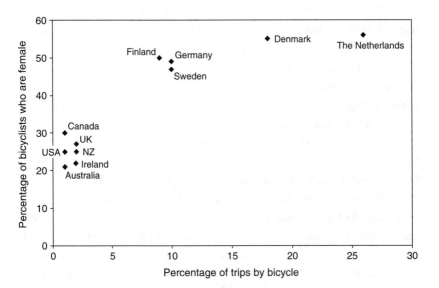

Figure 10.1
Bicycle mode share of trips and percentage of female cyclists, country-level data. *Sources:* Pucher and Buehler 2008, 2010; Geddes 2009.

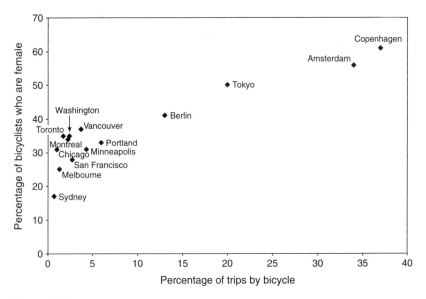

Figure 10.2
Bicycle mode share of trips and percentage of female cyclists, large cities. *Note:*
Data for Tokyo include bicycle-only and bicycle-train trips. *Sources:* See chapters
12–14; MLITT 2008.

features that are both associated with higher rates of commuter cycling
(Krizek, Forsyth, and Baum 2009).

Similar patterns occur in the relatively high-cycling cities in the United
States. In the city of Portland, Oregon, cyclist counts show that locations
with the highest share of women cyclists (40–45%) tend to be closer to
the city center where total bicycle counts are higher, whereas those with
the lowest shares (10–15%) are farther from the city center and/or in
hilly areas where the total counts are lower (City of Portland 2010). In
Davis, California, which has one of the highest bicycle mode shares in
the United States (see chapter 12), the gender differences in bicycling are
significant but much less than in the United States as a whole. High
proportions of females in the general population report cycling regularly
(50%) (Emond, Tang, and Handy 2009). Nearly 57 percent of students,
faculty, and staff at the University of California at Davis who live in
Davis cycle to campus (Lovejoy 2010). Among high school students, a
high proportion of both girls (30%) and boys (43.4%) bicycle to school
(Emond and Handy 2011).

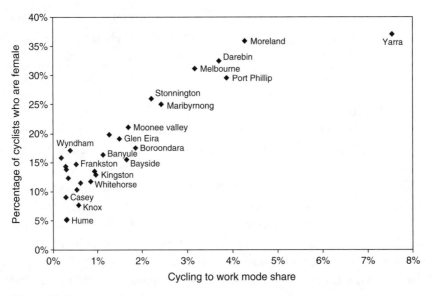

Figure 10.3
Bicycle mode share of commuter trips and percentage of female cyclists by local government area in the Melbourne Metropolitan Area. *Sources:* Analysis of Australian Bureau of Statistics, 2006 Census conducted for VicRoads by Cameron Munro, Sinclair Knight Merz Pty Ltd.

Gender differences in cycling also vary by age. In low-cycling countries such as the United States, cycling declines markedly among adolescent girls, followed by small increases among young adult women, and then further declines among older women (Sibley 2010). Data from Dublin, Ireland, demonstrate the dramatic drop in cycling among adolescent girls: 25.3 percent of 5- to 12-year-olds, but only 5.5 percent of 13- to 18-year-olds who cycle are female (Geddes 2009). Bonham and Wilson (2011) note that women in low-cycling countries tend to move in and out of cycling at various stages of their lives. In contrast, women in high-cycling countries such as the Netherlands move seamlessly between cycling as a child, adolescent, young adult, and older adult (Netherlands Ministry of Transport, Public Works, and Water Management 2009).

Gender differences in cycling for different types of trips also vary internationally. Although high-cycling countries have relatively high rates of commuter bicycling for both men and women, women represent even higher proportions of noncommuting trips. In Tokyo, for example, men and women both report high rates of weekly cycling—68 and 65.8 percent, respectively—but women are only half as likely as men to bicycle to work—14 versus 29 percent—and are more likely to cycle for non-commuting trips (MLITT 2008).

Trends over Time

Trends in female cycling over time also vary widely by location. For example, household travel surveys conducted in 2001 and 2009 in the United States showed that cycling (for thirty minutes or more) increased slightly for men (+0.2%) but decreased for women (−0.1%) (Pucher et al. 2011). In Germany, the proportion of the population who reported any cycling on a travel day increased from 12.1 to 14.1 between 2002 and 2008, with similar increases for men and women (Buehler et al. 2011). There is, however, some evidence that increasing rates of cycling may be associated with greater levels of cycling among women over time, and vice versa. For example, intercept counts in Portland, Oregon, show that the share of cyclists who are women increased from 21 percent in 1992 to 30 percent in 2010—a time period during which overall levels of cycling increased significantly (City of Portland 2010). In contrast, between 1986 and 2006 in Ireland, the overall decline in bicycle trips to work, school, or college was accompanied by a decrease in the proportion of female cyclists (Geddes 2009); see figure 10.4.

Understanding Female Participation in Cycling

Many factors have been proposed as explanations for the large gender difference in utility cycling in the low-cycling countries. Although direct evidence of their impact is slim, much indirect evidence points to a number of possible factors.

Do Women Dislike Cycling?

Transportation researchers have examined a range of individual and environmental factors that influence travel mode choices, such as cost, convenience, and accessibility. Less commonly researched is the extent to which travel mode choices are influenced by people's attitudes toward the different modes. That is, do people find the activity of driving, walking, cycling, or using a train or bus inherently enjoyable or unpleas-

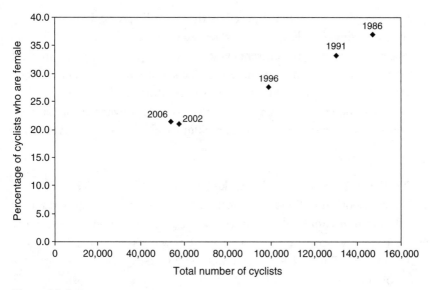

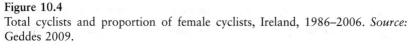

Figure 10.4
Total cyclists and proportion of female cyclists, Ireland, 1986–2006. *Source:*
Geddes 2009.

ant, and do these feelings affect their choice of mode? If so, then gender
differences in these attitudes could help to explain gender difference in
cycling.

In fact, surveys conducted in the United States and Australia indicate
somewhat mixed attitudes toward cycling, with men's attitudes tending
to be slightly more positive than women's (NHTSA 2008; Emond, Tang,
and Handy 2009; Garrard et al. 2006). In a study of six small US cities,
for example, women were somewhat less likely than men to agree with
the statement "I like riding a bike" (Emond, Tang, and Handy 2009).
When the same question was asked of residents in the Portland, Oregon,
region, gender differences in attitudes toward bicycling were more substantial, though also more positive than in the study of six small US cities
(author's data).

The degree to which differences in women's and men's attitudes
toward bicycling contribute to gender differences in utility cycling is
unclear. Two issues in particular make interpretation of the available
evidence difficult: (1) the two-way interaction between behaviors and
attitudes and (2) the fact that women's attitudes to cycling are likely to

vary according to the type of cycling, that is, utility, recreational or sport/ fitness cycling (as discussed further later in this chapter). Additional research is required, but current evidence appears to provide little support for the possibility that an inherent dislike of cycling among women accounts for the large gender differences in utility cycling in low-cycling countries and cities, though less positive attitudes toward cycling among women than men may be a contributing factor in the low-cycling countries.

Do Women's Responsibilities Make Cycling More Difficult?

The transportation literature consistently documents that as a result of differing household roles, women have tighter time budgets and more complex travel patterns and make more serve-passenger trips than men (Gossen and Purvis 2005). Less well researched is the impact of these factors on utility cycling.

Childcare and household responsibilities are major contributors to gender differences in time use. Australian women spend thirty minutes more each day completing domestic duties than men and spend twice as much time on the direct child care of children aged fourteen years or less, even when both parents work full time (ABS 2008). In the United States, among married parents, women spent more time on childcare and household activities than men, and regardless of employment status, women were more likely to spend some time in travel related to their children: 40 percent of women versus 23 percent of men (Bureau of Labor Statistics 2008). Increased workforce participation in the absence of a commensurate reduction in time spent on household work and child care makes women more time-constrained than men, possibly making cycling a less attractive option for them.

Of course, the relevance of time as a constraint on women's use of the bicycle for transportation depends on whether bicycle trips actually take longer than comparable trips by car (see chapter 4). These differences, too, vary geographically. In the Netherlands, many of the daily trips undertaken by women are quicker by bicycle than by car, making cycling the mode of choice in terms of travel time (see chapters 12 and 13). Although this might also be the case in at least some low-cycling countries and cities, there is a lack of data available on mode-specific trip times for the daily trips commonly taken by women. Nevertheless, favorable bike/car travel times may help to explain higher rates of bicycle trips by women in high-cycling countries.

An additional but related factor is that due to differing household and work roles, women's travel patterns are often more complex than those of men. Women are more likely to trip chain and to take passengers— children or older adult parents—to their destinations. This pattern, too, may make cycling less viable. A US survey of women cyclists found that 19 percent cited the inability to carry children or other passengers as a factor that discouraged them from cycling for transportation, compared to only 7 percent of men (Scheider 2010).

At first glance, therefore, it appears that women's household and work responsibilities may constrain their use of the bicycle for transportation, though these factors appear to be less of a constraint in regions that have high rates of female utility cycling, including during the child-rearing years (van Kempen et al. 2010). As discussed in chapter 5, different styles of bicycles and bicycle use (as seen in high-cycling countries) make it easier for women to travel by bicycle with children and to carry shopping and other goods by bicycle.

Another possibility is that women may have more limited access to motor vehicles, making nonmotorized travel more of a necessity than a choice. However, in developed countries, gender differences in access to cars are small and more likely to be found in older cohorts of women (Lehner-Lierz 2003). Women surveyed in the United States who cycled in the past month were equally likely as men to have another mode of transportation available for their trip (86%) (NHTSA 2008). It is there-fore unlikely that gender differences in access to a motor vehicle explain high levels of utility cycling among women in countries such as the Netherlands, Denmark, Germany, and Japan or low levels of utility cycling among women in countries such as the United States.

Are Women More Constrained than Men by Personal Safety Concerns and Traffic Risks Associated with Cycling?

Gender differences in concerns about personal safety and traffic risks associated with cycling might also play a role, even though data suggest that actual traffic risks are not greater for women. Of the cyclists sur-veyed nationally in the United States in 2002, 3 percent of the women were injured while riding a bicycle in the past two years, compared to 4 percent of men (NHTSA 2008). A study that tracked bicycle commuters in Portland, Oregon, did not find different rates of trauma between men and women (Hoffman et al. 2010). Neither of these studies, however, controlled for distance cycled. An analysis of cycling injuries in the United Kingdom found that after adjusting for distance cycled, men were more likely to be injured than women and that the relative risk for men was greater for injuries of greater severity (Knowles et al. 2009). Thus, in terms of actual risk of injury, it appears that women are no more likely to be injured while cycling than men and may in fact be at lower risk, particularly for the more severe injuries.

Nevertheless, numerous studies indicate that in low-cycling countries, concerns about cycling safety are a major constraint on cycling and a greater constraint for women than men. Women are both more concerned about safety and more affected by safety concerns. The following research findings, principally from low-cycling, English-speaking countries, indicate that women's concerns about safety while cycling include traffic safety, aggressive driving, and personal security.

Data from the UK National Travel Survey indicate that a high proportion of adults are concerned about the safety of cycling but women are more likely to express concerns about safety (85%) than men (61%) (cited in Geddes 2009). In a survey in Victoria, Australia, women reported significantly higher levels of concern than men about "cycling in traffic" and "aggression from motorists" (Garrard, Crawford, and Hakman 2006). A UK study reported that 72 percent of noncycling women felt that cycling in traffic is frightening (Basford et al. 2002), with a Dublin study finding that men are more "traffic tolerant" than women (Geddes 2009, 136). In a survey in six small US cities, women reported lower bicycling comfort and greater concerns about bicycling safety (Emond, Tang, and Handy 2009), both overall and for specific concerns (see figure 10.5). Although both men and women expressed the most concern about being hit by a car, women were over twice as likely as men to say that they were very concerned about being mugged or attacked or crashing because of road hazards.

Greater concerns over safety translate into greater barriers to cycling for women. In a random telephone survey of adults in Portland, Oregon, 52 percent of women cited "too much traffic" as a barrier to cycling more, compared to 34 percent of men (author's data). Aggressive driving

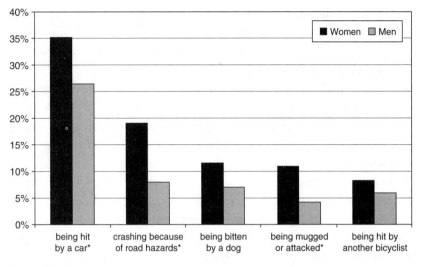

Figure 10.5
Percentage "very concerned" about potential hazards by gender, in six small US cities. *Note:* Asterisk (*) designates differences statistically significant at the 0.1 level. *Source:* Emond, Tang, and Handy 2009.

compounds gender differences in safety concerns about traffic. In the survey of cyclists in Victoria, Australia, women were more likely than men to report "aggression from motorists" as a constraint on cycling, even though men were more likely to have actually experienced harassment from motor vehicle occupants (Garrard, Crawford, and Hakman 2006). In another Australian survey, more women (46%) than men (38%) agreed that "aggressive drivers put me off cycling or walking" (Australian Associated Motor Insurers 2004).

Overall, these findings serve as a reminder that perceptions of risk may be as important as actual risks, particularly for women, and that "traffic risks" extend beyond risk of fatality or serious injury to include risk of "near misses" and harassment. Consequently, the concept of traffic risk as a barrier to cycling, particularly for women, might best be viewed as a "risk iceberg," with a small number of fatalities at the tip, followed by broadening layers of serious injuries, minor injuries, near misses, and harassment. In terms of risk assessment, which is often conceptualized as the product of potential harm and probability of occurrence (Kirch 2008), a large number of low-harm incidents can also contribute to substantially heightened risk concerns. The relative risk of fatality in low-cycling industrialized countries compared with high-cycling industrialized countries is lower than the relative risk for serious injury (Pucher and Buehler 2008, 2010; Garrard, Greaves, and Ellison 2010), so it may be that experiences and perceptions toward the base of the "risk iceberg" shape cycling behavior as much as, or possibly more than, the infrequent fatalities that form the tip of the iceberg.

Concerns about traffic appear to affect cycling behavior in terms of women choosing both not to cycle and, when they do cycle, to do so more cautiously than men. An observational study of commuter cyclists based on analysis of video recordings in Melbourne, Australia, found that women tended to cycle more cautiously than men, such as riding closer to the curb, less likely to use bike boxes at intersections, and less likely to merge through lanes of traffic to execute turns (Johnson 2010).

Safety concerns, particularly safety from motor vehicle traffic, also appear to affect women's bicycle route preferences and choices. Women in the survey of six small US cities reported being significantly less comfortable than men on all facility types except for quiet streets (Emond, Tang, and Handy 2009); their comfort level on off-street paths was high, but lower than for men, suggesting the possibility of some concern for personal safety. GPS monitoring of cyclists in Portland, Oregon, indicated that women were slightly more likely to go out of their way to use low-traffic streets and bicycle boulevards. Revealed route choice data and answers to questions about route choice priorities indicated that painted bike lanes on busy streets are not as appealing to women as to men (Dill and Gliebe 2008). Women's preferences for physically separated bicycle routes have also been reported in Melbourne, Australia (Garrard, Rose, and Lo 2008; Garrard, Crawford, and Hakman 2006), and Vancouver, Canada (Winters and Teschke 2010). Findings in the latter study suggested that women's preferences for cycling infrastructure may mirror those of other population groups underrepresented in utility cycling in low-cycling countries. The greater availability of separated facilities in high-cycling countries may thus contribute to higher levels of cycling for women: these countries do a better job of addressing women's safety concerns about cycling.

Although there is general acceptance that concerns about safety are a major barrier to cycling in many countries and a greater barrier for women than men, there is much debate about the origins and causes of these risk perceptions and their correspondence with actual risk. Stated simply: is it the case that cycling is as dangerous as many people (including greater numbers of women) believe, or is the "fear of cycling" largely based on psychological, social, and cultural factors operating independently of or interactively with actual risks?

Origins of Women's Concerns about Cycling Risks

Risk perceptions are often based on emotional responses to situations rather than rational analyses (Slovik et al. 2004). Emotional responses, in turn, are shaped by a range of psychological and social processes. Risk perception research has identified a number of biases that contribute to misjudgment of risk in general (Slovic et al. 2004) and may foster an inordinate fear of cycling, particularly among women. In particular, familiarity bias and control bias may reduce the perceived risks associated with car travel and increase the perceived risks for cycling—familiarity bias because in low-cycling countries, driving is a familiar activity but cycling for transportation is unusual, and control bias because in the myriad car/bicycle interactions that occur when cycling in traffic, cyclists are largely ceding control for their safety to car drivers. These biases may have a greater impact on women, who, in a range of contexts, have been shown to be more risk-averse than men (Byrnes, Miller, and Schafer 1999). The argument here is not that cycling risks are absent but rather that there is a perceptual element that appears to vary by gender.

For women, risks may also be exacerbated by the risk of "being on public display" while riding a bicycle (Horton 2007). The risk of being "blamed" for "risk-taking behavior" (i.e., cycling) may also constrain cycling and walking (Jacobsen, Racioppi, and Rutter 2009), particularly for women. In car-oriented countries, parents (usually mothers) are increasingly accused of behaving irresponsibly if they allow their children to cycle or walk to school or other neighborhood destinations independently (Skenazy 2009). They therefore expose themselves to the risk of being blamed (and indeed of blaming themselves) should an injury occur. These risk discourses, which vary between countries (Skenazy 2009), add another dimension, in the form of risk of guilt and blame, to the concepts of "cycling risk" and "fear of cycling" for women.

Other Possible Factors Contributing to Gender Differences in Utility Cycling

The greater effort often expended on cycling compared to walking (Ainsworth et al. 2000) may explain some of the gender differences in cycling, given that women tend to prefer less vigorous forms of physical activity such as walking (Armstrong, Bauman, and Davies 2000). Indeed, when asked why they did not bicycle, 13 percent of women in the United States indicated "physical difficulty" compared with 8 percent of men (NHTSA 2008).

Women's concerns about appearance, particularly in the workplace, may also contribute to reduced rates of cycling relative to men. US women who admitted to not wearing a helmet for all of their rides were more likely than men to say it was because it was too hot—53 percent compared to 44 percent of men. However, women and men were equally likely (45%) to say that helmets were uncomfortable (NHTSA 2008). It is interesting to note that in Tokyo, which has high rates of cycling for both women and men, men are more likely to commute to work by bicycle, but women are more likely to use the bicycle for nonwork trips (see chapter 14). This difference may be related to gender-specific work-related appearance issues, though gender differences in commute distance might also play a role.

Gender differences in self-efficacy for riding a bicycle may also be relevant. For example, among students, faculty, and staff at the University of California at Davis, 58.2 percent of women said that they are "very confident" riding a bicycle, compared to 80.9 percent of men (Lovejoy 2010). In the survey of residents of Davis and five other small US cities, 29 percent of women said they could fix a flat tire, compared to 83 percent of men, and 34 percent of men but only 3 percent of women said they could fix any problem (author's data). "Lack of confidence in bicycle maintenance" and "lack of confidence in cycling ability" were significantly more important constraints for women than men in the survey of 2,403 cyclists in Victoria, Australia (Garrard, Crawford, and Hakman 2006), though overall they were relatively minor constrains for both women and men.

Summary and Conclusions

As discussed in this chapter, several factors have been proposed as explanations for large gender differences in utility cycling in places with low levels of cycling for transportation. Each of these factors seems to play a role, but the evidence is perhaps most persuasive for concerns about personal safety and traffic risks. Not only do these concerns appear consistently in the literature, but in countries and cities where they have been addressed through improved cycling conditions, cycling rates are relatively high and gender differences largely absent.

Addressing women's safety concerns about cycling through an infra-structure strategy that relies mainly on painted bicycle lanes on busy streets may not succeed in attracting large numbers of new women cyclists. Separate paths, cycle tracks, and bicycle boulevards, together with good intersection treatments, are likely to be more effective. However, if these facilities are too far out of the way, women may not use them either. Utilitarian cyclists, both men and women, prefer direct routes. Moreover, if women have children with them, minimizing time and distance may be even more important. Therefore, a dense, well-connected network of facilities, complemented with low-speed, low-traffic neighborhood streets, is likely to increase the share of women cycling. It is also likely to increase cycling among men, children, and older adults as well, providing multiple benefits across the population.

In many low-cycling countries, efforts to increase transportation cycling have focused on encouraging bicycling to work, possibly reflecting road authorities' concerns with reducing traffic congestion during peak travel times. This bicycle-commute focus, and the neglect of every-day cycling for generally shorter trips within neighborhoods, may disadvantage women (including children, adolescents, and older women), who might be encouraged to cycle for multiple, short, local trips if neighborhood cycling conditions were comparable to those in the high-cycling countries.

Infrastructure and the physical environment are important, but so too are myriad other factors. Women, particularly in the United States, appear to have more negative attitudes than men toward cycling, possibly because the dominant images of cycling are of sport/fitness cycling rather than the more distinctive style of utility cycling seen in high-cycling countries. It is the latter form of cycling that seems to have greater appeal for women. The female share of utility cycling in low-cycling countries and cities is therefore likely to increase as the image and practice of cycling becomes more utility focused. Bicycle gear is likely to play a role, as discussed in chapter 5. The design of the bicycle will influence how comfortable women feel cycling, particularly in traffic. If women need to carry infants and young children, groceries, or other items with them while traveling, they will require large baskets and other carriers, cargo bikes, and extra seats in order to meet their daily travel needs on a bicycle. Chain guards, drop crossbars, and other components will also be important to enable women to cycle in everyday clothing, including cycling to work (see chapter 5).

The overall aim should be the normalization of utility cycling for women. Seeing women who look similar to themselves riding practical bicycles—women with children, women in dresses on their way to work, and women using bicycles to go shopping or to visit friends—can encourage more women to cycle. There may also be a role for marketing programs, particularly individualized marketing, buddy programs, and events such as ciclovías.[2] Based on interviews with women, Geddes (2009) recommended that marketing tools to promote cycling for women should include images of normal/standard bikes (rather than specialized bikes) and of women of all ages, social backgrounds, and ethnicities, rather than celebrities, attractive models, and "super-fit" competitive cyclists. The use of humor in marketing campaigns was also recommended. Special consideration needs to be given to addressing the dramatic decline in cycling among adolescent girls in many countries. A key challenge is to foster greater continuity of utility cycling across women's life-course as occurs in the high-cycling countries of Europe and Asia.

The Netherlands, in particular, has achieved one of the highest rates of female utilitarian cycling in the developed world (see figure 10.1) by establishing cycling as an appealing, convenient, and safe form of everyday travel for women of all ages, including during the child-rearing years. It is therefore an important model for other developed countries where few women cycle for transportation. As discussed in chapters 2, 12, and 13, the Netherlands has consistently implemented an integrated package of transportation, safety, and urban planning measures that systematically prioritizes cycling over car travel for the short- to medium-distance trips in urban areas that are commonly undertaken by women. Additional factors that make cycling appealing for women in the Netherlands include widespread use of bicycles appropriate for women's everyday travel needs and the absence of a legal requirement to wear a bicycle helmet. In addition, in the Netherlands, cycling is viewed as a convenient form of everyday travel, rather than a vigorous form of sport and exercise, which appear to have less appeal for women. What differentiates the Netherlands is not its cycling culture per se, but rather its *utilitarian* cycling culture. The Netherlands demonstrates that as bicycle travel is increasingly established as a convenient, safe, and enjoyable everyday transportation option, increasing numbers of girls, adolescents, and adult women will almost certainly go along for the ride.

Understanding the supports and barriers to utility cycling, particularly among underrepresented groups such as women, is crucial for developing policies aimed at increasing utility cycling. Apart from risk/fear, there appear to be few standout factors, but it is important to acknowledge that the accumulation of multiple small factors can add up to a substantial barrier to change. In addition to creating a cycling-friendly environment, increasing utility cycling among women will also require systematically addressing the "tyranny of small things" that often make driving a car an easier choice than riding a bicycle.

Note

1. For active commuting in general, which usually includes cycling.
2. Ciclovías are programs that close streets to cars and open them up to bicyclists, skaters, walkers, and other activities such as street theater.

References

AAMI (Australian Associated Motor Insurers). 2004. Personal communication.

ABS (Australian Bureau of Statistics). 2008. *How Australians Use Their Time, 2006. Cat. No. 4153.0.* Canberra, Australia: Commonwealth of Australia.

Ainsworth, Barbara E., William L. Haskell, Melicia C. Whitt, Melinda L. Irwin, Ann M. Swartz, Scott J. Strath, William L. O'Brien, et al. 2000. Compendium of Physical Activities: An Update of Activity Codes and MET Intensities. *Medicine and Science in Sports and Exercise* 32 (9 Suppl.): S498–S504.

Armstrong, Tim, Adrian E. Bauman, and Joanne Davies. 2000. *Physical Activity Patterns of Australian Adults.* Canberra, Australia: Australian Institute of Health and Welfare.

Australian Sports Commission. 2010. *Participation in Exercise, Recreation and Sport: Annual Report 2009.* Canberra, Australia: Australian Sports Commission.

Baker, Linda. 2009. How to Get More Bicyclists on the Road: To Boost Urban Cycling, Figure Out What Women Want. *Scientific American* 301 (4): 28–29.

Basford, L., S. Reid, T. Lester, J. Thomson, and A. Tolmie. 2002. Drivers' Perceptions of Cyclists. Transport Research Laboratory Report 549. Crownthorne, Scotland: Transport Research Laboratory.

Bonham, Jennifer, and Anne Wilson. 2012. Negotiating Cycling: The Start-Stop-Start Experiences of Women Riding Bicycles. *International Journal of Sustainable Transportation* 6 (4): 195–213.

Buehler, Ralph, John Pucher, Dafna Merom, and Adrian Bauman. 2011. Active Travel in Germany and the USA: Contributions of Daily Walking and Cycling to Physical Activity. *American Journal of Preventive Medicine* 41 (3): 241–250.

Bureau of Labor Statistics. 2008. *Married Parents' Use of Time, 2003–06.* USDL 08-0619. Washington, DC. http://www.bls.gov/news.release/pdf/atus2.pdf.

Byrnes, James P., David C. Miller, and William D. Schafer. 1999. Gender Differences in Risk Taking: A Meta-Analysis. *Psychological Bulletin* 125 (3): 367–383.

City of Portland. 2010. *Portland Bicycle Count Report 2010.* http://www.portlandonline.com/transportation/index.cfm?a=327783&c=44671.

de Geus, Bas, J. Joncheere, and Romain Meeusen. 2009. Commuter Cycling: Effect on Physical Performance in Untrained Men and Women in Flanders: Minimum Dose to Improve Indexes of Fitness. *Scandinavian Journal of Medicine & Science in Sports* 19 (2): 179–187.

Dill, Jennifer, and John Gliebe. 2008. *Understanding and Measuring Bicycling Behavior: A Focus on Travel Time and Route Choice.* Oregon Transportation Research and Education Consortium (OTREC), OTREC-RR-08-03, July. http://otrec.us/main/document.php?doc_id=966.

Emond, Catherine, and Susan L. Handy. 2011. Factors Associated with Bicycling to High School: Insights from Davis, CA. *Journal of Transport Geography* 20: 71–79.

Emond, Catherine, Wei Tang, and Susan L. Handy. 2009. Explaining Gender Differences in Bicycling Behavior. *Transportation Research Record* 2125: 16–24.

Forsyth, Ann, Kevin J. Krizek, and Daniel A. Rodríguez. 2009. Non-Motorized Travel Research and Contemporary Planning Initiatives. *Progress in Planning* 71 (4): 170–183.

Garrard, Jan. 2009. *Active Transport: Children and Young People. An Overview of Recent Evidence.* Melbourne: Victorian Health Promotion Foundation. http://www.vichealth.vic.gov.au/en/Publications/Physical-Activity/Active-transport/Active-Transport-Children.aspx.

Garrard, Jan, Sharinne Crawford, and Natalie Hakman. 2006. *Revolutions for Women: Increasing Women's Participation in Cycling for Recreation and Transport.* Melbourne: Deakin University. http://www.bv.com.au/file/Revs%20exec%20summary%20Final%2012Oct06.pdf.

Garrard, Jan, Stephen Greaves, and Adrian Ellison. 2010. Cycling Injuries in Australia: Road Safety's Blind Spot? *Journal of the Australasian College of Road Safety* 21 (3): 37–43.

Garrard, Jan, Geoffrey Rose, and Sing Kai Lo. 2008. Promoting Transportation Cycling for Women: The Role of Bicycle Infrastructure. *Preventive Medicine* 46 (1): 55–59.

Garvey, Ellen G. 1995. Reframing the Bicycle: Advertising-Supported Magazines and Scorching Women. *American Quarterly* 47 (1): 66–101.

Geddes, Mark. 2009. Gender and Cycling Use in Dublin: Lessons for Promoting Cycling. Master of Science (Spatial Planning) thesis. Dublin: Dublin Institute of Technology.

Giles-Corti, Billie, Sarah Foster, Trevor Shilton, and Ryan Falconer. 2010. The Co-Benefits for Health of Investing in Active Transportation. *New South Wales Public Health Bulletin* 21 (5–6): 122–127.

Gossen, Rachel, and Charles L. Purvis. 2005. Activities, Time, and Travel: Changes in Women's Travel Time Expenditures, 1990–2000. *Conference Proceedings 35, Research on Women's Issues in Transportation*, Vol. 2: Technical Papers, 49–56. Washington, DC: Transportation Research Board.

Graco, Marnie, Jan Garrard, and Andrea E. Jasper. 2009. Participation in Physical Activity: Perceptions of Women with a Previous History of Gestational Diabetes Mellitus. *Health Promotion Journal of Australia* 20 (1): 20–25.

Hamer, Mark, and Yoichi Chida. 2008. Active Commuting and Cardiovascular Risk: A Meta-Analytic Review. *Preventive Medicine* 46 (1): 9–13.

Harper, Ida H. 1983. *The Life and Work of Susan B. Anthony*, Vol. II. Salem, NH: Ayer Co.

Herlihy, David V. 2004. *Bicycle: The History*. New Haven, CT: Yale University Press.

Hoffman, Melissa R., William E. Lambert, Ellen G. Peck, and John C. Mayberry. 2010. Bicycle Commuter Injury Prevention: It Is Time to Focus on the Environment. *Journal of Trauma Injury Infection and Critical Care* 69 (5): 1112–1119.

Horton, David. 2007. Fear of Cycling. In *Cycling and Society*, ed. David Horton, Paul Rosen and Peter Cox, 133–152. Aldershot, Hampshire, England: Ashgate Publishing.

Hu, Gang, Pekka Jousilahti, Katja Borodulin, Noël C. Barengo, Timo A. Lakka, Aulikki Nissinen, and Jaakko Tuomilehto. 2007. Occupational, Commuting and Leisure-Time Physical Activity in Relation to Coronary Heart Disease among Middle-Aged Finnish Men and Women. *Atherosclerosis* 194 (2): 490–497.

Jacobsen, Peter L., Francesca Racioppi, and Harry Rutter. 2009. Who Owns the Roads? How Motorized Traffic Discourages Walking and Cycling. *Injury Prevention* 15 (6): 369–373.

Johnson, Marilyn. 2010. Preliminary Analysis of the Observed Behaviour of Female Commuter Cyclists in Melbourne. Melbourne BikeFest Forum, Cultural Shift—Women on Bikes, Melbourne, November 26.

Kavanagh, Anne, Lukar Thornton, Amanda Tattam, Lyndal Thomas, Damian Jolley, and Gavin Turrell. 2007. *Place Does Matter for Your Health*. Melbourne: Key Centre for Women's Health in Society, The University of Melbourne.

Kirch, Wilhelm. 2008. Risk Assessment. In *Encyclopedia of Public Health*, ed. Wihelm Kirch, 1261–1264. New York: Springer.

Knowles, J., S. Adams, R. Cuerden, T. Savill, S. Reid, and M. Tight. 2009. *Collisions Involving Pedal Cyclists on Britain's Roads: Establishing the Causes*. Wokingham, Berkshire, United Kingdom: Transport Research Laboratory.

Krizek, Kevin J., Ann Forsyth, and Laura Baum. 2009. *Walking and Cycling International Literature Review*. Melbourne: Victorian Department of Transport. http://www.transport.vic.gov.au/__data/assets/pdf_file/0004/31369/Walking CyclingLiteratureReview.pdf.

Lehner-Lierz, Ursula. 2003. The Role of Cycling for Women. In *Sustainable Transport: Planning for Walking and Cycling in Urban Environments*, ed. Rodney Tolley, 123–143. Cambridge: Woodhead.

Lovejoy, Kristin. 2010. *Results of the 2009–10 Campus Travel Survey*. Research Report UCD-ITS-RR-10-17, Institute of Transportation Studies, University of California, Davis. http://pubs.its.ucdavis.edu/publication_detail.php?id=1409.

Lusk, Anne C., Rania A. Mekary, Diane Feskanich, and Walter C. Willett. 2010. Bicycle Riding, Walking, and Weight Gain in Premenopausal Women. *Archives of Internal Medicine* 179 (12): 1050–1056.

Matthews, Charles E., Adriana L. Jurj, Xiao-Ou Shu, Hong-Lan Li, Gong Yang, Qi Li, Yu-Tang Gao, and Wei Zheng. 2007. Influence of Exercise, Walking, Cycling, and Overall Nonexercise Physical Activity on Mortality in Chinese Women. *American Journal of Epidemiology* 165 (12): 1343–1350.

McGuckin, Nancy, and Yukiko Nakamoto. 2005. Differences in Trip Chaining by Men and Women. In *Research on Women's Issues in Transportation, Report of a Conference, Volume 2: Technical Papers*, 49–56. Washington, DC: Transportation Research Board.

MLITT (Ministry of Land, Infrastructure, Transport, and Tourism). 2008. *Tokyo Person Trip Survey 2008*. Tokyo: Ministry of Land, Infrastructure, Transport and Tourism, Government of Japan. http://www.tokyo-pt.jp/.

NHSTA (National Highway Traffic Safety Administration). 2008. *National Survey of Bicyclist and Pedestrian Attitudes and Behavior, Volume II: Findings Report*. Report No. DOT HS 810 972. Washington, DC: U.S. Department of Transportation.

Nobis, Claudia, and Barbara Lenz. 2005. Gender Differences in Travel Patterns: Role of Employment Status and Household Structure. *Research on Women's Issues in Transportation, Conference Proceedings 35, Volume 2: Technical Papers*, 114–122. Washington, DC: Transportation Research Board.

Netherlands Ministry of Transport, Public Works, and Water Management. 2009. *Cycling in the Netherlands*. Utrecht, The Netherlands: Ministry of Transport, Public Works, and Water Management.

Pucher, John, and Ralph Buehler. 2008. Making Cycling Irresistible: Lessons from the Netherlands, Denmark, and Germany. *Transport Reviews* 28 (4): 495–528.

Pucher, John, and Ralph Buehler. 2010. Walking and Cycling for Healthy Cities. *Built Environment* 36 (4): 391–414.

Pucher, John, and Lewis Dijkstra. 2003. Promoting Safe Walking and Cycling to Improve Public Health: Lessons from the Netherlands and Germany. *American Journal of Public Health* 93 (9): 1509–1516.

Pucher, John, Jan Garrard, and Stephen Greaves. 2011. Cycling Down Under: a Comparative Analysis of Bicycling Trends and Policies in Sydney and Melbourne. *Journal of Transport Geography* 19 (2): 332–345.

Pucher, John, Ralph Buehler, Dafna Merom, and Adrian Bauman. 2011. Walking and Cycling in the United States, 2001–2009: Evidence from the National Household Travel Surveys. *American Journal of Public Health* 101 (S1): S310–S317.

Pucher, John, Lewis Thorwaldson, Ralph Buehler, and Nick Klein. 2010. Cycling in New York: Innovative Policies at the Urban Frontier. *World Transport Policy and Practice* 16 (Summer): 7–50.

Scheider, Kate. 2010. *Bicycle Leadership Conference Demographics Survey Report*. Boulder, CO: Bikes Belong Coalition. http://www.bikesbelong.org/assets/documents/uploads/BLCsurvey.pdf.

Sibley, Anna. 2010. *Women's Cycling Survey: Analysis of Results*. Cedarburg, WI: Association of Pedestrian and Bicycle Professionals. http://www.apbp.org/resource/resmgr/downloads/womens_cycling_survey_091420.pdf.

Sisson, S. B., and P. T. Katzmarzyk. 2008. International Prevalence of Physical Activity in Youth and Adults. *Obesity Reviews* 9:606–614.

Skenazy, Lenore. 2009. *Free-Range Kids: How to Raise Safe, Self-Reliant Children*. San Francisco: Jossey-Bass.

Slovic, Paul, Melissa L. Finucane, Ellen Peters, and Donald G. MacGregor. 2004. Risk as Analysis and Risk as Feelings: Some Thoughts about Affect, Reason, Risk, and Rationality. *Risk Analysis* 24 (2): 311–322.

Smith, Andy, Jim McKenna, Duncan Radley, and Jonathan Long. 2010. The Impact of Additional Weekdays of Active Commuting to School on Children Achieving a Criterion of 300+ Minutes of Moderate-to-Vigorous Physical Activity. *Health Education Journal* (September 1). DOI: 10.1177/0017896910379367.

Steindorf, Karen, Martina Schmidt, Silke Kropp, and Jenny Chang-Claude. 2003. Case-Control Study of Physical Activity and Breast Cancer Risk among Premenopausal Women in Germany. *American Journal of Epidemiology* 157 (2): 121–130.

Strange, Lisa S., and Robert S. Brown. 2002. The Bicycle, Women's Rights, and Elizabeth Cady Stanton. *Women's Studies* 31:609–626.

van Kempen, Elise, W. Swart, G. C. W. Wendel-Vos, P. E. Steinberger, A. B. Knol, H. L. Stipdonk, and M. C. B. Reurings. 2010. *Exchanging Car Trips by Cycling in the Netherlands: A First Estimation of the Health Benefits*. Bilthoven, The Netherlands: RIVM, National Institute for Public Health and the Environment.

Voss, Christine, and Gavin Sandercock. 2010. Aerobic Fitness and Mode of Travel to School in English School Children. *Medicine and Science in Sports and Exercise* 42 (2): 281–287.

Welke, Sylvia, and Jennifer Allen. 2004. Cycling Freedom for Women. *Women and Environments* (Spring/Summer): 34–37.

Winters, Meghan, and Kay Teschke. 2010. Route Preferences among Adults in the Near Market for Bicycling: Findings of the Cycling in Cities Study. *American Journal of Health Promotion* 25 (1): 40–47.

11
Children and Cycling

Noreen C. McDonald

Learning to ride a bicycle is an important milestone for children. The ability to control a bicycle provides evidence of the child's physical and cognitive development. For a child, riding a bicycle brings newfound independence and the ability to travel faster and farther, bringing within grasp destinations that previously were out of reach.

Beyond the excitement and sense of achievement that becoming a cyclist may bring to the child and the family, there are larger societal trends at play. Increasing levels of childhood obesity have been associated with declines in everyday physical activities such as cycling or walking (Tudor-Locke et al. 2003). Biking around the neighborhood or to destinations such as school and parks is a healthful activity that is increasingly rare, for a variety of reasons discussed in this chapter. Although no known studies establish a causal link between children's cycling and reduced levels of obesity, chapter 3 and other studies show that being active is good for children's health and that being active as a child may promote healthy lifelong habits (Steinbeck 2001).

Although we know that cycling is good, it turns out that how much children bicycle varies widely from country to country and, within countries, from family to family. Opportunities for cycling are highly dependent on the child's own skills and attitudes; family rules about when and where children are allowed to bicycle; whether the community provides safe routes to important destinations like schools, parks, and shops; and topography and weather. This chapter explores these factors and provides data on the quantity, patterns, and safety of cycling among children across the globe. The chapter also describes in detail policies affecting biking to school, particularly decisions related to city planning and community design, and discusses what it means to create a community children can navigate by bicycle.

Trends and Current Patterns

Despite the important role that learning to bicycle plays in many families and its relationship to important health and transportation issues, the formal study of children's cycling is limited. For example, little is known about how much children cycle for recreation. The time children spend riding in their neighborhood for fun or learning tricks on dirt tracks goes largely unrecorded by researchers. This lack of measurement does not mean it is unimportant. In fact, studies recording activity throughout the day show that boys who walk or cycle to school are more active throughout the day (Cooper et al. 2005). Recreational cycling yields most of the same benefits as bicycling for transportation and faces many of the same challenges, but we lack information about the volume and quality of such activity. Therefore, this chapter will focus on children's bicycling for transportation.

Most of our data on children's cycling comes from local and national travel surveys that record travel diaries for each household member. These diaries are good at cataloging trips for specific activities such as work or school. They are less effective at capturing children's trips to corner stores or their friend's house. Therefore, the most robust data on the level of cycling in various regions focus on the school trip. Rates of cycling to school are low (1–6%) in the United States and the United Kingdom and in cities in Canada and Australasia (table 11.1). By comparison, rates of walking to school are relatively high (25–50%) in the United Kingdom, Canada, and Australia.

In the Netherlands, 49 percent of primary schoolchildren bike to school and only 14 percent are driven. Biking is even more common than walking (at 37 percent). In Odense, Denmark, nearly 38 percent of 9-year-olds and two-thirds of 15-year-olds biked to school. Nearly two-thirds of 12- to 14-year-olds biked to school in Jiangsu Province, China. Biking to school is the norm in these countries, though likely for very different reasons. Although motorization is increasing rapidly in China, most families do not have the option to drive their child to school. Students there may bike because they have few other choices. In contrast,

Table 11.1
Children's school travel mode

	Survey year	Respondent ages	Bike (%)	Walk (%)	Auto (%)	Other (%)
Countries						
Netherlands	2000s	5–12	49	37	14	0
Switzerland	2005	6–14	17	55	14	15
Germany	2008/9	5–14	14	33	19	34
United Kingdom	2009	5–10	1	50	42	7
United Kingdom	2009	11–16	3	38	22	37
United States	2009	5–14	1	10	51	36
Regions/cities						
Jiangsu Pr., China	2002	12–14	B: 66 G: 63	B: 25 G: 21	n/a	n/a
Odense, Denmark	1999	9	B: 38 G: 38	B: 28 G: 24	B: 21 G: 25	B: 13 G: 13
Odense, Denmark	1999	15	B: 67 G: 64	B: 21 G: 21	B: 3 G: 3	B: 9 G: 12
Umea, Sweden	1994	6 & 9	31	41	18	10
Perth, Aust.	1994	6 & 9	6	31	62	1
Melbourne, Aust.	1994	6 & 9	3	35	61	1
Victoria, Aust.	2006	5–12	4	23	64	9
Ontario, Canada	2000	5–14	4	58	28	10
Toronto, Canada	2006	11–13	2	45	26	27
Toronto, Canada	2006	14–15	1	43	34	22
Montreal, Canada	1994	6 & 9	2	48	14	36
Auckland, NZ	1994	6 & 9	1	40	55	4
Baltimore, US	1994	6 & 9	0	55	38	7

Sources: Buliung, Mitra, and Faulkner 2009; Cooper et al. 2006; Department for Transport 2010c; Netherlands Ministry of Transport, Public Works, and Water Management 2009; Garrard 2009; Grize et al. 2010; McDonald et al., 2011, O'Brien 2001; Roberts et al. 1997; Shi et al. 2006; Sirard and Slater 2008.
Note: In the last four columns, "B" designates boys and "G" designates girls.

the European households choose to bike to school even though public transportation and autos are available.

Although rates of walking to school have decreased sharply in many countries (McDonald et al. 2011; Pooley, Turnbull, and Adams 2005), the trends in cycling to school are less clear. In the United States and United Kingdom, the decrease in the proportion of children cycling to school is low, but because the rates of cycling are low, this decrease can represent more than a 50 percent decline in percentage terms. For example, 2 percent of high school students biked in 1977 compared to only 1 percent in 2009 (McDonald 2007; McDonald et al. 2011). The statistics in the United Kingdom are similar, with relatively low rates of cycling. There, biking among 11- to 16-year-olds declined four percentage points or more than 50 percent between 1975 and 2009 (table 11.2). In Switzerland, the share of students biking to school declined significantly, from 20.9 percent in 1994 to 16.9 percent in 2005 (Grize et al. 2010). Because longitudinal data are not available for other countries, it is difficult to analyze the trends in countries with high levels of cycling.

Who Is Biking?

As shown in chapters 2 and 10, individual factors such as age and gender have direct associations with biking. Most children do not learn to ride bicycles until somewhere around age 5–7. Once children are physically able to ride, they still need to learn road rules, traffic safety, and more advanced bicycle handling skills. Thus, children cycle more as they get older, at least until teens reach driving age (Orsini and O'Brien 2006). As children mature, parents become more comfortable with their children's ability to safely negotiate roads and are more likely to let their children bicycle without supervision.

In countries where biking is more the exception than the rule, boys bike more than girls. However, in countries where cycling is the norm, there are no observed gender differences (table 11.1). For example, Roberts et al. (1997), in their study of school travel in six cities in the United States, Canada, Australia, and Sweden during the mid-1990s, found rates of biking to school that were approximately two times higher for 9-year-old boys than girls in Melbourne, Perth, and Auckland, and

Table 11.2
Longitudinal trends in cycling to school in the United Kingdom, the United States, Canada, and Switzerland

Country	Age (years)	Year	Bike mode share (%)
United Kingdom	5–10	1975/6*	2
		1985/6*	1
		1995/7	0.3
		2009	1.2
	11–16	1975/6*	7
		1985/6*	6
		1995/7	2.0
		2009	3.1
United States	5–14	1995	1.3
		2001	1.0
		2009	0.9
	15–18	1995	0.5
		2001	0.3
		2009	0.7
Greater	11–13	1986	2.7
Toronto Area,		1996	1.8
Canada		2001	1.5
		2006	0.9
	14–15	1986	2.2
		1996	1.2
		2001	1.1
		2006	1.2
Switzerland	6–14	1994	20.9
		2000	17.1
		2005	16.9

Sources: Buliung et al. 2009; Department for Transport 2010c; Grize et al. 2010; McDonald et al. 2011; Pooley, Turnbull, and Adams 2005.
Note: Asterisk (*) denotes years in the UK for which more precise data were not available.

approximately three times higher in Montreal. However, in Umea, Sweden, there were no observed differences in biking to school, with 40 percent of both boys and girls traveling to school by bicycle. In Odense, Denmark, 9-year-old girls and boys exhibited the same levels of cycling to school (38%), and the rates for 15-year-olds were close (Cooper et al. 2006). Similar gender differences exist among adults. As shown in chapters 2, 10, and 13, women in the United States are less likely to bike than men, but many northern European countries show no differences between the sexes (Garrard, Rose, and Lo 2008).

There is no definitive explanation for the gender differences. Among children, parents may restrict behavior perceived as dangerous or risky more in girls than boys (Valentine 1997). Studies in adults suggest that there are also gender differences in bicycle route choice, with women preferring low-traffic streets and bike-specific infrastructure, for example, bicycle boulevards (Dill and Gliebe 2008).

Characterizing how levels of cycling vary with other demographic characteristics is more difficult. Only limited published data break out cycling behavior by income, race, or household type. In the United States, whites had higher rates of cycling to school than nonwhites between 1977 and 2001 (McDonald 2007). Although cycling is a low-cost means of travel, children still need to have access to a bicycle to participate. Unfortunately, there is little data on the relationship between family economic resources and how much children bike. However, a number of nonprofit organizations have emerged that provide youths from low-income households with bicycles and training on how to repair them. Trips for Kids is one example of an international nongovernmental organization that works with disadvantaged children to provide mountain biking trips and teach bicycle safety and maintenance. Youth participating in the program have the opportunity to earn their own bicycle or need bicycle parts. The program currently has sixty chapters in the United States, Canada, and Israel.

Role of Families

The bicycle affords children independence, but there is evidence that parents are increasingly restricting children's neighborhood wanderings because of safety concerns and schedule constraints.

Children's Independent Mobility

In 1971, just over 40 percent of British 7- to 10-year-olds were allowed to cross roads alone; by 1990, the share was approximately 20 percent (Hillman, Adams, and Whitelegg 1990, 44). The reduction in independent mobility applied to cycling as well. Between 1971 and 1990, the share of British 7- to 10-year-olds allowed to cycle on roads decreased from 67 percent to 25 percent (Hillman, Adams, and Whitelegg 1990, 43). Even in recent years, children's independent mobility decreased in the United Kingdom. In 2002, 78 percent of 7- to 10-year-olds were accompanied by their parents to school, and in 2009 the share was 84 percent (Department for Transport 2010a). In the Netherlands, the age when children travel to school without a parent has increased from 8 in the 1970s to 10 today (Wassenberg and Milder 2008).

What has motivated this decrease in travel freedom across Western countries? There are several likely causes. The most prominent and oft-cited concern is safety, both traffic danger and stranger danger (Department for Transport 2010a; Hillman, Adams, and Whitelegg 1990; Martin and Carlson 2005). Although most countries have not seen marked increases in traffic injuries and fatalities or in child abductions, there have been dramatic changes in how those events are reported. Authors in the United Kingdom and the United States link some changes in the perception of safety to well-publicized abductions of children in the United Kingdom and the United States (O'Brien et al. 2000; Stearns 2004).

It is also important to note that even though travel freedom has declined across countries, there are still sharp differences in travel freedom across countries. German children had much more travel freedom than their English or Australasian counterparts in the early 1990s (Hillman, Adams, and Whitelegg 1990; Tranter 1996). Nearly 90 percent of German 9-year-olds were allowed to cross roads alone; half of the English or Australasian children had this privilege. Some of this difference has been attributed to varying cultural norms around monitoring children in public. In Germany, parents expected strangers to monitor children's behavior and intervene if necessary.

Family Schedules

Beyond safety concerns, some of the decline also can be attributed to changes in family work schedules and economic resources. The third-most-cited reason for British parents accompanying children is that it is convenient (Department for Transport 2010a). With both parents employed in many families, it becomes easier to drop off the child on the way to work (McDonald 2007; Joshi and MacLean 1995; Bradshaw 1995). In countries such as the United States where both parents usually drive to work, it is unlikely that parents will let a child cycle to school. In countries such as the Netherlands, where many adults bike to work, most children cycle to school either alone or accompanied by their parents, who are also on bike.

Parents' Biking and Attitudes to Biking

Beyond resources and safety concerns, it is clear that how much the parent bikes and enjoys biking affects whether children ride, particularly in the United States, where biking is the exception rather than the rule. A recent study looked at how children got to weekend soccer practice in Davis, California, a famously bicycle-friendly city (see chapter 12). In households where parents rode every day, 34 percent of children biked to soccer (Tal and Handy 2008). However, in families where parents never biked, only 2 percent of children rode to soccer. So the children of parents who cycled daily were approximately seventeen times more likely to cycle than children whose parents never cycled.

Children's Attitudes

Less considered in the academic literature is the role of children and adolescents' attitudes to transportation and activity choices. Decisions to bike, whether for recreation or to activities, are the result of negotiation between parents and children. Some youths show strong modal preferences. Zwerts et al. (2010) found preferences for bicycling and walking among a sample of Belgian children. These nonmotorized modes appealed to many children because of the opportunity to experience nature on the trip, assume responsibility, and opportunities for social interaction. Similarly, de Bruijn et al. (2005) found that attitudes to bike use were associated with bicycling to school. Practitioners recognize the importance of children's attitudes. Most programs to encourage bicycling and walking to school include a social marketing component to raise excitement about using active modes and to get children to ask to walk or bike more frequently.

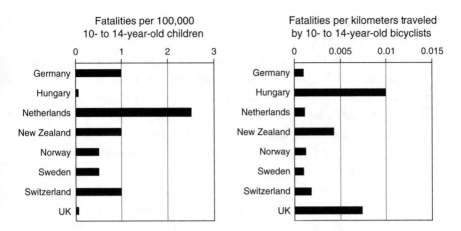

Figure 11.1
Cycling fatality rates for 10- to 14-year-old children relative to population and distance cycled. *Source:* Christie et al. 2004.

How Safe Is Cycling?

As shown in chapters 2, 7, 13, and 14, the safety of cycling as judged by injury and fatality rates varies greatly from country to country and from city to city. Cyclist fatality rates per 100,000 children aged 10–14 years old varied from 0.5 (Sweden) to 2.5 (the Netherlands) (see figure 11.1). However, after accounting for how much children bike in each country, the fatality rates vary from 1 per 1,000 kilometers traveled (the Netherlands) to 10 (Hungary). Rates of cycling fatalities are lowest in countries where children cycle the most. This relationship may indicate "safety in numbers" as discussed in chapter 7 (Jacobsen 2003; Geyer et al. 2006). Alternatively, parents may restrict cycling in places with poor safety records, or children may be better skilled and confident in countries with better safety ratings. No studies exist to disaggregate these effects.

International comparisons suggest that there are policies that can reduce cycling fatalities. However, within each country, cycling generally has higher fatality rates than cars after adjusting for exposure. For US students who bike to school, the fatality rate per million cycling trips was 9.6, approximately six times the rate when adults drive students to school and double the rate when students walk to school (National Research Council 2002). A longitudinal study of child (ages 0–14) fatality rates in England and Wales by mode found that deaths had declined 75 percent for pedestrians and 35 percent for cyclists between 1985 and 2003 (Sonkin et al. 2006). However, the fatality rate per cycling kilometer was fifty-five times the rate per motorized kilometer. Even in a country such as the Netherlands, which has one of the lowest fatality rates per kilometer biked, bike fatality rates are higher than auto fatality rates per kilometer of exposure. For Dutch children ages 0–14, the fatality rate is just over five per billion kilometers, compared to about one per billion kilometers for cars (SWOV 2009a). Even this apparently clear-cut statistic illustrates the difficulty of assessing safety. Fatality rates for children cycling in the Netherlands are five times that of children being driven per unit distance. But the US cycling fatality rate for school trips is approximately fifteen times that of the Dutch rate.

Safety Education and Regulations

To improve cycling safety, most countries focus on education programs or regulations on helmet use. Programs differ in design and the skills considered "age-appropriate." Dutch children receive school-based traffic education starting at age 4. The training emphasizes "master[ing] practical skills" and recognizes that school-based education provides inadequate practice and children need to practice skills, such as bicycle riding, every day in the company of adults (SWOV 2009b). Other countries are more hesitant about letting children practice road skills. A 2003 European Commission report on road safety education recommended delaying introducing children to bicycles until seven or eight and stated that early (ages 6 and 7) cycle training "should by no means encourage children . . . to cycle in real traffic!" (Kuratorium fur Verkehrs Sicherheit 2005). Unfortunately, there is little evaluation of the effectiveness of different education programs in different contexts, making it difficult to identify the most effective education strategies.

An ongoing debate exists about the population health effects of helmets. It is clear that helmets usually decrease the severity of head injuries in a bike crash. This protective effect in crashes has led many governments and medical groups to encourage mandatory cycle helmet laws, particularly for children. In the United Kingdom, the British Medical Association supports mandatory rules (British Medical Association

2010). In the United States, twenty-one states and the District of Columbia have mandatory helmet laws for children (Bicycle Helmet Safety Institute 2010). As noted in chapter 7, critics of mandatory helmet laws maintain that the decrease in cycling levels that is associated with the laws outweighs the health benefits of the decrease in head injuries (Carnall 1999).

Finally, the legal framework for liability likely also influences safety. Several continental European countries—including France, Germany, and the Netherlands—have strict liability laws that place most responsibility for traffic injuries on drivers (Fedtke 2003). The Anglo-American legal system places no such special responsibility on drivers.

Neighborhood Design and Bicycle Infrastructure

Bicycle-friendly environments for children depend on two elements: the spatial distribution of homes, schools, and other destinations and the connections between those destinations. Cycling becomes an option when destinations (schools, recreation centers, shops, parks) are nearby and children have safe routes to travel. The connectedness of destinations depends on the spatial layout of communities. This "built environment" is determined by history, developer investment decisions, and community land use planning guidelines. Distance between destinations varies not only on their actual locations, but also on the street network linking them. Areas with well-connected street and bicycle networks provide more options. The natural environment also influences how much children cycle. Steep hills may discourage cycling to destinations.

Although we cannot define reasonable cycling distances, we know that closer is better than farther away. In Davis, California, among children living within a half-mile of the soccer field, 60 percent of children cycled to soccer practice; this number dropped to approximately 10 percent for children living 2.4–6.4 km (1.5–4.0 miles) from the soccer field (Tal and Handy 2008). In the United Kingdom, the proportion of children cycling to school was highest for trips between one and two miles (Department for Transport 2010b). Reasonable cycling distances also depends on age, fitness, and cycling skills. For many 6-year-olds, a one-mile trip would be long. That same trip would be short for most teenagers.

Figure 11.2
Safe bicycle infrastructure is crucial for children, even when parents are cycling with them, as seen here in Portland, Oregon. *Credit:* John Pucher.

Bicycle Infrastructure

Safe connections between home, school, and other destinations are necessary for children to cycle and, critically, for parents to feel comfortable letting children cycle or ride without them. For example, the provision of bicycle infrastructure in Portland, Oregon, has increased cycling and likely led more children to bicycle (figure 11.2). The data on rates of cycling to school suggest a correlation between bicycle-specific infrastructure and biking. As shown in chapters 2 and 6, the northern European countries that have invested most heavily in infrastructure for biking have dramatically higher rates of cycling. Pucher and Buehler (2008) have used case studies of northern European countries compared with the United Kingdom and the United States to suggest that the history of investing in separate bicycle facilities promotes biking.

Analyses of the cycling frequency of six- to eleven-year-old Dutch children found that children cycled more in neighborhoods with recreation facilities and narrow streets with low traffic speeds (de Vries et al. 2010). Alhough there are few studies linking investments in cycling infrastructure to changes in how much children cycle, analyses of adult behavior suggest critical factors. The first is that the needs of cyclists vary. Less experienced adult cyclists prefer to travel on low-volume streets or use dedicated bicycle infrastructure (Dill 2009). It is likely that children—particularly younger ones (or their parents)—would prefer such facilities. Chapter 6 shows that communities have many options for providing this infrastructure, including bike boulevards, bike lanes, and multiuse paths (Pucher, Dill, and Handy 2010). Connectivity of the street network is also critical. Local governments can increase connectivity for children cyclists by providing direct bicycle and pedestrian connections. Such a strategy is particularly effective in suburban environments where the street network may not be well connected. Southworth and Ben-Joseph (2004) showed how paths could be used to retrofit suburban neighborhoods.

Although bike-specific infrastructure is critical, the short distances that children travel restrict most of their trips to local streets rather than separated bicycle infrastructure. The Dutch have addressed this issue by slowing traffic on neighborhood streets. Implemented as *woonerf* in the Netherlands and home zones in the United Kingdom, these areas require vehicles to travel slowly, with speed limits of 15 km/h (about 10 mph). Such neighborhood streets are generally quite narrow and do not provide separate zones for pedestrian, cyclists, and drivers (Alan M. Voorhees Transportation Center 2004). The resulting negotiation for right of way encourages slower automobile travel.

Although the infrastructure improvements described thus far would benefit all residents, there are some important interventions specific for children. Secondary schools in some Dutch cities are investing in guarded bicycle parking to encourage students to ride to school. A small secondary school in The Hague found a tenfold increase in the number of students cycling after installing a guarded parking facility (Netherlands Ministry of Transport, Public Works, and Water Management 2009). Another Dutch strategy for increasing safe mobility is Delft's effort to create *kindlint* or "child ribbons" (Netherlands Ministry of Transport, Public Works, and Water Management 2009). These ribbons connect destinations important to children, such as schools and playgrounds, and provide a safe route with special markings and traffic calming to connect the destinations. This type of intervention can be used in new communities or to retrofit existing developments.

Siting of Schools and School Cycling Policies

Recently, more attention has been paid to how decisions about school location affect how students travel. American school planning guidelines were developed for rapidly growing suburban areas and emphasized acquiring large school sites with sufficient room for recreation facilities and future expansion (McDonald 2010). These forces encouraged the building of large campuses, generally fifteen or more acres for an elementary school and thirty or more for a high school. Finding such large sites was often impossible in developed areas, and many districts built schools away from existing population (Gurwitt 2004). The result is that most US school pupils live far from school. American elementary students traveled an average of 5.8 km (3.6 miles) to school in 2009, compared with 2.4 km (1.5 miles) for British 5- to 10-year-olds and Swiss 6- to 14-year-olds (Department for Transport 2010c; Grize et al. 2010).

Schools also influence cycling through their policies. There are examples of schools actively encouraging and discouraging cycling to school. Liability and safety concerns have caused some schools to prohibit or make it difficult to bike to school. No large-scale analyses have cataloged this effect, but an informal survey by a Chicago nonprofit organization found bicycle bans in place in several suburban school districts. For example, Oak Park, a Chicago suburb, had bicycle bans in place at five of eleven schools, and a nearby school district banned bicycles at two of twenty-seven schools (Glowacz 2004). In the United Kingdom, schools cannot ban cycling, but they can prohibit students from bringing bicycles onto school property. One British secondary school took this approach (Schlesinger 2009). The result was several stolen bicycles and concerns that fewer students would cycle to school.

In contrast, many schools are working to encourage students to walk and bike to school. Government policies and nonprofit organizations in many countries have partnered with schools to increase levels of cycling and walking. In the United Kingdom, the government promotes "safe and healthy journeys to school which in turn can also help to reduce the use of the car" (Department for Transport 2010d). Schools are encouraged to develop School Travel Plans that facilitate cycling and walking and may be eligible for governmental grants to assist with implementation. In the United States, the 2005 federal transportation bill included $612 million for the Safe Routes to School program. This program funds education and infrastructure improvements near schools that will encourage more children to travel by foot and bicycle and make the journey safer. Some areas have used these governmental programs to improve conditions in low-income communities. For example, the Illinois Department of Transportation funded a nonprofit group to work with ten low-income communities to develop Safe Routes to School plans (Safe Routes to School National Partnership 2009).

Although there are no large-scale evaluations of the effectiveness of programs designed to increase cycling to school, anecdotal evidence suggests that they can increase the number of children biking to school. Early success was seen in Marin County's program, which doubled levels of biking to school in only two years (Staunton, Hubsmith, and Kallins 2003). Bear Creek Elementary School in Boulder, Colorado, reduced driving students to school by 36 percent by encouraging travel by bicycle and foot (National Center for Safe Routes to School 2008).

Creating Bikeable Communities for Children

If we accept the axiom that cycling is good for children, families, and communities, then we must ask: how can biking be promoted as an everyday activity for children across the globe? Several factors must be addressed: first, communities need to provide safe environments for children to cycle. In neighborhoods, this goal will require slowing traffic, and on larger roads, it may require specialized facilities. Although design is a necessary condition, it is not sufficient to get more children riding. Understanding and addressing parental concerns about cycling as well as their schedule constraints is critical to making change on the ground. Bicycles provide very low-cost mobility—but only once a child has a bicycle. Ensuring access to bicycles across the income spectrum requires attention. Finally, there is a need for much better information on children's cycling.

Community Design

A necessary condition for children to cycle is that they can safely reach needed activities from their homes. That desired proximity requires placing schools, recreation centers, and shops within reasonable distances of children's residences and creating connections between the two that meet the safety requirements of parents and children. Safe connections can be provided by separate bicycle infrastructure or by ensuring that vehicle traffic moves slowly on streets. The design solutions will vary with community preferences and existing character.

Parental Concerns

Policies to increase cycling among children must address infrastructure needs but must also recognize the complex parent-child negotiations that govern children's travel. Younger children will be accompanied by their parents; older children require parental permission to bike on their own. Parents' work schedules and their own feelings about biking will affect how much children bike. Getting more children to bike will require addressing parental safety concerns through infrastructure improvements but also through rigorous safety education in the schools. Nonprofit organizations or local government can try to address time constraints by providing supervision of children while they are biking to school. The provision of trained, adult crossing guards at intersections provides reassurance to parents. Similarly, volunteers or neighborhood parents can be organized to take a group of children to school or soccer practice. By sharing responsibility for biking with children, families may be able to create more opportunities to bike.

Equity Considerations

Any consideration of children and cycling must recognize that there is uneven access to bicycles, safe cycling environments, and parental availability to supervise children. Each of these could lead children in low-income communities to have fewer opportunities to cycle safely. Nonprofit organizations have been actively working to introduce disadvantaged children to cycling and provide opportunities for them to get their own bicycle. Governments have addressed equity concerns by targeting funding to low-resource areas.

Finding Out More about Children and Cycling

A key step in creating more bikeable communities for children is improving our understanding of what education programs and infrastructure investments are most effective. Currently, we can only make educated guesses about the type of bicycle infrastructure that is important for children, but we lack detailed studies. We also do not understand how cycling as a child affects cycling as an adult. Many advocacy groups have hypothesized a connection, but data have not been available to test the hypothesis. One study that tried to obtain such data—an analysis of travel in six western US cities—did not find a link between adult cycling and cycling as a child (Xing, Handy, and Buehler 2008). More in-depth research on these complex relationships is needed.

Conclusion

Learning to ride a bicycle provides children with one of the first concrete steps to independence. Establishing cycling as an accepted and valued mode of travel for children, and fostering lifetime habits that benefit individuals and communities, will require changes and improvements in current education, planning, and transportation practices. Children (and adults) need infrastructure to provide safe conditions for cycling along good routes connecting key destinations. The design of the infrastructure will vary with local conditions, but the most effective initiatives will consider children's mobility needs from project inception. Safe cycling can also be part of primary education, particularly in physical education classes. These actions can lay the foundation for establishing or maintaining a culture of cycling.

References

Alan M. Voorhees Transportation Center. 2004. *Home Zone Concepts and New Jersey*. New Brunswick, NJ: Alan M. Voorhees Transportation Center. http://policy.rutgers.edu/vtc/bikeped/reports/HomeZonesFinal12-8-04.pdf.

Bicycle Helmet Safety Institute. 2010. *Helmet Laws for Bicycle Riders*. 2010. Arlington, VA: Bicycle Helmet Safety Institute. http://www.bhsi.org/mandator.htm.

Bradshaw, Ruth. 1995. Why Do Parents Drive Their Children to School? *Traffic Engineering & Control* 36 (1): 16–19.

British Medical Association. 2010. *Promoting Safe Cycling*. London: British Medical Association. http://www.bma.org.uk/health_promotion_ethics/transport/promotingsafecycling.jsp?page=1.

Buliung, Ronald N., Raktim Mitra, and Guy Faulkner. 2009. Active School Transportation in the Greater Toronto Area, Canada: An Exploration of Trends in Space and Time (1986–2006). *Preventive Medicine* 48 (6): 507–512.

Carnall, Douglas. 1999. Cycle Helmets Should Not be Compulsory. *British Medical Journal* 318:1505.

Christie, Nicola, Elizabeth Towner, Sally Cairns, and Heather Ward. 2004. *Children's Road Traffic Safety: An International Survey of Policy and Practice*. London: Department for Transport, Road Safety Research Report No. 47.

Cooper, Ashley R., Lars B. Andersen, Niels Wedderkopp, Angie S. Page, and Karsten Froberg. 2005. Physical Activity Levels of Children Who Walk, Cycle, or Are Driven to School. *American Journal of Preventive Medicine* 29 (3): 179–184.

Cooper, Ashley R., Niels Wedderkopp, Han Wang, Lars B. Andersen, Karsten Froberg, and Angie S. Page. 2006. Active Travel to School and Cardiovascular Fitness in Danish Children and Adolescents. *Medicine and Science in Sports and Exercise* 38 (10): 1724–1731.

de Bruijn, Gert-Jan, Stef P. J. Kremers, Herman Schaalma, Willem van Mechelen, and Johannes Brug. 2005. Determinants of Adolescent Bicycle use for Transportation and Snacking Behavior. *Preventive Medicine* 40 (6): 658–667.

de Vries, Sanne, Marijke Hopman-Rock, Ingrid Bakker, Remy Hirasing, and Willem van Mechelen. 2010. Built Environment Correlates of Walking and Cycling in Dutch Urban Children: Results from the SPACE Study. *International Journal of Environmental Research and Public Health* 7 (5): 2309–2324.

Department for Transport. 2010a. Table NTS0616. Whether Children are Accompanied to School by an Adult and the Reasons: Great Britain, 2002 to 2009. London: Department for Transport.

Department for Transport. 2010b. Table NTS0614. Trips to School by Main Mode, Trip Length and Age: Great Britain, 2008/09. London: Department for Transport.

Department for Transport. 2010c. Table NTS0613: Trips to and from School per Child per Year by Main Mode: Great Britain, 1995/97 to 2009. London: Department for Transport.

Department for Transport. 2010d. School Travel. London: Department for Transport.

Dill, Jennifer. 2009. Bicycling for Transportation and Health: The Role of Infrastructure. *Journal of Public Health Policy* 30:S95–S110.

Dill, Jennifer, and John Gliebe. 2008. Understanding and Measuring Bicycling Behavior: A Focus on Travel Time and Route Choice. Portland, OR: Oregon Transportation Research and Education Consortium, OTREC-RR 08–03.

Fedtke, Jörg. 2003. Strict Liability for Car Drivers in Accidents Involving "Bicycle Guerrillas"? Some Comments on the Proposed Fifth Motor Directive of the European Commission. *American Journal of Comparative Law* 51 (4): 941–957.

Garrard, Jan. 2009. *Active Transport: Children and Young People*. Melbourne: VicHealth.

Garrard, Jan, Geoffrey Rose, and Sing Kai Lo. 2008. Promoting Transportation Cycling for Women: The Role of Bicycle Infrastructure. *Preventive Medicine* 46 (1): 55–59.

German Ministry of Transport. 2010. *Mobility in Germany 2008/2009*. Berlin: German Ministry of Transport.

Geyer, Judy, Noah Raford, David Ragland, and Trinh Pham. 2006. The Continuing Debate about Safety in Numbers—Data from Oakland, CA. Berkeley, CA: University of California Traffic Safety Center, UCB-ITS-TSC-2006-3.

Glowacz, Dave. 2004. Safe Routes to Suits: Cracking the Liability Lies in Walking and Biking to School. http://www.mrbike.com/rants.php.

Grize, Leticia, Bettina Bringolf-Isler, Eva Martin, and Charlotte Braun-Fahrländer. 2010. Trend in Active Transportation to School among Swiss School Children and Its Associated Factors: Three Cross-Sectional Surveys 1994, 2000, and 2005. *International Journal of Behavioral Nutrition and Physical Activity* 7:28.

Gurwitt, Rob. 2004. Edge-Ucation: What Compels Communities to Build Schools in the Middle of Nowhere? *Governing Magazine*, March.

Hillman, Mayer, John Adams, and John Whitelegg. 1990. *One False Move . . . : A Study of Children's Independent Mobility*. London: Policy Studies Institute.

Jacobsen, Peter L. 2003. Safety in Numbers: More Walkers and Bicyclists, Safer Walking and Bicycling. *Injury Prevention* 9 (3): 205–209.

Joshi, Mary S., and Morag MacLean. 1995. Parental Attitudes to Children's Journeys to School. *World Transport Policy and Practice* 1 (4): 29–36.

Kuratorium fur Verkehrs Sicherheit. 2005. Good Practice Guide on Road Safety Education. SER-B27020B-E3-2003-Good Practices-S07.28326. Brussels: European Commission.

Martin, Sarah L., and S. Carlson. 2005. Barriers to Children Walking To or From School: United States, 2004. *MMWR (Morbidity and Mortality Weekly Report)* 54 (38): 949–952.

McDonald, Noreen C. 2007. Active Transportation to School: Trends among U.S. Schoolchildren, 1969–2001. *American Journal of Preventive Medicine* 32 (6): 509–516.

McDonald, Noreen C. 2010. School Siting: Contested Visions of the Community School. *Journal of the American Planning Association*. 76 (2): 184–198.

McDonald, Noreen C., Austin Brown, Lauren Marchetti, and Margo Pedroso. 2011. U.S. School Travel 2009: An Assessment of Trends. *American Journal of Preventive Medicine* 41 (2): 146–151.

National Center for Safe Routes to School. 2008. Bear Creek Elementary School in Boulder, Colorado Wins Oberstar Award. http://www.saferoutesinfo .org/about-us/newsroom/our-newsletter/article/congressman-jim-oberstar -presents-oberstar-safe-routes-scho.

National Research Council. 2002. *The Relative Risks of School Travel: A National Perspective and Guidance for Local Community Risk Assessment*. Washington, DC: Transportation Research Board.

Netherlands Ministry of Transport, Public Works, and Water Management. 2009. *Cycling in the Netherlands*. The Hague, The Netherlands: Ministry of Transport, Public Works, and Water Management.

O'Brien, Catherine. 2001. *Ontario Walkability Study: Trip to School, Children's Experiences and Aspirations*. Toronto: York Centre for Applied Sustainability.

O'Brien, Margaret, Deborah Jones, David Sloan, and Michael Rustin. 2000. Children's Independent Spatial Mobility in the Urban Public Realm. *Childhood* 7 (3): 257–277.

Orsini, Arthur F., and Catherine O'Brien. 2006. Fun, Fast and Fit: Influences and Motivators for Teenagers Who Cycle to School. *Children, Youth and Environments* 16 (1): 121–132.

Pooley, Colin G., Jean Turnbull, and Mags Adams. 2005. The Journey to School in Britain since the 1940s: Continuity and Change. *Area* 37 (1): 43–53.

Pucher, John N., and Ralph Buehler. 2008. Making Cycling Irresistible: Lessons from the Netherlands, Denmark and Germany. *Transport Reviews* 28 (4): 495–528.

Pucher, John N., Jennifer Dill, and Susan L. Handy. 2010. Infrastructure, Programs, and Policies to Increase Bicycling: An International Review. *Preventive Medicine* 50:S106–S125.

Roberts, Ian, John B. Carlin, Catherine M. Bennett, Erik Bergstrom, Bernard Guyer, Terry Nolan, Robyn K. Norton, I. Barry Pless, Ravi Rao, and Mark R. Stevenson. 1997. An International Study of the Exposure of Children to Traffic. *Injury Prevention* 3 (2): 89–93.

Safe Routes to School National Partnership. 2009. Addressing the Needs of Low-Income Communities through the Federal Safe Routes to School Program: Best Practices from and for State SRTS Programs. http://www.saferoutespartnership.org/ media/file/Addressing_the_Needs_of_Low_Income_Communities_FINAL.pdf.

Schlesinger, Fay. 2009. Cotton-Wool Culture Blamed as School Bans All 1,000 Pupils from Bringing Their Bikes to School. *The Daily Mail*, November 17.

Shi, Zumin, Nanna Lien, Bernadette N. Kumar, and Gerd Holmboe-Ottesen. 2006. Physical Activity and Associated Socio-Demographic Factors among School Adolescents in Jiangsu Province, China. *Preventive Medicine* 43 (3): 218–221.

Sirard, John R., and Megan E. Slater. 2008. Walking and Bicycling to School: A Review. *American Journal of Lifestyle Medicine* 2 (5): 372–396.

Sonkin, Beth, Phil Edwards, Ian Roberts, and Judith Green. 2006. Walking, Cycling and Transport Safety: An Analysis of Child Road Deaths. *Journal of the Royal Society of Medicine* 99 (8) (August 1): 402–405.

Southworth, Michael, and Eran Ben-Joseph. 2004. Reconsidering the Cul-de-sac. *Access* 24:28–33.

Staunton, Catherine E., Deb Hubsmith, and Wendi Kallins. 2003. Promoting Safe Walking and Biking to School: The Marin County Success Story. *American Journal of Public Health* 93 (9): 1431–1434.

Stearns, Peter N. 2004. *Anxious Parents: A History of Modern Child-Rearing in America.* New York: New York University Press.

Steinbeck, Katherine S. 2001. The Importance of Physical Activity in the Prevention of Overweight and Obesity in Childhood: A Review and an Opinion. *Obesity Reviews* 2 (2): 117–130.

SWOV (Institute for Road Safety Research). 2009a. SWOV Fact Sheet: Road Safety of Children in the Netherlands. Leidschendam, The Netherlands: SWOV. http://www.swov.nl/rapport/Factsheets/UK/FS_Children.pdf.

SWOV (Institute for Road Safety Research). 2009b. SWOV Fact Sheet: Traffic Education of Children 4–12 Years Old. Leidschendam, The Netherlands: SWOV. http://www.swov.nl/rapport/Factsheets/UK/FS_Traffic_education_children.pdf.

Tal, Gil, and Susan L. Handy. 2008. Children's Biking for Nonschool Purposes: Getting to Soccer Games in Davis, California. *Transportation Research Record, Journal of the Transportation Research Board* 2074:40–45.

Tranter, Paul J. 1996. Children's Independent Mobility and Urban Form in Australasian, English and German Cities. In *World Transport Research Proceedings of the 7th World Conference on Transport Research*, ed. D. Hensher, J. King, and T. H. Oun, 31–44. Oxford: Pergamon Press.

Tudor-Locke, Catrine, Barbara E. Ainsworth, Linda S. Adair, and Barry M. Popkin. 2003. Objective Physical Activity of Filipino Youth Stratified for Commuting Mode to School. *Medicine and Science in Sports and Exercise* 35: 465–471.

Valentine, Gill. 1997. "Oh Yes I Can." "Oh No You Can't": Children and Parents' Understandings of Kids' Competence to Negotiate Public Space Safely. *Antipode* 29 (1): 65–89.

Wassenberg, Frank, and Jody Milder. 2008. *Child-Friendly Routes Evaluated: The Kindlint Project.* Delft, The Netherlands: OTB Research Institute.

Xing, Yan, Susan L. Handy, and Theodore J. Buehler. 2008. Factors Associated with Bicycle Ownership and Use: A Study of 6 Small U.S. Cities. Washington, DC: Presented at the Annual Meeting of the Transportation Research Board. Washington, DC.

Zwerts, Enid, Georges Allaert, Davy Janssens, Geert Wets, and Frank Witlox. 2010. How Children View Their Travel Behaviour: A Case Study from Flanders (Belgium). *Journal of Transport Geography* 18 (6): 702–710.

12

Cycling in Small Cities

Susan Handy, Eva Heinen, and Kevin J. Krizek

Efforts to promote cycling in large cities have garnered much attention in recent years (see chapters 13 and 14), but efforts within small cities also merit recognition. Many smaller European cities have cycling levels that exceed those in larger cities. In the United States, the most bike-oriented small cities have much higher shares of trips by bicycle than the most bike-oriented large cities. Although cycling overall accounts for just 1 percent of trips in the United States, cycling has long been a vital mode of transportation in some small cities. The experiences of cities like Davis, California, and Boulder, Colorado, provide a foundation for the efforts underway in larger cities like Portland, Oregon, and Los Angeles, California, and they have inspired other small cities as well.

Cycling offers unique opportunities for small cities. Cycling may be especially viable in small cities for a variety of reasons: their smaller geographic size, lighter traffic, and closer relationships among residents. Although cycling has benefits for cities of all sizes, it may be even more useful in smaller cities. More limited transit service in smaller cities gives cycling greater importance as an alternative to driving, and cycling can be an efficient way to access transit stops that are farther apart than in large cities. Limited capital budgets may necessitate more modest projects in smaller cities, potentially favoring bicycle investments. As an added plus, promoting cycling can be a way for smaller cities to "make their mark" as a part of "green city" efforts.

Small cities, defined here as having populations under 300,000, come in many different forms with respect to both internal structure and relationship to other cities. There are standalone cities, separated by farmland or open space from other cities, and there are small cities embedded within metropolitan areas, where one city blends into another. Some

smaller cities are home to colleges or universities and have disproportionately young populations; others skew toward older populations
because of an exodus of young people or an influx of retirees. Cycling
will be more or less viable depending on such characteristics, and bicycle
planning must account for the specific characteristics of each community
(Forsyth and Krizek 2011). Nevertheless, small cities share many of the
same opportunities as well as challenges, and many strategies for increasing cycling are potentially adaptable from one small city to another.

In this chapter, we examine how some small cities have succeeded in
promoting cycling, looking not just at the strategies they have adopted
but also at the broader set of factors that have led to the adoption of
these strategies. We consider first the natural advantages that small cities
may have in promoting cycling. Second, we focus on two small cities in
the United States where bicycle planning efforts are widely considered
to be exemplary—Davis, California, and Boulder, Colorado—and identify the factors that have contributed to their success. We then examine
the experiences of small cities elsewhere in the western world, focusing
on Odense, Denmark, and Delft, the Netherlands, to illustrate common-
alities and differences with European cities with respect to the sets of
factors that have come together to support cycling. We conclude with
some general reflections on the implications for other small cities.

Small City Advantages

Smaller cities face the same broad challenges as larger cities in their
efforts to increase cycling. The first challenge is to identify sets of strategies that will enhance the cycling environment, both physical and social—
strategies that may vary among communities. The second challenge is to
implement those strategies. Small cities may have an advantage over
larger cities in meeting these challenges.

First, their physical characteristics may be naturally more supportive
of cycling or at least more easily modified. The smaller geographic scale
of these cities means that a greater portion of the city is likely to be
within distances reasonable for cycling. Lower population and employment densities than in urban centers generally mean lower traffic densities as well, creating more attractive conditions for cycling, provided that
densities are not so low that distances between destinations are too great

for cycling and car speeds are too high. A key destination, such as a college campus, town center, or major employer, may dominate travel patterns within the community and thus provide a natural target for investments in bicycle infrastructure. These advantages are more likely in standalone cities than in the smaller cities embedded within a metropolitan region.

Second, the social characteristics of small cities may also facilitate support for cycling in a variety of ways. Because people are influenced, directly and indirectly, by the people to whom they are socially connected (Marsden and Friedkin 1993), the tighter social networks often present in smaller cities may mean that residents who bicycle have a greater chance of influencing others to bicycle as well. Citizens of small cities tend to be more closely connected to their local government than those of larger cities through greater participation in civic activities; greater participation is tied to the greater likelihood of residents mobilizing their neighbors for political activity in smaller cities (Oliver 2000). Thus, a group of residents who believe the community should invest in bicycle infrastructure will likely have an easier time building political support in small cities. Additionally, a cycling-friendly community is more likely to attract cycling-oriented residents, who are then likely to perpetuate support for bicycle investments (Tiebout 1956; Handy, Xing, and Buehler 2010).

Added to these advantages is the greater ease of documenting the effects of bicycle investments and other strategies in small cities. Evidence that a particular strategy has been effective in increasing cycling in one community helps other communities justify the adoption of that strategy (Krizek, Forsyth, and Slotterback 2009). The best such evidence comes from before-and-after studies that measure changes in cycling from before to after the implementation of the strategy. Such studies are hard to do well (Krizek, Handy, and Forsyth 2009) but may be easier in small cities, given easier identification of those affected by the strategy and fewer potential confounding factors. Small cities thus offer potential as "pilot studies" for new strategies.

American Case Studies: Davis and Boulder

Overall, small cities have about the same amount of cycling as cities of other sizes, with 1 percent of trips by bicycle, according to the 2009

National Household Travel Survey. However, in some small cities, the rate of cycling is much higher. Among small cities (with populations under 250,000) that the League of American Bicyclists has designated as bicycle-friendly cities at the silver, gold, or platinum level, 4.4 percent of workers usually commute to work by bicycle, compared to 0.6 percent for the country as a whole, according to the 2005–2009 American Community Survey. Not surprisingly, many of the small cities with high levels of cycling are home to major universities, and many of the others are vacation destinations (figure 12.1). Davis and Boulder especially stand out with 15.5 percent and 9.6 percent of workers, respectively, reporting that they usually commuted by bicycle in the 2005–2009 American Community Survey. Their ratings as platinum-level bicycle-friendly communities recognize their efforts in developing comprehensive approaches to promoting cycling in the United States. Understanding how these cities succeeded—the strategies they employed and the conditions that contributed to their adoption—is useful to other small cities aiming to increase their own levels of cycling.

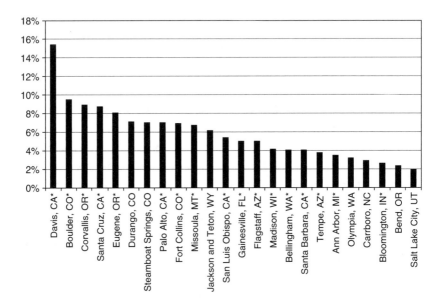

Figure 12.1
Share of workers commuting by bicycle for small bicycle-friendly US cities. *Note:* Cities with major universities are designated with an asterisk (*). *Source:* U.S. Census Bureau 2009.

Davis and Boulder have a number of natural advantages for cycling: they are college towns, they have good weather for at least three seasons (Davis can get stifling hot in summer, Boulder has spells of cold and snowy weather in winter), and they are relatively flat (especially Davis). These factors have contributed to the success of cycling in these cities, but they did not guarantee it: the bicycle-friendly environment in each city is a result of infrastructure investments, land-use policies, and other specific bicycle programs, all fostered by and in turn enhancing a cycling-supportive culture. In this section, we review the evolution of cycling efforts in each community and highlight key factors that contributed to their success.

Davis

Davis is a city of about 62,000 residents located 15 miles to the west of Sacramento in the Central Valley of California. Extending about 3 miles north-to-south and 5 miles east-to-west, the city is relatively compact, by American standards, and is surrounded by agricultural land. The major employer in the city is the University of California at Davis, with more than 30,000 students and nearly as many employees. Education levels and incomes are high for the Sacramento region. The city is known as a family-oriented community with a high quality of life.

Davis had a reputation as a bicycle-friendly town as early as the 1950s (Buehler and Handy 2008). Plans for an expanded University of California campus in Davis in the late 1950s featured extensive bicycle paths. But the city's first investments in bicycle infrastructure did not come until a decade later, in response to pressure from a citizen's group. In 1967, the city striped the first bicycle lanes in the United States. In the years that followed, city staff experimented with a variety of facility designs, and the university invented the bicycle roundabout to handle the large number of bicyclists on campus. The city also developed innovative intersection designs, including bike-activated signals, special turn lanes, and advanced stop lines.

Today, Davis has more than 50 miles of on-street bike lanes and more than 50 miles of off-street bike paths in an area of less than 10 square miles, with twenty-five bike tunnels and bridges, including overpasses over the two freeways that divide the city. Although the city made several significant investments in new bicycle infrastructure in earlier years, its recent efforts focus more on maintaining the system rather than expanding it. Davis has not yet implemented some of the European techniques now being used in other US cities, such as colored bicycle lanes and bicycle boxes (advance stop lines) at intersections. City officials cite a lack of funding for such projects, but a lack of political will might also be a factor. Some have argued that such innovations are not needed in Davis, where cycling is already common and traffic is generally light (Buehler and Handy 2008).

Land-use policies have furthered the cycling cause in Davis. In the 1970s, the city adopted a general plan designed to avert many of the negative impacts of suburban sprawl. Guided by this plan, the city adopted policies to encourage infill development, distribute multifamily housing throughout the city, and locate services conveniently within each neighborhood. The explicit goal was to moderate the length of trips and to facilitate walking, biking, and public transportation as alternatives to driving. At the same time, policies have long supported the centrally located downtown as the commercial heart of the city. Also critical to cycling has been a long-standing policy that requires a high level of connectivity between new developments and existing ones through the layout of the street network but also the network of off-street paths. As a result, travel distances can be considerably shorter for bicyclists than for drivers.

Bicycle programs were also important in building a culture of cycling in Davis. During the 1970s, the city sponsored a wide range of cycling programs, including subsidized helmet programs, elementary school education programs, removal of abandoned bikes from racks, and strict enforcement of traffic laws (Buehler and Handy 2008). Many of these programs have continued, but the city now devotes little funding for promotional programs, focusing on "bike rodeos" at the elementary schools and various activities during Bike Month (May). A local advocacy group has sponsored many events in recent years, including an annual bicycle film festival, and worked with the city in 2007 to mark the Davis Bicycle Loop, a twelve-mile bike route through Davis. In 2009, Davis became the permanent home of the US Bicycling Hall of Fame, the result of a coordinated campaign on the part of the city, the university, and local cycling advocates.

Davis faces many challenges in sustaining its high level of cycling. Although still higher than elsewhere in the United States, the share of workers usually cycling to work has declined by half since 1980 (Buehler and Handy 2008). Underlying this decline is a significant shift in commuting patterns in the region: fewer Davis residents work in Davis than in the past, instead commuting to Sacramento or the San Francisco Bay Area. Moreover, fewer university employees now live in Davis, owing in part to the high housing prices in the city. After the establishment of a shuttle bus system, the share of trips to campus by university students by bike fell from 75 percent in the 1970s to 45 percent in 2009 (Buehler and Handy 2008; Lovejoy 2010). Recent budget cutbacks limit the ability of the city and the university to improve and expand its cycling infrastructure. Nevertheless, state policy on greenhouse gas emissions and the burgeoning cycling culture elsewhere in the United States are generating new commitment within Davis to reverse these trends. Indeed, the latest census data show a slight increase since 2000 in the share of workers usually cycling to work.

Boulder
Boulder is located 35 miles northwest of Denver Colorado, nestled against the foothills of the Rocky Mountains, and has about 97,000 residents in 25 square miles (U.S. Census Bureau 2000). The city is home to the University of Colorado at Boulder, with nearly 30,000 students. The community is well known for attracting elite athletes from all over the world as a place to live and train. Moreover, several international publications for cycling and triathlon, as well as Bikes Belong, a national bicycle advocacy coalition, are based there. This mix, though oriented toward recreational cycling, provides a uniquely favorable climate for bicycle planning in general, and the city has successfully increased utilitarian cycling through investments in infrastructure, land-use planning, and other programs.

In 1989, the city adopted a transportation plan that brought together previously disparate initiatives to reduce vehicle travel (Rutsch 2008). The plan underscored the need for an interconnected system of sidewalks, multiuse paths, and bicycle lanes (Roskowski and Ratzel 2008). Six years later, the 1995 update to the plan further supported nonmotorized modes (Charlier 2008) by being the first plan in the United States to set a goal of reducing vehicle miles of travel. The plan has guided an ambitious program of infrastructure investments. Funding comes in part from a dedicated sales tax adopted in 1967, and in the last several years, almost half of the transportation budget from the general fund has been apportioned to bicycling, walking, and public transportation. Since 1989, the city has expanded the bicycle system at a rate of 1 mile of off-street path, half a mile of on-street bicycle lanes, and two underpasses each year, producing a system that now has more than 150 centerline miles of bicycle facilities, in comparison to 205 centerline miles of roadways (Ratzel 2008). The system includes 52 miles of multiuse paths, with 76 underpasses and 2 overpasses; 95 percent of major arterials have bike lanes or adjacent pathways (Krizek and Langegger 2009) (figure 12.2).

Land-use practices have complemented these infrastructure investments. In 1967, Boulder became the first US city to institute a sales tax dedicated to the purchase of open space and the funding of transportation infrastructure. Revenues have been used to create a band of 43,000 acres of permanent open space encircling the city and preventing its outward growth (City and County of Boulder 2005). The city adopted a comprehensive plan in 2005 that supports in-fill development and redevelopment to ensure that any destination in the city is within a reasonable cycling distance (City and County of Boulder 2005).

Several innovative programs further support the effort to promote cycling. The city's "GO Boulder" department is responsible for public transportation, walking, and cycling initiatives and works with other city departments to coordinate land use and transportation planning with input from citizens and advocacy groups (Roskowski and Ratzel 2008). The city has launched an Internet-based bicycle route finding system, sponsored a community "bike summit" to identify and address issues, spearheaded Bike to Work Day events, and worked to bring advocacy groups and neighborhood organizations into the planning process (Ratzel 2008).

In response to these and other efforts, the share of workers commuting by bike has more than doubled since 1980, and the city prides itself in consistently achieving between 10 and 20 percent of all trips via cycling. Looking forward, the city continues to seek new and creative strategies, though the economic downtown has made this more challenging. The city is pursuing other sources of funding, including federal and regional

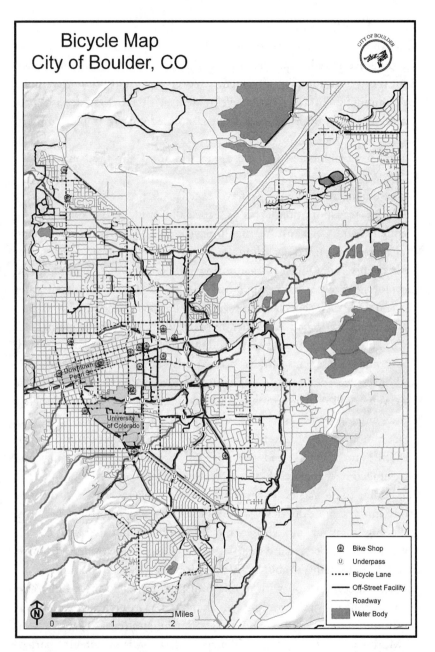

Figure 12.2
Cycling facilities in Boulder, Colorado. *Source:* Prepared by the Active Communities Transport Research Group, University of Colorado, Denver.

sources as well as new local taxes. It is difficult to meet the needs of all types of cyclists in the city, from families to competitive cyclists, without building overly redundant facilities. Despite current financial challenges, a local organization will implement a bicycle-loan/share system in 2011. By combining infrastructure development with other aggressive programs, Boulder endeavors to achieve continued growth in bicycle use.

European Case Studies: Odense, Denmark, and Delft, the Netherlands

Many small cities in Europe have excelled at promoting cycling as a mode of transportation. This is especially true in the Netherlands, Denmark, and Germany, but small bicycle-friendly cities are also found in Sweden, the United Kingdom, and many other countries. There are at least twenty-five OECD (Organisation for Economic Co-operation and Development) cities with populations under 250,000 with cycling rates in the double digits and six more with populations under 300,000 (figure 12.3). Contrary to popular belief, in many of these cities cycling has not always been as widely used as it is today. Driven by concerns over growth in automobile use, city officials consciously set out to reverse the trend and have succeeded to a remarkable degree, as shown by De la Bruhèze and Veraart (1999) for multiple western European cities, particularly Dutch cities.

Common to all of these cities is a comprehensive program of infrastructure investments and promotional programs, encouraging and encouraged by a culture of cycling, as was the case in Davis and Boulder. But adding to the success of these programs are several critical differences from most small American cities. First, favorable land-use patterns, including compact, mixed-use land development and a strong central commercial district, ensure that destinations are within cycling distance. Second, high-quality public transportation service promotes the use of bicycles in conjunction with public transportation as a means of travel to and from the train station (see chapter 8). Groningen (the Netherlands) and Münster (Germany) are good examples (table 12.1).

More generally, in these cities bicycle planning is an integral part of transportation planning, and transportation planning is closely coordinated with land-use planning. As a result, residents of these cities have more and better alternatives to driving than their counterparts in small

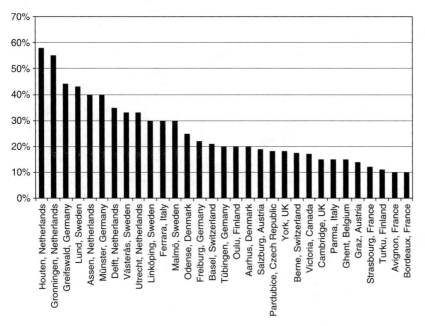

Figure 12.3
Cycling share of trips within city for small cities in Europe. *Source:* Colville-Andersen 2011.

cities in the United States. In addition, small cities in Europe employ a variety of deterrents to driving, particularly car-free zones in the center of the city and restricted parking, speed reductions, and traffic calming measures (table 12.1). As noted in chapter 2, the efforts of northern European cities are supported by strong national policy supporting cycling as a mode of transportation through both infrastructure investments and promotional campaigns, as well as deterrents to driving (Pucher and Buehler 2008, 2010).

To illustrate these points, we describe the experiences of Odense, Denmark, and Delft, the Netherlands, while summarizing efforts in a selection of other small cities (table 12.1). We describe the approach taken in each city to increase levels of cycling. Odense provides an interesting case because of the notable increase in cycling rates that resulted from its aggressive, creative, multifaceted promotional campaign. Delft is of interest for using an approach focusing mainly on infrastructure investments.

Table 12.1
Bicycling levels and programs in selected European cities

	Bicycling	Infrastructure	Programs	Auto deterrents
Groningen, NL[a] 187,197 pop.; 48,921 students	• 40 percent of all trips; 59 percent of trips within the city	• 220 km of separated facilities in 2006 • All outlying residential areas connected by several separated bicycle facilities • Cycling in two directions allowed on one-way streets • 29 guarded bike parking facilities, 16 at schools, 4 in the city center, 2 at the railway station, and others around recreational and sport facilities • 1,700 new bicycle parking places in the city center in 2015 and 1,500 at the railway station in 2012 • Bicycle accommodations at intersections, including advance stop lines, bike boxes, bicycle access lanes, signal priority for bicycles, right turn on red, waiting time forecast, rain sensor and two times green light in one cycle	• No special programs to promote cycling • Mandatory bicycling education for all schoolchildren	• Car-free zone and limited car parking in city center • Most residential streets traffic-calmed at 30 km/h

Table 12.1
(continued)

	Bicycling	Infrastructure	Programs	Auto deterrents
Münster, Germany[b] 282,000 pop.; 55,000 students	• 37.6 percent of all trips	• 457 km of separated paths and lanes in 2010, including 4.5 km bicycle promenade around the city and sixteen bicycling streets • Cycling in two directions allowed on one-way streets; cyclists allowed to make left and right turns in some places where cars are not • Cycling sometimes allowed in pedestrian areas and bus lanes • Bicycle accommodations at intersections, including advance stop lines, signal priority for bicycles • Bike station at main train station and in shopping district • Directional signage	• Wide range of special bicycle rides and promotional events • Bicycle chosen as official symbol of the city • Annual bicycling festivals • Mandatory bicycling education for all schoolchildren • Bicycle map and online route finder	• Car-free zone in city center and limited car parking in city center • Most residential streets traffic-calmed at 30 km/h with many home zones at 7 km/h

Table 12.1
(continued)

	Bicycling	Infrastructure	Programs	Auto deterrents
Freiburg, Germany[c] 220,000 pop.; around 30,000 students	• 22 percent of all trips; 28 percent of all local trips; 204 percent increase in bicycle trips between 1976 and 2007	• 420 km of bicycle facilities, including 170 km of bicycle paths, 130 km of 30 km/h streets, and 120 km on country roads • Cycling in two directions allowed on one-way streets • Bike station at main train station	• Mandatory bicycling education for all schoolchildren	• Car-free zone and limited car parking in city center • All residential streets traffic-calmed at 30 km/h with 177 home-zones at 7 km/h and two car-free neighborhoods • Number of lanes on arterial streets decreased
Malmö, Sweden[d] 294,000 pop.; around 23,900 students	• 25 percent of all trips; 30 percent of trips in inner city; 40 percent of commute and school trips	• 430 km of cycling paths • Bike-only streets in the city center	• Bicycling promotional programs starting in 1996 • "No Ridiculous Car Journeys" campaign to encourage cycling for trips less than 5 km	• Car-free zone in city center • Convenience of private cars reduced in neighborhoods

Table 12.1
(continued)

	Bicycling	Infrastructure	Programs	Auto deterrents
		• Radar sensors to prioritize cyclists at twenty-eight intersections • Three new large-scale bicycle parking garages • Other amenities, including signage, air pumps, "cycling barometers"	• The Friendly Road to School project to promote cycling and walking to school • Businesses on Bikes program; bicycle fleet for city employees to use during day • Bicycle map and online route finder	• Car-free zone and limited car parking in city center
Linköping, Sweden[e] 97,000 pop.	• 33 percent of all trips	• Around 400 km of cycle paths, including 100 km forming an "interconnected thoroughfare" with uniform signposts	• Radio commercials promoting bicycling • Bicycle parties with competitions, performances, and information • Cycling magazine distributed to households • Bicycle maps and brochures	

Table 12.1
(continued)

	Bicycling	Infrastructure	Programs	Auto deterrents
Cambridge, UK[f] 180,000 pop.; 30,000 students	• 21 percent of all trips; 26 percent of journeys to work; highest levels of cycling in UK	• Improvements to and expansion of facilities under the Cycling Demonstration Town program • Cycling in two directions allowed on some one-way streets • Mandatory development fees to support bicycling infrastructure	• Bicycle training for adults and elementary school children • Subsidies to employers to provide bicycle parking • Annual promotional events	• Car-free zone and limited car parking in city center • 20 mph speed limits on streets in city center

Sources: [a]Pucher, Dill, and Handy 2010; Pucher and Buehler 2007; Dutch Bicycle Council 2006; City of Groningen 2008; [b]Pucher, Dill, and Handy 2010; Pucher and Buehler 2007; Dutch Bicycle Council 2006; [c]Buehler and Pucher 2011; Pucher, Dill, and Handy 2010; Dutch Bicycle Council 2006; [d]City of Malmö, n.d.; City of Malmö 2010; [e]City of Linköping 2008; [f]Cambridgeshire County Council 2011; Cambridge Cycling Campaign 2011; Cycling England 2010; Joyce 2011.

Odense

Odense has a population of 185,000 and is the third largest city in Denmark; it is the largest city on the island Funen, located between Denmark's mainland to the west and the island of Seeland, the location of Copenhagen, to the east. The city serves as the market center for Funen and is home to the largest campus of the University of Southern Denmark, with more than 16,320 students. In the late 1990s, the connection to other parts of Denmark improved dramatically with the construction of a bridge for rail and car traffic linking the two main islands. Travel time by train between Odense and Copenhagen is now seventy-five minutes, and trains run about every twenty minutes.

The environment in Odense is naturally conducive to cycling because the city and surrounding areas are relatively flat and temperatures are relatively mild (although winter temperatures average –6.5°C/21°F) (DMI 2011). The distance from the outskirts of the city to the city center is about 5 kilometers (over 3 miles), making cycling an option for many trips. As of the 1980s, the city had 350 kilometers of bicycle paths and lanes (Dutch Bicycle Council 2010). This infrastructure supported high levels of cycling, but city officials became concerned about a downward trend. Motivated by both environmental and health concerns, the city undertook an ambitious program to promote cycling and achieved a remarkable turnaround, with cycling increasing by 80 percent between 1984 and 2002. As of 2010, 26 percent of all trips were made by bicycle, and 80 percent of children bicycle or walk to school (City of Odense 2010).

Although the city has expanded the bicycle system to 510 km (City of Odense 2010), the key to the turnaround was a four-year program of experiments conducted from 1999 to 2002 with financial support from the Danish Ministry of Transport (see chapter 2 and Dutch Bicycle Council 2010). The aim was to increase bicycle use by 20 percent through promotional activities and the construction of innovative bicycle facilities. At a total cost of €2.5 million, sixty projects were completed. The share of bicycle use increased from 22.5 percent in the period 1994–1997 to 24.6 percent in the period 1999–2002. Safety also improved: over the four years of the program, there were 20 percent fewer serious cycling injuries (Dutch Bicycle Council 2010).

Odense promotes cycling using a wide range of imaginative promotional programs for all age groups, building on its successful experiments.

Schoolchildren receive mandatory cycling education, and the city runs extensive safety programs. Three hundred safe routes to school projects have been implemented since 1979 (Andersen 2011). Bicycle trailers are loaned to parents of children in kindergarten, and the Odense cycle mascot, a chicken named Cycle Anton, visits schools. Guided cycling tours are offered for older residents. A bicycle training program is offered for immigrant women who are not familiar with cycling. Individual cyclists can make use of a bicycle route planner via cell phone or the Internet. In addition to the city's efforts, many companies provide bicycles for employees to use during the day.

This city is currently focusing on maintaining and upgrading bicycle infrastructure to improve traffic safety and bicycle comfort and convenience. Special accommodations for bicyclists at intersections include advance stop lines, a bike box at one intersection, bicycle access lanes, and "green wave" signal timing for cyclists along one route. The city has expanded and improved bicycle parking, including secured indoor parking facilities at the train station and lighted and covered parking in the town center. Air pumps are also available in the town center, and the city operates a facility where shoppers who cycle to the town center can check their purchases until they are ready to cycle home. An extensive system of well-designed signage directs cyclists to destinations throughout the city and to routes to neighboring communities. Some facilities serve a promotional purpose as well; for example, ten "cycling barometers" display the number of cyclists passing by each day.

In addition to improvements to bicycle infrastructure, the city has worked to reduce and restrict auto use. The city center is a car-restricted zone, similar to that in many other European cities (see table 12.1). Some car parking has been converted to bicycle parking. Special attention has been given to reducing car speeds. Speed reductions were implemented starting in 1979 on routes to and around schools to increase safety for bicyclists and pedestrians. The city's recently adopted Traffic and Mobility Plan sets a goal of reducing car traffic by 16 percent and aims to eliminate car traffic in the inner city, while increasing cycling by another 35 percent (City of Odense 2010). New policies for cycling are integrated into traffic policies, with priority given to bicycles over cars—an approach increasingly common in at least some European countries.

Delft

Delft is city of 96,000 residents located in the western part of the Netherlands, 15 kilometers from Rotterdam and 10 kilometers from The Hague. Delft University of Technology, with over 15,000 students, is a major employer in the town. The population of Delft is highly educated, and the city has a large foreign community compared to Dutch towns of similar size, probably due to the presence of the university. The city is well connected by rail to Rotterdam (12 minutes), The Hague (12 minutes), and Amsterdam (54 minutes) with at least two trains per hour. Bicycles are a common mode of travel to the rail station with abundant bicycle parking available. Delft is encircled by two major highways, but traffic congestion is a significant problem in the region.

Many factors contribute to a 27 percent cycling mode share for trips within the city. Cycling is easy and convenient (Heinen and Handy 2011) and it is seen as a normal means of transportation. The topography is flat, and the city has a moderate maritime climate characterized by relatively cool summers. Temperatures exceed 30°C only two days per year, on average, and the temperature falls below freezing only six to eight days per year (RNMI 2011). With an old city center and high-rise development from the second part of the twentieth century, the city is denser than Davis and Boulder. Strict national building regulations prevent urban sprawl, although in the last ten years new neighborhoods have been constructed farther from the city center, leading to an increase in car use (City of Delft 2005a).

As in Odense, Delft began to actively encourage cycling in the 1980s, although bicycle use was already common. The City of Delft wanted to build a bicycle network, and the Netherlands Ministry of Transport wished to learn from this experiment (Netherlands Ministry of Transport 1994). Between 1982 and 1987, the city constructed a bicycle system consisting of three interconnected networks: an urban network, a district network, and a neighborhood network. Together these networks were to provide an interconnected grid of bicycle facilities covering the entire urban area, with spacing between facilities of 500, 200 or 300, and 100 meters, respectively (Netherlands Ministry of Transport 1994). The city completed 60 percent of the envisioned system. The networks differ from each other in function and design with respect to both size and materials.

The result was a 7 percent increase in the number of bicycle trips between 1982 and 1987 in the neighborhoods in which the constructed networks were most complete (Netherlands Ministry of Transport 1998) and a total increase from 40 to 43 percent in the bicycle share for all trips within the boundaries of the city (Netherlands Ministry of Transport 1994). An evaluation of the system showed that the increase came mainly from residents who already cycled but started to cycle more often and for longer distances than they had before. In 1993, however, a second evaluation showed no further increase in the cycling mode share, though it did show an increase in cycling safety and a reduction in severe accidents.

Delft is now aiming to become one of the top cycling cities of the Netherlands (City of Delft 2005a), and bicycle planning is integrated into all transportation planning in the city. Infrastructure and parking improvements are the city's main focus. One goal is to identify and construct the missing links in the three-network system. The city is investing in improvements to existing bicycle infrastructure and more facilities separated from car traffic, as well as safe routes for children and bicycle parking. Traffic signals are being reprogrammed to reduce the waiting time for cyclists at intersections (City of Delft 2005b). The city is also investing in additional measures to promote cycling: information about parking and infrastructure is circulated via maps and the Internet and at train stations; attention is being given to reducing bicycle theft; at secondary schools a program offers mechanical checks of bicycles for students; and paid but subsidized guarded bike parking is provided in the city center (City of Delft 2005b).

Delft also encourages bicycle use through policies that deter driving. Starting in 2000, the city gradually limited the entry of car traffic to the city center. Movable posts now prevent cars from entering the historical city center but allow entry for buses and cars for deliveries of goods or persons (during restricted times). The city has maintained the total number of parking spaces at just under 4,000 but eliminated all free parking (DHV Group 2005). These measures have not resulted in an increase in bicycle use, but the accessibility of the center by bicycle is rated much higher than accessibility by car (8.2 compared to 5.7 out of 10 in 2005) (DHV Group 2005). More than 50 percent of the residents bicycle when going to the city center (City of Delft 2005a).

Complementing Delft's efforts are those of neighboring cities and of the national government. Within the Netherlands, cycling planning has recently focused on bicycle routes between cities as part of a special project of the Netherlands Ministry of Transport (n.d.) called *fiets filevrij* (cycle congestion free), based on a similar initiative in Delft called ZOEF (for *zorgeloos, onbelemmerd, eenvoudigweg fietsen*—carefree, unimpeded, simple cycling) (City of Delft, n.d.). Several connections have been upgraded to bicycle "highways." In an effort to increase the share of bicycle commuters, the existing cycling route between Delft and Rotterdam was transformed in 2007 to a direct route with facilities that are mostly separated from car traffic, with limited intersections, not a single traffic light, and red pavement; cyclists always have right-of-way along the route. Promotional programs at the national level complement local efforts, including campaigns for traffic safety, many subsidized programs encouraging cycling, and subsidies for buying a bicycle.

Discussion

In the United States, Davis and Boulder have succeeded in establishing cycling as a significant mode of transportation—more so than walking and, in Davis, public transportation—through infrastructure investments, complementary land-use policies, and a variety of supportive programs. Many small European cities have achieved even higher levels of cycling through these same strategies, though often at a much larger scale and almost always combined with several other important factors: historically compact development with strong city cores, coordination of cycling with good transit systems, integration of cycling into transportation planning and integration of transportation with land-use planning, implementation of deterrents to driving, and strong national policies supportive of cycling. These additional factors can be found also in the United States but to a far lesser degree.

It is important to understand how these cities adopted these strategies and were able to build comprehensive cycling programs. In all four cases presented here, a problem came together with a potential solution and political will to create the opportunity for noteworthy change in the city's approach to transportation (Zahariadis 2007). The problem was defined as too much driving, variously driven by concerns over traffic, environmental impacts, safety, and/or health. The solution was to increase cycling, and the culture of the community fueled the political will needed to carry out this solution. In all cases, committed city officials supported by engaged citizens were instrumental in both implementing a comprehensive bicycle program and sustaining these efforts over time. These cities overcame many challenges along the way, and they are likely to face more challenges ahead.

What lessons do the case study cities in this chapter have for other small cities in the United States as well as in countries like Canada and Australia where cycling accounts for a small share of travel? Many cities are already following the examples of Davis and Boulder by investing in bicycle infrastructure, adapting land-use policies, and implementing bicycle supportive programs and policies. But another important lesson from Davis and Boulder is that becoming a bicycle-friendly community takes time—especially true when a city must "retrofit" existing areas in contrast to incorporating infrastructure and supportive land use patterns into newly developing areas from the start. The challenges of retrofitting will differ by city. Newer cities (i.e., those built largely after World War II) are likely to have more space for infrastructure, given the wider streets common in these cities. But lower-density, single-use development patterns mean that destinations are likely to be more dispersed. In such cities, bicycle infrastructure may be used more for recreation than transportation, especially if the city builds off-street bicycle paths. For older cities, more compact, mixed-use development patterns keep destinations within cycling distance but the city may have less space for new bicycle infrastructure and a greater intensity of vehicle traffic from which to protect cyclists. Distances may make utilitarian cycling feasible in these cities, but creating a perception of safety is challenging.

Some older and more urban small cities in North America have been making good progress by using creative approaches to accommodating cyclists (table 12.2). Cambridge, Massachusetts, for example, has been installing bicycle lanes and other facilities as streets are repaved, installing bicycle parking throughout the city, and running a bicycle safety campaign in schools and elsewhere (City of Cambridge 2011). As of 2009, 5.8 percent of workers living in Cambridge commuted to work by bicycle, and bicycle counts more than doubled between 2002 and 2008; the number of bicycle crashes was virtually unchanged. Berkeley, California, adopted its first bicycle plan in 2000 (City of Berkeley 2011). At the core of the plan is an extensive bikeway network made up primarily of on-street bicycle lanes and designated bicycle routes, including nine "bicycle boulevards" with extensive traffic control devices to improve safety for bicyclists. The city's Public Health Division runs bicycle safety programs in the schools and after-school programs and funds training programs for adults. Victoria, British Columbia, has had similar success in promoting cycling through off-street bicycle trails, on-street bicycle lanes, marked shoulders, and bicycle-activated signals (Pucher and Buehler 2005). The community now has the highest level of cycling in Canada, with 4.8 percent of all trips by bicycle.

Cambridge and Berkeley highlight the additional challenges faced by small cities that are embedded within a metropolitan region. In these cities, travel patterns are likely to span city boundaries, so the viability of cycling depends also on infrastructure in neighboring cities. Within metropolitan regions, the efforts of individual cities are critical but more effective if coordinated with efforts at the regional level. The City of Cambridge coordinates its efforts with the 2007 Boston Region Bicycle Plan, which in turn is coordinated with the 2008 Massachusetts Bicycle Transportation Plan. The Paul Dudley White Bicycle Path along the Charles River, for example, which runs through Cambridge, is designated as a major state bicycle route. Similarly, the City of Berkeley coordinates its bicycle plans with the Alameda County Bicycle Plan and the Regional Bicycle Plan, adopted by the nine-county Metropolitan Transportation Commission. This coordination ensures that the networks in all three plans are consistent and interconnected. The Berkeley segment of the San Francisco Bay Trail, for example, appears in all three plans. Coordination across jurisdictions is perhaps more natural in Europe, where planning functions are more centralized and political boundaries less fragmented. As noted previously, the Dutch government is now focusing on intercity bicycle facilities.

Most of the small cities with high cycling rates in both the United States and Europe have a strong university presence, providing them with several advantages: a younger population with limited financial resources that naturally gravitates to cycling, a campus with parking that is likely to be limited and unlikely to be free, thriving central cores and compact city boundaries, and a progressive culture more receptive to a variety of

Table 12.2
Cycling levels and programs in selected small North American cities

	Cycling	Infrastructure	Programs
Cambridge, MA[a] 105,200 pop.; 24,000 students	• 5.8 percent of workers commuted by bicycle in 2009; bicycle counts show doubling in cycling levels between 2002 and 2008	• Extensive network of multiuse paths, bike lanes, cycle tracks, and shared lane pavement markings • Three bike repair stands with air pumps and tools • Signage to indicate routes connecting major bikeways • Bicycle parking for private developments required by zoning ordinance	• Bicycle network map and bicycle parking map • Annual Bike Week Events, including Bicycle Commuter Appreciation Day • Themed community bicycle rides hosted by the Cambridge Bicycle Committee
Berkeley, CA[b] 113,600 pop.; 29,000 students	• 6.5 percent of workers commuted by bicycle in 2009, up from 5.6 percent in 2000	• Fifty designated bikeways, including seven bicycle boulevards on which bicycles are given priority over cars • Bicycle/pedestrian bridge over interstate highway, linking city with waterfront • Bike stations at regional rapid transit stations, with free valet parking and bicycle repair shop	• Cycling and walking map • In-school and after-school safety education programs • Funding for adult bicycle training courses

Table 12.2
(continued)

	Cycling	Infrastructure	Programs
		• Public bicycle rack installation program • $2 million spent on bicycle improvements between 2000 and 2005	• Vehicle code enforcement effort • Program to reduce cycling on sidewalks
Victoria, Canada[c] 312,000 pop.	• 4.8 percent of all trips are by bicycle	• 377 km of bike routes, including 67 km of mixed-use off-road trails, 62 km of bike lanes, and 131 km of roadways with paved marked shoulders • Cyclist-activated traffic signals at forty intersections; special bike access lanes and bike boxes at many intersections • Most buses and ferries equipped with bike racks • Neighborhood traffic calming	• Mandatory cycling courses for school children ages 7–13 years • Annual Bike to Work Week and other promotional events • Detailed route maps including information for each bike route on steepness, traffic volumes, and difficult intersections

Sources: [a]City of Cambridge 2011; [b]City of Berkeley 2011; City of Berkeley 2005; [c]Pucher and Buehler 2005.

progressive and environment-based programs. This set of advantages does not imply, however, that smaller towns without universities cannot succeed in promoting cycling as a mode of transportation. In the United States, a growing number of smaller cities not dominated by a college or university are also working to promote cycling. Folsom, California, Bend, Oregon, and Olympia, Washington, for example, have achieved silver status as rated by the League of American Bicyclists (2010). The challenges may be greater in these cities, but they are not insurmountable. In the Netherlands, many noncollege towns have cycling shares over 20 percent, consistent with the high cycling share for the country as a whole.

Given the aging of the population in these countries, it is important to consider whether cycling can work as a mode of transportation in small cities with older populations. In the Netherlands, Denmark, and Germany, the answer is a definitive yes. Older people, including older women, bicycle as much as younger people in these countries (see chapters 2, 10, 11, 13, and 14). Encouraging older people to bicycle in places where it is not already common requires investments in off-street bicycle paths or at least cycle tracks that give cyclists a greater sense of protection from traffic. Providing access to appropriate equipment, such as adult tricycles and electric-assist bicycles, might also help (see chapter 5). In the United States, many private retirement communities (e.g., the Del Webb Sun City communities) rely on golf carts for getting around within the community; bicycles might be a viable substitute for many residents.

Conclusions

Small cities have unique natural advantages when it comes to utilitarian cycling, most prominently their bikeable geographic scale. But these advantages do not guarantee that cycling will thrive in these cities without concerted efforts to encourage it, and promoting cycling is not necessarily easier in smaller cities than in larger ones. Their natural advantages do, however, suggest a vast potential, untapped in the United States and many other countries, to increase cycling by focusing on the potential intrinsic to smaller cities. The experiences of cities that have succeeded— such as those described in this chapter—clearly demonstrate that efforts to increase cycling depend on a comprehensive approach comprising several critical components and that these efforts must be sustained over time to sustain cycling levels over time. Small cities have an essential role to play in the burgeoning cycling movement around the world.

References

Andersen, Troels. 2011. Personal communication, March 30.

Buehler, Ralph, and John Pucher. 2011. Sustainable Transport in Freiburg: Lessons from Germany's Environmental Capital. *International Journal of Sustainable Transportation* 5:43–70.

Buehler, Ted, and Susan Handy. 2008. Fifty Years of Bicycle Policy in Davis, CA. *Transportation Research Record* 2074:52–57.

Cambridge Cycling Campaign. 2011. Cycling Vision 2016. Cambridge: Cambridge Cycling Campaign. http://www.camcycle.org.uk/vision2016/.

Cambridgeshire County Council. 2011. Cycling and Walking. Cambridge: Cambridgeshire County Council. http://www.cambridgeshire.gov.uk/transport/around/cycling/.

City and County of Boulder. 2005. *Boulder Valley Comprehensive Plan—2005 Update*. Boulder: City and County of Boulder.

City of Berkeley. 2005. *2005 Berkeley Bicycle Plan Update*. Berkeley, CA: City of Berkeley. http://www.ci.berkeley.ca.us/uploadedFiles/Public_Works/Level_3_-_General/2005%20Berkeley%20Bicycle%20Plan%20Update.pdf.

City of Berkeley. 2011. Bicycling in Berkeley. Berkeley, CA: City of Berkeley. http://www.ci.berkeley.ca.us/ContentDisplay.aspx?id=6560.

City of Cambridge. 2011. Bicycle Programs. Cambridge: City of Cambridge. http://www2.cambridgema.gov/cdd/et/bike/index.html#about.

City of Delft. 2005a. *Local Traffic and Transport Plan 2005–2020. Delft Lastingly Accessible*. Delft, The Netherlands: City of Delft.

City of Delft. 2005b. *Delft Cycles! Bicycle Action Strategy II 2005–2010*. Delft, The Netherlands: City of Delft.

City of Delft. N.d. ZOEF. http://www.zoefroute.nl.

City of Groningen. 2008. *Get On! Bicycle Measures 2009–2010*. Groningen, The Netherlands: City of Groningen.

City of Linköping. 2008. *Cycle Plan for Linköping, 2008–2028*. Linköping, Sweden: City of Linköping. http://www.linkopingskommun.org/Global/Bygga%20och%20bo/Planer%20och%20byggprojekt/%c3%96versiktsplaner/Cykelplan/Cykelplan_del_3.pdf?epslanguage=sv.

City of Malmö. 2009. *Climate-Smart Malmö: Making Sustainability Reality*. Malmö, Sweden: City of Malmö. http://www.malmo.se/download/18.58f28d93121ca033d5e800091/Klimatbroschyr_090409EN.pdf.

City of Malmö. 2010. Final Application for the European Green Capital Award. Malmö, Sweden: City of Malmö.

City of Malmö. N.d. *Improving Malmö's Traffic Environment*. Malmö, Sweden: City of Malmö. http://www.malmo.se/download/18.58f28d93121ca033d5e 800077/SMILE_Malmo_+final+brochure.pdf.

Charlier, Jim. 2008. Personal communication. June 20.

City of Odense. 2010. City Cycle Odense. Odense, Denmark: City of Odense. http://www.expo.odense.dk/Topmenu/Cyclism/Cycle%20City%20Odense .aspx.

Colville-Andersen, Mikael. 2011. The World's Most Bicycle-Friendly Cities. http://www.copenhagenize.com/2009/07/worlds-most-bicycle-friendly-cities .html.

Cycling England. 2010. *Cycling City and Towns Programme Overview*. London: Department for Transport.

De la Bruhèze, Adri Albert, and Frank C. A. Veraart. 1999. *Bicycle Traffic in Practice and Policy in the Twentieth Century*. RWS-serie nr 63. Conducted by the Foundation for the History of Technology, Technical University of Eindhoven. The Hague: Dutch Ministry of Transport, Public Works and Water Management.

DHV Group. 2005. Monitor Inner City Limited-Traffic. Delft, The Netherlands: DHV Ruimte en Mobiliteit BV.

DMI (Danish Meteorological institute). 2011. Weather Archives. http://www .dmi.dk/dmi/en/vejrarkiv?region=5&year=2010&month=1.

Dutch Bicycle Council. 2006. *Continuous and Integral: The Cycling Policies of Groningen and Other European Cycling Cities*. Publication number 7. Amsterdam, The Netherlands: Dutch Bicycle Council.

Dutch Bicycle Council. 2010. *Bicycle Policies of the European Principals: Continuous and Integral*. Publication number 7. Utrecht, The Netherlands: Dutch Bicycle Council.

Forsyth, Ann, and Kevin J. Krizek. 2011. Urban Design: Is There a Distinctive View from the Bicycle? *Journal of Urban Design* 16:531–549.

Handy, S., Y. Xing, and T. Buehler. 2010. Factors Associated with Bicycle Ownership and Use: A Study of Six Small U.S. Cities. *Transportation* 37:967–985.

Heinen, Eva, and Susan L. Handy. 2011. Similarities in Attitudes and Norms and the Effect on Bicycle Commuting: Evidence from the Bicycle Cities Davis and Delft. *International Journal of Sustainable Transportation* 6 (5): 257–281.

Joyce, Patrick. 2011. Personal communication, March 7.

Krizek, Kevin, Ann Forsyth, and Carissa Schively Slotterback. 2009. Is There a Role for Evidence-Based Practice in Urban Planning and Policy? *Planning Theory & Practice* 10 (4): 459–478.

Krizek, Kevin J., Susan L. Handy, and Ann Forsyth. 2009. Explaining Changes in Walking and Bicycling Behavior: Challenges for Transportation Research. *Environment and Planning B* 36:725–740.

Krizek, Kevin J., and Siegmund J. Langegger. 2009. Bicycling in Boulder: Researching Initiatives Worth Replicating? Presented at the Annual Meeting of the Transportation Research Board, Washington, DC, January.

League of American Bicyclists. 2010. *Current Bicycling-Friendly Communities—September 2010.* Washington, DC: League of American Bicyclists. http://www.bikeleague.org/programs/bicyclefriendlyamerica/communities/pdfs/bfc _masterlist_09_10.pdf.

Lovejoy, Kristin. 2010. *Results of the 2009–10 Campus Travel Survey. UCD-ITS-RR-10–17, Institute of Transportation Studies, University of California, Davis.* Davis, CA: Institute of Transportation Studies.

Marsden, Peter V., and Noah E. Friedkin. 1993. Network Studies of Social Influence. *Sociological Methods & Research* 22 (1): 127–151.

Netherlands Ministry of Transport. 1994. *Space for the Bicycle, Examples of Cities in the Netherlands, Denmark, Germany and Switzerland.* The Hague: Netherlands Ministry of Transport and Association of Dutch Municipalities.

Netherlands Ministry of Transport. 1998. *Final Report Masterplan Bicycle. Summary, Evaluation and Overview of the Project Part of Masterplan Bicycle, 1990–1997.* The Hague: Netherlands Ministry of Transport.

Netherlands Ministry of Transport. N.d. Cycle Congestion Free. http://www.fietsfilevrij.nl.

Oliver, J. Eric. 2000. City Size and Civic Involvement in Metropolitan America. *American Political Science Review* 94 (2): 361–373.

Pucher, John, and Ralph Buehler. 2005. Cycling Trends and Policies in Canadian Cities. *World Transport Policy and Practice* 11:43–61.

Pucher, John, and Ralph Buehler. 2007. At the Frontiers of Cycling: Policy Innovations in the Netherlands, Denmark, and Germany. *World Transport Policy and Practice* 13 (3): 8–57.

Pucher, John, and Ralph Buehler. 2008. Making Cycling Irresistible: Lessons from the Netherlands, Denmark, and Germany. *Transport Reviews* 28 (4): 495–528.

Pucher, John, and Ralph Buehler. 2010. Walking and Cycling for Healthy Cities. *Built Environment* 36 (5): 391–414.

Pucher, John, Jennifer Dill, and Susan Handy. 2010. Infrastructure, Programs, and Policies to Increase Bicycling: An International Review. *Preventive Medicine* 50:S105–S125.

Ratzel, Marni. 2008. Personal communication, June 2.

RNMI (Royal Netherlands Meteorological Institute). 2011. Averages of 1981–2010. http://www.knmi.nl.

Roskowski, Martha, and Marni Ratzel. 2008. *How to Be Like Boulder. Bike/Ped Professional Newsletter* 2. Cedarburg, WI: Association of Pedestrian and Bicycle Professionals.

Rutsch, Randall. 2008. Personal communication, July 9.

Tiebout, Charles M. 1956. A Pure Theory of Local Expenditures. *Journal of Political Economy* 64 (5): 416–424.

U.S. Census Bureau. 2000. U.S. Census Journey to Work Data. http://www .census.gov/main/www/cen2000.html.

U.S. Census Bureau. 2009. 2005–2009 American Community Survey. http://www .census.gov/acs/www/.

Zahariadis, Nikolaos. 2007. The Multiple Streams Framework: Structure, limitations, prospects. In *Theories of the Policy Process*, ed. Paul Sabatier, 65–92. Boulder: Westview Press.

13
Big City Cycling in Europe, North America, and Australia

Ralph Buehler and John Pucher

The national data presented in chapter 2 hide variations in cycling conditions, trends, and policies within each country. In fact, cycling rates and policies vary widely among cities and regions. Moreover, it is at the city level that cycling policies are actually implemented, even if funding is provided by the state or federal levels of government. Thus, it is crucial to examine cycling trends and policies at the local level. This chapter focuses on large cities, which we define as having at least half a million residents in their metropolitan area. Over two-thirds of the populations in developed countries live in such metropolitan areas, and their share of total population has been increasing (Brookings Institution 2010; OECD 2006).

Conditions for cycling in large cities are quite different from those in the small cities discussed in chapter 12. Large cities usually have a greater mix of incomes, races/ethnicities, educational attainments, and lifestyles (Brookings Institution 2010; OECD 2006). Moreover, large cities typically have younger populations and are at the vanguard of economic and societal trends, which are often pioneered in large cities and later spread throughout the country (Brookings Institution 2010). Transportation systems and land-use patterns in larger cities, however, generally deter cycling (Heinen, van Wee, and Maat 2010). Motor vehicle traffic volumes are generally higher, and roads are more congested (Texas Transportation Institute 2009). Trip distances are longer due to the greater land area of large cities. Finally, public transportation services are generally more extensive and provide more competition to cycling in larger cities (Heinen, van Wee, and Maat 2010).

Although large cities present special challenges to cycling, they would benefit from the economic and environmental advantages cycling has to offer. Bikes require little space for operation and storage and might help mitigate roadway congestion and crowding of public transportation during peak hours. Bikes are less polluting and less noisy than motor vehicles and thus offer the potential for cleaner air and quieter streets. A modal shift to cycling might also provide financial relief to big city governments; provision of bike infrastructure is far less expensive than building highways (City of Copenhagen 2011). Because bikes are affordable for virtually everyone, they have the potential to provide mobility for low-income households, which are often concentrated in large cities (STPP 2004; USDOL 2010).

For this overview of cycling trends and policies in large cities, we examine thirteen cities on three continents. Most of the case study cities have been among the most successful large cities in their respective countries at improving conditions for cycling and raising cycling levels. We contrast cycling in less car-dependent European cities (Amsterdam, Berlin, and Copenhagen) with more car-oriented urban areas in Australia (Melbourne and Sydney), Canada (Montreal, Toronto, and Vancouver), and the United States (Chicago, Minneapolis, Portland, San Francisco, and Washington).

Data Sources and Characteristics of Case Study Cities

The case study cities cover a broad range of locations, climates, demographics, densities, histories, and urban structures. Moreover, the cities comprise the full range of cycling policies and programs that are implemented in OECD countries to encourage more cycling and make it safer. Data for the case study analysis originate from (1) federal, state, and local government statistics and reports; (2) transportation plans, official documents, and transportation sections of each city's official website; (3) national level cycling organizations and research centers; and (4) unpublished information gathered though in-person, phone, and email correspondence with bike planners, city and transportation planners, and representatives from cycling organizations in each city.

Table 13.1 summarizes some key demographic, economic, and climatic characteristics of the case study cities. Population size of the cities ranges from 3.4 million in Berlin to 82,000 in Melbourne. International differences in definitions of administrative city boundaries distort this

Table 13.1
Demographic and climatic characteristics of case study cities

	Population (1,000)		Population density (per km²)		Gross domestic product (US$)		Percent car-free households	Percent university students	Annual climate normals		
	City	Metro region	City	Metro region	Total (in bn US$)	Per capita			Precipitation (cm)	Days ≤ 0°C	Days ≥ 32.2°C
Amsterdam	751	2,160	4,581	1,587	47	32,900	63	11	78	64	—
Berlin	3,395	4,500	3,806	3,750	95	21,300	50	4	57	80	7
Copenhagen	531	1,700	6,015	1,850	49	33,500	70	7	70	76	—
Chicago	2,741	9,570	4,633	1,500	574	45,600	26	8	92	129	17
Minneapolis	361	3,230	2,524	1,050	194	53,000	18	12	75	154	14
Montreal	1,621	3,636	4,439	1,850	148	29,100	—	10	105	164	9
Portland	560	2,207	1,584	1,300	110	41,800	15	8	94	40	11
San Francisco	809	4,275	6,600	2,350	301	62,300	29	9	57	1	3
Toronto	2,503	5,113	3,972	2,650	253	34,900	—	5	83	107	10
Vancouver	578	2,117	5,039	1,650	95	32,000	—	8	120	46	0
Washington	592	5,358	3,700	1,300	375	61,600	36	11	100	68	36
Melbourne	82	3,590	1,570	1,500	172	32,700	—	—	66	0	32
Sydney	177	4,120	2,040	2,100	213	35,000	14	—	122	0	25
Average	1,131	3,967	3,885	1,880	202	39,669	36	8	86	71	15

Source: City of Amsterdam 2010; City of Berlin 2010; City of Copenhagen 2010b; City of Melbourne 2011; City of Sydney 2007; Environment Canada 2010; Statistics Canada 2010; USDOC 1980–2000, 2010.
Note: In this table gross domestic product has been converted to US dollars using the methodology of purchasing power parity. Precipitation and temperature are thirty-year averages from 1970 to 2000: 0°C = 32°F, 32.2°C = 90°F.

comparison, however. The local government areas of Melbourne and Sydney are very small—comparable to downtowns in North America and city centers in Europe. Sydney and Melbourne can be compared to the other cities only in terms of their metropolitan areas, which range in population from 5.5 million in Washington to 1.7 million in Copenhagen.

Studies suggest that larger cities tend to have lower cycling levels due to their greater land area, longer trip distances, and more extensive public transportation systems (Heinen, van Wee, and Maat 2010). Higher densities of larger cities might be expected to facilitate cycling due to the concentration of many origins and destinations, but density might also discourage cycling due to high traffic volumes on roads and limited space for bikeway facilities. Population density of the cities varies by a ratio of 4 to 1: from 6,600 inhabitants per km^2 in San Francisco to 1,584 per km^2 in Portland. Population densities in the cities are about twice as high as for their metropolitan areas as a whole, which also include lower-density suburban areas.

San Francisco is the most affluent case study city, with a gross domestic product (GDP) per capita ($62,300), which is three times as high as Berlin's ($21,300). Overall, the American case study cities have roughly 40 percent higher GDP per capita than the other large cities. Automobile ownership is correlated with income and influences cycling more directly than differentials in GDP (Dill and Carr 2003; Heinen, van Wee, and Maat 2010). Causation probably runs in both directions: lower levels of car ownership encourage more cycling, and households that cycle more may choose to own fewer cars. The percentage of households without cars ranges from roughly 15 percent in Sydney and Portland to more than 60 percent in Amsterdam and Copenhagen. The share of car-free households is almost twice as high in the three European cities as in the North American and Australian cities. The lower level of car ownership in Europe may be explained by better walking, cycling, and public transportation alternatives to the car as well as national government policies that make car ownership and use more expensive (DIW 2005).

Studies show that cities with large student populations tend to have higher bike mode shares (Dill and Carr 2003; Nelson and Allen 1997). This factor is especially important in small university towns, where students account for a large share of the population, as discussed in chapter 12. Students generally account for a small share of the population in large cities, ranging from about 4 percent in Berlin to roughly 10 percent in Amsterdam, Minneapolis, and Washington.

Several studies find that climate and topography can affect cycling levels (Dill and Carr 2003; Heinen, van Wee, and Maat 2010; Pucher and Buehler 2006b, 2011). Most studies suggest that high precipitation levels discourage cycling. Very cold or hot weather may also discourage cycling. As shown in table 13.1, there is a ratio of 2 to 1 in the amount of precipitation per year, ranging from 122 cm in Sydney to 57 cm in San Francisco. The average number of days with temperature below freezing (0°C) ranges from 164 in Montreal to none in Sydney and Melbourne. The average number of days with temperature of 32.2°C or higher ranges from thirty-six in Washington to none in Vancouver. There are no comparable statistics for humidity, which raises the heat index and further discourages cycling during hot summers.

Similarly, we could not find standardized statistics on topography, but San Francisco is probably the hilliest of the case study cities, followed by Vancouver and Portland, whereas Amsterdam, Chicago, Copenhagen, Berlin, and Minneapolis are quite flat. Cycling in some cities, such as Minneapolis, is favored by flat topography, but their harsh climates would be expected to discourage cycling. Conversely, cities with hilly topography, such as San Francisco, have mild climates that favor cycling. Other physical characteristics can also pose barriers to cycling. For example, the large Sydney harbor with its many inlets, bays, and rivers interrupts the transportation network—and the few bridges allow for only a limited number of direct travel routes and increase travel distances (Pucher, Garrard, and Greaves 2011).

Trends in Cycling Levels and Safety

Over the past two decades, cycling has increased in all the case study cities, but cycling rates in the European cities are much higher than in Australia, Canada, and the United States. Figure 13.1 shows trends in the share of commuters who bike to work, the only comparable statistic for all cities. In 2010, Portland, Minneapolis, and Vancouver had the highest share of bike commuters in North America and much higher bike

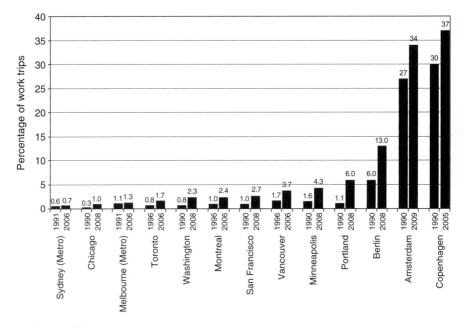

Figure 13.1
Trend in share of workers commuting by bike in large North American, Australian, and European cities, 1990–2009. *Sources:* City of Amsterdam 2010; City of Berlin 2010; City of Copenhagen 2010b; City of Melbourne 2011; City of Sydney 2007; Statistics Canada 2010; USDOC 1980–2000, 2010.

commuting levels than the two Australian cities. However, data in figure 13.1 for Sydney and Melbourne refer to their metropolitan areas, including large car-dependent suburbs. Both cities report significantly higher cycling levels for their city centers: 4.0 percent in downtown Melbourne and 2.1 percent in central Sydney.

In Portland, the bike mode share rose more than fivefold between 1990 and 2008, from 1.1 percent to 6.0 percent—the largest increase among the thirteen cities. All eight North American cities at least doubled their bike share of work commuters. Cycling levels increased at a slower rate in the three European cities but from much higher starting levels than in North America. Between 1990 and 2009, the share of bike commuters rose from 27 to 34 percent in Amsterdam and from 30 to 37 percent in Copenhagen. During the same time period, Berlin more than doubled its bike share for commute trips from 6 to 13 percent. The slowest increases were in Australia, where bike commuting rose from

0.6 to 0.7 percent in Sydney and from 1.1 to 1.3 percent in Melbourne between 1991 and 2006.

Aside from the commute data shown in figure 13.1, most of the case study cities have their own sources of information on cycling levels, either through travel surveys or cordon counts of cyclists at particular locations. Without exception, they also confirm growth in cycling (Pucher and Buehler 2008; Pucher, Buehler, and Seinen 2011; Pucher, Garrard, and Greaves 2011). We do not report those survey results here, however, because the cities use different methodologies, trip definitions, geographic coverage, and timing and are thus incomparable.

There is considerable spatial variation in cycling levels within cities. Cycling rates tend to be higher near the city center. Such bike-friendly neighborhoods are usually located within close cycling distance of university campuses and downtown jobs and feature a mixture of residential and commercial land uses. For example, the bike mode share exceeds 10 percent in several of the central neighborhoods of both Toronto and Vancouver compared to less than 1 percent in most of their outlying residential districts (City of Toronto 2010b; City of Vancouver 2010). The Inner Northeast and Inner Southeast sections of Portland have bike commute mode shares of 13 percent, more than six times higher than the 2 percent bike share in outlying districts such as Outer East Portland (City of Portland 2010a). In the central Berlin neighborhood of Friedrichshain-Kreuzberg, cycling accounts for 21 percent of all trips, compared to 6 percent in the outlying neighborhood of Marzahn-Hellersdorf (City of Berlin 2010). The bike share of commuters living in the city of Copenhagen is 55 percent, compared to 37 percent for all metropolitan area commuters, including suburbanites cycling to Copenhagen (City of Copenhagen 2010a). Similarly, Melbourne reports 4 percent of all commutes by bike in the city center, but only 0.5 percent in the suburbs (Pucher, Garrard, and Greaves 2011). In short, all the cities exhibit much higher bike mode shares in central versus outer neighborhoods, with yet lower cycling rates in suburbs.

Gender Differences

Similar to the national statistics presented in chapter 2, cycling is far more male-dominated in large cities in North America and Australia than in Europe. In both Copenhagen and Amsterdam, women account for the

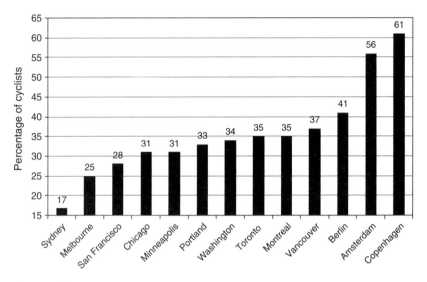

Figure 13.2
Share of women among cyclists in large North American, Australian, and European cities, 2008. *Sources:* City of Amsterdam 2010; City of Berlin 2010; City of Copenhagen 2010b; City of Melbourne 2011; City of Sydney 2007; Statistics Canada 2010; USDOC 1980–2000, 2010.

majority of cyclists (56% and 61%, respectively). The 41 percent share of female cyclists in Berlin is slightly higher than the 35–37 percent of bike commuters in Vancouver, Montreal, and Toronto. Those Canadian cities, in turn, have higher female shares than any of the American and Australian cities (figure 13.2). Washington and Portland come closest to the Canadian cities at 34 percent and 33 percent, respectively. Sydney has, by far, the lowest percentage of women bike commuters: only 17 percent.

Cycling Safety

Figure 13.3 shows the cyclist fatality rate per 10,000 daily commuter cyclists in each of the cities, ranging from 8.3 in Sydney to 0.3 in Copenhagen—a ratio of more than 20 to 1. Similar to national cycling safety levels described in chapter 2, European cities have the safest cycling, followed by Canadian, American, and Australian cities, in that order. Vancouver has the safest cycling in North America. Because the number of cyclist fatalities fluctuates from year to year, we calculated the average number of fatalities over the past five years for each city. For

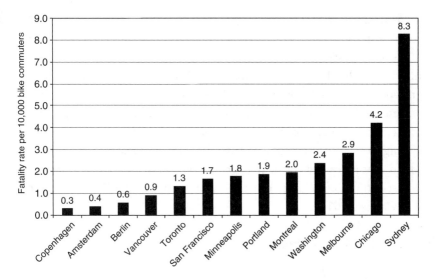

Figure 13.3
Five-year average annual cyclist fatalities per 10,000 daily bike commuters in
North American, Australian, and European cities, 2008. *Sources:* City of Amsterdam 2010; City of Berlin 2010; City of Copenhagen 2010b; City of Melbourne
2011; City of Sydney 2007; Statistics Canada 2010; USDOC 1980–2000, 2010.

the exposure rate, we used the number of daily commuter cyclists because
those data are derived from large census surveys that can be disaggre-
gated to the city level. There is no other source of internationally comparable and statistically reliable data on cycling levels in each city. The
problem with this methodology is that the number of fatalities in the
numerator is due to cycling for all trip purposes, whereas the number of
cyclists in the denominator includes only work commuters. Despite its
limitations, the indicator provides the only feasible adjustment for different levels of cycling and thus different exposure rates across the cities.

The relationship between cycling levels in figure 13.1 and cyclist fatality rates in figure 13.3 is consistent with the principle of safety in
numbers discussed in chapter 7. Cities with the highest bike mode shares
have the safest cycling; and cities with the lowest bike mode shares have
the most dangerous cycling. It is likely that causation runs in both directions: safer cycling encourages more cycling, and more cycling encourages greater safety. Trends in cycling levels and injuries in the case study
cities also support the principle of safety in numbers. For example, from

1996 to 2008, the share of bike commuters in Copenhagen increased from 30 to 37 percent, while the number of cyclist injuries declined by 50 percent (City of Copenhagen 2009, 2010a). In Amsterdam, cyclist injuries fell by 40 percent between 1980 and 2005, in spite of strong growth in cycling levels (City of Amsterdam 2010; Langenberg 2000; Osberg and Stiles 1998). Whereas safer cycling has encouraged more cycling in Europe, dangerous conditions are an important deterrent to cycling in North America and Australia. For example, a Sydney survey found that perceived traffic danger was the main reason why infrequent cyclists do not cycle more often (City of Sydney 2006; Pucher, Garrard, and Greaves 2011).

Cycling Policies and Programs

All the case study cities have been implementing infrastructure, programs, and policies to promote cycling. European cities have implemented bike-friendly measures to a greater extent and for a longer period of time than cities in North America and Australia. European cities have also done far more to restrict car use and make it more expensive by establishing car-free zones and traffic-calmed neighborhoods while raising taxes and other charges on car ownership, use, and parking.

Expansion and Improvement of the Bikeway Network

Without exception, cycling policy in all the cities has included the expansion, integration, and improvement of bikeway facilities as discussed in chapter 6, including on-street bike lanes, cycle tracks, and off-street bike paths. As shown in figure 13.4, Amsterdam, Portland, Minneapolis, and Copenhagen have the largest supply of bike lanes and paths per 100,000 population, ranging from 61 to 79 km. At the other end of the spectrum, Chicago and Toronto have the fewest bike lanes and paths per 100,000 population: 9 km and 12 km, respectively. Both Chicago and Toronto are making progress, however, having roughly doubled their bikeway networks between 2000 and 2010 (CDOT 2010; City of Toronto 2010a, 2010b).

The largest increase on a per-capita basis was in Minneapolis, which added 29 km per 100,000 population over the ten-year period (City of Minneapolis 2008, 2010a). The supply of bike paths and lanes in Sydney

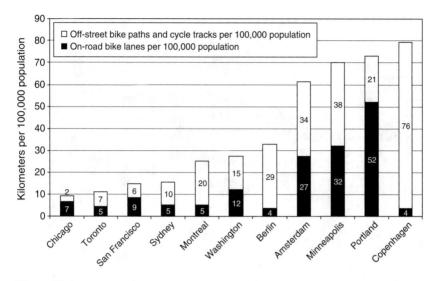

Figure 13.4
Supply of bike paths and lanes per 100,000 residents in large North American, Australian, and European cities. *Sources:* Calculated by the authors based on data from City of Amsterdam 2010; City of Berlin 2010; City of Copenhagen 2010b; City of Melbourne 2011; City of Sydney 2007; Statistics Canada 2010; USDOC 1980–2000, 2010.

is similar to that in San Francisco, albeit with a greater focus on off-road facilities in Sydney and less connectivity of individual segments. Comparable data for Melbourne are not available.

As shown in figure 13.4, the bikeway networks in some of the cities such as Chicago, Portland, and San Francisco consist mainly of on-street bike lanes (Buehler and Pucher 2012). In other cities, such as Copenhagen, Berlin, and Montreal, separate bike paths or physically separated on-street cycle tracks account for the majority of the bikeway network. Copenhagen has the longest tradition of favoring separate paths and cycle tracks over on-street lanes—dating back to the 1930s (City of Copenhagen 2002, 2007). Copenhagen cycle tracks are generally on both sides of the street, located between the roadway and the sidewalk (figure 13.5). Cycle tracks in Copenhagen are usually curb elevated (7–12 cm) and between 2.2 and 2.5 meters wide, but on especially busy commuter routes, they are widened to 3 meters (City of Copenhagen 2002, 2010a). The city has plans to build an additional 65 km of cycle tracks over the next decade.

Figure 13.5
Copenhagen's extensive network of integrated cycle tracks provides physical separation from motor vehicles. *Photo:* Ralph Buehler.

Montreal was the first large city in North America to install cycle tracks, which are bidirectional in Montreal and located on one side of the street (75 km in 2010) (Pucher and Buehler 2006a; City of Montreal 2010). There are also cycle tracks on three streets in Washington (figure 13.6), two streets in Portland, and on two bridges and one street in Vancouver (City of Portland 2010b; City of Vancouver 2010; DDOT 2010).

Most bike paths and lanes in Amsterdam have been built since the early 1980s. In fact, Amsterdam did not finalize the plan for its primary bicycle network until 2005 ("Hoofdnet Fiets"). In 2009, the Hoofdnet Fiets was 450 km long and consisted mainly of separate bicycle paths

Figure 13.6
The cycle track on Pennsylvania Avenue in Washington, D.C., extends from the White House to the Capitol. *Photo:* Ralph Buehler.

with a minimum width of 1.8 m per directional lane (Buehler and Pucher 2010). The network also included stretches of traffic-calmed roads (30 km/h) with low traffic volumes, which the city's bike planners consider safe enough for cyclists to share the road comfortably with automobiles. The aim of the Hoofdnet Fiets is to provide bicycle travel routes that minimize intersections with car traffic. As of 2011, 90 percent of Amsterdam roads were considered bike friendly. To avoid the dooring of cyclists, the network does not place any bike lanes immediately next to parked cars (City of Amsterdam 2010).

Similar to Copenhagen and Amsterdam, most of Berlin's cycling network consists of separate bike paths along roads (650 km), off-road bikeways through parks and forests (190 km), and traffic-calmed neighborhoods (3,800 km) (City of Berlin 2010). Between 2002 and 2010, Berlin focused on expanding on-road cycling facilities, tripling the extent of its bike lanes (from 40 km to 125 km) and more than doubling the length of its shared bus-bike lanes (from 30 km to 80 km). Berlin's increasing emphasis on bike lanes instead of bike paths has been partly due to the lower cost of lanes. In North America, most recent investment has also been in on-street bike lanes. Between 2000 and 2010, for example, the overall length of bike lanes increased more than twice as much as the overall length of bike paths in Toronto, Portland, Washington, Minneapolis, and Chicago (CDOT 2010; City of Minneapolis 2010a; City of Portland 2010a; City of Toronto 2010a).

As discussed previously, traffic-calmed residential streets can serve as convenient, comfortable, and safe bike routes, even without any special bike facilities. In Berlin, Amsterdam, Portland, and Vancouver, traffic-calmed neighborhood streets are an integral part of the cycling network and often provide crucial links between otherwise unconnected bike lanes and paths. Traffic calming combines low speed limits with infrastructure modifications, such as street narrowing, chicanes (obstructions and curves that force zigzag routing), traffic circles, speed humps, median islands, curb extensions, raised intersections and crosswalks, special pavement, diverters, and mid-block street closures with pass-throughs for bikes (Pucher and Buehler 2008).

Traffic calming is less common in North America and Australia and is often limited to isolated streets and not area-wide as in Europe. An exception is Vancouver, which has been at the forefront of traffic calming in North America. Vancouver has focused on providing safe and convenient bike routes on low-volume, traffic-calmed streets instead of building extensive systems of bike lanes and paths (City of Vancouver 2010; TransLink 2009). Bicycle boulevards are a modification of traffic-calmed streets specifically designed to facilitate cycling. Special pavement markings and signage reinforce bicycle priority on such streets, which includes right-of-way when riding through most intersections (i.e., stop signs for traffic crossing bike boulevards) and special bike traffic signals to cross arterials. In 2010, there were 129 km of bike boulevards in Vancouver, 58 km in Portland (with another 30 km planned and funded), and 16 km in Minneapolis (City of Minneapolis 2010a; City of Portland 2010a; City of Vancouver 2010).

Similar to Berlin, Copenhagen, and Amsterdam, North American cities like Portland, San Francisco, and Vancouver have been painting some of their bike lanes bright green, blue, or red to enhance visibility and increase cycling safety, especially where conflicts between cars and bikes are most problematic. Portland and Washington have installed buffered bike lanes (City of Portland 2010a; DDOT 2010). Unlike cycle tracks, they provide no physical barriers from cars but offer some separation from motor vehicles via a diagonally striped lane between the bike and car lanes.

Although the recent focus of some cities has been on expanding bike lanes, off-street bike paths are often the most heavily used and highest-profile cycling facilities (Pucher, Buehler, and Seinen 2011). In North America and Australia, most separate bike paths are located in parks or along rivers, lakes, or harbors. In contrast to Europe, where bike paths and pedestrian walkways are generally separated, most bike paths in North America and Australia are multiuse paths shared with pedestrians. That can lead to cyclist-pedestrian conflicts and slower cycling speeds, especially on weekends, when such facilities are most heavily used.

Most of the large cities examined in this chapter have been installing bike boxes with advance stop lines for cyclists at key intersections. Cyclist stop lines are about 3–5 meters ahead of the stop line for cars, thus enhancing cyclist visibility and safety. In 2010, there were 20 bike boxes in Vancouver, 17 in Portland, 6 in Minneapolis, and 2 in San Francisco and Washington (City of Minneapolis 2010a; City of Portland 2010b; DDOT 2010; SFMTA 2010). Berlin and Copenhagen also provide advance stop lines for bikes ahead of stopped cars but only on the right hand side of the road within the width of the bike lane—and not stretching across the entire road. In Copenhagen, 117 key intersections are equipped with advance stop lines, traffic signal priority, and special blue lane markings for cyclists (City of Copenhagen 2010a).

Copenhagen and Amsterdam synchronize some of their traffic lights to give cyclist consecutive green lights—a so-called green wave. In 2010, Copenhagen had green waves on four major arterials (City of Copenhagen 2010a). In 2007, Amsterdam implemented its first green wave for cyclists on the Raadhuisstraat with a green light for cyclists at eleven traffic signals synchronized to a cycling speed of 18 km/h (City of Amsterdam 2010).

Overall, European cities have more extensive and better integrated systems of bike paths, lanes, and cycle tracks than North American and Australian cities. In Copenhagen, Amsterdam, and Berlin, cyclists can reach virtually any destination by bike without riding on roads with heavy

Figure 13.7
Improvements of cycling facilities in Portland, Oregon, led to a 516 percent increase in bike trips across four Willamette River bridges from 1991 to 2010. *Photo:* Greg Raisman.

car traffic volumes and high travel speeds. Most intersections accommodate cyclists with advance bicycle stop lines for visibility and safety, advance green lights, or green waves for cyclists. Some North American cities such as Portland (figure 13.7), Minneapolis, and Vancouver are rapidly expanding their bikeway networks. Other cities such as Sydney, Chicago, and Washington continue to lag far behind.

Bike Parking
Just as car parking is essential to car use, bike parking is essential to cycling. All the case study cities have greatly increased their supply of public bike parking since 2000. As shown in figure 13.8, Amsterdam has by far the most bike parking per 100,000 residents: five times more than Copenhagen, the city with the second most bike parking. Even 225,000 bike parking spaces in Amsterdam do not suffice, however. During peak hours on workdays, bike parking demand far exceeds existing supply at

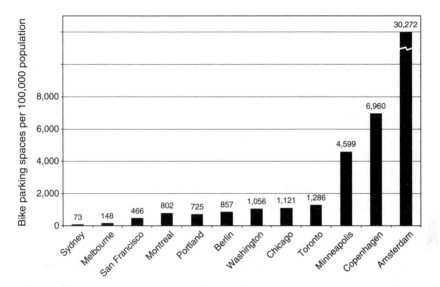

Figure 13.8
Bike parking spaces per 100,000 residents in large North American, Australian, and European cities, 2008. *Sources:* City of Amsterdam 2010; City of Berlin 2010; City of Copenhagen 2010b; City of Melbourne 2011; City of Sydney 2007; Statistics Canada 2010; USDOC 1980–2000, 2010.

many popular downtown destinations, such as Central Station. Similarly, in a biannual survey Copenhagen cyclists regularly rate the lack of good bike parking as the worst aspect of cycling conditions in the city (City of Copenhagen 2009).

Toronto has the most bike parking spaces in North America (32,200), but Minneapolis has the most bike parking spots per 100,000 residents. Chicago, Minneapolis, and Toronto have been expanding public bike parking in sidewalk racks by about 1,000 additional racks each year (Bike Walk Twin Cities 2008; CDOT 2010; City of Minneapolis 2008; City of Toronto 2010b). Sydney and Melbourne have incomplete inventories of their bike parking facilities, but the available statistics indicate that they have the least bike parking per capita of our case study cities.

In addition, most of the case study cities have laws requiring the private provision of bike parking in both commercial and residential buildings (Dutch Bicycle Council 2006, 2010; Pucher, Buehler, and Seinen 2011; Pucher, Garrard, and Greaves 2011). Some cities, such as

Washington and Vancouver, and some states, such as New South Wales and Victoria in Australia, offer financial incentives for the provision of shower and locker facilities for cyclists in newly constructed buildings.

Integration with Public Transportation and Bikesharing

The case study cities have made impressive progress at integrating bicycling with public transportation, and many cities have implemented bikesharing schemes. Chapters 8 and 9 focus on bike-transit integration and bikesharing, respectively. In this chapter, we only highlight key aspects of each city's policies. Most North American cities have equipped all of their buses with bike racks. The exception among the case study cities is Montreal. Most European cities do not allow bikes on city buses; nor are buses equipped with bike racks. Instead, European cities provide ample bike parking at public transportation stops. Buses in Sydney and Melbourne are not equipped with bike racks, and bike parking at bus stops or public transportation terminals is far more limited than in Europe.

Rail systems in all the case study cities permit bikes on board trains, but most systems restrict bikes to off-peak hours and/or to cars specifically designated for bicycles. European systems usually charge a special fee for taking bikes on board. Over the last decade, rail systems in the case study cities have vastly improved bike parking at stations by providing racks for short-term parking and bike lockers and bike stations for long-term parking.

Most Dutch, Danish, and German train stations provide bike rentals of some sort (Dutch Bicycle Council 2010; German Railways 2007). Recently introduced bikesharing schemes offer a more flexible form of bike rental, as explained in chapter 9. In 1965, Amsterdam pioneered bikesharing by distributing fifty unlocked bicycles painted in white in the inner city for use by everyone—free of charge (Dutch Bicycle Council 2006; Shaheen, Guzman, and Zhang 2010). In 1995, Copenhagen introduced a coin-operated bikesharing system with 1,100 bikes located at 110 bike kiosks throughout the city (City Bicycle Foundation 2010). In North America, Montreal, Washington, Minneapolis, and Chicago have bikesharing systems with bike kiosks. Toronto and San Francisco have plans to open similar bikesharing systems. In contrast to the other systems, the "Call-a-Bike" program in Berlin allows bike rentals by cell phone without a fixed bike kiosk.

Cyclist and Driver Training and Education

All of the case study cities have some sort of bike training programs for children as well as adults, but German, Dutch, and Danish schools have the most comprehensive bike training and traffic education programs (Pucher and Buehler 2008). In Berlin, for example, school children have to take part in cycling training and pass a cycling skills test between third and fourth grade (City of Berlin 2010). Police officers first supervise cycling lessons on off-street training grounds with miniature roads and traffic signals. After children have mastered traffic signs on the training course, the police accompany them for a ride on city streets, bike lanes, and paths. Dutch school children participate in similar bicycle training courses at school. In Amsterdam, bicycles are made available to schools for free so that children who do not own a bicycle can learn at school how to cycle safely (City of Amsterdam 2007). Most Dutch, German, and Danish children become familiar with cycling as a mode of transportation when cycling with their parents.

In contrast to northern Europe, cycling training programs in North America and Australia are offered in only a small percentage of schools, thus reaching a limited number of children. All of the American case study cities have schools taking part in the Safe Routes to School program as discussed in chapter 11. In Australia, 30 percent of schools in the state of Victoria and 10 percent of schools in New South Wales offer cycling education or Ride to School programs for children (Bauman et al. 2008).

There are many other cycling training programs in the case study cities, often coordinated with community outreach, such as the Bicycling Ambassador programs in Toronto, Chicago, Minneapolis, and Portland, which send well-trained cyclists into neighborhoods throughout their cities to promote cycling and offer bike training (CDOT 2010; City of Minneapolis 2010b; City of Portland 2010b; City of Toronto 2010b). Many courses target specific groups with special needs, such as children, women, older adults, and recent immigrants. In addition to courses, all the case study cities offer some form of bike camps, rodeos, races, and festivals for children.

Another important aspect of cycling safety is training motorists to be aware of cyclists on the roadway and to avoid endangering them. In general, motorist training in the Netherlands, Denmark, and Germany is far more extensive, more thorough, and more expensive than in the United States, Canada, and Australia. In the Netherlands and Germany, motorists are legally responsible for collisions with children and elderly cyclists, even if they are cycling in the wrong direction, ignoring traffic signals, or otherwise behaving contrary to traffic regulations (German Ministry of Transport 2002; Netherlands Ministry of Transport 2009; Pucher and Buehler 2008). The priority legal status of cyclists puts motorists on the defensive and forces them to drive with special attention to avoiding endangering cyclists.

Some of the case study cities in North America have made a special effort to educate motorists about cyclist rights and their legal responsibility to avoid endangering cyclists. Portland employs plainclothes police to catch motorists guilty of endangering cyclists and then requires the offending motorists to take a special "share the road" safety class (City of Portland 2010b). Chicago, Minneapolis, Portland, San Francisco, and Washington provide their police with special training on cyclist rights (ABW 2012; CDOT 2010; SFMTA 2010).

Information and Promotional Programs

All of the case study cities distribute free printed bike maps as well as interactive, online versions that permit trip planning. The cities also offer some form of online bike route planning, often integrated with Google Maps (City of Berlin 2010; Su et al. 2010). The cities feature a wide range of group bike rides and races, bike festivals and art shows, food and wine tours by bike, and fundraising rides for special causes. Portland offers more than 4,000 rides, races, festivals, and special cycling events per year (City of Portland 2010b). Most other cities have similar group rides, such as the Sternfahrt in Berlin, with 200,000 participants in 2010; Bike the Drive in Chicago, with about 20,000 participants; and the Portfolio Partners Rides in Melbourne and Sydney, with 14,000 and 11,000 participants, respectively.

An increasing number of cities throughout the world have been closing down parts of their street network to motor vehicle traffic on some weekends (Sarmiento et al. 2010). Cycling, walking, and other nonmotorized modes can use the car-free streets for recreation and physical activity, encouraged by a wide range of educational and fun events. Chicago, Portland, and San Francisco have offered such "ciclovía" events since 2008. Participation in those three cities ranges from 15,000 to 50,000 per ciclovía, and the number of ciclovías has been increasing each year. Unlike some group bike rides, ciclovías are designed to appeal to all age groups and skill levels. In addition to organized rides and officially sanctioned ciclovías, there are Critical Mass rides, which started in San Francisco in 1992 and eventually spread to more than 300 cities worldwide, including most of the other case study cities (Blickstein and Hanson 2001).

Policy Implementation

Comprehensive, long-range bike plans have been crucial in almost all of the case study cities for guiding overall strategies to increase cycling, coordinating a range of programs, and phasing infrastructure investments over time so they are most effective (CDOT 2006; City of Amsterdam 2007; City of Berlin 2010; City of Copenhagen 2007; City of Minneapolis 2010b; City of Montreal 2008; City of Sydney 2007; City of Vancouver 1999; DDOT 2005; SFMTA 2009). These plans set overall goals and lay out in detail the measures that will be taken to increase cycling. They also provide a look back at recent trends in cycling levels and cycling safety and recap what has been done so far.

The city of Copenhagen was first among the case study cities to use a biannual survey of cyclists (Bicycle Account) to help guide development of cycling policies and priorities (City of Copenhagen 2009). Every two years, cyclists themselves evaluate the actual performance of the cycling system in the city and provide suggestions for its improvement. They are asked, for example, about their degree of satisfaction with the extent and width of bike paths, crowding of facilities, road and path maintenance, bike parking, coordination with public transportation, and safety. The biannual survey permits cycling planners to track progress over time since 1995.

Since 2006, Amsterdam has followed Copenhagen's example by implementing an annual cyclist satisfaction survey (City of Amsterdam 2010). The survey asks residents to evaluate cycling conditions in the city. Survey scores help the city determine its progress toward specific transportation policy goals. In addition to monitoring cyclist satisfaction with the current system, the Bicycle Account also provides information on cycling levels, extent of facilities, safety, trip purpose, and cyclist characteristics, thus supplementing the information from cordon counts of cyclists and other travel surveys. In 2007, the City of Melbourne conducted the first Melbourne Bicycle Account. The annual survey is modeled after the Copenhagen Bicycle Account and tracks progress toward reaching goals outlined in the city's bike plan (City of Melbourne 2011). San Francisco's Report Card on Cycling serves a similar purpose and is published by the San Francisco Bicycle Coalition (SFBC 2010).

In 2003, the City of Berlin founded the Berlin Bicycle Council (City of Berlin 2010). The council consists of cycling experts from different departments of the City of Berlin, experts from research centers, representatives from the bicycle industry, bike advocacy groups, and public transportation providers. The group meets regularly to discuss relevant cycling issues in the city and participates actively in formulating Berlin's cycling strategy.

It is difficult to compare cycling funding between cities and across countries because of differences in the timing of infrastructure investments; the mix of local, regional, and federal funding sources; and data reporting requirements. Investments in cycling infrastructure can vary greatly from year to year. Moreover, cycling infrastructure is often part of larger projects, such as the construction of a new bridge, redeveloping a park, or repaving of a road. Exact funding amounts for the cycling portion of these projects are not usually available. Nevertheless, the available data permit a rough comparison of annual spending. For example, the City of Amsterdam spent about €70 million ($98 million) on cycling projects between 2007 and 2010, including federal and regional matching funds. The city also spent about €10 million ($14 million) per year on traffic safety related to cycling. Amsterdam spends an average of about €20 million ($28 million) a year on bicycling, or €27 ($38) per inhabitant (City of Amsterdam 2010). The City of Berlin intends to increase the budget for bicycling to €15 million ($21 million) annually by 2015—about €5 ($7) per inhabitant per year. In recent years, the City of Copenhagen has spent €10–€15 million ($14–$21million) on cycling per year—€19–€28 ($27–$39) per inhabitant. In sharp contrast, the Rails-to-Trails-Conservancy (2008) estimates that Portland, the most bike-friendly large city in the United States, spends about $4 (€3) per inhabitant on cycling per year, about a tenth the level in Amsterdam and Copenhagen. Although these funding estimates are rough and largely incomparable, they indicate much larger investment in cycling in European cities.

Complementary Policies and Restrictions on Car Use

Sales taxes on fuel and new car purchases, import tariffs, registration fees, license fees, driver training fees, and parking fees are much higher in Europe than in the United States, Canada, and Australia (Kenworthy and Laube 2001; Nivola 1999; TRB 2001). These higher taxes and fees result in overall costs of car ownership and use two to three times higher in Europe. The higher cost discourages car use and thus promotes alternative ways of getting around, including cycling, which is one of the cheapest means of travel.

European cities also have a longer history of discouraging driving though parking restrictions and parking fees. For example, since the 1970s, the City of Amsterdam has reduced the amount of car parking in the city center while sharply increasing fees for the remaining parking spaces. In 1992, citizens voted to continue reducing the supply of parking spaces in the city center (Dutch Bicycle Council 2006; Langenberg 2000). By 2010, the city assessed fees for virtually all car parking spots within the A-10 beltway. Reducing parking and increasing its price has proven to be an effective transportation demand management tool. If parking is limited and expensive, it discourages car trips to the city (City of Amsterdam 2010).

Land-use and urban-design policies in Dutch, Danish, and German cities are generally much stricter than in the United States, Canada, and Australia and provide more government controls on low-density sprawl and the long-trip distances it generates (Kenworthy and Laube 2001; Nivola 1999; Schmidt and Buehler 2007). Moreover, mixed-use zoning and transit-oriented developments have a longer history in northern Europe. They facilitate the proximity of residential areas to commercial establishments, schools, churches and a range of services. The resulting trip distances are shorter and thus more bikeable than those in the United States, Canada, and Australia. For the most part, these complementary taxation, parking, and land-use policies are not specifically intended to promote cycling. Nevertheless, they provide stronger incentives for cycling in Europe.

Case Study Highlights and Lessons

Over the past two decades, cycling levels have increased in all the large cities examined in this chapter. The cities have encouraged cycling through the same sorts of measures but to varying extents and with different timing. As noted in the previous section, the biggest difference is the far greater use of car-restrictive measures in Europe. Table 13.2 lists policy highlights for the thirteen large cities examined in this chapter.

Compared to cities in Australia and North America, European cities have much higher cycling levels, at least partly due to the greater extent and longer history of efforts to increase cycling. Amsterdam, Berlin, and Copenhagen have extensive, well-connected, and integrated networks of bike lanes and paths. Amsterdam and Copenhagen in particular have a long history of continuously expanding and improving their separate cycling infrastructure. Over the past four decades, both cities have been at the forefront of cycling innovations such as synchronized traffic-signal timing at cycling speeds (green waves), cycle tracks, intersection design, bike stations, bicycle accounts, and cycling training. Moreover, all three of the European cities have implemented a range of measures to reduce car use. Berlin and Amsterdam, for example, have implemented traffic calming and limiting speeds in most of their neighborhood streets to 30 km/h. Similar to many other German and Dutch cities, Berlin and Amsterdam have increasingly implemented home zones (Spielstrassen/ Woonerven) with further speed reductions to 7 km/h (Berlin) and 15 km/h (Amsterdam) and streets that are fully shared by nonmotorized and motorized users. Amsterdam and Copenhagen have implemented and successively expanded car-free pedestrian zones in their city centers while reducing car parking supply and increasing its price.

Portland is the large North American city that comes closest to the European cities in implementing a truly comprehensive, well-integrated, long-term package of infrastructure, programs, and policies to promote cycling. The city is most notable for its bike boulevards, dense bikeway network, innovative bike corrals, large number of cycling events, and lively bike culture. Minneapolis has an extensive system of off-street bike paths—the most bike parking per capita of any North American city—and offers an impressive adaptation of cycling to cold, snowy winters. Vancouver has been a model of traffic calming, bike boulevards, and bike-transit integration. San Francisco has been at the vanguard of bike culture in the United States for two decades, leading the way in bike advocacy and cyclist rights as well as bike-transit integration. Montreal has North America's largest and oldest network of cycle tracks, as well as the largest bikesharing system. Washington has the oldest bikesharing program in the United States, excellent bike-transit integration (including a bike station), and an extensive mixed-use trail network that extends into the entire region. Toronto stands out for its bike parking and pioneering role in bike training and community outreach with the bicycling ambassador program. Chicago has led the way in bike-transit integration, bike parking, community outreach, and enforcement of cyclist rights.

In Australia, cycling levels in Melbourne are higher and have been growing faster than in Sydney. However, limited data make it difficult to assess the effect of bicycle policies on cycling levels in Melbourne and Sydney. Available statistics suggest more favorable cycling policies in Melbourne, which has a better integrated cycling network and more extensive cycling promotion programs than Sydney.

Overall, the case studies highlight the importance of transportation policies that encourage cycling while simultaneously restricting car use, such as in the three northern European cities, which have implemented the entire gamut of policies in a coordinated way over many years. Even without implementing car-restrictive measures, however, the North American and Australian cities examined in this chapter have made considerable progress at raising cycling levels. For example, car-dominated American cities such as Portland and Minneapolis have increased their bike mode shares by sixfold and fourfold, respectively. Although North American and Australian cities lag far behind their European counterparts, the improvement of cycling conditions provides their populations with greater choice in travel while contributing to a cleaner environment, reduced energy use, and more livable cities.

Table 13.2
Policy highlights in the case study cities

Europe	
Amsterdam	• Most bike parking (225,000) and most bike parking per 100,000 population (30,272) of any case study city • Car-free zones in city center; many residential streets are traffic-calmed at 30 km/h, including home zones with a 7 km/h limit • Bike training for all children in school. Special bike training programs target groups that traditionally cycle less • OV-fiets (public transportation bikes) for convenient, cheap, short-term rental at key train stations
Berlin	• 3,800 km of streets (72% of road network) traffic-calmed to 30 km/h (19 mph) or less • Network of separate bicycling facilities tripled from 271 km in 1970 to 920 km in 2008 • Required bike-training courses for all school children in third or fourth grade • Call-a-Bike program of German railways with more than 3,000 bikes for short-term rental, unlocked for use via mobile phones
Copenhagen	• Car-free zones and reduced car parking in city center; many residential areas are traffic-calmed at 30 km/h or 20 km/h • Largest network of cycle tracks that are 2.2–3 m wide, grade separated from motorized traffic, and marked in blue color at intersections • Biannual survey of cyclists tracks satisfaction with bicycling conditions since 1995 (Bicycle Account) • Traffic signals are synchronized at cyclist speeds for consecutive green lights for cyclists on four major arterials (green wave)

North America	
Chicago	• Good bike parking at transit stations, racks inside stations for shelter and security. Largest bike station in United States (300 spaces) • Over 12,000 parking spaces in sidewalk racks, with continuous expansion every year based on usage survey • Extensive bicycling ambassador program for community outreach, bike training, and cycling promotion • New bike safety ordinance increases penalties for motorists who endanger cyclists or block bike lanes

Table 13.2
(continued)

North America	
Minneapolis	• Most bike parking per capita in North America. Annual dedicated cost sharing fund for bike racks for private businesses • Metro area received $25 million from federally funded Nonmotorized Transportation Pilot Program (NTPP) • Extensive network of off-street bike paths serves as backbone of the city's bikeway network • The city plows all multiuse paths within twenty-four hours of the end of a snowfall
Montreal	• Most extensive off-street path network of North American case study cities (328 km) • North America's largest network of cycle tracks • Largest bikesharing system in North America (BIXI), with more than 5,000 bikes • During cold winter months, BIXI is discontinued and cycle tracks are used for snow storage
Portland	• Tightly connected bike network with access to bike facilities within three to six blocks from anywhere in the city • Extensive network of bike boulevards with traffic calming and priority for bicycles • Lively bike culture, including bike education, promotion, and fun events such as ciclovías (up to 25,000 participants) • Regulations require new or reconstructed roadways to include bike facilities
San Francisco	• Good bike-transit integration, with most bike stations of any city in North America • Extensive road-based bike network, including numerous road diets and traffic calming programs • North American leader in bike training and education, including bike clubs at high schools, bike safety courses, and special off-road bike training facilities • Strong bike advocacy, lively bike culture, and originator of Critical Mass rides, which spread throughout the world
Toronto	• Iconic post-and-ring bike racks doubled from 7,500 to over 16,000 from 2000 to 2010 • Bike station at Union Station offers parking for 180 bicycles; two more bike stations under construction • First city with bicycling ambassador program, providing community outreach and range of bike training programs • Length of bikeway network more than doubled between 2001 and 2010, from 166 km to 425 km

Table 13.2
(continued)

North America	
Vancouver	• Only case study city in North America with helmet law for adults
	• Extensive bike training programs for all age groups
	• Most extensive bike boulevard network in North America (139 km)
	• North American leader in traffic calming and intersection treatments to accommodate cyclists
	• Strong regional bike-transit integration under TransLink
Washington	• Extensive regional mixed-use trail network
	• First regional bikesharing program in North America (Capital Bikeshare)
	• All Metrorail stations have elevators for easy bike access during off-peak hours
	• Bike station at Union Station offers parking for 150 bicycles, bike rentals, and bike repair

Australia	
Melbourne	• Bicycles allowed on rail vehicles at all times without extra charge
	• Regional rail network provides parking in eighteen secure bike parking cages (for twenty-six bicycles each) with plans to add ten additional cages
	• The Melbourne Bicycle Account tracks the City's progress toward reaching goals outlined in the bicycle plan
	• The Portfolio Partners Rides in Melbourne attract up to 14,000 participants
Sydney	• Cyclists can bring their bikes on public transportation at all times, but have to pay a special fee during peak times
	• The Sydney Portfolio Partners Rides attract 11,000 cyclists
	• Cycle Strategy and Action Plan 2007–2017 includes the goal of constructing 55 km of cycle tracks by 2012

Source: Information collected by the authors directly from the case study cities.

References

ABW (Alliance for Biking and Walking). 2012. *Bicycling and Walking in the United States: 2012 Benchmarking Report.* Washington, DC: Alliance for Biking and Walking. http://www.peoplepoweredmovement.org/benchmarking.

Bauman, Adrian, Chris Rissel, Jan Garrard, Ian Kerr, Rosemary Speidel, and Elliot Fishman. 2008. *Getting Australia Moving: Barriers, Facilitators and Interventions to Get More Australians Physically Active through Cycling.* Melbourne: Cycling Promotion Fund.

Bike Walk Twin Cities. 2008. *Snapshot Minneapolis: Bicycling and Walking.* St. Paul: Bike Walk Twin Cities.

Blickstein, Susan, and Susan Hanson. 2001. Critical Mass: Forging a Politics of Sustainable Mobility in the Information Age. *Transportation* 28 (4): 347–362.

Buehler, Ralph, and John Pucher. 2010. Cycling to Sustainability in Amsterdam. *Sustain, A Journal of Environmental and Sustainability Issues,* no. 21, (Fall/ Winter 2010): 36–40.

Buehler, Ralph, and John Pucher. 2012. Cycling to Work in 90 Large American Cities: New Evidence on the Role of Bike Paths and Lanes. *Transportation* 39 (2): 409–432.

Brookings Institution. 2010. *State of Metropolitan America. On the Front Lines of Demographic Transformation.* Washington, DC: The Brookings Institution.

CDOT (City of Chicago Department of Transportation). 2006. *Bike 2015 Plan.* Chicago: CDOT.

CDOT (City of Chicago Department of Transportation). 2010. *Bicycle Program.* Chicago: CDOT, Chicago Bike Program.

City of Amsterdam. 2007. *Choosing for the Cyclist: Bicycle Program 2007–2010.* Amsterdam: City of Amsterdam.

City of Amsterdam. 2010. *Amsterdam Paves the Way for Cyclists.* Amsterdam: City of Amsterdam.

City of Berlin. 2010. Cycling in Berlin 2010. Berlin: Department of Urban Development.

City Bicycle Foundation. 2010. *Copenhagen City Bike.* Copenhagen: City Bicycle Foundation.

City of Copenhagen. 2002. *Cycle Policy.* Copenhagen: City of Copenhagen.

City of Copenhagen. 2007. *Cycle Policy—Revision of Goals.* Copenhagen: City of Copenhagen.

City of Copenhagen. 2009. *Copenhagen. City of Cyclists—Bicycle Account 2008.* Copenhagen: City of Copenhagen.

City of Copenhagen. 2010a. *Cycling Indicators.* Copenhagen: City of Copenhagen.

City of Copenhagen. 2010b. *A Metropolis for People.* Copenhagen: City of Copenhagen.

City of Copenhagen. 2011. *Cycling Statistics—Cycle Track Costs*. Copenhagen: City of Copenhagen.

City of Melbourne. 2011. *Melbourne Bicycle Account*. Melbourne: City of Melbourne.

City of Minneapolis. 2008. *Bicycle Friendly Community Application*. Minneapolis: City of Minneapolis.

City of Minneapolis. 2010a. *Bicycling in Minneapolis*. Minneapolis: City of Minneapolis, Department of Public Works.

City of Minneapolis. 2010b. *Draft Bicycle Master Plan*. Minneapolis: City of Minneapolis.

City of Montreal. 2008. *Transportation Plan*. Montreal: City of Montréal.

City of Montreal. 2010. *Ville De Montréal Transportation*. Montreal: City of Montreal.

City of Portland. 2010a. *Bicycles*. Portland, OR: City of Portland, Bureau of Transportation.

City of Portland. 2010b. *Portland Bicycle Plan for 2030*. Portland, OR: City of Portland, Bureau of Transportation.

City of Sydney. 2006. *Sydney Cycling Research: Internet Survey*. Sydney: City of Sydney.

City of Sydney. 2007. *Cycle Strategy and Action Plan 2007–2017*. Sydney: City of Sydney Council.

City of Toronto. 2010a. *Bikeway Network Project Status*. Toronto: City of Toronto.

City of Toronto. 2010b. *Cycling in Toronto*. Toronto: City of Toronto.

City of Vancouver. 1999. *1999 Bicycle Plan: Reviewing the Past and Planning the Future*. Vancouver: City of Vancouver.

City of Vancouver. 2010. *Cycling*. Vancouver: City of Vancouver.

DDOT (District Department of Transportation). 2005. *DC Bicycle Master Plan*. Washington, DC: DDOT.

DDOT (District Department of Transportation). 2010. *Bicycle Program*. Washington, DC: DDOT.

Dill, Jennifer, and Teresa Carr. 2003. "Bicycle Commuting and Facilities in Major U.S. Cities: If You Build Them, Commuters Will Use Them—Another Look." *Transportation Research Board Annual Meeting*. Washington, DC: TRB.

DIW (German Institute for Economic Research). 2005. *Automobile Taxes in Europe 2005*. Berlin: DIW.

Dutch Bicycle Council. 2006. *Continuous and Integral: The Cycling Policies of Groningen and Other European Cities*. Amsterdam: Dutch Bicycle Council.

Dutch Bicycle Council. 2010. *Bicycle Policies of the European Principals: Continuous and Integral*. Amsterdam: Dutch Bicycle Council.

Environment Canada. 2010. *National Climate Data and Information Archive: Climate Data Online*. Downsview, Canada: Environment Canada.

German Ministry of Transport. 2002. *Ride Your Bike!* Berlin: German Ministry of Transport.

German Railways. 2007. *Call a Bike*. Berlin: German Railways.

Heinen, Eva, Bert van Wee, and Kees Maat. 2010. Bicycle Use for Commuting: A Literature Review. *Transport Reviews* 30 (1): 105–132.

Kenworthy, Peter, and Felix Laube. 2001. *Millennium Cities Database*. Brussels: UITP.

Langenberg, Peter. 2000. *Cycling in Amsterdam: Developments in the City*. Amsterdam: Velo Mondial 2000 Conference.

Nelson, Arthur, and David Allen. 1997. If You Build Them, Commuters Will Use Them. *Transportation Research Record* 1578:79–83.

Netherlands Ministry of Transport. 2009. *Cycling in the Netherlands*. Rotterdam: Netherlands Ministry of Transport.

Nivola, Pietro S. 1999. *Laws of the Landscape. How Policies Shape Cities in Europe and America*. Washington, DC: Brookings Institution Press.

OECD (Organization for Economic Co-operation and Development). 2006. OECD Territorial Reviews. Competitive Cities in the Global Economy. Paris: OECD.

Osberg, J. Scott, and Sarah C. Stiles. 1998. Bicycle Use and Safety in Paris, Boston, and Amsterdam. *Transportation Quarterly* 52 (4): 61–76.

Pucher, John, and Ralph Buehler. 2006a. Cycling Trends and Policies in Canadian Cities. *World Transport Policy and Practice* 11 (1): 43–61.

Pucher, John, and Ralph Buehler. 2006b. Why Canadians Cycle More Than Americans: A Comparative Analysis of Bicycling Trends and Policies. *Transport Policy* 13 (3): 265–279.

Pucher, John, and Ralph Buehler. 2008. Making Cycling Irresistible: Lessons from the Netherlands, Denmark, and Germany. *Transport Reviews* 28 (4): 495–528.

Pucher, John, and Ralph Buehler. 2011. *Analysis of Cycling Policies and Trends in Large American and Canadian Cities*. Washington, DC: US Department of Transportation, Research, and Innovative Technology Administration.

Pucher, John, Ralph Buehler, and Mark Seinen. 2011. Bicycling Renaissance in North America? An Update and Re-Assessment of Cycling Trends and Policies. *Transportation Research Part A: Policy and Practice* 45 (6): 451–475.

Pucher, John, Jan Garrard, and Stephen Greaves. 2011. Cycling Down Under: A Comparative Analysis of Bicycling Trends and Policies in Sydney and Melbourne. *Journal of Transport Geography* 18 (2): 332–345.

Rails-to-Trails Conservancy. 2008. *Active Transportation for America*. Washington, DC: Rails-to-Trails Conservancy.

Sarmiento, Olga, Andrea Torres, Enrique Jacoby, Michael Pratt, Thomas L. Schmid, and Gonzalo Stierling. 2010. The Ciclovía-Recreativa: A Mass Recreational Program with Public Health Potential. *Journal of Physical Activity & Health* 7 (S2): S163–S180.

Schmidt, Stephan, and Ralph Buehler. 2007. The Planning Process in the U.S. and Germany: A Comparative Analysis. *International Planning Studies* 12 (1): 55–75.

SFBC (San Francisco Bicycle Coalition). 2010. *Cycling in the Bay Area*. San Francisco: SFBC.

SFMTA (San Francisco Municipal Transport Authority). 2009. *San Francisco Bicycle Plan*. San Francisco: SFMTA.

SFMTA (San Francisco Municipal Transport Authority). 2010. *San Francisco Bicycle Program*. San Francisco: SFMTA.

Shaheen, Susan, Stacey Guzman, and Hua Zhang. 2010. Bikesharing in Europe, the Americas, and Asia: Past, Present, and Future. *89th Annual Meeting of the Transportation Research Board*. Washington, DC: TRB.

Statistics Canada. 2010. *Canadian Census 2006*. Ottawa: Statistics Canada.

STPP (Surface Transportation Policy Project). 2004. *Mean Streets*. Washington, DC: STPP.

Su, Jason, Meghan Winters, Melissa Nunes, and Michael Brauer. 2010. Designing a Route Planner to Facilitate and Promote Cycling in Metro Vancouver, Canada. *Transportation Research Part A: Policy and Practice* 44 (7): 495–505.

Texas Transportation Institute. 2009. *Urban Mobility Report*. College Station, TX: Texas Transportation Institute.

TransLink. 2009. *Regional Cycling Strategy Background Study*. Burnaby, Canada: TransLink.

TRB (Transportation Research Board). 2001. *Making Transit Work: Insight from Western Europe, Canada and the United States*. Washington, DC: TRB, National Research Council, National Academy Press.

USDOC (U.S. Department of Commerce). 1980–2000. *United States Census*. Washington, DC: USDOC, U.S. Census Bureau.

USDOC (U.S. Department of Commerce). 2010. *U.S. Climate Normals: Comparative Climatic Data*. Washington, DC: National Climatic Data Center.

USDOL (U.S. Department of Labor). 2010. *Consumer Expenditure Survey*. Washington, DC: U.S. Department of Labor, Bureau of Labor Statistics.

14

Cycling in Megacities: London, Paris, New York, and Tokyo

John Pucher, Emmanuel de Lanversin, Takahiro Suzuki, and John Whitelegg

Cycling in megacities faces challenges similar to those discussed for large cities in chapter 13 but generally more extreme. Heavy traffic on noisy, congested streets makes cycling in megacities more stressful, more intimidating, and more dangerous than in smaller cities—at least it is perceived that way by many people, thus discouraging cycling. Moreover, the large geographic extent of megacities generates many long trips that are difficult to cover by bike, especially for the commute to work. Another special problem of megacities is their density and lack of space, forcing cyclists to share space with motor vehicles on clogged roadways and with pedestrians on crowded sidewalks. Space constraints make it more expensive and politically difficult to install separate cycling facilities, although they are the most needed in such situations.

Cycling has more competition in megacities than in smaller cities. The density of land use in very large cities generally favors walking, especially in combination with public transportation. Megacities have extensive public transportation systems, but they are usually congested, making it difficult to take bikes on board trains and buses. Viewed positively, however, the overcrowding of public transportation in megacities may provide a rationale for promoting cycling. A modal shift to cycling might help remove passengers from the most crowded, central portions of public transportation systems, where many trips are short enough to cover by bike. Moreover, on the outer portions of the route network, cycling can provide a cheap and effective way to expand the service area of metro and suburban rail stations far beyond walking distance. Thus, to some extent, public transportation and cycling have the potential to work together especially well in megacities.

In short, megacities pose special opportunities as well as challenges. Moreover, the economic and political dominance of megacities within their countries focuses media attention on them. Cycling in megacities is not just different but potentially iconic, influencing views on cycling far beyond the cities' own borders. If cycling can thrive even under the difficult conditions of a megacity, that provides hope for cycling elsewhere.

Yet another reason to examine megacities is the rapidly growing number of urban areas in the world with more than ten million residents, from only two in 1950 to twenty in 2005 (Pacione 2009; United Nations 2006). Projections indicate further growth in the coming years, making it increasingly important to explore ways to promote cycling in megacities. We focus this chapter on four megacities in industrialized countries with high per capita incomes and democratic governments: London, Paris, New York, and Tokyo. London is especially interesting because of the complementary policy of congestion charging. Paris is notable for its large bikesharing program. New York has led the way in the United States, with innovations in cycling infrastructure. Tokyo has extraordinarily high levels of cycling in spite of the lack of separate cycling facilities. We examine recent trends in cycling levels and policies in each city and draw lessons for other large cities seeking to promote cycling.

Demographics and Climate

As shown in table 14.1, Tokyo is by far the largest of the four megacities, with 36 million residents in its greater metropolitan area, almost twice the population of metropolitan New York and more than three times the populations of metropolitan London and Paris. The populations listed for the central cities are based on the official boundaries of each megacity's central political jurisdiction. The Tokyo Metropolitan Prefecture has the largest population: 12.6 million compared to 8.4 million in New York City, 7.6 million in the Greater London Authority, and only 2.2 million in the City of Paris. The much smaller population for Paris is due to its much smaller land area: only 105 km^2 versus 2,188 km^2 in Tokyo, 1,572 km^2 in London, and 791 km^2 in New York. Indeed, the City of Paris includes only about a fifth of its metropolitan area population. Because most available statistics are only for the central political

Table 14.1
Demographic and climatic characteristics of four megacities, 2010

	Population (in 1,000s) of		Population per km^2	% univ. students	% car-free households	Annual precipitation (cm)	Annual days ≤ 0°C	Annual days ≥ 30°C*
	city	metro						
New York	8,364	19,007	10,576	7	54	126	77	17
London	7,557	11,917	4,807	n.a.	42	58	0	0
Paris	2,193	11,089	20,807	6	55	65	29	n.a.
Tokyo	12,577	35,921	5,749	6	58	149	9	47

Sources: MIC 2001, 2005, 2009; USDOC 2010a, 2010b; TfL 2010b; JMA 2009; MEXT 2009, 2010.
Note: Precipitation and temperature data are thirty-year averages from 1970 to 2000.

jurisdiction, the much smaller size of the City of Paris may distort some of the comparisons among the cities. For example, the far more restrictive boundaries of the City of Paris help explain why its population density is so much higher than the other central cities. Conversely, the political jurisdiction of the Greater London Authority extends far beyond the city center, including about three-fourths of the population of the metropolitan area and accounting for the relatively low density reported for London.

As shown by several studies, cycling rates tend to be higher among students and car-free households (Baltes 1997; Dill and Carr 2003; Heinen, van Wee, and Maat 2010). All four of the central cities have roughly the same percentage of university students, so this factor would not explain differences in cycling levels. New York, Paris, and Tokyo all have a majority of households without cars, suggesting a greater incentive to cycle there than in London, where only 42 percent of households are car-free.

Climate can influence cycling levels, with heavy precipitation as well as extreme heat or cold discouraging cycling (Dill and Carr 2003; Pucher, Buehler, and Seinen 2011; Heinen, van Wee, and Maat 2010). Of the four cities, London has the least average annual precipitation but the most days with precipitation (145). New York and Tokyo have the most precipitation but the fewest days with precipitation (96 and 100, respectively). London has the fewest days below freezing or above 30°C; New York and Tokyo have the most days with temperature extremes (WMO 2011). Topography can also influence cycling levels. Although there are some hilly portions of the four megacities, they are mostly flat and thus offer topography highly conducive to cycling.

Trends in Cycling

Figure 14.1 summarizes trends in bike mode shares derived from travel surveys in each of the four cities. In 2008, cycling accounted for 16.5 percent of all trips in Tokyo, almost ten times as high as the bike share in the other three cities. The lowest bike share is in New York City (0.6%), less than half the bike shares in London and Paris (about 2%). Cycling has been growing in all four cities. Over the period 1978 to 2008, the bike mode share in Tokyo rose from 13.5 to 16.5 percent. Over

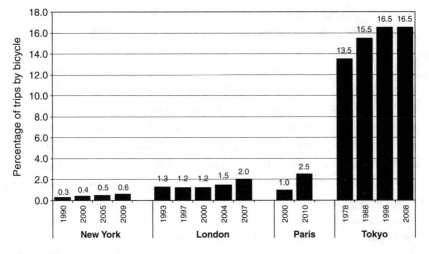

Figure 14.1
Trends in bike mode shares in New York, London, Paris, and Tokyo. *Note:* Bike modal shares shown for New York are percentages of daily work commuters; the other three cities report bike share of trips, all trip purposes. *Sources:* USDOT 2010b; MLITT 1998, 2008c; TfL 2009; City of Paris 2008.

much shorter periods, the bike mode share roughly doubled in each of the other three cities. The growth in cycling in London, Paris, and New York has been mainly since 1995; growth in Tokyo was mainly between 1978 and 1998.

Cordon counts of cycling volumes on major roads or crossing points also indicate considerable growth in cycling. Transport for London reports a 107 percent increase in cycling volumes on major roads in Greater London between 2000 and 2008 (TfL 2010a). The City of Paris reports a 154 percent increase in cycling volumes on six major arterials between 1997 and 2008 (City of Paris 2008). New York City reports a 155 percent increase in cyclists entering Lower Manhattan at six crossing points between 2000 and 2008 (NYCDOT 2010).

Cycling levels are not uniform throughout metropolitan areas. In New York City, for example, the bike mode share of daily work commuters ranges from about 2 percent in Lower Manhattan and northwestern Brooklyn to only 0.2 percent or less in eastern Brooklyn and Queens, the Bronx, and Staten Island, just about the same low rate as in the suburbs (Pucher et al. 2010). This spatial pattern holds in virtually all

North American cities, with bike mode shares falling sharply from the center to the periphery of urban areas (Pucher, Buehler, and Seinen 2011). Similarly, the bike mode share in the City of Paris is more than twice as high as in the Ile de France region as a whole: 2.5 percent versus 1.0 percent) (STIF 2010). Central London has a slightly higher bike mode share than Greater London as a whole (3% versus 2%), but there are also differences among the outer boroughs, with bike shares of 2 percent in South London and West London but only 1 percent in North London and East London (TfL 2009). Cycling rates are high throughout the Tokyo Prefecture, but they are slightly lower in the twenty-three wards of the traditional old city than in the prefecture as a whole (14% versus 16.5%).

Trip purposes of cycling vary considerably among the four cities. In Tokyo, cycling is almost entirely for utilitarian purposes: more than 95 percent of bike trips are for commuting to work or school, accessing train stations, shopping, or conducting personal business (TMG 2006 and 2008). Sports and recreation are far more important reasons for cycling in the other three megacities: about 30 percent in both Paris and London and more than 50 percent in New York City (City of Paris 2008; NYCDOT 2010; NYCDOH 2010; TfL 2009).

Cyclist Characteristics

The profile of cyclists in Tokyo is very similar to that of cyclists in the Netherlands, Denmark, and Germany, as described in chapter 2: all age groups cycle at high rates, and women cycle more than men (MLITT 1998, 2008c; Pucher and Buehler 2008; TMG 2006, 2008). In 2008, for example, 36 percent of women were daily cyclists in Tokyo, compared to 27 percent of men (TMG 2008). The age groups with the highest percentage of daily cyclists were 40–49 (39%) and 60–69 (36%) (TMG 2008). The lowest percentage of daily cyclists was for persons ages 70 and older (22%), but that is a much higher percentage of daily cyclists than for any age category in the other three megacities (TMG 2008). By comparison, 86 percent of women in New York City never cycle at all, and only 5 percent cycle a few times a month. Similarly, 93 percent of New Yorkers ages 65 and older never cycle at all, and only 3 percent cycle a few times a month (NYCDOT 2010; Pucher et al. 2010). Only

20 percent of cyclists in New York are women, compared to 54 percent of cyclists in Tokyo.

Cycling is not quite as male-dominated in Paris and London. Women account for 41 percent of bike trips in Paris (City of Paris 2008) and 30 percent of bike trips in London (TfL 2009). In both Paris and London, the highest rates of cycling are for ages 25–44, but unlike in New York, seniors account for a nonnegligible percentage of all bike trips: 8 percent in Paris and 5 percent in London. Perhaps due to generational differences in travel behavior, women and men in London in the age group 45–59 average roughly the same number of bike trips per day, whereas the bike trip rate is two to six times higher for men than for women in other age categories (TfL 2009).

Trip purpose also varies by gender and age. In Tokyo, for example, commuting to work by bike, either directly or in combination with public transportation, is much more common among men than women (31% versus 15% of bike trips) (TMG 2006). By comparison, women cycle mainly for shopping, personal business, and to accompany children to school (TMG 2006). Cycling to work declines sharply for the age groups 60–69 and 70 and older (TMG 2008). Similarly, in London cycling to school or university occurs mainly among the age groups 5–16 and 17–24, whereas cycling to work occurs mainly in the age groups 25–44 and 45–59 (TfL 2009).

Almost 70 percent of Tokyo residents cycle at least once a week, and more than a third cycle four or more times per week—mostly for short, utilitarian trips with purposes that vary by age and gender (TMG 2006, 2008). Cyclists in London, Paris, and New York are a small minority, composed disproportionately of young men, and cycling there is often for recreation, sports, or exercise.

Cycling Safety

As shown in figure 14.2, there are large differences in cycling safety among the four megacities. Relative to population and cycling mode share, the fatality rate in New York is almost twenty times higher than in Tokyo and roughly four times as high as in London and Paris. The much greater danger of cycling in New York City, both real and perceived, is an important deterrent to cycling there, and may also account

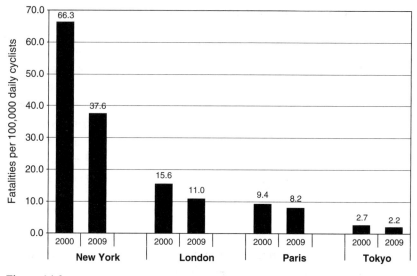

Figure 14.2
Decline in cyclist fatality rates per 100,000 daily cyclists, 2000–2009. *Note:* The fatality rate shown here is calculated as average annual fatalities over a five-year period divided by population weighted by bike mode share. Thus, it is only a rough approximation of the fatality rate relative to different exposure levels in the four cities. *Sources:* NYSDMV 2001–2010; City of Paris 2000–2009; TfL 2009, 2010a; MPD 1999–2009.

for the very low percentage of women and senior cyclists. By comparison, the much greater safety of cycling in Tokyo might help explain why cycling rates are so high among women and seniors there, especially compared to the other three megacities. The fatality rates shown in figure 14.2 are only approximate indices because there are no fully comparable exposure data for the four cities. Ideally, one would prefer to compare fatalities to the number, distance, or duration of cycling trips, but such information is not available. The population and bike mode share data were thus used as proxies for exposure. Nevertheless, even these rough approximations suggest truly dramatic differences in cycling safety among the cities. They also reveal improvement in cycling safety in all four cities, with the fatality rate declining from 2000 to 2009 by 43 percent in New York City, 29 percent in London, 13 percent in Paris, and 19 percent in Tokyo.

It is difficult to compare nonfatal injury data across cities because each city collects its injury data in a somewhat different way, using different definitions and methodologies. Yet all four cities report declining numbers of serious cyclist injuries relative to cycling levels. In New York City, for example, the number of serious injuries per hundred daily bike commuters fell from an average of 2.56 over the period 1999–2001 to 1.53 in 2005–2007, a 40 percent decline (Pucher et al. 2010). In Paris, the number of serious cyclist injuries rose by 41 percent between 2000 and 2008, while the number of bike trips rose by 127 percent, indicating a 38 percent fall in the rate of serious injuries relative to the number of bike trips (City of Paris 2008, 2000–2009). In London, the number of killed or seriously injured cyclists rose by 18.3 percent from 2000 to 2009, while the number of bike trips rose by 117.5 percent over the same period, indicating a 46 percent decline in the serious injury rate (TfL 2010a). In Tokyo, the number of serious injuries fell from 302 in 2002 to 163 in 2009 during a period of stable bike mode share, also indicating a sharp reduction in the serious injury rate per bike trip (MPD 1999–2009).

In summary, both the fatality rates in figure 14.2 and the cities' time-trend data on serious injuries suggest significant improvement in cycling safety in all four cities over the past decade. Yet the differences in cycling safety among the cities remain large. There are several possible reasons for the observed time trends and differences among cities. For example, as discussed in chapter 7, the theory of "safety in numbers" suggests that as cycling levels rise, cycling becomes safer because cyclists become more visible to motorists, who can thus adjust their driving behavior to avoid collisions with cyclists (Elvik 2009; Jacobsen 2003). Moreover, as a higher percentage of the population cycles, more motorists are likely to be sensitive to the safety concerns of cyclists and to respect their rights on the roadway. Thus, the very low fatality rate in Tokyo might be a function of the very high level of cycling there among a broad spectrum of social groups. Conversely, the very high fatality rate in New York might be a function of the low level of cycling and the concentration of cycling among young men. Safety in numbers might also help explain the reduction in cycling fatality rates over the past decade in New York, London, and Paris.

Our interviews with transportation planners and cycling experts in the four cities suggested some other reasons both for differences among cities and trends over time. As noted later in this chapter, New York,

London, and Paris have invested heavily in expanded and improved infrastructure for cycling, roughly tripling the extent of bike lanes and paths since 1995. To varying degrees, they have also offered bike training programs and reduced motor vehicle speeds in some residential neighborhoods. All of these measures were at least partly intended to enhance cycling safety.

The much greater safety of cycling in Tokyo is harder to explain. Several experts we interviewed suggested an important cultural difference, with the Japanese custom of politeness, mutual respect, and considerate sharing of space accounting for fewer dangerous clashes between motorists, cyclists, and pedestrians than in European or North American cities. They also cited the slower speeds of motor vehicles on residential streets in Tokyo, due not to deliberate traffic-calming measures but to high levels of congestion on the narrow, winding roads in many neighborhoods. Cycling itself tends to be at lower speeds as well, partly due to the almost complete lack of cycling infrastructure, with most cycling on crowded sidewalks or on the shoulders of roads, as discussed later in this chapter.

Cycling Infrastructure

Expansion and improvement of cycling infrastructure has been central to the cycling promotion strategies in New York, London, and Paris. The network of bike lanes and paths in New York almost quadrupled between 2000 and 2010, increasing from 202 km to 745 km (NYCDOT 2010; Pucher et al. 2010). Most of the new cycling facilities feature improved design. For example, the city has been building on-street cycle tracks separated from motor vehicle traffic by physical barriers and further protected at intersections by traffic signals that restrict car turns into crossing cyclists. Even ordinary, unprotected bike lanes have generally been widened, and many have been painted bright green for higher visibility. Some on-street lanes have been insulated with diagonally striped buffer zones, offering more protection from motor vehicles than usual bike lanes.

London doubled its network of bike paths and lanes between 2001 and 2010, from 435 km to 875 km. In addition to cycle tracks, bike lanes, and mixed-use paths shared with pedestrians, the London Cycle

Figure 14.3
Since 2008, New York City has been installing physically separated on-street bike paths (cycle tracks), such as this one on 9th Avenue, with special signage, priority traffic signals, and pavement markings. *Photo:* New York City Department of Transportation.

Network in 2010 comprised 308 km of bus lanes that permit use by cyclists and 1405 km of bike routes on roadways without any segregation from motor vehicles (TfL 2010b, 2010c). Since July 2010, London has been establishing so-called cycling superhighways, radial bike routes that provide cyclists with safer, faster, and more direct journeys into the city center (GLA 2010). The superhighway bike lanes are 1.5 meters wide and painted blue for increased visibility, but they are not physically segregated from motorized traffic. As of early 2011, two cycling superhighways (40 km) were already completed, with ten more planned.

Paris almost tripled its network of cycling facilities between 1999 and 2008, from 151 km to 439 km, an annual growth rate of about 10 percent (City of Paris 2008). Most of the cycling routes are shared bus-bike lanes, which were first established in 2001. Other facilities include bike-only lanes on the street and bike lanes on sidewalks. Recently, the city has begun installing counterflow bike lanes on a few streets.

Improving intersection design is crucial for reducing bike conflicts with motor vehicles. Most cyclist fatalities and serious injuries occur at or near intersections. The main approach to this problem in New York has been the installation of bike boxes, which are advance stop lines for cyclists, about 3–5 meters ahead of the stop line for cars. Some of the bike boxes are painted the same bright green as the specially marked bike lanes in order to raise visibility and alert motorists to the presence of cyclists. As of 2010, there were 252 bike boxes at key intersections, almost always connected to on-street bike lanes. In addition, there are special pavement markings ("chevrons") at many intersections to alert both motorists and cyclists to the presence of a bike route or lane crossing the intersection. London has installed advance stop lines for cyclists at 640 intersections, some with bike turning lanes, cyclist-activated traffic signals, and roadside safety mirrors. Moreover, London's new cycling superhighways feature blue lane markings that continue through intersections to increase cyclist visibility where conflicts with motorists are most frequent (GLA 2010; TfL 2010b).

In sharp contrast to the other three cities, Tokyo has few cycling facilities of any kind. As of 2008, the Tokyo Metropolitan Prefecture had 44 km of bike paths along rivers, 23 km of special bike lanes on sidewalks, 2 km of on-street bike-only lanes, and 4 km of extra-wide road shoulders for cycling (MLITT 2008b; Yai 2010). The total 73 km of cycling facilities in Tokyo is only a tenth of the 745 km in New York and one-twentieth of the 1,425 km in London, even though Tokyo's population is twice that of the other two cities. Most cycling in Tokyo is on sidewalks shared with pedestrians or on lightly traveled roads, but with no special separation in either case. Table 14.2 summarizes the supply of cycling infrastructure in the four cities, both in total and on a per-capita basis.

Bike Parking and Integration with Public Transport

Although Tokyo lags far behind the other cities in the provision of bike paths and lanes, its supply of bike parking is five times greater than for the other cities combined. There are more than 800,000 bike parking spaces in the Tokyo Metropolitan Prefecture itself and more than 2.1

Table 14.2
Supply of bike lanes and paths and bike parking in four megacities, 2010

	Bike lane and path network				Bike parking	
	On-street lanes (km)	Off-street paths (km)	On-street lanes and off-street paths (km)	Kilometers of bike paths and lanes per 100,000 population	Bike parking spaces	Bike parking spaces per 100,000 population
New York	517	228	745	9	12,800	153
London	550	875	1425	19	126,000	1,669
Paris	n.a.	n.a.	439	20	32,700	1,493
Tokyo	6	67	73	1	804,607	6,398

Source: Information collected by the authors directly from the case study cities.
Note: The 67 km of paths reported for Tokyo include paths along rivers as well as specially marked bike paths on extra wide sidewalks.

million bike parking spaces in the Greater Tokyo metropolitan area (Government of Japan 2009). The Tokyo Prefecture's per capita supply of bike parking is roughly forty times higher than in New York and about four times higher than in Paris and London. Much of Tokyo's vast bike parking is located at the hundreds of metro and suburban train stations along its extensive rail network. Indicative of cycling's role as an access mode for public transportation, 37 percent of all bike trips in Tokyo are made for the purpose of getting to and from train stations (MLITT 2008a, 2008c). Indeed, provision of ample bike parking is Tokyo's main policy for encouraging bike and ride. Some of the parking facilities are technologically advanced bike stations storing thousands of bikes and enabling automatic deposit and retrieval of bikes in less than a minute (Government of Japan 2009; MLITT 2008b).

Of the four cities, New York has done the least to provide bike parking. It provides few bike racks and no secure bike parking at the city's most important train and bus terminals. The New York City subway system provides no bike parking at any of its 467 subway stations, although some racks are available on nearby sidewalks (Pucher et al. 2010). London and Paris have done far more than New York but nothing approaching the scale of bike parking in Tokyo. Since 2000, for example,

London has added about 5,000 bike parking spaces at its underground and suburban rail stations (TfL 2010b; GLA 2010).

In all four of the megacity case studies, integration of cycling with public transportation is mainly through the provision of bike parking at stations and not by facilitating carriage of bikes on board vehicles. None of the cities provide bike racks on their buses. London, Paris, and Tokyo prohibit bikes on their metro and suburban trains at most times. New York's official policy is to allow bikes on the subway, but in fact, less than 5 percent of stations have elevators, and the many steps from street level to the platform make it difficult to get bikes on board (Pucher et al. 2010).

As noted in the next section, many of the docking stations of the bikesharing systems in Paris and London are located at or near public transportation stations. Surveys indicate that many public transportation riders rely on the cheap and convenient availability of these public access bikes to get to and from public transportation. In that respect, bikesharing systems are also a way to integrate cycling with public transportation.

Public Bikesharing Systems

As analyzed in detail in chapter 9, public bikesharing systems have been rapidly proliferating in cities around the world. Paris's Vélib' is the world's most famous bikesharing scheme. It began in 2007 and is generally considered a huge success. As of 2010, it offered more than 20,600 bikes and 1,451 docking stations, with 162,000 annual subscribers (City of Paris 2007, 2011). Vélib' is used mainly for short trips. A 2009 survey found that 79 percent of Vélib' trips are for accessing metro and suburban rail stations, confirming the important role of bikesharing as a complement to public transportation (TNS Sofres 2009). Although Paris had undertaken other measures to increase cycling since the mid-1990s, all studies indicate that Vélib' provided an extraordinary stimulus to cycling, generating widespread interest in cycling and attracting users who had rarely cycled before (Nadal 2007, 2008; Pucher, Dill, and Handy 2010; Shaheen, Guzman, and Zhang 2010). Between 2006 (before Vélib') and 2008 (one year after its inception), the city's cordon counts of cycling volumes on major streets registered a 56 percent increase (City of Paris 2008). Electronic usage records indicate that Vélib' generates 70,000 to 145,000 bike trips per day, depending on season of the year and day of the week. As discussed in chapter 9, there have been problems with vandalism and maintenance, but Vélib' remains a popular program that has given cycling a big boost in Paris.

London initiated a bikesharing scheme of its own in July 2010: Barclays Cycle Hire (TfL 2011). With about 6,000 bikes and 400 docking stations, the London program in 2010 was about a fourth of the scale of Vélib' in Paris, but significant expansion is planned for the coming years. Preliminary reports indicate that Barclays Cycle Hire generates about 20,000 bike trips per day (TfL 2011). The program focuses on serving short trips, especially by people who work in central London but do not live there. A survey in late 2010 found that most bike hire users are affluent, white males between the ages of 25 and 44, and that 60 percent were cycling in central London for the first time (TfL 2010b). Almost two-thirds of trips with the Cycle Hire bikes were for the commute to work, and 34 percent were to access train stations, considerably less than in Paris but still indicating an important role as feeder to public transportation. Only 1 percent of Barclay bike users had previously made their trips by car; instead, they were drawn from public transportation (60%), walking (29%), or private bike (5%). On net, therefore, there was virtually no modal shift away from the private car.

For several years New York and Tokyo have been considering bikesharing. New York will introduce North America's largest bikesharing system in 2013 with 10,000 bikes and 600 docking stations, mainly in lower Manhattan and northwestern Brooklyn, financed in part by $41 million from Citibank (NYCDOT 2012). For two months in 2009, Tokyo ran an experimental bikesharing program with 4,649 bikes at docking stations near rail stations (Government of Japan 2009).

Restrictions and Charges on Car Use

As noted by several studies, reducing the speed and volume of motor vehicle traffic on residential streets can greatly increase the safety, comfort, and convenience of cycling (Herrstedt 1992; Pucher, Dill, and Handy

2010; Morrison, Thomson, and Petticrew 2004). Most residential neighborhoods in German and Dutch cities, for example, benefit from a range of traffic-calming measures that generally limit speeds to 30 km/h but further restrict speeds to 7 km/h in "home zones" where streets are equally shared by motorized and nonmotorized users (Pucher and Buehler 2008).

Of the four megacities examined in this chapter, Paris has done the most in this respect, having established thirty-eight "quartiers verts," extensive traffic-calmed neighborhoods with speed limits of 30 km/h or less, car-free zones, narrowed roadways, and widened sidewalks (City of Paris 2010). Roughly a fourth of Paris streets incorporate traffic-calming measures. There is also a special program for weekends and holidays called "Paris respire" ("Paris breathes"), when districts close their streets to cars and reserve them for nonmotorists. As of spring 2011, twenty-one districts participated in this program. In addition, the city has established six "civilized travel corridors" of restricted motor vehicle access and is converting a major highway along the Seine River to a promenade reserved for pedestrians and cyclists.

London has also been introducing traffic calming in many residential neighborhoods through 20 mph (32 km/h) speed limits and roadway design modifications that include pass-throughs (shortcuts) for cyclists and pedestrians to provide more convenient, faster connections. There are no comprehensively traffic-calmed neighborhoods in New York, but the city has introduced speed humps, street narrowing, sidewalk widening, and bulbouts (curb extensions) at various locations throughout the city. A few isolated but iconic portions of streets, such as Broadway from Herald Square to Times Square, have been made car-free.

Tokyo does not implement any traffic-calming infrastructure measures to slow down traffic, but the city's mostly narrow, winding, congested streets naturally reduce speeds. In addition, traffic signals on many neighborhood streets are timed to slow down traffic via the reverse of a "green wave," forcing motorists to stop at almost every intersection. The speed limit throughout the city is 30 km/h, and the average motor vehicle speed of all roads in the Tokyo metropolitan area is only 26 km/h (MLITT 2008a). Thus, motor vehicle speeds on most of Tokyo's residential streets are slow, and thus more compatible with cycling, even without explicit traffic-calming measures.

Tokyo discourages car use, and thus indirectly encourages cycling, by imposing many fees, taxes, and restrictions on car ownership and use. For example, anyone wanting to purchase a car must first document the availability of a private, off-street parking space where the car can be parked (MPD 2010). In 2007, the average annual cost of a parking space in the Tokyo Metropolitan Prefecture was ¥304,752 (US$3,710, or roughly $10 per day) (MIC 2007). Taxes on car ownership and use in Japan are also considerable: 4.54 times higher than in the United States, 1.92 times higher than in France, and 1.47 times higher than in the United Kingdom (JAMA 2010).

Congestion charging in London has been an especially innovative approach to reducing car use in central London (TfL 2003–2008). Introduced in 2003, this program imposes a fee of £8 per day to cross into the charging area, which is 21 km²—only 1.3 percent of Greater London's land area, but it includes the City of London (the financial district) and the West End, an important commercial and entertainment center. It is unclear to what extent the congestion charge has encouraged cycling because explicitly pro-cycling policies were introduced at the same time. It is likely, however, that the charge contributed to the 27 percent growth in cycling volumes on major London roads between 2002 (before the congestion charge) and 2004 (after imposition of the charge). TfL (2003–2008) estimates that the western extension of the congestion charging zone in 2008 (rescinded in December 2010) raised cycling volumes by 15 percent. The main purpose of congestion charging was to discourage car use and encourage public transportation, but a side benefit has been the stimulus to cycling.

Cycling Training and Promotion

The four megacities offer cycling training of some sort, both for children and adults, but there are no comparable statistics on their extent. All of London's schools offer cycle training, and about 40,000 children received training in 2010. Most of London's thirty-three boroughs also offer cycle training for adults; this amount far surpasses educational programs in New York, where only a few schools offer cycle training. The nonprofit organization Bike New York has tried to fill the void and currently offers a range of courses for different ages and skill levels, reaching about 10,000 trainees in 2010 (Bike New York 2011). Many different organizations provide cycling training courses in Paris, but the most important is Animation, Insertion et Culture Velo (AICV 2011), which offers a wide range of courses for both children and adults, including training in bike repair and special skills for city cycling. As in New York, however, cycle training in Paris is not provided by the schools and charges a modest fee, so it is less likely to reach all children. Every year, more than a million Japanese school children take cycle training courses, but there are no statistics on cycle training specifically in Tokyo schools.

London, Paris, and New York all offer a wide range of bike rides for various skill levels to promote cycling. Some of these are high-profile, large group rides such as the Skyride in London (85,000 participants in 2010), the Five Borough Bike Ride in New York (30,000 cyclists in 2010), and the Convergence in Paris (20,000 cyclists). Most of these rides are organized by nonprofit organizations, which also offer a wide range of other, smaller rides. Some of the cycling events are part of ciclovías, in which part of the road network is closed to motor vehicle traffic and reserved for cyclists, pedestrians, inline skaters, and other nonmotorized uses. Summer Streets in New York, for example, has been attracting more than 50,000 participants on the three Saturdays in August when it has been held since 2008 (NYCDOT 2010). Paris-Plages is a prominent event in the French capital that has been attracting over 5 million nonmotorized participants during the four weeks each summer when a major highway along the Seine River is closed to motor vehicle traffic (City of Paris 2010).

London, New York, and Paris have strong cycling advocacy organizations that support laws and funding to improve cycling conditions, offer bike training, and coordinate many of the group rides and special events noted previously. The London Cycling Campaign (LCC) is the largest and most important of these advocacy groups, with 11,000 members in 2010 (LCC 2011). The LCC has played a role in almost every recent cycling development in London. It campaigned successfully for the creation of a dedicated cycling unit at Transport for London (TfL) and lobbied for increased funding for cycling, which rose from only £5 million in 2002 to more than £100 million in 2010. In partnership with TfL, LCC helped produce and distribute the fourteen London cycle route maps, which cover all of Greater London. When congestion charging was introduced, LCC campaigned widely to promote cycling as an alternative to driving. Every year LCC organizes the London Skyride and about 500 local rides and events, as well as promoting cycle training, running repair workshops, and providing input to hundreds of city traffic schemes and bike route projects. LCC works with TfL on community cycling projects aimed at specific groups. Most recently, LCC campaigned for the creation of a police task force (now up and running) to reduce bike theft, pushed for the reduction of road danger from trucks (for which an action group has been implemented), and set up a web map that enables people to indicate where bike parking is needed. LCC offers cycling information through a free advice phone line, a popular website, electronic newsletter, magazine, and web-based networks like Facebook (LCC 2011).

Bicycling advocacy in New York City is led by Transportation Alternatives (TA), whose membership tripled between 2000 and 2010 from 2,600 to 8,000 (TA 2011). TA works closely with local government officials, the media, and other groups advocating for the environment, sustainable transportation, and social justice. TA has vigorously supported expansion of New York's bikeway network and organizes large group rides such as the Century Ride, the Tour de Brooklyn, and the Tour de Bronx (Pucher et al. 2010).

The main cycling advocacy organization in Paris is Mouvement de Défense de la Bicyclette (MDB). It engages in similar activities as LCC and TA but is much smaller, with fewer than a thousand members, and is far less influential (MDB 2010). The Fédération Française des Usagers de la Bicyclette (FUB), Club des Villes Cyclables (CVC), and Animation, Insertion et Culture Velo (AICV) are three other cycling organizations that have also supported probike policies in Paris (AICV 2011; CVC 2009; FUB 2011). Advocacy for cycling is minimal in Tokyo, perhaps because cycling is already at high levels for most of the population.

Just as London leads the way in cycling advocacy, it also has the best record on cooperation of the police to protect cyclists, reduce bike theft, and enforce cyclist rights. The Metropolitan Police Service established a Cycle Task Force of forty police officers patrolling on bike to reduce bike theft and enforce good road user behavior (TfL 2010a, 2010b). The police work closely with cycling education programs in London schools and facilitate group bike rides (TfL 2011). In sharp contrast, relations between police and cyclists have been highly confrontational in New

York, as documented in a report by the NYC Department of City Planning, with many cyclists accusing the police of harassment, mistreatment, and ignoring the needs of cyclists (NYCDCP 2005; Pucher et al. 2010). Moreover, the police have targeted group bike rides that are not approved in advance, thus terminating the monthly Critical Mass rides and other impromptu group rides. New York's police have seriously undermined cyclist safety by refusing to protect bike lanes from blockage by motor vehicles (Pucher et al. 2010; Tuckel and Milczarski 2009). The police have not been willing to intervene proactively to enforce cyclists' legal right use the roads, probably because most NYC police do not believe cyclists should have that right. Police opposition to cycling has undercut the impressive expansion of cycling facilities by the NYC Department of Transportation.

The situation in New York contrasts with Paris and Tokyo, where the police have contributed to cycling safety by strictly ticketing motorists who speed or encroach on bike lanes. In Paris, for example, motorcyclists had been illegally riding in bike lanes and causing many crashes with serious cyclist injuries. After the police cracked down in 2008 and strictly ticketed motorcyclists, motorcyclist use of bike lanes fell from 25 percent of motorcyclists to only 3 percent (City of Paris 2000–2009). The police in Tokyo contribute to cycling safety not due to any deliberate policy of favoring cyclists but by strictly enforcing speed limits and other traffic regulations for motorists. They rarely ticket cyclists riding on sidewalks, even in situations where it is illegal.

Conclusions

Table 14.3 lists the highlights of cycling trends and policies in each of the four megacities. Clearly, the situation in Tokyo is very different from that in London, New York, and Paris. The bike mode share in Tokyo is about ten times higher than in the other three cities, and a broad cross-section of Tokyo's residents cycle, very similar to the situation in Dutch, Danish, and German cities. By comparison, the bike mode share is very low in the other three cities, where cycling is dominated by young men.

Another striking difference is the almost complete lack of cycling infrastructure in Tokyo, with the sole exception of the massive amounts of bike parking provided. New York, London, and Paris have all greatly expanded their networks of bike paths and lanes as the key approach to increase cycling. Tokyo does not even explicitly employ traffic-calming measures in its residential neighborhoods by modifying roadway design. Finally, Tokyo does little to promote cycling through group rides, special events, informational campaigns, and cycling advocacy, which have been an important part of the overall policy package in the other three cities.

One of the reasons for the high cycling levels in Tokyo is the high user cost of owning, parking, and driving a car there, combined with the inconvenience, frustration, and slow speed of car use in Tokyo. Surely, there are cultural factors as well, but there can be little question that disincentives to car use are an important, if not the most important, reason for so much cycling in Tokyo. The example of Tokyo highlights to need for disincentives to car use as part of any policy package for increasing cycling.

The other three megacities have invested heavily in cycling infrastructure and programs but have not implemented the sorts of strong car disincentives dominating travel behavior in Tokyo. London, New York, and Paris have made impressive gains in cycling levels, but without serious policy "sticks" to discourage driving, it seems unlikely that bike mode share will reach even the 5 percent official goal set by London, for example (TfL 2011).

Tokyo leads the way on combining cycling with public transportation. With more than 2 million bike parking spaces at metro and suburban rail stations in the Greater Tokyo Metropolitan Area, cyclists can easily cover the short distances to the stations by bike and then take the train for the long portion of the journey. As Tokyo demonstrates, cycling and public transportation can have a symbiotic relationship. New York's lack of bike parking at its subway and suburban train stations represents an important foregone opportunity to increase public transportation use as well as cycling.

Another lesson from this comparison of the four cities is the need to implement complementary, mutually reinforcing policies. New York's Department of Transportation has been expanding its network of bike lanes at record speed (more than 300 additional miles just between 2006 and 2010), but police antipathy toward cyclists has diminished their benefits. The refusal of New York's police to keep bike lanes clear of motor vehicles leads to frequently blocked bike lanes, which can be more

Table 14.3
Policy highlights in the four megacities

New York	• Built 540 km of bike lanes and mixed-use paths between 2000 and 2010
	• Innovative infrastructure including cycle tracks, advance stop lines, green bike lane markings, and bike only traffic signals
	• Worst bike-transit integration of the case-study cities; no racks on buses, no bike parking at subway stations or major transit terminals
	• Limited public bike parking of any kind and no secure bike parking at all; no bike lockers or bike stations
	• In 2009, introduced requirements for provision of bike parking in commercial and residential buildings
	• Police failure to enforce bike lanes leads to frequent blockage of lanes by motor vehicles
	• Confrontational relation between police and cyclists, with frequent police harassment, ticketing, arrests
	• Summer Streets ciclovía introduced in 2008 with more than 100,000 participants
London	• Congestion charging in Central London, imposing £8 (US $13) per day fee for private cars workdays, 7:00–18:00
	• Expansion of bikeway network since 2000, mainly with bike routes on lightly travel streets and 875 km of separate facilities
	• 12 Cycle Superhighways planned, 2 finished by 2010: 1.5 m wide, blue road markings, radial express routes to city center
	• 640 intersections with advance stop lines for cyclists, some with bike-turning lanes and cyclist-activated traffic signals
	• More than 60,000 new bike parking spaces since 2000, including 15,000 at schools and 5,000 at public transportation stops
	• Free printed bike route maps covering all 33 boroughs of London, plus interactive bike route planning via Internet
	• Barclays Cycle Hire bikesharing opened July 2010 with 6,000 bikes and 400 docking stations, with expansion planned
	• Widespread introduction of bicycling training since 2000, now in all 33 boroughs, at over 600 schools in London in 2008
	• Skyride ciclovía on 12 km of central London streets grew from 30,000 participants in 2006 to 85,000 in 2010
Paris	• More than tripling of bike lane network from 122 km in 1998 to 439 km in 2010, including many bus-bike lanes
	• Increase in bike parking on sidewalks from 2,200 in 2000 to over 10,000 in 2010, plus 22,700 other parking spaces
	• In 2007, started Vélib' bikesharing program, now with more than 20,000 short-term rental bikes and 1,200 docking stations

Table 14.3
(continued)

	• Thirty-eight "quartiers verts," traffic-calmed neighborhoods with 30 km/h speed limit, narrowed roadways, and widened sidewalks • Cycling training courses for adults offered twice a month in alternating arrondissements throughout Paris • Cycling training courses in many schools with bicycle safety permits issued in fifth grade • Improved street signage for cyclists; bike route map and website with interactive bike route planning
Tokyo	• By far the highest bike mode share of any high-income, industrialized megacity: 16.5% in 2008 • Cycling is not mainly for recreation but for practical purposes like shopping, school, work trips, and family business • Women cycle as often as men in Tokyo; cycling is male-dominated in the other three cities • Most cycling is at low speeds on practical city bikes • Very few separate cycling facilities: most cycling is on roadway shoulders and on sidewalks shared with pedestrians • Vast amounts of bike parking, especially at rail stations: more than 800,000 spaces in Tokyo, more than 2.1 million in metro region • Extremely high cost of car ownership, parking, and use in Tokyo encourages cycling as a cheap alternative

Source: Information collected by the authors directly from the case study cities.

dangerous than no bike lanes at all. On many streets, cyclists are forced to swerve in and out of motor vehicle traffic almost every block. Clearly, police cooperation is essential for promoting cycling safety, as shown by the successful example of London.

Perhaps the most important conclusion from this analysis is that cycling is possible even in very large cities. Tokyo is the world's largest megacity and presents all the challenges to cycling noted in the introduction to this chapter: high traffic volumes, long trip distances, crowded sidewalks and streets, and intense competition from other uses of scarce space. Yet cycling accounts for 16.5 percent of all trips in Tokyo and is safe and convenient enough to permit women, children, and the elderly to cycle. In short, with the right policies, cycling can indeed thrive in megacities.

References

AICV (Society for the Cultural Integration of Cycling). 2011. *Bicycle Culture.* Paris: AICV.

Bates, Michael. 1997. Factors Influencing Nondiscretionary Work Trips by Bicycle Determined from 1990 US Census Metropolitan Area Statistical Area Data. *Transportation Research Record*, no. 1538: 96–101.

Bike New York. 2011. *Bike Education.* New York: Bike New York.

City of Paris. 2000–2009. *Bike Accidents in Ile de France.* Paris: City of Paris, Department of Transportation.

City of Paris. 2007. *Vélib' Statistics 2007.* Paris: City of Paris, Department of Transportation.

City of Paris. 2008. *Travel in Paris.* Paris: City of Paris, Mobility Observatory.

City of Paris. 2010. *Paris-Beaches.* Paris: City of Paris, Department of Transportation.

City of Paris. 2011. *Bike Sharing in Paris.* Paris: City of Paris, Department of Transportation.

CVC (Association of Bike Friendly Cities). 2009. *Bike and City.* Paris: CVC.

Dill, Jennifer, and Theresa Carr. 2003. Bicycle Commuting and Facilities in Major US Cities: If You Build Them, Commuters Will Use Them—Another Look. Transportation Research Record, no. 1828: 116–123.

Elvik, Rune. 2009. The Non-Linearity of *Risk* and the Promotion of Environmentally Sustainable Transport. *Accident: Analysis and Prevention* 41 (4): 849–855.

FUB (French Cyclist Association). 2011. *Bicycle Use in France.* Paris: FUB.

GLA (Greater London Authority). 2010. *Mayor's Transport Strategy.* London: GLA.

Government of Japan. 2009. *Bikes Parked at Public Transport Stations.* Tokyo: Government of Japan, Cabinet Office.

Heinen, Eva, Bert van Wee, and Kees Maat. 2010. Commuting by Bicycle: An Overview of the Literature. *Transport Reviews* 30 (1): 59–96.

Herrstedt, Lene. 1992. Traffic Calming Design—A Speed Management Method: Danish Experiences on Environmentally Adapted through Roads. *Accident; Analysis and Prevention* 24 (1): 3–16.

Jacobsen, Peter. 2003. Safety in Numbers: More Walkers and Bicyclists, Safer Walking and Bicycling. *Injury Prevention* 9 (3): 205–209.

JAMA (Japanese Automobile Manufacturers Association, Inc.). 2010. *Automobile Taxes in Japan Compared to Other Countries.* Tokyo: JAMA.

JMA (Japan Meteorological Agency). 2009. *Climate Statistics: 1971–2009.* Japan: Government of Japan, JMA.

LCC (London Cycling Campaign). 2011. *Bicycling in London.* London: LCC.

MDB (Mouvement de Défense de la Bicyclette). 2010. *Minutes of the Annual General Meeting 2010.* Paris: MDB.

MEXT (Ministry of Education, Culture, Sports, Science and Technology). 2010. *National Education Survey.* Tokyo: Government of Japan, MEXT.

MEXT (Ministry of Education, Culture, Sports, Science and Technology). 2009. *School Basic Survey 2009.* Tokyo: Government of Japan, MEXT.

MIC (Ministry of Internal Affairs and Communications). 2001. *Census of Japan 2001.* Tokyo: Government of Japan, Bureau of Statistics, MIC.

MIC (Ministry of Internal Affairs and Communications). 2005. *Census of Japan 2005.* Tokyo: Government of Japan, Bureau of Statistics, MIC.

MIC (Ministry of Internal Affairs and Communications). 2007. *2007 National Survey of Prices.* Tokyo: Government of Japan, Bureau of Statistics, MIC.

MIC (Ministry of Internal Affairs and Communications). 2009. *2009 National Survey of Family Income and Expenditure.* Tokyo: Government of Japan, Bureau of Statistics, MIC.

MLITT (Ministry of Land, Infrastructure, Transport and Tourism). 1998. *Tokyo Person Trip Survey 1998.* Tokyo: Government of Japan, MLITT.

MLITT (Ministry of Land, Infrastructure, Transport and Tourism). 2008a. *10th Urban Road Traffic Census.* Tokyo: Government of Japan, MLITT.

MLITT (Ministry of Land, Infrastructure, Transport and Tourism). 2008b. *Progress Report on Improving Cycling Conditions.* Tokyo: Government of Japan, MLITT.

MLITT (Ministry of Land, Infrastructure, Transport and Tourism). 2008c. *Tokyo Person Trip Survey 2008.* Tokyo: Government of Japan, MLITT.

MOE (Ministry of the Environment). 2009. *Press Release on 2009.08.03.* Tokyo: Government of Japan, MOE.

Morrison, David, Hilary Thomson, and Mark Petticrew. 2004. Evaluation of the Health Effects of a Neighborhood Traffic Calming Scheme. *Journal of Epidemiology and Community Health* 58 (10): 837–840.

MPD (Metropolitan Police Department). 1999–2009. *Metropolitan Police Statistics 1999–2009.* Tokyo: Tokyo Metropolitan Prefecture, MPD.

MPD (Metropolitan Police Department). 2010. *Parking Certificate.* Tokyo: Tokyo Metropolitan Prefecture, MPD.

Nadal, Luc. 2007. Bike Sharing Sweeps Paris Off Its Feet. *Sustainable Transport,* no. 19: 8–13.

Nadal, Luc. 2008. Vélib' One Year Later. *Sustainable Transport,* no. 20: 8–9.

NYCDCP (New York City Department of Planning). 2005. *The State of Cycling in New York City.* New York: NYCDCP.

NYCDOH (New York City Department of Health and Mental Hygiene). 2010. *Epiquery: NYC Interactive Health Data System—Community Health Survey 2007.* New York: NYCDOH.

NYCDOT (New York City Department of Transportation). 2010. *Bicycling*. New York: NYCDOT.

NYCDOT (New York City Department of Transportation). 2012. New York City Bike Share. New York: City of New York. www.nyc.gov/bikeshare/.

NYSDMV (New York State Division of Motor Vehicles). 2001–2010. *Summary of New York City Motor Vehicle Accidents*. New York: NYSDMV.

Pacione, Michael. 2009. *Urban Geography: A Global Perspective*. London: Routledge.

Pucher, John, and Ralph Buehler. 2008. Making Cycling Irresistible: Lessons from the Netherlands, Denmark, and Germany. *Transport Reviews* 28 (4): 495–528.

Pucher, John, Jennifer Dill, and Susan Handy. 2010. Infrastructure, Programs and Policies to Increase Bicycling: An International Review. *Preventive Medicine* 50 (S1): S106–S125.

Pucher, John, Lewis Thorwaldson, Ralph Buehler, and Nick Klein. 2010. Cycling in New York: Innovative Policies at the Urban Frontier. *World Transport Policy and Practice* 16 (1): 7–50.

Pucher, John, Ralph Buehler, and Mark Seinen. 2011. Bicycling Renaissance in North America? An Update and Re-Assessment of Cycling Trends and Policies. *Transportation Research Part A: Policy and Practice* 45 (6): 451–475.

Shaheen, Susan, Stacey Guzman, and Hua Zhang. 2010. Bikesharing in Europe, the Americas, and Asia: Past, Present, and Future. *Transportation Research Record*, no. 2143: 159–167.

STIF (Greater Paris Regional Transport Association). 2010. *Mobility and Transport in Greater Paris*. Paris: STIF.

TA (Transportation Alternatives). 2011. *Walking and Cycling in New York*. New York: TA.

TfL (Transport for London). 2003–2008. *Central London Congestion Charging: Impacts Monitoring, Annual Report*. London: TfL.

TfL (Transport for London). 2009. *Travel in London, Report 1: Key Trends and Developments*. London: TfL.

TfL (Transport for London). 2010a. *Cycling Safety Action Plan*. London: TfL.

TfL (Transport for London). 2010b. *Travel in London, Report 3*. London: TfL.

TfL (Transport for London). 2010c. Data on the specific length of different kinds of cycling facilities in London in 2010 were obtained directly from Transport for London as the result of a Freedom of Information request, September 29, made by John Whitelegg.

TfL (Transport for London). 2011. *Cycling Revolution London: End of Year Review*. London: TfL.

TMG (Tokyo Metropolitan Government). 2006. *2006 TMG Web Survey on Bicycling Policy*. Tokyo: TMG, Bureau of Citizens, Culture and Sports.

TMG (Tokyo Metropolitan Government). 2008. *2008 TMG Public Survey on Life in Tokyo*. Tokyo: TMG, Bureau of Citizens, Culture and Sports.

TNS Sofres. 2009. *Vélib Satisfaction Survey*. Paris: TNS Sofres.

Tuckel, Peter, and William Milczarski. 2009. *Bike Lanes or Blocked Lanes? An Observational Study of Vehicular Obstructions of Bike Lanes in Manhattan*. New York: Hunter College, Departments of Sociology and Urban Planning.

United Nations. 2006. *World Urbanization Prospects: The 2005 Revision Working Paper No. ESA/P/WP/200*. New York: United Nations, Department of Economic and Social Affairs, Population Division.

USDOC (US Department of Commerce). 2010a. *U.S. Climate Normals: Comparative Climatic Data*. Washington, DC: USDOC, National Climatic Data Center.

USDOC (US Department of Commerce). 2010b. *American Fact Finder: 2000–2008 American Community Survey, Journey to Work*. Washington, DC: USDOC, U.S. Census Bureau.

WMO (World Meteorological Organization). 2011. *Weather, Climate, and Water*. Geneva: WMO.

Yai, Tetsuo. 2010. *Bicycling Space in Tokyo*. Tokyo: Tokyo Institute of Technology.

15

Promoting Cycling for Daily Travel: Conclusions and Lessons from across the Globe

John Pucher and Ralph Buehler

Cycling for Sustainable Transportation and Livable Cities

As documented in this book, cycling for daily travel can provide a wide range of benefits that far outweigh the costs of cycling infrastructure, equipment, and programs. Chapter 3, for example, reviews the extensive scientific evidence of the health benefits of cycling, which greatly exceed the traffic dangers of cycling and yield economic benefits for individuals and society as a whole. Chapter 4 shows that cycling for transportation is often faster than motorized alternatives and offers substantial cost savings for individuals. There are many other indirect benefits as well. Cycling has the potential to reduce energy use, noise and air pollution, greenhouse gas emissions, roadway congestion, and other harmful impacts of cars. By reducing dependence on the car, cycling can help increase the sustainability of transportation systems and the livability of cities. Thus, there are many compelling justifications for governmental efforts to increase cycling.

This concluding chapter draws on the preceding chapters to summarize key lessons for promoting cycling from experience around the world. To identify the most promising strategies, we focus on two groups of countries and cities: (1) those that have maintained or increased their already high levels of cycling and (2) those that have significantly increased cycling from low starting levels.

Success Stories Reveal the Potential of Cycling

One encouraging finding of this book is that cycling can thrive in countries with high levels of income and car ownership. As shown in figure

2.1, the bike share of daily trips is 26 percent in the Netherlands, 18 percent in Denmark, 10 percent in Germany, and 9 percent in Sweden and Finland, all of which are affluent countries. With cars readily available, the residents of these northern European countries cycle out of choice and not economic necessity. Moreover, cycling in those countries has grown considerably in recent decades—in spite of increasing incomes, car ownership, and suburbanization. Between 1978 and 2008, average daily kilometers cycled per inhabitant increased from 0.6 to 1.0 km in Germany, from 1.3 to 1.6 km in Denmark, and from 1.7 to 2.5 km in the Netherlands. Over the same period, cyclist fatalities fell by more than 60 percent in each country, as shown in figure 2.7.

This pattern holds for individual German, Dutch, and Danish cities as well. Some large cities achieved big increases in cycling. From 1990 to 2008, the bicycle share of trips in Berlin rose from 6 percent to 13 percent, while serious cyclist injuries fell by 38 percent. From 1970 to 2005, the bicycle share of trips in Amsterdam rose from 25 percent to 34 percent, while serious bicyclist injuries fell by 40 percent. From 1975 to 2005, the bicycle share of trips in Copenhagen rose from 22 percent to 35 percent, while serious injuries fell by 60 percent. Smaller cities also achieved growth in cycling. Freiburg, Germany, almost doubled the bicycle share of trips from 15 percent in 1982 to 27 percent in 2007. Muenster, Germany, raised its already high bike share of trips from 29 percent in 1982 to 38 percent in 2007. Many smaller Dutch and Danish cities increased cycling over the period 1975 to 2005 while reducing cyclist fatalities (Dutch Bicycle Council 2010). The strong relationship between safety and cycling volumes observed at both the country and city level is consistent with the principle of safety in numbers explained in chapter 7.

Another encouraging finding is that cities with low levels of cycling can dramatically increase cycling with the right set of policies. As noted in chapter 13, for example, the bike mode share in Portland, Oregon, rose almost sixfold between 1990 and 2009 (from 1.1% to 6.0%). Over the same period, the bike mode share roughly tripled in Chicago (from 0.3% to 1.0%), Minneapolis (from 1.6% to 4.3%), San Francisco (from 1.0% to 2.7%), and Washington (from 0.8% to 2.3%). Over the shorter period from 1996 to 2006, cycling levels more than doubled in Canada's three largest cities—Vancouver (from 1.7% to 3.7%), Montreal (from 1.0% to 2.4%), and Toronto (from 0.8% to 1.7%). In each of these seven large North American cities, cyclist fatality rates fell as cycling levels rose, again consistent with safety in numbers.

Chapter 12 reports that many smaller cities in North America, mostly college towns, have also raised cycling levels considerably. The most notable example is Boulder, Colorado, which tripled its bike share of work commuters from 3.8 percent in 1980 to 12.3 percent in 2009. The large increases in cycling in some North American cities far exceed the average increases for the United States and Canada as a whole. Nevertheless, even the modest growth observed for both countries over the past two decades is encouraging, especially because it has been accompanied by falling cyclist fatality rates, as shown in chapter 2.

Megacities offer special challenges and opportunities for cycling, as noted in chapter 14, which reports roughly a doubling of cycling rates in Paris, London, and New York since 2000. Most impressive, perhaps, is the very high level of cycling in Tokyo (16.5% of trips in 2008). In short, cities of all sizes with very different land use patterns, histories, and cultures have succeeded in increasing cycling and making it safer. That, in itself, is good news and provides hope to other cities wanting to do the same.

Lessons for Cycling Promotion

Examining the transportation policies of successful cities and countries reveals how to promote cycling even where it must compete with the car. The lessons that follow draw not only on the detailed city case studies of chapters 12, 13, and 14 but also on other chapters that deal with some of the specific measures to increase cycling and improve safety. We organize the lessons into two categories: policies and implementation strategies (see table 15.1).

Infrastructure, Policies, and Programs to Increase Cycling

As noted throughout this book, there are many ways to increase cycling. Listed here are the ten most important aspects of a successful policy package.

1. Provide a comprehensive package of integrated measures.

Perhaps the most important lesson drawn from the case studies is that no single measure suffices. A coordinated package of infrastructure provisions, promotional programs, and transportation and land-use policies

Table 15.1
Key lessons for cycling promotion and successful implementation of cycling policies

---

Infrastructure, policies, and programs to increase cycling

---

1. Provide a comprehensive package of integrated measures
2. Build a network of integrated bikeways with intersections that facilitate cycling
3. Provide good bike parking at key destinations and public transportation stations
4. Implement bikesharing programs
5. Provide convenient information and promotional events
6. Introduce individualized marketing to target specific groups
7. Improve cyclist education and expand bike-to-school programs
8. Improve motorist training, licensing, and traffic enforcement
9. Restrict car use through traffic calming, car-free zones, and less parking
10. Design communities to be compact, mixed-use, and bikeable

---

Implementation strategies

---

1. Publicize both individual and societal benefits
2. Ensure citizen participation at all stages of planning and implementation
3. Develop long-range bike plans and regularly update them
4. Implement controversial policies in stages
5. Combine incentives for cycling and disincentives for car use
6. Build alliances with politicians, cycling organizations, and other bike-friendly groups
7. Coordinate bike advocacy and planning through national organizations

---

is the trademark of every city that has succeeded at significantly raising cycling levels and improving safety. That is also the conclusion of previous international reviews (Dutch Bicycle Council 2010; Heinen, van Wee, and Maat 2010; Krizek, Forsyth, and Baum 2009; Pucher, Dill, and Handy 2010; Reynolds et al. 2009).

The city case studies examined in chapters 12, 13, and 14 of this book suggest that a comprehensive approach has a much greater impact on cycling than individual measures that are not coordinated. The impact of any particular measure is enhanced by synergies with complementary measures in the same package. However, the more successfully a city implements a wide range of policies and programs, and simultaneously and fully integrates them with each other, the more difficult it becomes to disentangle the separate impacts of each measure. For example, the impacts of improved bike parking, cycling training, and individualized marketing are probably influenced by the extent and quality of the bikeway network. Similarly, bike-to-school and bike-to-work programs are more likely to be successful if motor vehicle speeds and volumes are reduced in residential neighborhoods through traffic-calming measures. In short, efforts to promote bicycling are interactive and synergistic and must be coordinated.

The European cities examined in this book generally employ a wider range of pro-bike measures, implement them more extensively, and do a better job of coordinating them than American, Canadian, and Australian cities. Moreover, the most successful North American cities (Portland, Minneapolis, and Vancouver) come closest to the comprehensive European model.

2. Build a network of integrated bikeways with intersections that facilitate cycling.

No city in Europe or North America has achieved a high level of cycling without an extensive network of well-integrated bike lanes and paths that provide separation from motor vehicle traffic. Bikeways are the trademark of bike-oriented cities in the Netherlands, Denmark, and Germany. Bike paths and lanes must be combined with intersection modifications such as advance stop lines, special lane markings, extra turning lanes, and advance green lights for cyclists. As explained in chapter 6, physical separation from motor vehicle traffic is crucial for enabling risk-averse and/or vulnerable groups to cycle. Virtually all surveys report that separate cycling facilities are needed to encourage noncyclists to cycle—especially for women, seniors, and children. As shown in chapter 2, those traffic-sensitive groups have high rates of cycling in countries such as the Netherlands, Denmark, and Germany, with their extensive separate cycling facilities, but low rates in countries where most cycling is on roads with heavy traffic and no separation for cyclists. As noted in chapter 10, some researchers consider women an "indicator species" for cycling policies. Where cycling rates among women are high, cycling conditions are generally safe, comfortable, and convenient, leading to high overall cycling rates among all groups. Separate cycling facilities are a crucial first step toward increasing cycling and making it socially inclusive.

3. Provide good bike parking at key destinations and public transportation stations.

As noted in chapters 8, 13, and 14, safe and convenient bike parking is crucial to urban cycling and, in particular, to the integration of cycling with public transportation. Countries and cities with the highest rates of cycling provide ample bike parking, including sheltered and secure parking at key locations. Good bike parking at train stations is the main approach to integrating cycling with public transportation in northern Europe. Full-service bike stations are perhaps the most famous parking provision, but simple bike racks, often sheltered, make up the bulk of parking in the Netherlands, Denmark, and Germany. The United States and Canada have focused far more on installing bike racks on buses, but those two countries have also been increasing parking at rail stations.

4. Implement bikesharing programs.

As noted in chapter 9, there has been a worldwide boom in bikesharing since 2005. By 2011, there were bikesharing programs in more than 160 cities on five continents. Cycling has increased in virtually all cases for which studies have compared cycling levels before and after implementation of bikesharing (Pucher, Dill, and Handy 2010). In only a few years, for example, the percentages of trips made by bicycle almost doubled in Paris, Lyon, and Barcelona. The percentage increases have been smaller in cities with high initial cycling levels (such as Hangzhou, China, and Copenhagen, Denmark) and where bikesharing systems are first implemented on a small scale (such as Washington, D.C.). Although bikesharing must be combined with improved infrastructure and other programs, evidence suggests that it can greatly boost interest in cycling and raise cycling levels. Bikesharing also facilitates integration of cycling with public transportation because many docking stations are located near rail stations.

5. Provide convenient information and promotional events.

It is important to provide the general public with a wide range of easily accessible information about cycling facilities and programs, especially for beginning cyclists, who are less likely to be well-informed. Many cities distribute free printed bike maps and offer interactive, online versions that permit trip planning. City departments of transportation often have extensive websites offering a wide range of information on cycling routes, bike parking, safety, training, special events, and recent and proposed projects.

Cities throughout the world employ a wide range of special events to generate interest in cycling. In countries with low cycling rates, such as Australia, Canada, and the United States, there are often bike-to-work and bike-to-school days, weeks, or months, usually coordinated with the Safe Routes to Schools programs. Many cities offer group bike rides and races, bike festivals and art shows, food and wine tours by bike, and fundraising rides for special causes. Some group rides have special themes, such as the World Naked Bike Ride, which took place in seventy cities in twenty countries in 2010 (WNBR 2011).

Ciclovías are an important development of recent years. An increasing number of cities throughout the world have been closing down parts of their street network to motor vehicle traffic on selected weekends to promote cycling and walking for recreation and physical activity, encouraged by a wide range of educational and fun events (Sarmiento et al. 2010). Unlike some group bike rides, ciclovías are designed to appeal to all age groups and skill levels. In addition to organized rides and officially sanctioned ciclovías, there are Critical Mass rides, which started in San Francisco in 1992 and eventually spread to more than three hundred cities worldwide (Blickstein and Hanson 2001). Critical Mass rides often involve hundreds of riders, usually meeting on the last Friday evening of the month at a prearranged place but without a predetermined route and then proceeding spontaneously.

6. Introduce individualized marketing to target specific groups.

Individualized marketing schemes may be especially useful for focusing on particular groups, and a recent review documented their significant impacts on cycling levels (Yang et al. 2010). Unlike general promotional programs, individualized marketing offers advice on how to reduce car use based on the specific situation and preferences of each particular household. Although such interventions are almost never aimed exclusively at increasing cycling, that is often the result (Brög et al. 2009).

7. Improve cyclist education and expand bike-to-school programs.

As discussed in chapter 11, it is especially important to promote cycling among children because habits learned while young tend to persist throughout life. Most Dutch, German, and Danish children receive extensive education in traffic safety by the third or fourth grade, usually including classroom instruction about cycling safety and traffic regulations, police-administered training sessions on special off-street bike training facilities, and in-traffic cycling training with police officers on local streets (see chapter 2). By comparison, few American, Canadian, and Australian schools provide cyclist training for children, and participation by students is voluntary.

Instead of comprehensive traffic education and training, the United States, Canada, and Australia have been implementing Safe Routes to School (SRTS) programs, generally coordinated by state or provincial departments of transportation. In the United States, for example, the SRTS program supports both infrastructure improvements (such as sidewalks, crosswalks, bike paths, and better signage) and education and enforcement efforts to improve conditions for children walking and cycling to school (PBIC and FWHA 2010). This initiative has been the most important program for increasing walking and cycling by children in the United States for decades, but it reached less than 7 percent of the 98,706 primary and secondary schools in the country in 2010 (NCES 2010). SRTS programs should be greatly expanded to include most schools and combined with the sort of mandatory traffic education in northern European schools.

8. Improve motorist training, licensing, and traffic enforcement.

Improving motorist behavior toward cyclists is perhaps the most overlooked measure to promote cycling. As noted in chapters 2, 7, 10, and 13, driver training varies greatly from one country to another, both in terms of overall rigor and comprehensiveness, and especially regarding the obligation to avoid endangering cyclists and pedestrians. Compared to the United States, Canada, and Australia, motorist training in the Netherlands, Germany, and Denmark focuses far more on the needs of cyclists and pedestrians. Tests for driver licensing are much stricter in northern Europe and specifically examine whether potential drivers respect the legal rights and special needs of nonmotorized travelers, especially children and seniors.

Surveillance of motorist behavior is also far stricter in most northern European countries, with tickets and severe fines levied for failing to yield to cyclists where they have the right of way. Motorists in these countries are held legally responsible for the financial costs of crashes with nonmotorists, forcing drivers to exert special care to avoid endangering cyclists. As a result, motorist behavior in the Netherlands, for example, is drastically different from driving practices in the United States or Australia. In the Netherlands, cyclists can be confident that motorists look out for them and consciously avoid endangering them. Careful and considerate driving makes cycling safer, less stressful, and more comfortable in the Netherlands, totally aside from the extensive cycling infrastructure there.

It is crucial that motorist training, licensing, and traffic enforcement be improved, especially in car-oriented countries such as the United States, Australia, and Canada. Ignoring the needs of cyclists and pedestrians unquestionably endangers them and heightens the perception of traffic danger because many cyclists feel threatened by motor vehicles. Vulnerable traffic participants in car-oriented countries deserve the same respect and consideration they receive in the Netherlands, Denmark, and Germany. Improving the behavior of motorists is not easy, but it is key to improving cycling safety and raising cycling levels.

9. Restrict car use through traffic calming, car-free zones, and less automobile parking.

The most severe impediment to cycling in North American and Australian cities is the absence of restrictions on car use that are common in most northern European cities. Although such restrictions are not usually intended to promote cycling, they are probably as important as cycling infrastructure and programs for making cycling safe and comfortable. Car-free zones, home zones, and traffic-calmed streets are the most obvious restrictions on car use (figure 15.1). They make streets bikeable even without separate facilities. As shown in chapter 7, motor vehicles are the main source of danger to cyclists. Limiting motor vehicle access and speeds, especially in residential areas, is key to improving cycling safety. Many Dutch, Danish, and German cities channel motor vehicle traffic around city centers while cyclists have direct and convenient access. Similarly, car parking has generally been curtailed and made more expensive in city centers. Such car-restrictive measures reduce the noise, air pollution, and traffic danger faced by cyclists on trips to the center, facilitating cycling while discouraging car use by making it more circuitous, slower, less convenient, and more expensive.

Figure 15.1
Car-free zones, such as here in Freiburg, Germany, encourage cycling and walking, as well as the use of public transportation, and enhance the livability of city centers. *Credit:* Ralph Buehler.

As discussed in chapter 2, national policies in northern Europe also make car use more expensive through higher sales taxes and registration fees for cars, higher fuel taxes, and higher driver training and licensing fees. With the overall costs of car use roughly twice as high in northern Europe as in North America and Australia, there is obviously a much greater economic incentive to cycle in countries such as the Netherlands, Denmark, and Germany.

10. Design communities to be compact, mixed-use, and bikeable.

It is important to encourage more compact, mixed-used development, which facilitates shorter trip distances that can be covered by bike. At the very least, it is necessary to revoke existing prohibitions on mixed-used, higher-density developments, which interfere with consumer preferences in many American cities (Levine 2006). Moreover, official planning guidelines should specifically recommend the inclusion of cultural centers, shopping, and service establishments within residential developments.

The specific design of new communities can also foster cycling—by placing car parking behind buildings and bike parking in front on sidewalks, for example. Similarly, overall street design and landscaping can encourage cycling. The Complete Streets guidelines in the United States are specifically intended to provide space and a pleasant, safe riding environment for cyclists on newly built or reconstructed streets (ABW 2010, 2012; PBIC and FHWA 2010).

Implementation Strategies

Although there are many ways to increase cycling, each city's situation is unique and requires a tailored mix of measures. Any city seeking to promote cycling faces three main tasks. First, it must garner the necessary public and political support. Second, it must determine the most appropriate mix of measures. Third, it must develop a method for long-term implementation and ongoing feedback from cyclists, other key stakeholders, and the public at large. Listed here are seven lessons for facilitating implementation.

1. Publicize both individual and societal benefits of cycling.

Perhaps the most important first step in promoting cycling is a public information campaign to explain the wide range of benefits of cycling to individuals and society at large. Voters and their elected officials will support the measures necessary to increase cycling only if they are convinced that cycling generates significant benefits. As noted in chapters 1, 3, and 4, there are both economic and health benefits to individual cyclists. Those personal benefits should be highlighted in campaigns to convince more people to cycle on a daily basis. The message is that cycling pays off for the individual even on the basis of selfish considerations of one's own finances, time, health, and recreation. To generate widespread public support, information campaigns should also convey cycling's broader societal benefits, which include reduced noise, air pollution, energy use, and traffic congestion as well as improved public health and more travel options for everyone. The message is that even noncyclists should support cycling because of these social and environmental benefits of cycling that go beyond the direct benefits to cyclists themselves.

Similar to the decades-long campaign to discourage smoking, there could be a national advertising program to highlight the many benefits of cycling. The informational campaign should be as diverse as possible to emphasize the many possible reasons people might have to support cycling. In addition to national efforts, there should also be state and local information campaigns reflecting the special opportunities and needs in any particular state or metropolitan area.

As noted in measure no. 6 in the previous listing, individualized marketing is an even more specific informational strategy aimed at particular households, explaining how individual households can increase cycling, walking, and public transportation use given their own specific situation.

2. Ensure citizen participation at all stages of planning and implementation.

Ongoing citizen involvement is important for garnering public support and for developing a package of policies that is most appropriate to the needs and preferences of the local population. The planning process must be transparent, sending a clear message that policies are not being imposed from above but that they are generated in close consultation with key stakeholders, neighborhood groups, and all interested citizens. Because the goal is to increase daily cycling among the general population, citizen feedback is crucial for choosing those measures that would most encourage them to cycle more often.

Citizen involvement can take many forms. As noted in chapters 12–14, some cities have established "bicycle accounts"—periodic surveys of cycling levels, safety, and opinions about cycling conditions and needed improvements in cycling infrastructure and programs. Such bicycle accounts provide trend data over time to help measure progress in meeting goals established in long-term bike plans and to update and adjust those plans to respond to changing conditions over time. In addition to regular surveys, many cities have cycling advisory boards composed of cyclists, bike planners, and other stakeholders who provide frequent feedback to city officials. Yet another form of citizen input is facilitated by city websites that enable cyclists and other interested citizens to report problematic situations and suggest specific improvements. Many cities, for example, permit online suggestions of locations where more bike parking is needed. Some websites invite reporting of cycling facilities that need repair.

When new bike paths or lanes are being considered, it is essential to meet with neighborhood residents to discuss the specific design of the facilities and to resolve possible conflicts before they are installed by making necessary adjustments. Cycling advocacy organizations should be consulted as well to ensure that the facilities serve their needs and are well-designed.

3. Develop long-range bike plans and regularly update them.

Most cities with successful cycling policies have long-term bike plans that establish goals for the future and systematically lay out the categories of measures they intend to implement. Such plans usually include a status report on the current situation, evaluation of past and current initiatives, examination of available funding sources, and explanation of future plans. Bike plans are almost always developed by city officials in close consultation with cycling advocacy organizations, transportation planners, other key stakeholders, and interested citizens. Bike plans should be flexible and adaptable. All of the forms of citizen participation mentioned in strategy no. 2 can be used to help develop the bike plan and to improve it over time as it is periodically updated in response to changing community needs. Bike plans provide an important opportunity to coordinate efforts across different government agencies and to ensure citizen involvement throughout the planning and implementation process.

4. Implement controversial policies in stages.

As noted in many of the city case studies in chapters 12, 13, and 14, it is wise to start off with relatively uncontroversial projects that almost everyone can agree on and that have a high probability of success. For example, provision of good bike parking at rail stations and other key locations is inexpensive and does not seriously conflict with other users. In contrast, installation of bike lanes usually means taking roadway space from motor vehicles, either as traffic lanes or parking spaces. Judiciously choosing less heavily trafficked routes for bike lanes may reduce opposition from motorists as well as offer a safer, less stressful riding environment for cyclists. Reduced speed limits and comprehensive traffic calming should be introduced first in neighborhoods where there is widespread support from residents, especially where citizens proactively request traffic calming to reduce noise, pollution, and traffic dangers.

5. Combine incentives for cycling with disincentives for car use.

Whenever car use is restricted, it is important to improve alternatives to the car. Providing better cycling, walking, and public transportation services increases the political feasibility of car-restrictive measures by making it more feasible for communities and individuals to reduce car use. Improving alternatives to the car expands the range of travel options for everyone, which also facilitates the desired mode shift from the car.

6. Cultivate alliances with politicians, cycling organizations, and other bike-friendly groups.

Strong leadership by charismatic and/or powerful individuals has been crucial to the implementation of pro-bike policies and programs in some cities. Bertrand Delanoë (Paris), Enrique Peñalosa (Bogotá), Ken Livingstone and Boris Johnson (London), Sam Adams (Portland), Janette Sadik-Khan and Michael Bloomberg (New York), and Richard Daley (Chicago) are examples of politicians whose strong support has been crucial to the success of cycling in their cities.

Especially in cities with low levels of cycling, it is crucial to form alliances to generate sufficient political support to get the necessary policies adopted and implemented (Birk 2010; Mapes 2009; Wray 2008). City departments of transportation often work with bike advocacy groups and other nongovernmental organizations devoted to the environment, livable cities, and sustainable transportation. It takes the coordinated efforts of many different individuals and interest groups to offset the minority status of cyclists in car-oriented cities in North America and Australia.

7. Coordinate bike advocacy and planning through national organizations.

Most of the countries examined in this book have national cycling organizations that help coordinate the advocacy efforts of local cycling groups. They lobby the national government for funding and pro-bike legislation; organize promotional events and cycling training; help develop design standards for cycling facilities; collect and disseminate information about cycling; and provide advice on national bike plans. Examples of such national organizations are the League of American Bicyclists (United States), Alliance for Biking and Walking (United States),

National Center for Bicycling and Walking (United States), Cycling Promotion Fund (Australia), Fietsersbond (the Netherlands), Cycling Touring Club (United Kingdom), Dansk Cyklist Forbund (Denmark), and Allgemeiner Deutscher Fahrrad-Club (Germany). The European Cyclists Federation promotes cycling throughout Europe.

The Future of Cycling

Many cities in Europe, North America, and Australia have witnessed impressive growth in cycling over the past two decades. It seems likely that the coming years will bring continued growth. Many studies predict shortages in oil supplies and rising energy prices, which would increase the cost of car use and enhance the relative cost savings of cycling (Black 2010; Ewing et al. 2008; Sperling and Gordon 2009). With slowing economic growth and falling real per-capita incomes in some countries, those cost savings may become even more important as an economic incentive to cycle rather than drive.

At the same time, developed countries everywhere are faced with a worsening obesity epidemic and concerns about the range of health problems caused by car dependence and sedentary lifestyles fostered by car-oriented suburban sprawl (Frank, Engelke, and Schmid 2003; Frumkin 2003). The public health benefits of walking and cycling have generated much support for active travel in recent years, with more pro-bike government policies likely in the future. Increased attention to quality of life, personal and public health, livable cities, environmental protection, and climate change seem certain to provide cycling with a growing base of public, political, and financial support.

Shifting cultural attitudes among younger generations may also stimulate cycling. For many decades, rates of car ownership and use rose higher and higher for successive generations of Europeans, Americans, Canadians, and Australians. Recent evidence, however, suggests a possible turnaround. Younger generations in some affluent countries now have lower rates of car ownership and use than their parents (Kuhnimhof, Buehler, and Dargay 2012). Cycling instead of driving is becoming central to the lifestyles and identities of increasing numbers of young adults. It is unclear whether this nascent generational shift will become a long-term trend and spread to other countries. At the very least, however, cycling is no longer viewed as an outdated, old-fashioned mode of transportation. Especially among younger adults, cycling has become cutting edge and is viewed as a cool way to get around.

Perhaps the greatest strength of cycling is that it provides enormous benefits both to the individual and to society as a whole. Everyone benefits from cycling. As noted previously, communicating the societal benefits is crucial to generating the necessary political and public support to implement the necessary policies to promote cycling. Communicating the individual benefits of cycling is crucial to getting more people on bikes.

Cycling offers a healthy, cost-effective, equitable way to improve the sustainability of urban transportation systems and build more livable cities. As shown throughout this book, cycling is indeed a path to more sustainable transportation.

References

ABW (Alliance for Biking and Walking). 2010. *Bicycling and Walking in the United States: 2010 Benchmarking Report.* Washington, DC: Alliance for Biking and Walking.

ABW (Alliance for Biking and Walking). 2012. *Bicycling and Walking in the United States: 2012 Benchmarking Report.* Washington, DC: Alliance for Biking and Walking. http://www.peoplepoweredmovement.org/benchmarking.

Birk, Mia. 2010. *Joyride: Pedaling toward a Healthier Planet.* Portland, OR: Cadence Press.

Black, William. R. 2010. *Sustainable Transportation: Problems and Solutions.* New York: Guilford Press.

Blickstein, Susan, and Susan Hanson. 2001. Critical Mass: Forging a Politics of Sustainable Mobility in the Information Age. *Transportation* 28 (4): 347–362.

Brög, Werner, Erhard Erl, Ian Ker, James Ryle, and Rob Wall. 2009. Evaluation of Voluntary Travel Behavior Change: Experiences from three Continents. *Transport Policy* 16 (6): 281–292.

Dutch Bicycle Council. 2010. *Bicycle Policies of the European Principals: Continuous and Integral.* Amsterdam: Dutch Bicycle Council.

Ewing, Reid, Keith Batholomew, Steve Winkelman, Jerry Walters, and Don Chen. 2008. *Growing Cooler: The Evidence on Urban Development and Climate Change.* Washington, DC: Urban Land Institute.

Frank, Larry, Peter Engelke, and Thomas Schmid. 2003. *Health and Community Design: The Impact of the Built Environment on Physical Activity.* Washington, DC: Island Press.

Frumkin, Howard. 2003. Healthy Places: Exploring the Evidence. *American Journal of Public Health* 93 (9): 1451–1456.

Heinen, Eva, Bert van Wee, and Kees Maat. 2010. Bicycle Use for Commuting: A Literature Review. *Transport Reviews* 30 (1): 105–132.

Krizek, Kevin, Anne Forsyth, and Laura Baum. 2009. *Walking and Cycling: An International Literature Review*. Melbourne: Department of Transport, State of Victoria.

Kuhnimhof, Tobias, Ralph Buehler, and Joyce Dargay. 2012. A New Generation: Travel Trends among Young Germans and Britons. *Transportation Research Record: Journal of the Transportation Research Board* 2230: 58–67.

Levine, Jonathan. 2006. *Zoned Out: Regulation, Markets, and Choices in Transportation and Metropolitan Land Use*. Washington, DC: Resources for the Future.

Mapes, Jeff. 2009. *Pedaling Revolution: How Cyclists are Changing American Cities*. Corvalis, OR: Oregon State University Press.

NCES (National Center for Education Statistics). 2010. *Fast Facts*. Washington, DC: National Center for Education Statistics, U.S. Department of Education.

PBIC and FHWA (Pedestrian and Bicycling Information Center and Federal Highway Administration). 2010. *The National Walking and Bicycling Study: 15-Year Status Report*. Chapel Hill, NC, and Washington, DC: PBIC and FHWA/USDOT.

Pucher, John, Jennifer Dill, and Susan Handy. 2010. Infrastructure, Programs, and Policies to Increase Bicycling: An International Review. *Preventive Medicine* 48 (S1): S106–S125.

Reynolds, Conor C. O., M. Anne Harris, Kay Teschke, Peter Cripton, and Meghan Winters. 2009. The Impact of Transportation Infrastructure on Bicycling Injuries and Crashes: A Review of the Literature. *Environmental Health* 8 (47). DOI: 10.1186/1476-069X-8-47.

Sarmiento, Olga, Andrea Torres, Enrique Jacoby, Michael Pratt, Thomas L. Schmid, and Gonzalo Stierling. 2010. The Ciclovía-Recreativa: A Mass Recreational Program with Public Health Potential. *Journal of Physical Activity & Health* 7 (S2): S163–S180.

Sperling, Dan, and Deborah Gordon. 2009. *Two Billion Cars: Driving Toward Sustainability*. New York: Oxford University Press.

WNBR (World Naked Bike Ride). 2011. World Naked Bike Ride: List of rides. Portland, OR: WNBR. http://www.worldnakedbikeride.org.

Wray, Harry. 2008. *Pedal Power: The Quiet Rise of the Bicycle in American Public Life 2008*. Boulder: Paradigm Publishers.

Yang, Lin, Shannon Sahlqvist, Alison McMinn, Simon J. Griffin, and David Ogilvie. 2010. Interventions to Promote Cycling: Systematic Review. *British Medical Journal* 341. DOI: 10.1136/bmj.c5293.

Index

Urban and Industrial Environments

Series editor: Robert Gottlieb, Henry R. Luce Professor of Urban and Environmental Policy, Occidental College

Eran Ben-Joseph, *The Code of the City: Standards and the Hidden Language of Place Making*

Nancy J. Myers and Carolyn Raffensperger, eds., *Precautionary Tools for Reshaping Environmental Policy*

Kelly Sims Gallagher, *China Shifts Gears: Automakers, Oil, Pollution, and Development*

Kerry H. Whiteside, *Precautionary Politics: Principle and Practice in Confronting Environmental Risk*

Ronald Sandler and Phaedra C. Pezzullo, eds., *Environmental Justice and Environmentalism: The Social Justice Challenge to the Environmental Movement*

Julie Sze, *Noxious New York: The Racial Politics of Urban Health and Environmental Justice*

Robert D. Bullard, ed., *Growing Smarter: Achieving Livable Communities, Environmental Justice, and Regional Equity*

Ann Rappaport and Sarah Hammond Creighton, *Degrees That Matter: Climate Change and the University*

Michael Egan, *Barry Commoner and the Science of Survival: The Remaking of American Environmentalism*

David J. Hess, *Alternative Pathways in Science and Industry: Activism, Innovation, and the Environment in an Era of Globalization*

Peter F. Cannavò, *The Working Landscape: Founding, Preservation, and the Politics of Place*

Paul Stanton Kibel, ed., *Rivertown: Rethinking Urban Rivers*

Kevin P. Gallagher and Lyuba Zarsky, *The Enclave Economy: Foreign Investment and Sustainable Development in Mexico's Silicon Valley*

David N. Pellow, *Resisting Global Toxics: Transnational Movements for Environmental Justice*

Robert Gottlieb, *Reinventing Los Angeles: Nature and Community in the Global City*

David V. Carruthers, ed., *Environmental Justice in Latin America: Problems, Promise, and Practice*

Tom Angotti, *New York for Sale: Community Planning Confronts Global Real Estate*

Paloma Pavel, ed., *Breakthrough Communities: Sustainability and Justice in the Next American Metropolis*

Anastasia Loukaitou-Sideris and Renia Ehrenfeucht, *Sidewalks: Conflict and Negotiation over Public Space*

David J. Hess, *Localist Movements in a Global Economy: Sustainability, Justice, and Urban Development in the United States*

Julian Agyeman and Yelena Ogneva-Himmelberger, eds., *Environmental Justice and Sustainability in the Former Soviet Union*